FOCUS ON BUSINESS

4th edition

Ausgabe Nordrhein-Westfalen

von

Shaunessy Ashdown

Michael Benford

Isobel Williams

Steve Williams

unter Mitarbeit
der Verlagsredaktion

Cornelsen

Verfasser/innen:	Shaunessy Ashdown, Berlin Michael Benford, Bochum Isobel Williams, Berlin Steve Williams, Corio Bay Media, Melbourne
Berater/innen:	Anne Arheiliger, Neuss Marc Engels, Erkelenz Dr. Hans Oestreich, Lemgo Bianca Sonnenschien, Erkelenz
Projektleitung:	Andreas Goebel
Verlagsredaktion:	Kari-ann Seamark
Außenredaktion:	Janan Barksdale, Berlin
Redaktionelle Mitarbeit:	Gemma Duggan, Simone Conrad, Ingrid Raspe (Wörterverzeichnisse)
Layout:	Oxana Rödel, Absatz DTP-Service, Teltow
Technische Umsetzung:	Sabine Theuring, Berlin
Umschlaggestaltung:	werkstatt für gebrauchsgrafik, Berlin
Titelfotos:	Fotosearch; shutterstock/Brian Jackson; shutterstock/hxdbzxy; shutterstock/wavebreakmedia
Bildredaktion:	Gertha Maly
Illustrationen:	Oxford Designers & Illustrators
Entwicklung Modellunternehmen Fly Bike Werke GmbH:	Hans-Peter von den Bergen, Alfons Steffes-lai

Erhältlich sind auch:

Workbook mit Audio-CD	ISBN: 978-3-06-450386-1
Handreichungen zum Unterricht mit Lehrer-CD und 2 Audio-CDs	ISBN: 978-3-06-450389-2
Webcodes und Online-Zusatzmaterialien auf www.cornelsen.de/cbb	

www.cornelsen.de

Die Links zu externen Webseiten Dritter, die in diesem Lehrwerk angegeben sind, wurden vor Drucklegung sorgfältig auf ihre Aktualität geprüft. Der Verlag übernimmt keine Gewähr für die Aktualität und den Inhalt dieser Seiten oder solcher, die mit ihnen verlinkt sind.

1. Auflage, 1. Druck 2013

Alle Drucke dieser Auflage sind inhaltlich unverändert und können im Unterricht nebeneinander verwendet werden.

Druck: Mohn Media Mohndruck, Gütersloh

ISBN 978-3-06-450383-0

Inhalt gedruckt auf säurefreiem Papier aus nachhaltiger Forstwirtschaft.

VORWORT

Focus on Business 4th Edition Ausgabe Nordrhein-Westfalen wurde speziell für die Höhere Berufsfachschule in Nordrhein-Westfalen entwickelt. Das Lehrwerk führt vom mittleren Abschluss in zwei Jahren zur Fachhochschulreife und deckt alle Anforderungen des neuen Bildungsplans ab.

Focus on Business besteht aus sechs **Topics**, die die Anforderungssituationen des Bildungsplans in der vorgeschriebenen Reihenfolge abdecken. Diese Topics sind in Unterthemen gegliedert, die zentrale Wirtschaftsthemen behandeln und alle Zielformulierungen der jeweiligen Anforderungssituationen abdecken. Die Reihenfolge der Bearbeitung kann jedoch variieren, wenn fächerübergreifender Unterricht geplant wird.

Der Aufgabenapparat der Topics ist klar **kompetenzorientiert**; die jeweils behandelten Kompetenzen werden in den Aufgabenüberschriften beschrieben. Auch das **Hörverstehen** wird im Rahmen der Vorbereitung auf die Abschlussprüfung intensiv trainiert.

Die aktuellen Themen wurden oft in **Handlungsrahmen** und **Situationen** eingebettet, daher spielen rollenbasierte Aufgaben eine wichtige Rolle. *Scenarios* (Simulationen) am Ende jedes Abschnitts fördern gezielt kompetenz- und anwendungsorientiertes Lernen durch das Modellunternehmen Fly Bike Werke GmbH, das im Sinne eines **fächerübergreifenden Unterrichts** auch in den übrigen Lehrwerken des Cornelsen Verlags für die Höhere Berufsfachschule Wirtschaft und Verwaltung thematisiert wird.

Der **Anhang** enthält viele ergänzende Materialien; neben den Partner files sind dies vor allem:

Business glossary: wichtige Materialien zum Nachschlagen wie z. B. die Incoterms© 2010 oder *Terms of payment*,

Skills: ein anwendungsbezogener Leitfaden zu Lernstrategien, auf den im Verlauf der Topics verwiesen wird,

Grammar summary: eine übersichtliche Zusammenfassung der wichtigsten Grammatikstrukturen

sowie umfangreiche **Wörterverzeichnisse.**

Zur **Differenzierung** und selbstständigen Weiterarbeit stehen zum jeden Topic Webcodes zur Verfügung, die mit klaren Verweisen gekennzeichnet sind und von den Lernenden auf www.cornelsen.de/cbb abgerufen werden können.

Die **Handreichungen** bieten auch Differenzierungsvorschläge sowie Hinweise zum kompetenzorientierten Unterricht u. a. auf der Lehrer-DVD mit zahlreichen editierbaren und differenzierenden Kopiervorlagen, darunter Arbeitsblätter, Klassenarbeitsvorschläge (mit Audio-Dateien) oder Zusatztexte. Videos vertiefen Themen und üben Geschäftskommunikation. Das **Workbook** enthält weitere Übungsmaterialien zu Wortschatz, Grammatik, Kompetenzen und Prüfungsvorbereitung. Die beigelegte Audio-CD bereitet gezielt auf den neuen Prüfungsteil Hörverstehen vor.

Wir hoffen, dass Ihnen die Arbeit mit **Focus on Business 4th Edition Ausgabe Nordrhein-Westfalen** Freude bereitet und das Lehrwerk zu einem erfolgreichen Unterricht beiträgt.

Die Autoren und der Verlag

Appendix

▸BWR/HF 4 = fächerübergreifende Bezüge auf BWR-Handlungsfelder möglich

1 Welcome to the world of work

FOCUS

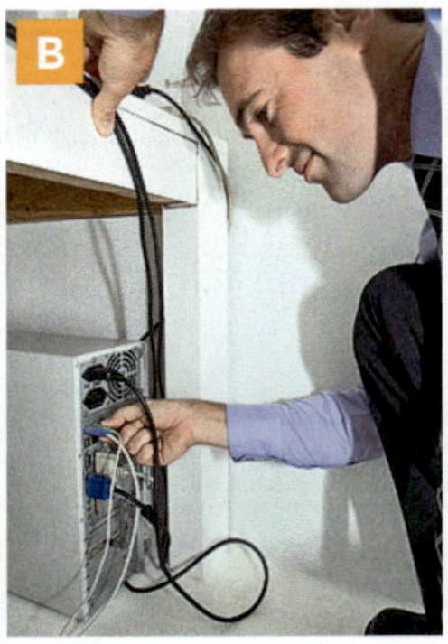

1 Match the people in the photos to the jobs. What are the positions called in German?

1 automobile sales management assistant
2 bank business management assistant
3 hotel management assistant
4 information technology officer
5 management assistant for retail services
6 management assistant in freight forwarding

2 Who does what? Match the quotes below to the people in the photos. Sometimes more than one answer is possible.

1 'I deal with people from different countries so I speak English a lot of the time.'
2 'I do general paperwork, fill out forms, make telephone calls and make sure the goods get safely from A to B.'
3 'I have to keep up to date with current developments on the market so that I can give advice to customers.'
4 'In order to be able to advise my customers properly, I must know absolutely everything about my products.'
5 'I take people out for test drives and I often have to prepare credit contracts.'
6 'I run a lot of tests. Keeping up to date with technological developments is important.'

3 Talk about what you are studying. Say what jobs you may be interested in and why.

A Work experience

1 READING A BLOG POST

You are interested in learning about work experience in the UK so you go online and find Luke's blog. Luke is from Bristol in the South-West of England and he writes a weekly blog post about his life. This week he is doing work experience.

1 2

http://www.lukes_blogspot.co.uk/blog52

Apple (12) ▾ Amazon eBay Yahoo! News (255) ▾

About me | Blogs | Archive | Comments | Contact me

Luke's Blog

Work experience! **Wednesday, 12 November, 8 p.m.**

I'm tired this evening – very tired. Why?

I'm doing work experience this week. I get up at half past five every morning – the bus into town leaves at a quarter past six, so I'm always in a hurry. I don't get home until about six o'clock in the evening. Working life is HARD! Hmm, wait a minute. Maybe you don't live in the UK and don't know about work experience. OK, here's how it works:

In England, students do work experience when they're in year 10 or year 11 (14–16 years old). It's an opportunity to try a job while you're still at school or college. You choose the type of work, write letters and phone employers and maybe go for an interview – just like a real job. The work placement – or experience (it's the same thing) – usually lasts about two weeks.

What about me? I'm working in a big computer store in town. It's good because I'm interested in IT and retail. This week I'm working in the office. Maybe that doesn't sound so interesting, but it is: there are a lot of different jobs to do here. There's the purchasing department – they order the stock; there's the customer service department – they handle customer queries and problems; there's the accounts department – they keep financial information, and so on. It's surprising how many people work 'behind the scenes' in a big store like this: customers who use the store rarely see these people. Everyone's nice to me here and I'm learning a lot. I do a different job every day – that's cool. Today I worked in purchasing, tomorrow I'm in the personnel department. They keep records for all the employees, write job advertisements, things like that.

So what do I actually do at work? Sometimes I work on the computer, updating records and completing form letters. Sometimes I photocopy paperwork or send faxes, answer the phone or make the tea and coffee. In other words, I do a lot of the things a normal employee does.

Do I want to work here when I leave school? I'm not sure yet, to be honest. But that doesn't matter: I'm finding out about the world of work.

That's all for tonight, folks – I'm off to bed!

(376 words)

A **Answer the questions on the text.**

1. Why does Luke find working life hard?
2. How do students in England get a work placement?
3. Where is Luke's work placement?
4. Why does Luke say that the office staff work 'behind the scenes'?
5. How are the staff treating Luke?
6. What does Luke like about his work placement?
7. What administrative tasks does Luke do in the office?
8. What is Luke not sure about?

B **Write a short comment for Luke's blog. Tell him about work experience in Germany. The expressions below will help you.**

In Germany, students do work experience when they are ...
It usually lasts for ...
It is organized by ...

2 WRITING AN E-MAIL

A British friend has asked you what you think about work placements. Make a list of the advantages and disadvantages. Then write your friend an e-mail telling him or her your opinion.

A work placement is useful / not very useful if ...
In my opinion/view, work placements are ... because ...

3 WORKING WITH WORDS

A **Replace the words in *italics* with a word of a similar meaning. The words that you need are in the same order in the text on page 7.**

1. It's sometimes *difficult* to be nice to customers all day.
2. Work experience is *a chance* to try a job that interests you.
3. English students *normally* organize their own work placements.
4. In a big *shop* like PC World, there are several office staff.
5. *Many* companies take work experience students.
6. The customer service department *deals with* customer complaints.
7. You should phone them if you have a *question* about your purchase.
8. I'm not *certain* that this is the right job for me.

B **Find the words or expressions in the text on page 7.**

1. a person who pays other people to work for him/her
2. business which involves selling goods to the public
3. concerning money
4. a notice in a newspaper or a website
5. to change (a document etc.) so that it contains the latest information
6. a type of letter which has gaps to fill in
7. all types of printed documents
8. a person who works for a company

4 TALKING ABOUT WORK

A Make sentences to explain what these people do in their jobs.

EXAMPLE
> Accounts manager – make financial decisions
> *The accounts manager makes financial decisions.*

Grammar Summary, simple present, p. 212

1 Purchasing manager – order new stock
2 Personnel assistant – update employee records
3 Sales assistants – serve customers
4 Accounts assistant – keep financial records
5 Customer service representatives – handle customer queries
6 Personnel manager – write job advertisements
7 Work experience students – try different jobs
8 Luke – make the tea and coffee
9 Julie – photocopy paperwork and answer the phone
10 Purchasing assistant – complete forms and send faxes

B Luke has some questions to ask Lucy, a sales assistant. Write questions in the simple present.

EXAMPLE
> we / have / a coffee break / every morning?
> *Do we have a coffee break every morning?*

1 how long / be / the coffee break ?
2 where / I / put / these keyboards ?
3 how / the cash register / work ?
4 the customers / ask / a lot of questions ?
5 what time / the store / close / this evening ?
6 how many customers / you / serve / each day ?
7 when / you / usually / go / to lunch ?
8 where / you / have / lunch ?
9 you / have / a boyfriend ?
10 what / you / do / on Saturdays ?

C Make sentences to explain what is happening now, today or this week.

EXAMPLE
> Ahmed (do) work experience with us this week.
> *Ahmed **is doing** work experience with us this week.*

Grammar Summary, present progressive, p. 212

1 I (work) in the accounts department at the moment.
2 Anna (make) us some coffee – would you like a cup?
3 Everyone (enjoy) the nice weather this week.
4 We (write) letters to employers this afternoon.
5 Luke (not work) hard at the moment. He (have) a cup of tea.
6 Jules and Barry (update) customer records today.
7 You (work) with them this week.
8 I (do) a training course this afternoon.
9 That's Emma over there – she (handle) a customer query.
10 Julie and Chloe (not enjoy) their work experience this week.

D Ask Luke questions about his work experience. Use the present progressive.

EXAMPLE
> you / learn / a lot here ? > *Are you learning a lot here?*

1 you / enjoy / your work placement ?
2 you / make / new friends ?
3 the other employees / help / you ?
4 the work / become / boring ?
5 your boss / give / you / lots of feedback ?
6 why / you / work / in a computer store ?
7 you / write / a report about your work experience ?
8 your friends / do / work experience too ?
9 where / they / work ?
10 they / write / blogs too ?

E **Present progressive or simple present? Choose the correct tense.**

EXAMPLE > The careers advisor generally ***helps*** / *is helping* students to get a work placement.

1 I *look / am looking* for a work placement at the moment.
2 Every year the students in year 10 *do / are doing* work experience.
3 Currently 20 students *work / are working* in different companies around town.
4 Usually they *find / are finding* it very enjoyable.
5 However, this year some students *don't enjoy / aren't enjoying* it much.
6 Sometimes employers *aren't giving / don't give* the students enough help.
7 All the same, you *always learn / are always learning* a lot from a work placement.
8 This week I *go / am going* for an interview with a law firm in the high street.

5 TRANSLATION

Translate the sentences into English. Use the simple present or the present progressive as appropriate.

1 Stefan versendet gerade ein Fax.
2 Birgit kocht immer Tee und Kaffee für die Mitarbeiter (*staff*).
3 Diese Woche arbeiten sie in der Buchhaltung (*accounts department*).
4 Ben benutzt gerade den Kopierer.
5 Die Praktikanten (*work experience students*) erledigen jeden Tag andere Aufgaben (*different tasks*).
6 Unsere Einkaufsleiterin bestellt (*order*) gewöhnlich die Produkte (*products*).
7 Ab und zu nehme ich Anrufe entgegen (*answer the phone*).
8 Arbeitet gerade jemand an diesem Computer?

6 DESCRIBING JOBS AND DUTIES

A job centre in the UK offers a regular podcast in which people across Europe are interviewed about their jobs and career choices. Today, John Smith is interviewing Meryem Özdemir, who is currently doing a work placement in a freight forwarding company in Dortmund.

A **Before you listen, decide with a partner which of the following words and phrases you might hear.**

- programming computers
- transport of goods
- importers and exporters
- routes for shipment
- writing job advertisements
- keeping the costs down
- customs and insurance
- suitable packing
- working with my hands
- keeping track of shipments

1 3

B **Now listen and check. Then summarize what Meryem said for someone who has not heard the interview.**

Begin like this:
Meryem trained as a freight forwarding agent because ...

C **Research a job you are interested in. Talk about what the job involves and describe some of the duties to a friend who does not speak German.**

Useful links: http://berufenet.arbeitsagentur.de or http://www.berufe.tv/BA/

B Working internationally

1 GET THAT JOB ABROAD

The Going Places magazine has an online forum where people can ask questions and share ideas. The discussion on the page below is about differences in pay and qualifications in various countries, and offers tips on getting a job abroad.

1 4

http://www.goingplacesmagazine.com/forum

Apple (12) Amazon eBay Yahoo! News (255)

Anna

I'm training to be an office management assistant and would love to work in the UK. My careers officer advised me to make enquiries at my local employment agency. They said there that British companies often take on German-trained office assistants, but they didn't have anything to offer me at the moment. I'm really keen to get away. I'd accept any job in the UK, as long as it was well paid.

Boris

Well paid – dream on, Anna. Young, foreign workers can only find work in low-paying sectors, so the wages are low. There's a national minimum wage in the UK, but you won't be offered any more than that. You do get a lot of holidays there, though. The problem is that you won't have much money to spend on them!

Cool Cal

Boris is too negative about wages in the UK. Anyone with qualifications has a chance of getting a well-paid job wherever they go. If you want to work anywhere in Europe, you should check out Europass. That's a good way to keep track of your employment record and qualifications. In some countries, you need to get your qualifications and professional experience officially recognized, but I don't think that's the case in the UK.

Dave the Dude

I agree with Cool Cal. It's important that you've completed an apprenticeship or a training course and you've got your qualifications. Here, in the USA, you'll also need a TOEFL certificate to prove that your English is good enough. You have to remember that if you're applying for work in a country where English isn't the first language, you should be fit in that language, too.

Ella

I'd just like to add one thing. I agree that training, qualifications and language skills are a must for any job, but it also helps if you have experience of working abroad. Voluntary work is a good way to get started. During my gap year, I worked in a refugee camp in Ethiopia for six months. I think that volunteering helped me get the job I'm in now, working in a bank in Spain. Employers usually see volunteering as something very positive.

(352 words)

A **Richtig oder falsch? Korrigieren Sie die falschen Angaben mit Informationen aus dem Forum.**

1 In Großbritannien stellen Unternehmen nicht gerne ausländische Arbeitnehmer ein.
2 Oft zahlen Arbeitgeber in Großbritannien jungen Arbeitnehmern so wenig wie möglich.
3 Ein Europass ähnelt einer Arbeitserlaubnis.
4 In einigen Ländern verlangen Arbeitgeber Nachweise für Qualifikationen und Arbeitserfahrung.
5 In den USA sind Unternehmen eher an Ihren Deutsch- als an Ihren Englischkenntnissen interessiert.
6 Freiwilligenarbeit ist nur eine gute Möglichkeit, die Zeit zwischen Jobs auszufüllen. Sie verhilft einem nicht zu einer „richtigen“ Arbeitsstelle.

B **Write a response to Ella's comment. If you have done voluntary work, say what you did and what you have learnt from the experience. If you have not done any voluntary work so far, say why not.**

2 TALKING ABOUT QUALIFICATIONS AND EXPERIENCE

A **Make sentences to describe what the people did while at school and the qualifications they got.**

> Grammar Summary, simple past, p. 213

EXAMPLE > Max (do) an apprenticeship last year.
> *Max **did** an apprenticeship last year.*

1 Irene (study) business administration at a vocational college. Her sister Mary (attend) the same school but she (not study) business administration.
2 Jane and Julie (enjoy) their work experience. They (work) together in the same firm.
3 Klaus (begin) to train as a sales assistant but he (leave) school before he (finish) the course.
4 While he was studying, Harry (have) a part-time job in a hotel. He (learn) a lot while he was there.
5 Martin (never try) hard at school but he still (get) excellent marks in his final exams.
6 Paul and Paula (not be) good at languages so their parents (pay) for extra English lessons.
7 Ian (take) a course in Excel but he (forget) to include that on his Europass.
8 Carmen (be) angry because she (not get) a place on the typing course.

B **Use the words in brackets to describe what has (not) happened.**

> Grammar Summary, present perfect, p. 214

EXAMPLE Luke (work) in a computer store.
*Luke **has worked** in a computer store.*

1 Martha (write) a lot of applications to foreign companies but she (have) no replies so far.
2 It's only Tuesday and Emily (sit) three of her final exams already.
3 Hannah (never have) any problems passing exams.
4 Eve (not do) her work experience yet. She plans to do it next month.
5 Ivan (just have) his first telephone interview in English.
6 Margot (never be) good at figures so her grades (always be) poor.
7 Tom (do) so many holiday jobs abroad, he (add) an extra page to his CV.
8 The teacher (give) us too much homework again.

C Make questions using the simple past or present perfect.

EXAMPLE what / you do / during your gap year?
*What **did** you **do** during your gap year?*
How long / you study / English?
*How long **have you studied** English?*

1 Jane / already supply / proof of her work experience ?
2 James / get the job / in Paris / that he apply for / last month ?
3 how long / you work / for this company ?
4 you read / any information about the firm / yet ?
5 why / be / the application forms for that job so complicated ?
6 how you do / at the interview?
7 you / ever do / voluntary work ?
8 when / Ella / work in Ethiopia ?

1 5

D In this week's podcast, John Smith has interviewed Axel Lang, a German trainee working in London. Complete the extract with the simple past or the present perfect of the verbs in brackets. Then listen to check your answers.

JOHN: Today, I'm interviewing Axel Lang. Axel works at my local bank, and we *met* (meet)[1] a few weeks ago when I *opened* (open)[2] an account there. Axel, how long (you be)[3] at the bank?
AXEL: Well, I officially (start)[4] work here three months ago.
JOHN Officially? So (you work)[5] here before?
AXEL: Yes. Before I (leave)[6] college, I (do)[7] a work placement as a teller. Then I (apply)[8] for a job.
JOHN: I see. Why (you decide)[9] to work in a bank?
AXEL: I (always love)[10] anything to do with figures. At college, I really (enjoy)[11] bookkeeping and accounts.
JOHN I believe you (just begin)[12] an internal training programme.
AXEL: That's right. I (be)[13] on the course since the beginning of the month.

3 TRANSLATION

Translate the sentences into English using the correct tense.

1 Meine Schwester hat sich um eine Stelle in London beworben.
2 Ich habe noch nie in einem Büro gearbeitet.
3 Mein Kollege hat sein Jahr Auszeit zwischen Schule und Ausbildung (*gap year*) in New York verbracht.
4 Wie lange sind Sie schon im Unternehmen?
5 Vor zwei Jahren arbeitete ich in der Schweiz.
6 Ich hatte viel Spaß bei dem Projekt.
7 Ich habe gerade meinen Lebenslauf aktualisiert (*to update*).
8 Hattest du schon einmal ein Bewerbungsgespräch auf Englisch?

Webcode: FOBNRWT101

C Jobs and job adverts

1 FINDING THE RIGHT JOB

Maria and Markus Müller are twins. They have recently completed their training courses and are now looking for their first permanent positions. They would both like to work in the UK or Ireland. Today, they have been checking adverts online.

A **Read the lists of jobs they have viewed and try to guess what each of them has studied.**

freight forwarding | information technology | office management | retail business

People who viewed this job also viewed

Receptionist for fast-growing entertainment company
£18–20K, depending on experience
PA for Sports Consultancy
London, salary negotiable
Secretary, some experience necessary
£18K per annum

Maria

Related jobs

- Product Marketing – well-established company based in Cork, Ireland €24,000 + benefits
- Sales and Marketing Co-ordinator basic salary £18K plus commission
- Telesales – Retail on-the-job training given

Markus

B **Study the two lists and find abbreviations and synonyms for these words and phrases:**

1 thousand (Hint: This is a letter.)
2 personal assistant
3 the company will decide how much you will earn after the interview
4 things like health insurance and payment into a pension fund
5 each year
6 the lowest amount of payment you will receive
7 if you work hard, you will earn more money
8 learning by doing

2 TWO JOB ADVERTS

A **Maria and Markus are interested in the positions advertised on the next page. Compare and contrast the two adverts. Talk about salary, type of contract, working hours, responsibilities, etc.**

B **Which job looks more attractive? Give reasons for your opinion.**

3 WORKING WITH WORDS

A **Find references in the adverts to personal qualities and skills. Make two lists.**

Personal qualities	*Skills*
a professional manner	*communication skills*

B **Brainstorm other characteristics and skills that might be useful in the jobs and add them to your lists.**

Area Sales Management Assistant, Oxford £22K basic + Commission + Benefits	
Job description:	Development of sales market for leading automotive manufacturer
Contract:	Permanent
Hours:	Full time

We are looking for a candidate who is dynamic, focused and results oriented.

You will demonstrate the company products to automotive professionals (garages, workshops, etc.), take orders and make follow-up visits. You will have the ability to understand what our clients are looking for and demonstrate our products professionally. An enthusiastic manner is a must.

You should also have commercial ability, effective communication skills, and good negotiation, persuasion and influencing skills.

This is an excellent opportunity to join a successful team within a well-established company that offers exciting fringe benefits. Some experience in the retail field is necessary.

Apply with CV

Receptionist / Office assistant, Property Management, City, 12K	
Job description:	Reception / general office duties
Contract:	Temporary
Hours:	Part time

Who we are: Property Management company based in London
What we need: A part-time receptionist who will make sure that all contact to the company is dealt with in a professional and polite manner. You should also be adaptable and have the ability to cope with a busy environment.

Responsibilities include welcoming visitors to the office and providing refreshments for guests; answering incoming calls and transferring or taking messages as required; assisting with incoming and outgoing mail.

The successful candidate will have excellent communication skills, working knowledge of computer programs, and at least one foreign language. No previous experience necessary.

Apply with CV

4 TRANSLATION

Translate the sentences into English using the most suitable modal auxiliaries or their substitutes.

> Grammar Summary, modal auxiliary verbs, p. 216

1 Man muss gute Qualifikationen haben, wenn man sich auf diese Position bewerben will.
2 Man muss seine Befähigungsnachweise nicht beglaubigen lassen.
3 Wenn man keine Green Card hat, darf man nicht in den USA arbeiten.
4 Du musst Englisch sprechen können, aber du musst es nicht fließend können.
5 Konntest Du den Interviewer verstehen, als er Englisch gesprochen hat?
6 Wenn ich hier keine Stelle bekomme, könnte ich mich im Ausland nach Arbeit umsehen.
7 Der erfolgreiche Kandidat sollte gute Kommunikationsfähigkeiten am Telefon besitzen.
8 Darf man das Internet auf der Arbeit nutzen?

5 MEDIATION: A JOB ADVERTISEMENT

Skills, p. 211

Ein britischer Freund würde gerne in Deutschland arbeiten. Er hat die nachstehende Anzeige gesehen und glaubt, dass er ein geeigneter Kandidat für die Stelle sein könnte. Bevor er sich bewirbt, bittet er Sie, ihm die Anzeige auf Englisch zu erklären.

ABC-Spedition GmbH

Praktikant (m/w) gesucht (Referenznr. 200-56-9898-S)

Wir sind: ein Speditionsunternehmen mit Sitz in Münster, das sich auf den Versand nach Großbritannien und Irland spezialisiert hat.

Wir suchen: eine/n Praktikant/in für unser Büro. Das Praktikum beträgt mindestens 6 Monate. Idealerweise suchen Sie einen Ausbildungsplatz zum Speditionskaufmann/- frau zum Sommer 20.. oder einen Einstieg in die Speditionsbranche.

Ihre Aufgaben: Unterstützung des Vertriebsinnendienstes; administrative Aufgaben; allgemeine Büroorganisation und Bedienung der Telefonzentral

Unser Anforderungsprofil: Sie sind kommunikativ und dienstleistungsorientiert; Sie bringen ein sehr gutes Ausdrucksvermögen in Wort und Schrift mit; Sie verfügen über sehr gute Englischkenntnisse; Teamarbeit macht Ihnen Spaß

Was wir Ihnen bieten: ein spannendes und eigenverantwortliches Aufgabengebiet; eine intensive Einarbeitung; nette Kollegen und einen modernen Arbeitsplatz

Bei entsprechender Eignung bieten wir Ihnen einen Ausbildungsplatz für den Sommer 20.. oder eine Festanstellung an.

Haben wir Ihr Interesse geweckt? Bitte senden Sie uns Ihre Bewerbungsunterlagen in englischer Sprache per E-Mail an bewerbung@abc-spedition.com Ansprechpartnerin: Frau Michendorf

6 EXPLAINING YOUR PREFERENCES

Choose one of the jobs mentioned in the book so far and explain why you would or would not like to do it. Use phrases from below to write your answer.

Introduction
Working as a ... would be ... (e.g. exciting/interesting/hard work)
The job of a ... is ...
If you work as a ..., you have to ... (e.g. like working with people / do shift work)
Own experience
I work in ... (e.g. a shop) at the weekends / two evenings a week / in the holidays
I once worked ... (e.g. in a shop/café/restaurant / on a farm)
I have never worked but my mother/father ... (e.g. works in a factory)
Opinion
I think / I believe / In my opinion, ...
I would/wouldn't like to ... (e.g. be an office worker / work abroad)
I like to work with ...
I think working in ... would be ...
I don't like ... (+ -ing)
It is important to ... (e.g. be my own boss / see how other people live / earn money)

7 FRINGE BENEFITS AND PERKS

You have been looking at job advertisements in English and keep coming across the words 'fringe benefits' and 'perks'. You are not really sure what the terms mean, so you have done a search on the internet and found the text below.

1 6

Fringe benefits then and now

What are you looking for when you start a new job? A good salary, a permanent position, nice colleagues, interesting work? What about the fringe benefits or perks? We're not talking about the benefits which are laid down by law – things like minimum wage, unemployment benefit and medical leave. We're talking about the extras which supplement these basic benefits.

What sort of things can you expect? Childcare, flexible working hours and discounts on company products and services are some of the most common fringe benefits. In some companies, where employees would like to improve their language skills, employers help by paying the fees or by giving employees paid leave of absence. In recent years, some companies have started to offer health club memberships. The list is endless.

It hasn't always been like this, of course. When your grandfather was younger, the boss had a company car and his own parking space. Employees, on the other hand, had to take whatever parking space was available – if there was staff car parking at all. Subsidized canteens provided factory workers with a hot meal at lunchtime, and some office workers in the big cities were given 'luncheon vouchers', which could be exchanged at specific cafes or restaurants for a meal.

The expression 'fringe benefits' came into common use in the late 1940s, when the world got back to work after World War II.

There were no fringe benefits aimed specifically at working women who had a young family. Private arrangements were made, and grandmothers or neighbours cared for babies and children. Many so-called 'career women' decided against having a family altogether.

Today, women in Britain make up nearly half of the workforce. If they decide to have a family, they can rely on the laws which grant them paid leave before and after the birth, and guarantee that their job will be open to them when they decide to return to work. As far as fringe benefits are concerned, some employers provide on-site childcare and a quiet room for mothers who are breastfeeding.

Employers today invest a lot of money in training employees. An employer who offers fringe benefits or perks will keep his workers happy and loyal to the company. *(348 words)*

Without benefits, there would be fewer women in the workplace.

A Read the text and do the tasks below in English.

> Skills, p. 203

1 Beschreiben Sie, was sich Menschen erhoffen, wenn sie eine neue Arbeitsstelle beginnen.
2 Erklären Sie den Unterschied zwischen Grundsicherung und Zusatzleistungen, indem Sie jeweils drei Beispiele aus dem Text verwenden.
3 Nehmen Sie Stellung zu den Leistungen, die Arbeitnehmern Mitte des 20. Jahrhunderts gewährt wurden.
4 Stellen Sie vergleichend die Situation von Arbeitnehmerinnen damals und heute gegenüber.
5 Erklären Sie, warum Arbeitgeber Zusatzleistungen anbieten.

B Translate the German expressions using words and phrases from the text.

1 unbefristete Stelle
2 Zusatzleistungen
3 Mindestlohn
4 ergänzen
5 Beurlaubung
6 subventioniert
7 Essensmarke
8 Mutterschutzgesetz
9 Arbeitsplatzgarantie
10 stillen

8 RESEARCHING AND REPORTING

A Prepare a list of questions in German. Then interview one or two older people about their working life. Take notes on the following:

> the working conditions when they first started to work and the fringe benefits they received
> how the benefits improved their lives back then
> how things have changed over the years
> what kinds of benefits they have now (if they are still working)

B Give a report in English to the class about the differences between then and now. The expressions below will help you.

I interviewed ...
In (year), he/she worked in a/an ... (e.g. company/factory/office/shop)
Then, ... / At that time, ... (Not: ~~In former times~~)
Now, ... / Nowadays, ...

D Applying for a job

1 AN ONLINE JOB ADVERTISEMENT

Janina Witt is in the final year of a two-year commercial course at a vocational training college in Essen. She registers with a number of online recruitment agencies and sees this job advertisement on one of their websites.

A Describe what the job advert says about the following:

1 Arbeitsort
2 Arbeitszeiten
3 Kleidervorschriften/Dresscode
4 Verpflegung
5 Vergütung
6 erforderliche Qualifikation

HOSPITALITY RECRUITMENT

HOME | CHECK YOUR E-MAIL | LATEST JOBS | REGISTER

JOB DESCRIPTION

Entry level hotel work (male or female)

We are looking for a full-time employee (37 hours a week) to work at a first-class hotel and conference venue in a major city in the north of England. Previous experience of hotel work is desirable but not necessary, and promotion prospects in this dynamic and exciting environment are excellent.

The successful applicant will receive training on the job and be paid £6.08 an hour for the first three months. We will then review your performance with a view to a pay rise. A uniform and meals are provided during working hours.

We expect a team player with:
- a good command of English
- a good command of at least one other foreign language
- a high standard of personal appearance
- a passion for the customer care industry

Please send your application to the address below quoting reference no. RHYO 232:

Ms Debbie Wharton
Human Resources Manager
Best Western Monkbar Hotel
St. Maurice's Road
YORK
YO31 7JA
UK

B Find words in the advertisement to match the following definitions.

1 someone who works for an employer
2 location
3 earlier, before now
4 needed
5 a higher position in the same company
6 very good
7 increase
8 great interest and enthusiasm

Applying for a job abroad

The most important part of a job application in an English-speaking country is your CV (curriculum vitae, American English: résumé). A CV, which should not be more than two pages long (12-point font), should list your skills and abilities and should be tailored to fit each job application.

Some employers also require a short cover letter or e-mail in which the applicant explains why he or she particularly wants this job. Others require a statement summarizing the applicant's skills.

It is not necessary to begin a CV with the heading CV or CURRICULUM VITAE.

2 A CV (CURRICULUM VITAE)

A Janina Witt decides to apply for the hotel job advertised. Look at her CV and the explanations 1–9 below. Make a list of the differences between an English and a German CV, including the following points:

> the information left out of an English CV
> the extra information in an English CV
> the order in which education and work experience are listed (chronological or reverse chronological order)

1 Make it easy for an employer to contact you by including your mobile number and e-mail. Make sure your e-mail address is acceptable to an employer (e.g. not lachdichkrumm@hihi.de).

2 The PROFILE section is the first thing an employer reads. Give a positive picture of yourself by listing your strongest points. This will make the employer read the rest of your CV. Remember: Most CVs are read in less than 60 seconds, so make sure your profile catches the reader's attention.

3 Check that the skills you list are what the employer is looking for. Use 'fluent', 'good command' or 'basic knowledge' to describe your language skills.

4 Begin in the present and work backwards. Leave out irrelevant information (e.g. primary school). Translate all German expressions into English.

5 This sections shows you know about the world of work. Make sure it is clear what types of employer you have worked for and what you did in each case.

6 Include any skills you have that may be relevant or useful for the job.

7 Include any activities which show what sort of person you are but make sure they are relevant for the job (e.g. do not put clubbing or computer games).

8 Make sure you write out the month as a word. Remember German starts with a capital 'G'.

9 The names of referees can be left out to save space.

Janina Witt
Tulpenweg 15, 44892 Bochum, Germany
Landline: +49 234 588167 Mobile: +49 176 8873321
E-mail: janina.witt@web.de 1

2 **PROFILE**

My ambition is to use my experience in the hospitality industry at a large hotel in the UK. I am highly motivated, hard-working, responsible and reliable, and I am very interested in languages and other cultures.

3 **KEY SKILLS**

Native speaker of German
Fluent in English
Good command of Spanish
Good command of Serbian

4 **EDUCATION AND QUALIFICATIONS**

Since August 20..	Two-year, full-time commercial course at Robert Schumann Berufskolleg für Wirtschaft und Verwaltung der Stadt Essen (Robert Schumann Vocational Training College for Business and Administration in Essen), Germany to obtain higher education entrance qualifications (English and Spanish)
20.. – 20..	Städtische Realschule (selective state secondary school), Bochum

5 **WORK EXPERIENCE**

March – April 20..	Work placement at Porto Azzuro Aparthotel Malta in reception and housekeeping
September 20..	Work placement as shop assistant at Mango boutique, Essen
June – July 20..	Work placement at Hotel Zira in Novi Sad, Serbia in reception and back office

6 **RELEVANT SKILLS**

Good command of Microsoft Office
Swimming teacher for children of primary school age
First aid certificate

7 **EXTRA-CURRICULAR ACTIVITIES**

Ballroom dancing
Riding
Travel

8 **PERSONAL DETAILS**

Date of birth: 11 November 19..
Marital status: Single
Nationality: German

9 **REFERENCES**

Available on request

B **Match the information from a CV (A–L) with the headings (1–6). There are two answers for each heading.**

1 PROFILE

2 KEY SKILLS

3 EDUCATION AND QUALIFICATIONS

4 WORK EXPERIENCE

5 RELEVANT SKILLS

6 EXTRA-CURRICULAR ACTIVITIES

A Full driving licence

B September 20.. Two-week placement at Softech Computers in workshop and shop.

C 20.. – 20.. Regular summer holiday job as play leader for primary school children

D June 20.. German school leaving certificate (Year 10)

E Member of Red Cross

F I wish to find a job in an English-speaking country where I can use my computer and language skills. I am highly motivated and extremely flexible.

G Fluent Polish / Good command of English and Russian

H 20.. – 20.. Duisburg state secondary school

I Experience of website design

J Badminton

K My goal is to gain experience of working in the US for at least six months. I have computer, language and administrative skills and am a reliable, flexible person.

L Fluent English / Basic knowledge of Spanish

C **Now use the headings (1–6) in exercise B to write facts about yourself. Invent more headings if necessary. Write on a separate piece of paper and compare your answers with those of two or three other students.**

D **How do you refer to your education, training and skills in English? Find the English equivalent (a–j) for each German expression (1–10).**

1 Allgemeine Hochschulreife (Abitur)
2 Berufsschule, Berufskolleg, Gewerbliche Schule
3 Fachhochschulreife
4 Führerschein Klasse 3
5 Mittlere Reife
6 Realschule
7 Hauptschule
8 Gymnasium
9 Streitschlichter
10 Schülersprecher/-in

a grammar school
b secondary school
c selective secondary school
d German university entrance qualifications
e German higher education entrance qualifications
f student representative
g student conflict mediator
h driving licence
i (BE) vocational training college, (AE) vocational school
j German Class 10 School Leaving Certificate

3 A COVER LETTER

Read Janina's cover letter and find the following information:

1 the location of the hotel
2 when Janina will be able to start work
3 what possibilities her course gives her
4 how she knows about the hospitality industry
5 what sort of atmosphere she likes to work in
6 what she sends with her letter

Tulpenweg 15
44892 Bochum
Germany

10 May 20..

Ms Debbie Wharton
Human Resources Manager
Best Western Monkbar Hotel
St. Maurice's Road
YORK
YO31 7JA
GROSSBRITANNIEN

Dear Ms Wharton

Vacancy for entry level hotel work, reference no. RHYO 232

With reference to your advertisement on the internet, I wish to apply for the above-mentioned post.

By June of this year I will have completed a two-year commercial course in business and adminstration at Robert-Schuman Vocational Training College in Essen, Germany. The course includes languages (English and Spanish), IT and a work placement with a local employer. It prepares students for a job in commerce or industry and also entitles them to attend a course in higher education.

My summer hotel jobs over the last two years have shown me that the hospitality industry is the field I wish to work in permanently. I enjoy working in a busy environment with people from all over the world and would love to have the chance to use the skills I have learned at college and on my work placements.

My CV is enclosed for your information and I am available for an interview at short notice.

I would be delighted if you would consider me for this post and hope to hear from you soon.

Yours sincerely

Janina Witt

Enc

4 WRITING A JOB APPLICATION

A Choose one of the jobs below and write:

> your own CV using the example on page 21 as a model.

> an 80–100 word summary of your skills (job 1) or a cover letter (job 2).

Use the list of useful phrases on page 25 to help you.

Entertainers/animators

Job 1

Sun-sand-fun.com is looking for young German speakers to train as all-round entertainers/animators at hotels in the Canary Islands.

Starting date: 01 July 20..

Requirements: You speak good English and Spanish. You are a top fit team player and a fun-loving person with a 'can-do' attitude. Previous experience is desirable but not necessary to do this job.

Training: We'll teach you how to entertain, dance, sing, and give classes to young and old.

Terms of employment: €500–600 per calendar month; board and lodging provided

Applications

Upload your CV here:		Browse...
Explain in 80–100 words why we should employ you.	Your statement:	

Successful applicants will be invited to a face-to-face interview and casting in Cologne.

German-speaking tour guide required in Brighton / South-East England

Job 2

Location: Brighton, UK

Salary: £1,500 per month

Job type: Temporary, full time

Reference: RSJ99

You will be responsible for accompanying German-speaking tourists on coach tours in South-East England. Duties and responsibilities include providing information on the destinations and sights visited; helping with accommodation, transport, food, hospitality issues; and providing round-the-clock assistance to ensure the well-being of all participants.

Person Specification

- Excellent spoken English
- Charming, friendly and helpful manner
- Strong communication skills
- Well-groomed appearance
- Able to learn quickly
- Effective team player with ability to be flexible

Applications

Upload your CV and cover letter for the attention of Ms Angela Chandler, Recruitment Director, Travel and Tourism Services UK.

B Now choose one of the jobs advertised on pages 15–16 and list the most important skills needed to get that job. Re-write your CV and cover letter or summary to make them fit that job description.

Introduction	**Einleitung**
I was extremely interested to read your advertisement in ... *(newspaper/magazine)*/ on the internet for the post of ...	Ich habe Ihre Anzeige in der ... *(Zeitung/Zeitschrift)*/ im Internet für eine Stelle als ... mit großem Interesse gelesen.
I wish to gain experience in ... / make use of my foreign language skills.	Ich möchte Erfahrungen auf dem Gebiet von ... sammeln / von meinen Fremdsprachenkenntnissen Gebrauch machen.
I feel sure that your company/organization has the post I am looking for.	Ich bin sicher, dass Ihr Unternehmen / Ihre Organisation die Stelle hat, die ich suche.
I believe I am particularly suited for the post advertised because ...	Ich denke, dass ich für die ausgeschriebene Stelle besonders geeignet bin, weil ...
Skills	**Fähigkeiten**
As a native speaker of German/French/ Spanish/Polish, I am also fluent in (spoken and written) ...	Als deutsche(r)/französische(r)/spanische(r)/ polnische(r) Muttersprachler(in) beherrsche ich auch die ... Sprache (in Wort und Schrift).
I am used to (e.g. working with people / working in a team).	Ich bin es gewohnt (z. B. mit Menschen umzugehen, im Team zu arbeiten).
Previous experience	**Bisherige Erfahrung**
Before/After/During my course at ..., I completed a work placement at ... in the ... department.	Vor/Nach/Während meiner Ausbildung am ... habe ich ein Praktikum bei ... in der ... Abteilung absolviert.
My experience/work placement at ... has confirmed my interest in ...	Meine Erfahrungen haben / Mein Praktikum hat mein Interesse an ... bestätigt.
My course has enabled me to use/develop my skills in ...	Meine Ausbildung hat es mir ermöglicht, meine Fähigkeiten auf dem Gebiet von ... zu gebrauchen/ entwickeln.
Availability	**Verfügbarkeit**
I am available for an interview at short notice / immediately / as from ...	Ich stehe für ein Vorstellungsgespräch kurzfristig / sofort /ab dem... zur Verfügung.
I would be prepared to move to ... and could start on ... *(date)*.	Ich wäre bereit, nach ... zu ziehen und könnte am ... *(Termin)* anfangen.
I would be able to start work any time after ...	Ich wäre in der Lage, jederzeit nach dem ... anzufangen.
References	**Referenzen**
Should you require references, the persons named in the enclosed/attached CV will be pleased to provide you with any information you may require.	Sollten Sie Referenzen benötigen, sind die im beiliegenden/beigefügten Lebenslauf genannten Personen gerne bereit, Ihnen alle benötigten Informationen zukommen zu lassen.
Suitable ending	**Angemessene Verabschiedung**
I very much look forward to hearing from you at your earliest convenience.	Über Ihre zeitnahe Antwort würde ich mich sehr freuen.
I would be delighted if you would consider me for this post and hope to hear from you soon.	Ich würde mich sehr freuen, wenn Sie meine Bewerbung für diese Stelle berücksichtigen würden und hoffe, bald von Ihnen zu hören.

E Job interviews

1 TIPS FOR JOB INTERVIEWS

A Read the tips for job interviews below. Then work with a partner to come up with at least two more tips.

1

Think about why you want the job and be able to put this into words. At first, you may only have a strong feeling that you want it, and this is a great sign and may be enough for you, but your employer will want to hear you talk about your interests and desires in connection with the position. This is also true for any written correspondence you have with potential employers.

2

Even if dress is normally casual at the employer's, you should still dress up. Wear a suit, if you have one. Everyone will know it is just for the interview and they will appreciate your effort. No one will worry that you will come to work every day overdressed.

3

If the position you are applying for is in another city, your interview may well take place via webcam, and you will need to prepare. Choose a tidy, professional-looking background to sit in front of. Make sure everything technical is working at your end: test the sound, the picture, the lighting in the room, etc. with a friend before the employer calls you.

4

If the job you are applying for is, well, not particularly attractive, nobody will expect you to say it is what you want to do for the rest of your life. For example, if it is a job passing out flyers, you do not have to say 'It's always been my dream to stand on a street corner and distribute information!' Nevertheless, you will have to say why you want this particular job. Say something like 'I enjoy contact with people and I want to practise approaching strangers.' You will also have to give the impression that you plan to do the job for a while and not quit after just one day.

B Ihre Schule führt eine Job-Info-Woche durch. Bereiten Sie hierfür ein Informationsblatt oder einen Aushang vor, in welchem Sie die Tipps von 1A auf Deutsch kurz zusammenstellen.

C With a partner, follow these steps to brainstorm what to say in an interview.

1. Think of three jobs and come up with good, realistic answers for the question 'Why do you want this job?' for each one of them. Refer to tips 1 and 4 in the text.
2. Then give another group your answers to this question and let them guess which jobs they relate to.

2 LISTENING: TWO TELEPHONE CALLS

1 7

A **Listen to two telephone interviews. First copy the table into your exercise book or onto your computer and then fill it in as you listen.**

	Tobias	Helena
1 Why this job?	…	…
2 Skills?	…	…
3 Strengths?	…	…
4 Weaknesses?	…	…
5 Future plans?	…	…
6 Own question(s)?	…	…

B **Which applicant do you think should get the job? Explain why in a short text.**

3 DOING A JOB INTERVIEW OVER THE PHONE

Follow the steps below to role-play a job interview.

1 Refer to the job advert for a tour guide on page 24. Angela Chandler has received some interesting applications from young people in Germany, so she now telephones them to see which ones are suitable.

2 Practise the telephone dialogue with a partner. Refer to page 135 for useful telephone phrases.

Partner A: You (own name)
Go to file 1 on page 174.

Partner B: Ms Angela Chandler
Go to file 7 on page 176.

3 Perform your dialogues in front of the class. The class should now judge which applicants are best suited for the job.

4 When you have finished, swap roles with your partner and do the role-play again.

TOP TEN INTERVIEW QUESTIONS

We asked 100 personnel managers: **'What are your top ten questions for recruitment interviews?'**

Here are the ten most popular requests and questions.

1 Please take us through your CV.
2 Are you a team player?
3 Do you have any hobbies?
4 What are your strengths?
5 What are your weaknesses?
6 Why do you want to become a …?
7 Why do you want this job?
8 Why should we employ you and not someone else?
9 What are your plans for the future?
10 Do you have any questions you'd like to ask?

4 LISTENING: A FACE-TO-FACE JOB INTERVIEW

Janina Witt is at the Best Western Monkbar Hotel in York for a job interview. She has prepared answers to the top ten interview questions on page 27.

A **Study Janina's CV on page 21 and write down how you think she will answer questions 2–10 on page 27.**

1 8

B **Listen to the interview and write down Janina's answers to questions 2–10. List the biggest differences between her answers and yours.**

C **Listen to the interview again and explain:**

1 why Janina has chosen to apply to this hotel
2 what she could do next instead of getting a job
3 why she was so happy in Malta
4 how she plans to help her parents

5 DOING A FACE-TO-FACE JOB INTERVIEW

Role-play a face-to-face job interview with a partner. Choose one of the jobs mentioned in the advertisements in this Topic and try to use phrases from below.

Taking the interviewer(s) through your CV
Profile
– *As you can see from my CV, my ambition is to ...*
– *I would describe myself as ... (>see PROFILE in the CV, p 21)*
Skills
– *My native language is ... / I can speak (and write) ... fluently / I have a good command of ... (e.g. English) / I have a basic knowledge of ... (e.g. Polish)*
Education and qualifications
– *At the moment I'm at ... (name of vocational training college) in ... (town/city) / I'm doing a two-year full-time commercial course / My course finishes in ... (e.g. June 20..)*
Work experience
– *I have a part-time job ... (e.g. serving in a shop) / I have been working at ... for ... (e.g. two years) / since ... (e.g. August 20..)*
Other relevant activities/skills
– *I am a member of a ... (e.g. football, chess) club / I do charity work helping ...*
Strengths and weaknesses
I would say I'm good at ... (e.g. working with people) / I find it easy to ... (e.g. work in a team)
I'm not very good at ... (e.g. maths etc.) / I haven't got much experience of ... (e.g. foreign travel)
Why this job?
I think I'm a good candidate for this job because ... (e.g. I have the right skills)
Plans for the future
I hope to ... (e.g. do a traineeship / get a permanent contract / save some money)
Own questions
Would it be possible to ... ? / If I got the job, would I be able to ... ?

> Grammar Summary, if-sentences type II, p. 220

Webcode: FOBNRWT102

F Scenario

Situation: Sie haben gerade Ihren Schulabschluss gemacht und suchen nun eine Stelle, bei der Sie Ihre Englischkenntnisse gut einsetzen können. Folgende Stellenanzeige erweckt Ihr Interesse.

Fly Bike Werke GmbH

We are a leading manufacturer of sport and leisure bicycles based in Oldenburg. We produce high-quality bicycles as well as cycle wear and cycle accessories.

To help us expand our cycle tour business in the English-speaking market we are looking for a

Sales and Marketing Assistant (m/f).

Responsibilities include assisting with incoming and outgoing mail, dealing with customer enquiries and taking orders. You will have the ability to understand what our clients are looking for and explain our products professionally. An enthusiastic manner is a must.

We are looking for a candidate who is dynamic, focused and able to work closely with other members of the team. You should have effective communication skills as well as good persuasion and influencing skills.

The successful candidate will have completed a course in business administration at a vocational college and have a working knowledge of computer programs, excellent German and English (spoken and written) and preferably some knowledge of one other foreign language. Work experience in a sales or marketing office is an advantage but not necessary.

Send your CV and cover letter (in English) explaining why you are suited to this post to:

Frau Veruschka Linden
Personalabteilung
Fly Bike Werke GmbH
Rostocker Straße 334
26121 Oldenburg

1 **Um entscheiden zu können, ob Sie sich für die Stelle bewerben möchten, machen Sie sich zunächst Notizen auf Deutsch zu den Eckpunkten der Anzeige.**

Stellenbeschreibung: ...
Geforderte Eigenschaften: ...
Notwendige Qualifikationen: ...
Gewünschte Unterlagen: ...

2 **Nach reiflicher Überlegung entscheiden Sie sich, sich bei Fly Bike Werke GmbH um die ausgeschriebene Stelle zu bewerben. Erstellen Sie Ihre Bewerbungsunterlagen auf Englisch.**

3 **Kurze Zeit später erhalten Sie eine Einladung zu einem Vorstellungsgespräch bei Fly Bike Werke GmbH. Dieses soll auf Englisch stattfinden, um Ihre Englischkenntnisse einzuschätzen. Als Vorbereitung auf dieses Gespräch sehen Sie sich den Internetauftritt der Firma an und machen sich auf Englisch Notizen zu den Eckdaten des Unternehmens, welche Ihnen beim Gespräch nützlich sein könnten.**

http://www.flybike.de

Apple (12) ▾ Amazon eBay Yahoo! News (255) ▾

Home | Produkte | **Über uns** | Anfahrt | Kontakt

Geschichte: Jan Ullmann und Björn Ries, die Gesellschafter der Fly Bike Werke GmbH, sind seit frühester Jugend befreundet und hatten immer ein gemeinsames Hobby, das Radrennfahren. Dirk Ries, Vater von Björn Ries, betrieb in Oldenburg einen Fahrradeinzelhandel. Klaus Ullmann, Vater von Jan Ullmann, produzierte in Oldenburg Standardfahrradrahmen aus Stahl für die Fahrradindustrie.
Die Erfahrungen, die Jan Ullmann als Hobbysportler gesammelt hatte, ließen sich gut mit dem Knowhow seines Vaters kombinieren. Die Geschäftsidee, eigene Freizeit-Sporträder aus Stahl zu entwickeln, erschien ihm so vielversprechend, dass er 1982 die Fly Bike Werke GmbH (als so genannte Ein-Mann-GmbH) gründete. Die Aufgaben eines Geschäftsführers übertrug er an den ebenfalls radsportbegeisterten Hans Peters.
Der Zwang zu modernen Fertigungsmethoden und die damit verbundenen Investitionen erhöhten den Kapitalbedarf zum Ende des ausgehenden Jahrhunderts erheblich. Da traf es sich gut, dass bei einem Radrennen Jan Ullmann seinen alten Freund Björn Ries traf, der spontan bereit war, sich an der Fly Bike Werke GmbH zu beteiligen. Anfang 2001 trat er als weiterer Gesellschafter in die GmbH ein.

Kontakt: Rostocker Str. 334, 26121 Oldenburg
Telefon 0441 885-0 Telefax 0441 885-9211
Internet: www.flybike.de
E-Mail: mail@flybike.de

Gesellschafter: Jan Ullmann, Björn Ries
Geschäftsführer: Hans Peters

Mitarbeiter: 12 Arbeiter, 26 Angestellte, 2 Auszubildende
Kunden: Großhändler, Filialisten, Cash-and-Carry-Märkte im Inland, Großhändler im Ausland

Produkte
Fahrräder: City-Räder, Mountainbikes, Rennräder, Jugendräder, Trekkingräder
Handelswaren: Fahrradbekleidung, Fahrradzubehör, Fahrradanhänger
Dienstleistungen: Vermittlung von Fahrradreisen

Home

4 **Sie sind nun zu einem Vorstellungsgespräch nach Oldenburg eingeladen. Arbeiten Sie mit einem Partner / einer Partnerin zusammen. Lesen Sie Ihre Rollenkarten und bereiten Sie sich darauf vor, das Interview auf Englisch zu führen.**

Partner A: Sie haben sich für die Stelle als Sales & Marketing Assistant bei Fly Bike Werke GmbH beworben und sind zu einem Vorstellungsgespräch nach Oldenburg eingeladen worden.

- Lesen Sie Ihre Bewerbungsunterlagen noch einmal durch.
- Lesen Sie die Informationen zur Firma Fly Bike Werke GmbH auf den Seiten 182–186 durch.
- Bereiten Sie sich auf das Vorstellungsgespräch vor und überlegen Sie sich eine oder zwei Fragen auf Englisch, die Sie zur Firma oder zu den Aufgaben als Sales & Marketing Assistant stellen könnten.

Partner B: Sie sind Frau Veruschka Linden aus der Personalabteilung bzw. Herr Ralf Gerland vom Vertrieb der Firma Fly Bike Werke GmbH. Sie werden ein Vorstellungsgespräch mit Partner A für die Stelle als Sales & Marketing Assistant durchführen.

- Lesen Sie die Bewerbungsunterlagen von Partner A genau durch.
- Lesen Sie die Informationen zur Firma Fly Bike Werke GmbH auf den Seiten 182–186 durch.
- Bereiten Sie sich auf das Vorstellungsgespräch vor und überlegen Sie sich Fragen auf Englisch, die Sie stellen könnten, um die Eignung des/der Kandidat/in für die Stelle herauszufinden.

Spielen Sie das Vorstellungsgespräch mit Ihrem Partner / Ihrer Partnerin durch.

2

In the workplace

FOCUS

1 Look at the four different types of charts and decide which one:

1 shows how a whole or total amount is divided up into different quantities.
2 shows how one factor changes from place to place.
3 shows how a figure or figures change with time.
4 shows performance month by month.

2 What do the charts show us? Describe two of them in about 50–80 words.

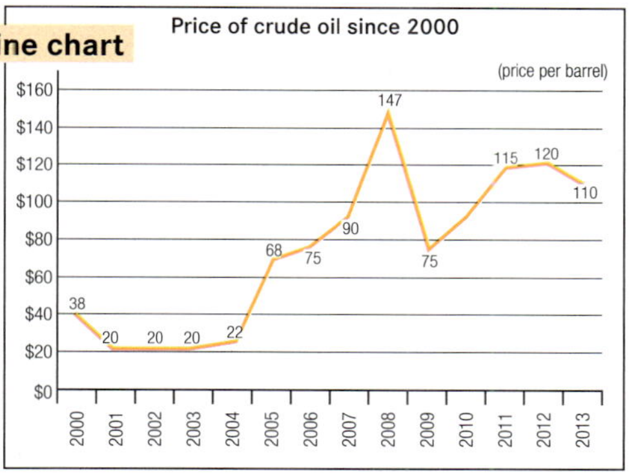

line chart

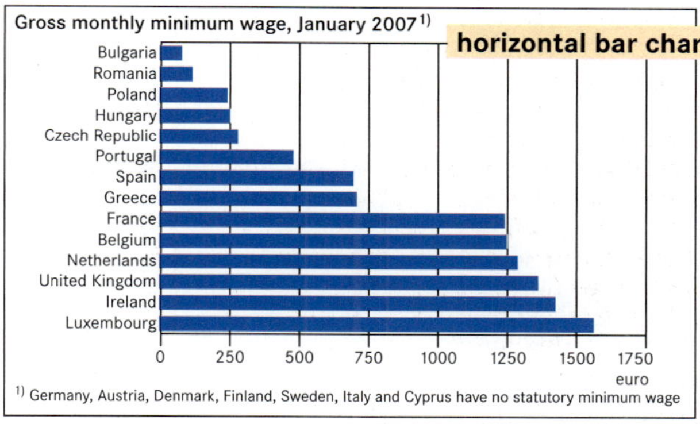

horizontal bar chart

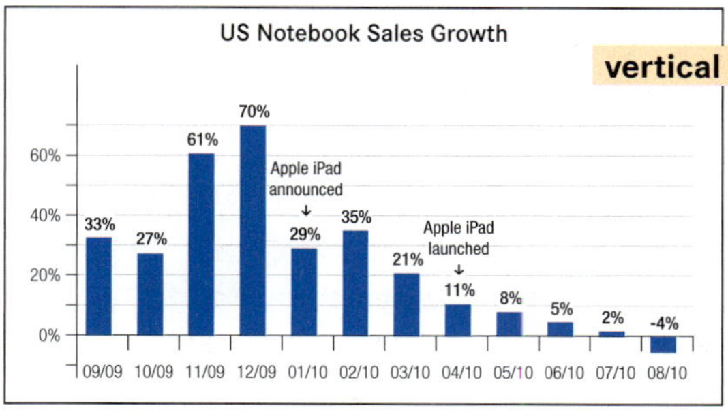

vertical bar chart

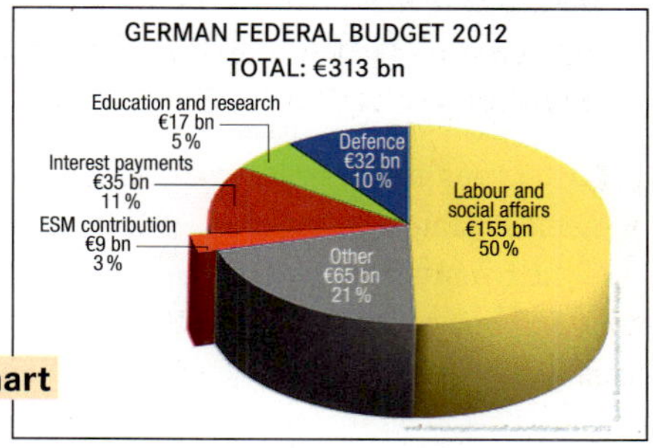

pie chart

3 Which type of chart would you use to describe the following?

> Skills, p. 209

1 the temperature changes in your town/city over the year
2 the relative price of diesel at six different petrol stations
3 the numbers of students in your class travelling to college by car, bus, train, bicycle and on foot
4 the different ages of students in your class
5 how much each student in your class spends on fast food and entertainment each month

4 Choose a topic from exercise 3 (or your own idea) and present the data to the class in a suitable chart.

A Europe at work

1 WORKERS ON THE MOVE

A With a partner make lists of all the languages spoken and different national backgrounds in your class. Then choose a suitable chart to present this data to the class.

Use these expressions:
In this class ...% of the students are from ...
We can that some/many/most/(almost) all of the girls/boys/students are ...

B Follow the steps below to discuss your feelings about leaving home to get a job.

1 Take three or four minutes to list the reasons why you would or would not move to another town/city or another country to work.
2 Turn to your neighbour and discuss the pros and cons of moving to another country in order to work there.
Begin like this: *I'd (I wouldn't) move away from home / to another country because then I would (wouldn't) ...*
3 Discuss with the whole class why people might wish to move to another country in search of work and what problems they might have to face.

C Study the following text and answer the questions in your own words.

1 Why did most people migrate at the beginning of the 21st century?
2 What sort of jobs did many new immigrants to the UK find in 2004? Can you imagine why?
3 What caused the European debt crisis in 2009?
4 Why did people leave countries like Spain, Portugal and Greece after 2008?

MIGRATION IN EUROPE

EU citizens are free to work and live in any member state and for most of the first decade of the twenty-first century many people moved to another country to find work, mainly from east to west. When, for example, Poland and nine other countries joined the EU in 2004, half a million migrant workers went to the UK and 64% of them were Polish. Whole sectors of the UK economy became dependent on immigrant labour, including the hotel business, catering, agriculture and the building trade. Until 2008 (see diagram, p. 33) the richer countries in the western part of the EU were not in financial difficulty and had work for immigrant labour.

A taste of home: A Polish shop in the UK

Everything changed after the US financial crisis of 2008–2009 leading to the European debt crisis in late 2009. The economies of Portugal, Ireland, Italy, Greece and Spain got into difficulty, so these countries were no longer attractive to immigrants. The Greek government became insolvent and needed massive help from the EU; the Spanish and Irish property bubbles burst in 2008 leaving thousands homeless, unemployed and in debt (see diagram *Youth unemployment*, p. 31). The new word heard all over Europe was austerity: cutting government spending. In consequence many people left the countries in difficulty in search of work wherever they could find it. In Europe countries of immigration became countries of emigration. We can only guess if and when things will change again in the future.

D Study the diagram and complete the following tasks.

1 Describe the general direction of migration until 2008.
2 Name the countries which were once countries of immigration and are now countries of emigration.
3 Explain why the inhabitants of some European countries have emigrated to Africa and South America.
4 List the larger countries in which there have been no major changes as regards immigration.
5 List the countries which have received most immigrants since 2009 and give possible reasons for this.

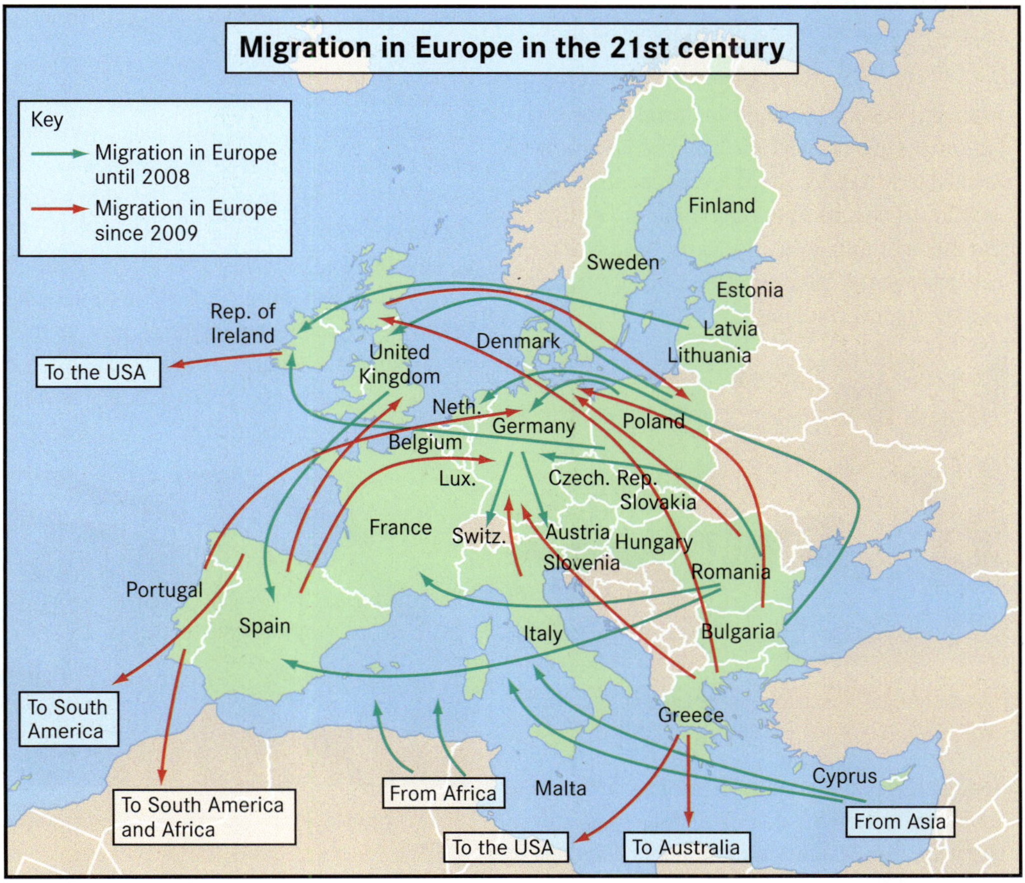

2 WORKERS FOR HIRE

A Read the text. What do the following numbers and expressions refer to?

60 | twice as much | 60,000 | two or three | 90

Germany needs you!

Germany needs qualified workers, while Spain and Portugal are struggling with high unemployment rates. When an article about job opportunities in a town in Baden-Württemberg appeared in a Portuguese newspaper, it started an avalanche of applications.

An employee at the job centre in Schwäbisch Hall takes up the story. “We were flooded with applications from the Iberian Peninsula,” she says, “and while we were trying to sort out all the CVs, about 60 unemployed Portuguese people simply turned up in our offices hoping to get work. A lot of the applicants didn’t have suitable qualifications, but when a planeload of qualified Spanish engineers flew to Stuttgart for a weekend of job interviews, most of them were hired.”

Alfonso Fonseca, an engineer from Lisbon, was one of the lucky ones. He has been working in Schwäbisch Hall for the last nine months. “There isn’t much chance of finding a job in Portugal at the moment and, even if you do have work, the pay isn’t good,” he says. “I’m earning twice as much here as I can make at home.”

Amalia Mendez, from lab technician in Spain to production engineer in Germany

You hear similar stories whoever you talk to. Take Amalia Mendez who qualified from a top university in Seville. Mendez is a production engineer in a high-tech company in Stuttgart. “I didn’t really want to emigrate,” she says, “but there are no openings for people with higher qualifications in Spain. The only job I was offered at home was as a laboratory technician.”

As Spain and Portugal watch their young specialists move north, local experts are starting to complain. “I can understand why they are moving away,” says a lecturer in Economics at one of Spain’s leading universities. “Everyone has the right to work, and there’s no work here. But our problem is the brain drain. A whole generation of highly qualified graduates is leaving. And they’re taking their knowledge and expertise out of the country. It costs about 60,000 euros to train an engineer, and Spain isn’t getting any return on that investment. Germany is reaping the benefit.”

While a spokesperson for a job agency in Schwäbisch Hall can understand the resentment, he also points out that everyone is benefitting from migration. “It’s true that we need qualified people to fill the gaps left by the young German engineers who are being headhunted by Asian companies, but, at the same time, Spain and Portugal are benefitting, too. We are relieving the pressure on their welfare state and giving job opportunities to what has quickly become known as the lost generation,” he says. “I don’t really see any conflict of interest there.”

Germany is relieving pressure on the Spanish welfare state

The conflict will begin, however, when the Iberian Peninsula recovers and wants its engineers back. The question is, when will that be? Most of the new arrivals say they hope to return home after two or three years and, if there is a turnaround in the economy in that time, economists expect around 90 per cent of these Spanish and Portuguese professionals to return home. If the recession holds on longer, however, many migrants are likely to settle permanently and never return to rebuild the economy in their own countries. If this is the case, economists envision a scenario in which the northern economies retain industry, and the southern countries are left with agriculture and tourism.

(546 words)

B **Work in groups to do the following tasks.**

1 Beschreiben Sie das Arbeitsmarktsverhältnis zwischen Deutschland und der Iberischen Halbinsel.
2 Erklären Sie, weshalb die spanischen Ingenieure eingestellt wurden, während andere Migranten keine Arbeitsstelle gefunden haben.
3 Zeigen Sie zwei Verbesserungen der Situation von Erwerbstätigen aus Spanien und Portugal auf, die diese in Deutschland erwarten können.
4 Erklären Sie, warum Absolventen die Iberische Halbinsel verlassen und geben Sie wieder, inwiefern die Region durch diese Abwanderung Schaden davonträgt.
5 Erörtern Sie die Vorteile für Deutschland, Spanien und Portugal, die bei der Abwanderung von Arbeitskräften entstehen.
6 Beschreiben Sie, was geschehen könnte, wenn die wirtschaftliche Erholung auf der Iberischen Halbinsel langsam vonstattengeht.

C **Match these words and phrases from the text with their definitions.**

no openings | brain drain | return on investment | reaping the benefit | turnaround | welfare state | lost generation | conflict of interest | headhunted

1 profit from money spent on something
2 found by an employer keen to persuade you to leave your present job and join his company
3 lack of vacancies in the workplace
4 people who started looking for work at a time of high unemployment
5 obtaining something good as the result of someone else's efforts
6 situation in which it is difficult for two or more parties to be treated equally
7 situation in which something changes from bad to good
8 system by which the government provide free services to people who need them
9 the movement of highly skilled and qualified people to another country where they can work in better conditions and earn more money

3 PRESENTATION

What is the European job market looking for? Follow these steps to give a short presentation.

1 Study the text *Germany needs you!* on page 34 again and, with a partner, draw up a profile of someone who is able to find work easily all over Europe. Think of things like education and training, age, family, gender, foreign language skills, cultures, the types of jobs available and wage levels. Include your own ideas and experience as far as possible.
2 Present the profile you draw up to your class and give reasons for

4 LISTENING: GOING HOME

1 10

A You are interested in the subject of migrant workers returning home and see the announcement of the radio programme on the right. Before you listen, work with a partner and brainstorm some reasons why the Polish workers might have decided to leave Britain. Then listen and check.

8.30 Business Talk Today
Host Bob Douglas talks to some Polish workers who are leaving the UK and returning home.

B Copy the table below into your exercise book or onto your computer, then listen again and complete.

Name	Reason for coming to the UK	Studied or trained as	Job in the UK	Reason for leaving
Ula	...	...	...	...
Jurek	...	...	...	...
Helena	...	...	...	...

C Complete these expressions from the radio programme with the most suitable word from the box. Then listen again and check.

after | away | for | in | into | on (x2) | up

1 to slide deeper ... recession
2 to look ... work
3 to go ... a position
4 to work one's way ...
5 to hand ... one's notice
6 to work ... the factory floor
7 to comment ... a fact
8 to take ... work from a British person

5 MIGRATION: WHO BENEFITS?

What do you think? Either write a comment for a forum about who benefits from migration and how, or have a discussion using the roles below. Whichever task you choose, think about the migrants, the country they emigrate to or from, and employers at home and abroad.

a recent migrant to another country

a migrant who has just returned home

an employer who has hired foreign workers

an employer who cannot find qualified staff

> Skills, p. 204 and p. 210

B Outsourcing and globalization

1 WHY OUTSOURCE?

A Before reading the text, look at the pie charts below. What reason for Germany's outsourcing of IT staff do they show?

Hourly wages of IT Workers

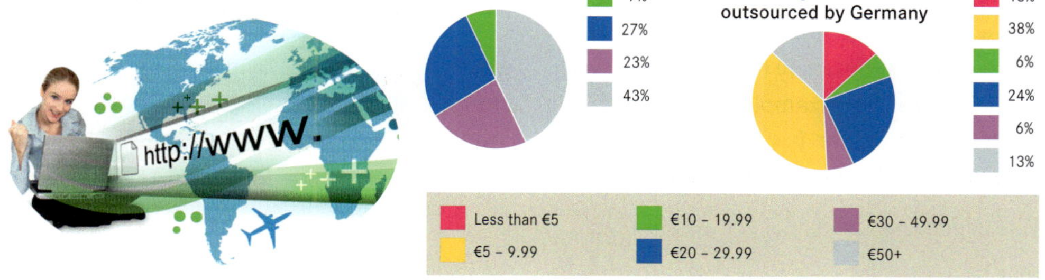

The outsourcing trend in IT

The competition between the internal IT department and the external provider

Companies which just a few years ago had huge IT departments are laying off staff and hiring other companies to meet their technology needs. This practice has become so popular that the value of IT outsourcing contracts in Western Europe in 2011 was estimated at €228 bn, with a yearly increase of about 5%. The reason for the popularity of outsourcing is that external IT providers have shown that they can adapt to companies' changing technology needs, and that they can do so at competitive prices.

One area in which internal IT departments are quickly losing this competition is the public sector, where budgets are getting smaller. The City Council of Cropping, England, for example, wants to have all of its IT services outsourced by 2017. British Telecom will run the communications, Fujitsu will run the infrastructure from Japan, and Tata will run the application management from India. 'This means,' says the Council's Chief Information Officer (CIO) Priya Waldorf, 48, 'that I need completely new skills on my internal IT staff.'

New career field: geek meets suit

Internal IT departments will still exist in some form. They will keep some of their highly skilled technical people who will decide the best strategy for the company's technology. And they will also hire new people who can deal with the changing needs of the department. Cornelia Neff, 27, is one of these people. She was hired by Waldorf earlier this year to manage the relationships between the Council's IT department and its external IT providers. 'I'm part geek, part suit,' Neff says, referring to her valuable mix of computer and business skills.

The business skills needed by today's internal IT departments go way beyond those of a typical programmer. Nowadays internal IT staff

Cornelia Neff: 'part geek, part suit'

have to know project management, supplier management and contract management. They have to be able to talk to, listen to and understand the needs of their company's IT users. And they have to use these skills to choose the best outsourcing contracts and get the most out of the relationships with their providers.

Neff studies a new outsourcing contract on her computer screen. 'I have to be very careful how I write this,' she says anxiously. 'I have to predict what flexibility the Council will need in the future. For example, the government might pass a minor law, and that could increase the data storage we need.'

Rise of the freelancer

Rick Forrest, 32, sits in his home office in Edinburgh, designing the new Web platform for the Council's public calendar of events. He has never spoken with Neff or anyone who works in Cropping. In fact, he has not been hired by the Council. He is working for one of the Council's external IT providers.

As a freelance worker, you might say Forrest is at the bottom of the outsourcing food chain – outsourced by the outsourced. When his former employer laid him off six years ago (and outsourced *his* job), he 'thought the world was going to end'. There are some drawbacks to working freelance: he has to pay his own health insurance and save money for his retirement by himself. But there are also some big advantages to freelancing: he can make his own work schedule and he does not have to worry about getting fired.

What about finding customers? 'That was difficult at the beginning,' says Forrest, 'but over the years I've developed a base of clients that like my work. I haven't had to look for work in a long time.' (560 words)

Freelancer Rick Forrest in his home office

B Do the following tasks in English.

1. Erklären Sie, warum Unternehmen die Größe ihrer IT-Abteilungen reduzieren und beschreiben Sie die Konsequenzen.
2. Stellen Sie heraus, weshalb ein IT-Projektmanager für eine moderne interne IT-Abteilung möglicherweise wertvoller ist als ein typischer Programmierer.
3. Vergleichen Sie Freiberufler mit Angestellten.

C Match the quotation with the speaker.

Priya Waldorf
Cornelia Neff
Rick Forrest

1 *It's my job to get our overseas suppliers to fulfil the needs of our customers. That can be difficult to coordinate.*

2 *I have no boss, so I can take a day off whenever I want, as long as my clients are taken care of.*

3 *We're looking to hire someone who has some IT experience but who can also manage our suppliers overseas.*

2 VISUALIZING THE PROCESS OF OUTSOURCING

A Complete the text with the words in the box.

budget | company | freelancer | skills | staff | suppliers

The outsourcing trend does not exist only in IT or in the public sector, it is happening in many industries. The first thing that usually happens is that a …[1] gets reduced. Then, the company lays off …[2] and outsources work areas. Finally, the company hires a smaller number of people to manage the …[3]. When a worker gets laid off, he or she sometimes goes to work for an external supplier, or he becomes a …[4]. If a worker learns supplier management …[5], he or she sometimes keeps the full-time job at the …[6].

B Copy the cause-and-effect diagram into your exercise book or onto your computer and complete it with the underlined phrases from the text above. Three answers have been done for you.

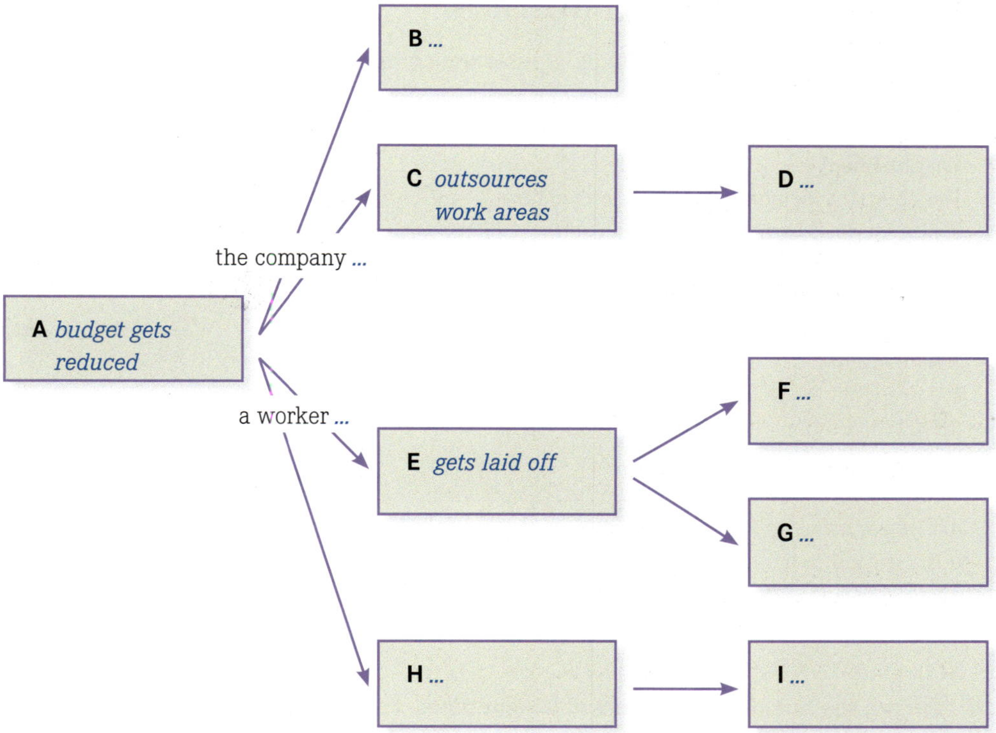

3 RESEARCHING ONLINE

Do some online research. Find three examples of companies that have outsourced jobs, either domestically or internationally. Make notes as in the example.

EXAMPLE

Company: British National Rail
Job: telephone hotline worker
Outsourced to: Comtech in India

> Skills, p. 201

4 WRITING A COMMENT

Comment on whether working as a company employee or as a freelancer would be better for you personally. Before you start writing, sort the following aspects into one of the four columns of the table.

> Skills, p. 204

dealing with company politics
freedom to work for whomever I want
setting my own hours
more structure and routine
more personal responsibility
having to motivate myself every day
working every day with the same colleagues
a boss checking my work
health insurance provided by the employer
being my own boss

working in a company		*working freelance*	
I would like ...	*I wouldn't like ...*	*I would like ...*	*I wouldn't like ...*
...	...	...	...

5 DISCUSSING A BUSINESS DECISION

A Read the text about Wright Bikes. How is the company's story similar to other stories you might have read about?

Wright Bikes

The company Wright Bikes has a long history. It was founded by the Wright family in the 1950s as a manufacturer of high-quality bicycles and bicycle parts. The company was very successful and grew to about 100 employees. Then, in 1975, the decision was made to close down the local factory and have the products made more cheaply in Taiwan. Since then, the company employs only about 30 full-time workers, all of whom get decent salaries, health insurance, six weeks' paid holiday, etc. Five of these full-timers make up the customer service department. It is their job to deal with customers via telephone and e-mail. Now an urgent need to cut costs makes it very tempting to 'let them go' (= fire/sack them) and hire service providers in other, poorer countries to replace them.

B You are the business managers at Wright Bikes. Form groups of three to discuss what your company should do.

> Skills, p. 210

Partner A: Go to file 4 on page 175.
Partner B: Go to file 11 on page 177.
Partner C: Go to file 25 on page 181.

C Write a letter to the board of directors explaining your point of view (according to your role card).

> Letter layout, p. 88

Webcode: FOBNRWT201

6 TALKING ABOUT EMPLOYMENT TRENDS

A Complete the text below with the words and numbers in the box.

2 | 30 | demand | early stages | growth | highly | include | labour intensive | less | manufacturing industry | outsources | material goods | replaces | society

ECONOMIC DEVELOPMENT AND JOBS

In the ...[1] of economic development, food production is very ...[2], so many people work in the agricultural sector. As a ...[3] becomes industrialized, technology does more and more work for the people. It ...[4] most of the agricultural workers and, later, some of the industrial workers, too. Another reason why jobs in these sectors disappear is that the developing country ...[5] more and more agricultural and industrial production to ...[6] developed countries. A reason for the ...[7] of the service sector is that, as the per capita income (income per person) rises, the ...[8] for services also rises.

Essen, Germany in 1864

Service-sector jobs are jobs which do not contribute to the production of ...[9]. These jobs ...[10] medics, teachers, bankers and police officers, just to name a few examples.

Germany is somewhat exceptional because it is a ...[11] developed economy which has maintained a large ...[12]. Today, only about ...[13]% of Germans work in agriculture, but approximately ...[14]% still work in industry.

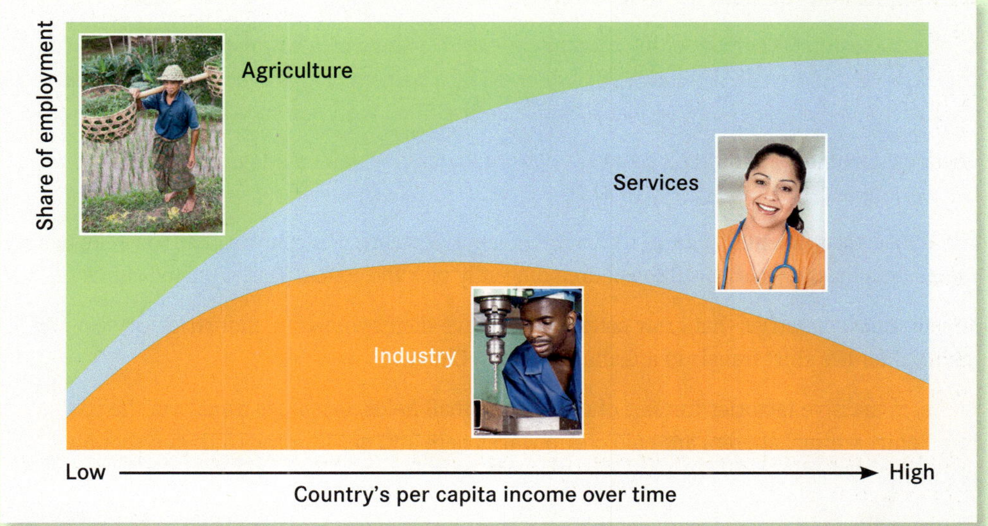

B Work with a partner. One of you should have your book open at page 41. Use information from the text and the diagram to do the following tasks. Use your own words as often as possible.

1. Describe the development of the three job sectors in relation to each other as an economy develops.
2. Point out what makes Germany different to some other developed countries.
3. As more and more people in developed countries work in service sector jobs, who is doing the jobs in industry and agriculture? Explain the implications this shift has on the way the world does business.

7 THE GLOBAL ECONOMY

A Before you read the article, talk in groups. What were the last three items of clothing you bought? Where did you buy them? Where were they made?

1 12

THE HUFFINGTON POST

THE INTERNET NEWSPAPER: NEWS BLOGS VIDEO COMMUNITY

FRONT PAGE | POLITICS | BUSINESS | ENTERTAINMENT | TECH | MEDIA | LIFE&STYLE | CULTURE | COMEDY | HEALTHY LIVING | WOMEN | LOCAL | MORE

Where is it from?

Craig and Marc Kielburger

"Nice T-shirt," I heard someone say. "Where's it from?"

The fashionista offered a store's name.

The question lingered.

Where is it from? Not just this shirt. Any shirt. Look at your own label. Where is it from? And who is it from?

In the beginning, there was a child.

He is in a cotton field in Uzbekistan, the second-largest cotton exporter in the world. He is working not because he wants to, but because he has to.

Cotton makes up 60 percent of his country's export earnings, so everyone is expected to contribute, even children. In 2000, UNICEF estimated 22.6 percent of kids aged 5 to 14 were harvesting the cotton. Some were given plastic water bottles filled with pesticide to spray on the crop.

The most fortunate child gets 3 cents for every kilogram picked – a kilogram worth $1.15 on the world market.

The Uzbek government maintains that no child labor exists in their country. Still, come September, rather than heading to school, the children diligently pick the cotton, pack it up and ship it off.

You see, most countries that grow cotton do not have their own textile industries. So, the raw material for the shirt travels to a manufacturer in China.

There, in massive factories the size of multiple football fields, machines transform the cotton into T-shirt fabric. Laborers are paid cheap wages here and produce the cloth at discounted prices before passing it on to a woman in Bangladesh.

There, cotton textile manufacturing is king. About 4000 garment factories fill the capital of Dhaka and employ 2.5 million people, mostly women.

The woman making our specific T-shirt arrives at work at 5 a.m. and spends 13 hours at her sewing machine. She is surrounded by younger workers, some under the legal working age of 13.

The woman makes about $25 monthly – the minimum wage – barely enough to afford food and her squalid living conditions.

Still, she works without complaint. Her fear is conditions getting better, because then the company might leave Bangladesh for a place with more employer-friendly laws. If that happens, she would face unemployment, hunger and potentially prostitution to keep her family alive.

So, she finishes the T-shirt and passes it on for its journey across the Pacific. In the hands of dockworkers, the shirt is loaded onto a ship and sent to North America.

In the back of a truck, someone drives it across the country to a shopping mall. It is unloaded and placed on a rack by a teenager.

That teen likely gets minimum wage. Currently, the U.S. federal minimum wage is $7.25.

From there, the item is bought – one of about 1.4 billion cotton T-shirts sold annually in North America. It is pulled over your head. It is thrown in the wash. It begs the question, "Where's it from?"

The short answer would be the store in the mall. But the short answer neither tells us the whole story nor makes us informed consumers.

T-shirts do not just magically appear on hangers. Chances are, they have crossed more borders than you. *(510 words)*

The Huffington Post, 6 February 2009,
www.huffingtonpost.com

B Copy and complete the flowchart showing the story of the T-shirt in the article. Then use the flow chart to explain the supply chain to your partner.

EXAMPLE
A child in Uzbekistan picks the cotton. Then the cotton is shipped to ... where ...

Where:	Uzbekistan		...2		...4			...8		
Who:	*a child* 1		labourers		a woman	...6		driver	...10	consumers
What:	picks the cotton		...3		...5	...7		...9	...11	...12

C Match each word to its definition.

1 afford
2 conditions
3 crop
4 discounted price
5 earnings
6 exporter
7 manufacturer
8 minimum wage
9 raw material
10 unemployment

a a person or company that produces goods in large quantities
b a person, company or country that sells goods abroad
c a large quantity of a farmed plant
d a reduced charge
e the lowest wage that an employer is allowed to pay by law
f basic ingredient that is used to make a product
g not having a job
h to have enough money to be able to buy or do something
i the circumstances in which people work or live
j the amount of money that has been made

D **Who from the story might have made these statements?**

1 *Why do I only get three cents per kilogram for this crop when it's worth $1.15? Someone is really stuffing their pockets here!*

2 *I hope our government doesn't make any new laws to protect us workers. If they do, my factory's customers will take their business elsewhere, and I will lose my job.*

3 *My pay is the lowest in the country, but since I'm in a developed country and not a developing country, it's not really very low.*

4 *Wow, this T-shirt only costs $6! I suppose some workers might have been exploited, but I'm going to buy it anyway. If I pay more at a different store, the big corporations will pocket the money; their workers won't see any of it.*

8 DISCUSSING GLOBALIZATION

Do you agree with what the consumer in the previous exercise says? Tell your partner why or why not. Use the following phrases.

I agree / I don't agree, because ...
That consumer is right/wrong, because ...
The consumer is partly right.
I agree somewhat.
I strongly disagree.
I think/believe/feel that ...

9 DESCRIBING EVENTS AT AN OVERSEAS FACTORY

> Grammar Summary, the passive, p. 219

Make the following active sentences passive.

EXAMPLE: Active: A factory in Bangladesh manufactures most of our goods.
Passive: *Most of our goods **are manufactured** in a factory in Bangladesh.*

1 Bangladeshi workers make cheap T-shirts seven days a week.
2 A Bangladeshi teenager loads and unloads the lorries.
3 Cameras record all vehicle movements.
4 A Bangladeshi company checked the safety precautions at the factory.
5 Last week a security guard locked the windows.
6 Guards check and lock all the exits every day.
7 A faulty electricity generator caused the fire.
8 The factory manager didn't make the emergency call to the fire brigade.
9 The water from the fire engines damaged the goods.
10 The fire killed over 200 workers.

10 ISSUES IN A GLOBAL ECONOMY

A When the things we buy are grown or produced abroad, it is not always clear how far environmental issues, workers' rights and safety are taken into consideration. How important is it for you to know that goods are produced in an ethical way? Which of these ethical food labels do you know?

B Complete the text below with relative pronouns, then summarize the text. Say whether you agree or not.

> Grammar Summary, relative clauses, p. 224

Fair Trade versus Food Miles

When you're shopping, are you one of these people *who/that*[1] looks for the Fairtrade logo? Buying goods ...[2] carry an ethical food label reassures us that we're supporting poor workers, most ...[3] live in faraway countries. It's nice to know that we're helping.

But, stop! Before you put that packet of organic beans into your trolley, how do you deal with the food miles – the distance ...[4] the food has travelled before it gets to the supermarket? Is it a good idea to choose food ...[5] has been brought to Europe on a plane ...[6] emitted tons of CO_2 into the atmosphere? And that's not the end of the journey. After the plane landed, the goods were loaded into refrigerated trucks ...[7] spewed out fumes as they travelled along the motorways to the supermarket. Apart from the pollution ...[8] is destroying the atmosphere, long-distance transportation of food means extra packaging, ...[9] uses up resources.

Aidan Young, ...[10] organization 'Buy Local' campaigns for regional products, says: 'Why do we import food ...[11] we could easily grow ourselves?' It's a question ...[12] everyone ...[13] is concerned about the problems ...[14] are caused by pollution should ask themselves.

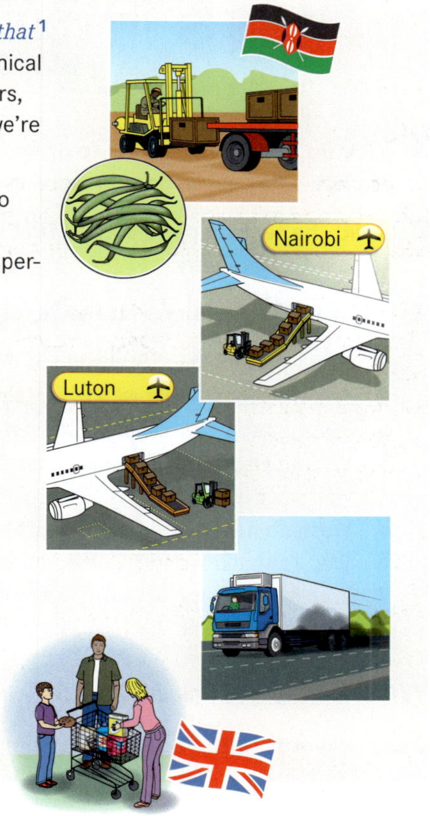

C Assess the attitude of your society or of your classmates towards consumption. Include the following in your text:

- whether or not you think that others are concerned about issues like workers' rights or the environment when they buy products
- arguments and facts to support your opinion
- a consideration of the counter-argument
- a suggestion on how awareness of ethical consumption issues could be improved

> Skills, p. 204

C Companies at work

1 RICHARD BRANSON: A FEARLESS ENTREPRENEUR

A **Why do people take risks to open their own business? Look at the pictures above and explain what some people want and what can go wrong.**

B **Read the text on page 47 and find out what sort of company Richard Branson prefers to run. Explain why.**

C **Answer the questions on the text in English.** > Skills, p. 203

1 Was wollte Richard Branson mit dem Gewinn der Weihnachtsbäume machen?
2 Aus welchem Grund ist Richard Branson im Alter von 18 Jahren nicht nach Bali gezogen?
3 Warum brauchte Richard Branson keinen Laden, als er begann, Schallplatten zu verkaufen?
4 Warum war Richard Branson bereit, Geld aufs Spiel zu setzen für neue, unbekannte Bands wie Boy George?
5 Weshalb hat er eine public limited company für seine Virgin Atlantic Airline gegründet?
6 Was kann man an der Börse kaufen und verkaufen?
7 Was war Richard Bransons Position bei der Virgin Group plc?
8 Warum kaufte er Virgin Atlantic mit seinem eigenen Kapital zurück?

2 WORKING WITH WORDS

Use the words in the box to complete the text.

amount | chairman | liability | lose | mail order | profit | public | responsibility | set up | shareholder

A lot of people buy books by … …[1] these days. The biggest company is Amazon, which was … …[2] in the USA in 1994. Amazon is a company with limited …[3], so investors can only …[4] the money they have invested in it. They have no …[5] for any mistakes the company makes. A big company like Amazon is a …[6] limited company because this type of company needs a large …[7] of capital to finance its activities. Someone who invests in a plc is called a …[8]. The head of a plc is the …[9]. Once a year he or she has to explain why the company has made a …[10] or a loss.

1 13

The Virgin Group

In 2010, Richard Branson, the famous inventor of the Virgin brand, was worth £2.6 bn and his empire included approx. 200 companies all over the world. In an interview in 2007 he said his first business venture had been at the age of nine when he planted some Christmas trees on a piece of land near his home in London. His plan was to sell them at 18 and move to the Indonesian island of Bali with the profits. Technically speaking, he was a sole trader because he did not intend to share the profits with anybody, he was his own boss and he had unlimited liability, meaning he bore all the risk. Rabbits ate his Christmas trees and he lost everything. Statistics show that 80% of all small businesses fail like Richard Branson's, but this did not stop him.

In 1970, he started again as a sole trader selling records by mail order and made a profit. In 1972, believing that the major record labels were not giving young people what they wanted, he set up Virgin Records Limited, which was a very different sort of company. He signed up unknown bands such as the Sex Pistols and Boy George. These rock and pop singers were more of a risk, so the company was a private limited company. The word limited (Ltd) in a company's name means its liability (financial responsibility) is limited, and the people who have put money into the company can only lose their investment and no more. (In contrast, sole traders have unlimited liability. If, for example, an electrician who is a sole trader makes a mistake working on a house and it burns down, he must pay for all the damage, even if it means he has to sell his personal property, e.g. his house, his car etc.) Richard Branson, therefore, had little to fear when there was fighting at the Sex Pistols' concerts because he could only lose the money he had put into his company.

Richard Branson added more and more private limited companies to the Virgin Group including an airline, Virgin Atlantic. In 1985 he needed a large amount of cash to fund his airline and other business activities so he formed a public limited company called The Virgin Group plc and sold shares in this company on the stock exchange. By selling shares to the public he was able to get the cash he needed to buy new planes for his airline, but he did not like his new role as the chairman of a public limited company because he had to tell the shareholders what he was doing and also show a profit. He was no longer free to do what he wanted, so in 1987 he bought back all the shares for £200 million and made his company into a private limited company again. (476 words)

3 CHOOSING THE TYPE OF COMPANY TO SET UP

A Read about the three ways to do business on the next page, then choose the right words to complete the sentences.

1 The person who bears most risk is *a member of a private limited company* / *a sole trader* / *a shareholder in a public limited company.*
2 A private limited company is owned by *the members* / *the public* / *a sole trader.*
3 A sole trader has *little freedom* / *the least freedom* / *the most freedom to make decisions.*
4 A shareholder in a plc *bears all the risk* / *gets all the profit* / *gets some of the profit.*
5 Members of the public can *buy shares in a private limited company* / *can buy shares in a public limited company* / *can buy a sole trader's business.*
6 Bankruptcy is a serious risk for *a sole trader* / *a director of a public limited company* / *a member of a private limited company.*

Three ways to do business

UK: Sole trader
US: Sole proprietor

- The company belongs to the sole trader.
- The sole trader takes decisions alone.
- He gets all the profit.
- He could lose everything.

UK: Private limited company (Ltd)*
US: Limited liability company (LLC)

- The company belongs to a closed circle of members.
- The members decide what is best for the company.
- The members share the profits.
- The members can only lose the money they have invested.

UK: Public limited company (plc)
US: Corporation (Corp./Inc.)

- The company belongs to the shareholders, who are members of the public.
- The directors decide what is best for the company and the shareholders.
- The shareholders share the profits.
- The shareholders can only lose the money they paid for the shares.

* In South Africa, Australia and New Zealand: Proprietary limited company (Pty Ltd)

B Match the companies in the box with the speakers.

East-West Fashions | Solar Power | Trekking and Mountaineering

1 John

My politics are green. I'm not rich but I have invested my extra money in a company which I hope will generate environmentally friendly energy. If the company does well, I'll get a share of the profits in a few years' time!

I worked for a big bank in the City of London for about 10 years and, as my hobby is travelling to distant places, I saved hard and set up a travel agency for trips to Africa and Asia with some close friends. We each invested £50,000 and so far the business has done well. If the worst came to the worst, I'd lose the money I invested but not everything I own!

2 Jill

3 Joanne

I opened a fashion boutique and imported clothes from India. For six months it was great and I made a lot of money for myself, but then the fashion changed and I suddenly had hundreds of dresses that nobody wanted. I couldn't pay the rent and then they cut off the phone. I went bankrupt.

C Decide what type of business each company above is: a sole trader, a private limited company or a public limited company. Explain your answer in a few sentences.

Begin like this:
I think / In my opinion ... is a ... (e.g. public limited company) / is owned by a ... (e.g. a sole trader) because ...

Webcode: FOBNRWT202

4 MINI AND MINIMALISM

A **Read the text and find as many examples of minimalism as you can.**

NO MORE THAN A MINI

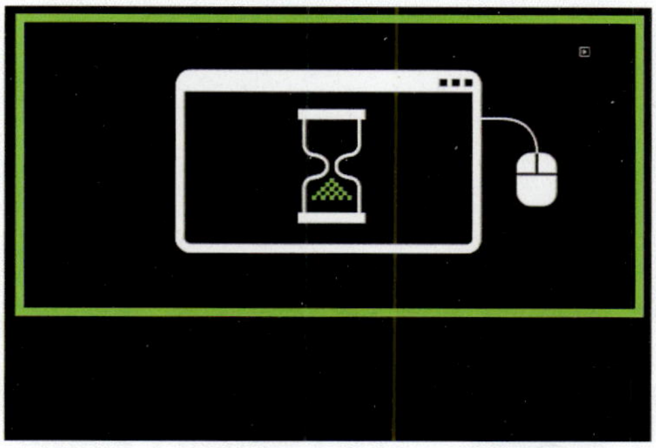

1 second of information

*http://archive.neverinneutral.com/mini_minimalism/microsite/index.html

The MINI manufacturers in the UK have chosen a clear message for their product: minimalism. A MINI is no more and no less than it needs to be. It is a small car but big enough for five passengers. It is fast but economical on fuel. Its stylish design has a big effect on people but its recyclable materials only have a small effect on the environment. If you only have time for a minimum of information on the MINI, you can go to the MINI website*, click on one of the MINI's features (e.g. engine intelligence) and listen to information for a minimum of time, e.g. exactly one second. The MINI manufacturers don't want to waste your time.

Minimalism or 'doing more with less' is an expression of MINI's corporate identity, as are concepts such as sustainability, efficiency, responsibility, social commitment, economy and, last but not least, fun. MINI drivers have fun driving, fun enjoying their freedom, fun being with each other and fun doing things for others. This is the message the makers of the MINI wish to give us, the consumers.

B **Find the English equivalents of these German expressions in the text.**

Freiheit | Leistungsfähigkeit | Nachhaltigkeit | soziales Engagement | Sparsamkeit | Spaß | Spaß am Miteinander | Umwelt | Verantwortung | Verbraucher | weniger ist mehr

C **How many of your answers in B can you make into adjectives?**

EXAMPLE *environment > environmental*

D **Ein/e amerikanische/r Gastschüler/in an Ihrer Schule möchte später, wenn er/sie wieder zu Hause ist, ein kleineres Auto kaufen und interessiert sich u. a. für einen Mini. Er/sie zeigt Ihnen eine Webseite (siehe Seite 50) und bittet Sie, ihm/ihr die wichtigsten Inhalte auf Englisch zu erklären.**

> Skills, p. 211

Rolle A
deutschsprachige/r Schülerin/-in
Beantworten Sie die Fragen des/der Gastschülers/-in zur Website und fügen Sie weitere Erklärungen nach Wahl hinzu.

Rolle B
amerikanische/e Gastschüler/-in
Stellen Sie Fragen zu den Überschriften, Texten und Bildern der Website. Stellen Sie weitere Fragen nach Wahl.

E **Use the extract from the MINI website to give a short presentation about the image the MINI manufacturers wish to give of their company. Consider the points below and add ideas of your own.**

> the colours used (how many? why these colours?)
> the use of photos and drawings (how many photos? how many drawings?)
> the amount of text used (why not more/less? colour/size of letters?)

5 SUSTAINABLE DEVELOPMENT

A Read the text and explain:

1 how industry has changed over the last 60–70 years.
2 what responsibilities companies have for their products.
3 the message the illustration has about the world as a whole.

1 14

The importance of being sustainable

Visit the website of any major company[1] and click on the section entitled *About us*, or *Corporate responsibility*, or *Our mission*. Very soon you will come across the word *sustainable*, so what does it really mean?

To understand it properly we need to look back to the middle of the 20th century when big industries were, at the most, national, but certainly not global. In those days companies manufactured and used products without worrying too much about the environment or the future. Coal was used to heat houses and power trains; chemicals were pumped into rivers and oceans, asbestos was used to insulate houses, etc. etc. If companies had carried on producing in this way, life as we know it would have stopped.

Nowadays, companies realize that the world is a small place in which everything they do has consequences for the whole planet. The International Institute for Sustainable Development (iisd) defines sustainable development in this way:

> *Environmental, economic and social well-being for today and tomorrow.*
> *All definitions of sustainable development require that we see the world as a system – a system that connects space; and a system that connects time.*

In simple terms, what we do in our own backyard will affect people on the other side of the planet (space). What people did in the past affects us now, and what we do now will affect people in the future (time). Companies must, therefore, balance both of these factors when they manufacture a product. If this balance is achieved, the product is sustainable.

Companies which believe in sustainable development accept responsibility for the present and the future. Their products and/or services are then described as *green*, *environmentally friendly*, *organic*, *bio-* (e.g. biofuel, biodiesel, biogas, biodegradable) and/or *recyclable*.

(289 words)

[1] Try it out with these companies: EDF (Britain's biggest electricity provider), Tesco plc (Britain's largest supermarket chain), Virgin Trains (a major British rail company) or BAE Systems (Britain's largest plane manufacturer).

B Find words in the first two paragraphs of the text on page 51 to match the definitions.

1 large
2 100 years
3 all over the world
4 the world around us
5 a soft grey heat-proof building material which is no longer used because it causes cancer
6 to keep heat out or in

C Do one of the research and writing tasks below.

1 With a partner use the internet to look up the websites mentioned in the text and some more of your own choice (e.g. major German companies with a website in English). Write down all the statements you find with the words 'sustainable' and 'sustainability'. Compare your results with those of other students. Do you think the companies all really do what they say on their websites? Write a comment.
2 Make a list of the products you and your family regularly buy (e.g. food, drinks, cosmetics, clothing, energy, electrical and electronic goods). Do research on the internet to find out about the companies that make them. Are any of them green? If so, how important is it to you that they are green? Write about your findings.

6 WORKPLACE STANDARDS

A Sie lernen eine/n englische/n Studenten/in kennen, der/die eine Arbeit über Arbeitsplatzstandards bei großen europäischen Firmen schreibt. Er/Sie findet einen Beitrag über Adidas auf Deutsch (siehe Seite 53) und bittet Sie, die wichtigsten Inhalte zu erklären.

B Schreiben Sie eine kurze schriftliche Zusammenfassung des Textes auf Englisch mit Hilfe der Wortliste.

> Skills, p. 211

Ansichten	*beliefs*
Bedingungen erfüllen	*to fulfil requirements*
Behinderung	*disability*
Diskriminierung	*discrimination*
Geschlecht	*gender*
Kinderarbeit	*child labour*
Leistung	*performance*
Merkmale	*characteristics*
Nationale Herkunft	*national origin*
Rasse	*race*
Ressourcen	*resources*
Sklavenarbeit	*slave labour*
Umweltgesetze	*environmental laws*
Umweltverschmutzung	*environmental pollution*
Vielfalt	*diversity*
Werte	*values*
Zulieferer	*supplier(s)*
Zwangsarbeit	*forced labour*

ttp://www.adidas-group.com/de/sustainability/Suppliers/Our_Workplace_standards/default.aspx

Apple (12) ▾ Amazon eBay Yahoo! News (255) ▾

ADIDAS Workplace Standards

LEISTUNG. LEIDENSCHAFT. INTEGRITÄT. VIELFALT

Dies sind die Grundwerte des Sports. Sport ist die Seele des adidas Konzerns. Wir messen uns nicht nur selbst an diesen Werten, sondern auch unsere Geschäftspartner.

...

Wir erwarten von unseren Geschäftspartnern, dass sie in ihren Produktionsstätten die folgenden Grundsätze und Verfahrensweisen umsetzen:

Zwangsarbeit

Geschäftspartner dürfen keine Zwangsarbeiter beschäftigen, weder in Form von Gefangenenarbeit, Sklavenarbeit oder einer sonstigen Form von Zwangsarbeit. ...

Kinderarbeit

Geschäftspartner dürfen keine Kinder unter 15 Jahren oder schulpflichtige Kinder in Ländern, in denen das schulpflichtige Alter über 15 Jahren liegt, beschäftigen.

Diskriminierung

Wir respektieren kulturelle Unterschiede. Geschäftspartner dürfen bei ihren Einstellungs- und Beschäftigungspraktiken niemanden diskriminieren. Entscheidungen über Anstellung ... dürfen nicht auf persönlichen Merkmalen oder Ansichten, auf Rasse, nationaler Abstammung, Geschlecht, Religion, Alter, Behinderung, Familienstand, Mitgliedschaft in einer Organisation, sexueller Orientierung oder politischer Überzeugung basieren. ...

Umweltbestimmungen

Unsere Geschäftspartner sollten sich um die ständige Verbesserung der Umweltbedingungen bemühen, unter denen sie selbst und ihre Zulieferer produzieren. Dies bedeutet: die Beachtung des Prinzips der Nachhaltigkeit bei betrieblichen Entscheidungen, der verantwortliche Umgang mit natürlichen Ressourcen, saubere Produktion, Verhinderung von Umweltverschmutzung und die Entwicklung und Verwendung von Materialien, Technologien und Produkten, die sich am Prinzip der Nachhaltigkeit orientieren.

7 GROUP DISCUSSION

The BBC radio discussion programme *World Have Your Say* is inviting listeners and Facebook users to take part in a debate about company values.

The topic is *"Buy Green, Think Green, Work Green. We all have a choice."*

In groups of 3-4, imagine the contributions the people described in your profiles would make on air and on Facebook, and then have a group discussion. Follow it up with a written contribution on Facebook from each person.

Partner A: Go to file 2 on page 174.
Partner B: Go to file 19 on page 180.
Partner C: Go to file 13 on page 178.
Partner D: Give your own point of view.

> Skills, p. 210

8 A COMPANY PRESENTATION

A **Die Industrie- und Handelskammer in Ihrer Nähe veranstaltet eine Jobbörse für Jugendliche, bei der Arbeitgeber aus mehreren EU-Ländern vertreten sind. Ihre Klasse hat den Auftrag, Firmenprofile und berufliche Perspektiven zu sammeln, um darüber im Unterricht zu berichten.**

1 15

Sie besuchen den Stand von TASTE UK, einer großen britischen Einzelhandelskette, und hören sich eine Präsentation in englischer Sprache über das Unternehmen an. Notieren Sie die wichtigsten Fakten in Ihrem Arbeitsheft mit Hilfe der Checkliste.

Checkliste

1 Name des Unternehmens
2 Unternehmensform
3 Branche
4 Sitz
5 Geschichte des Unternehmens
6 Beschäftigte
7 Märkte
8 Angebotene Stelle(n)
9 Arbeitsbedingungen
10 Vergütung
11 Unterschiede zu deutschen Bedingungen
12 Weitere Informationen

B **With a partner choose a European company (e.g. a car manufacturer, an energy or internet provider, a retail chain or a company where friends or family work), research it and give a short presentation to the class. Use the checklist from above and the expressions in the language box.**

Introductions

Hi / Good morning/afternoon/evening. My name's ... (first and surname, *e.g. Silke Meier*).
This is my colleague ... (first and surname).

Presentation

Background
- *The company was founded in ...* (date) *... by* (person/company).
- *The managing director / chief executive officer (CEO) / president is ...*
- *It has ... employees in ...* (locations).
- *Last year its turnover was ... (e.g. €8,000,000) and its profit margin was ... (e.g. 10%).*

Location
- *It's located in ... / Its headquarters are in ... / Its head office is in ... / The parent company is located in ...*
- *It has a subsidiary in ... / It has a factory in ... / It has agents in ...*

Products
- *Its ... (products) are made of ... (materials, e.g. pure wool / wood / steel / plastic).*
- *It's famous for ...* (goods/services).
- *Its products include ...* (goods/services).

Markets
- *It sells/exports its products/services to ... (e.g. customers all over the world).*
- *The goods are bought by ...* (customer) *in ...* (place).

Thanks

Thanks for listening. / Thanks for coming to this presentation.

Questions

If you have any questions, I'll/we'll be happy to answer them.

Webcode: FOBNRWT203

D The changing workplace

1 COMMUNICATION IN BUSINESS

A How long has the technology listed below been used commercially? Discuss in pairs and try to put the list into chronological order.

A e-mail
B facsimile (fax) machine
C internet
D mobile phone
E personal computer
F smartphone
G answerphone
H video conferencing software

B In groups, talk about what the office would be like without the technological advances above. How did the work get done?

People had to meet in person before there was video conferencing software.
Now office workers can ..., but they used to use ...

2 TELEWORKING

A Have you ever heard of teleworking? Try to find the best definition. Then read the text on the right to check your answer.

1 commuting to a factory or an office which is very far away from home
2 selling or dealing with complaints on the telephone
3 working at home or away, using communication tools to keep in touch with customers, colleagues and a central office

Telework or Teleworking *(noun)*: An option for employees to work away from the office one or more days a week using IT and telecommunication tools. Activities specially suited to teleworking include reading, writing, research, working with data and talking on the phone.

1 16

B You are interested in teleworking and have found a podcast on the internet in which a teleworker is interviewed. Before you listen, decide which of these statements you might hear.

1 *I have a password and can access a platform.*
2 *I go into head office twice a week.*
3 *I give face-to-face reports to my boss.*
4 *There are fewer distractions and people can concentrate better on their work.*
5 *I am in charge of two other teleworkers.*

Joy, 32, pharmaceutical sales representative

C Listen again and take notes on the following:

> Skills, p. 202

1 what Joy describes as 'a typical situation'
When the company has a new product on the market, Joy first ...
After a few weeks, she ...
Finally, she ...
2 what Joy sees as the benefits of teleworking

3 TELEWORKING FACTS AND FIGURES

After more internet research, you find the report on page 57 about telework in Europe.

A Read the text and do the following tasks.

1 Describe the diagram comparing and contrasting the sectors which were looked at during the study. Link the sectors to the occupations named and explain why some occupations are more suitable for telework than others.
2 Describe the benefits of telework for a) employers and b) employees.
3 Explain what makes a good tele-manager and describe the ideal teleworker.

B How were these German phrases expressed in the text? Match the verbs from box A to words and phrases from box B to find the translations used.

1 den Teammitgliedern vertrauen
2 der Versuchung widerstehen
3 eigenständig
4 gerne eigenverantwortlich arbeiten
5 jemanden unter Druck setzen
6 sich krank melden
7 sich verwöhnen
8 unbeaufsichtigt arbeiten

A

to call in
to trust
to pamper
to resist
to be left
to pressurize
to work
to not mind

B

working alone
sick
unsupervised
to get on with things
someone
temptation
the members of the team
oneself

C Do one of the writing tasks below.

> Skills, p. 204

1 The company where you are doing an internship is thinking about introducing teleworking and has asked for employees to say what they think of the idea. Write saying whether or not you would like to work from home and give reasons why (not).
2 You would like to telework but your boss is not keen on the idea. Write her an e-mail outlining the benefits of teleworking for the company and explain why you would be a good teleworker. Try to persuade your boss to agree to give you a chance to telework.

Telework in the European Union

A recent study conducted into teleworking threw up some interesting results.

The study looked at various sectors and discovered that a high percentage of employees in real estate, finance and education were doing telework, with professionals and senior managers topping the list of those who most often worked away from the office.

Telework by sector and occupation, EU27 (%)

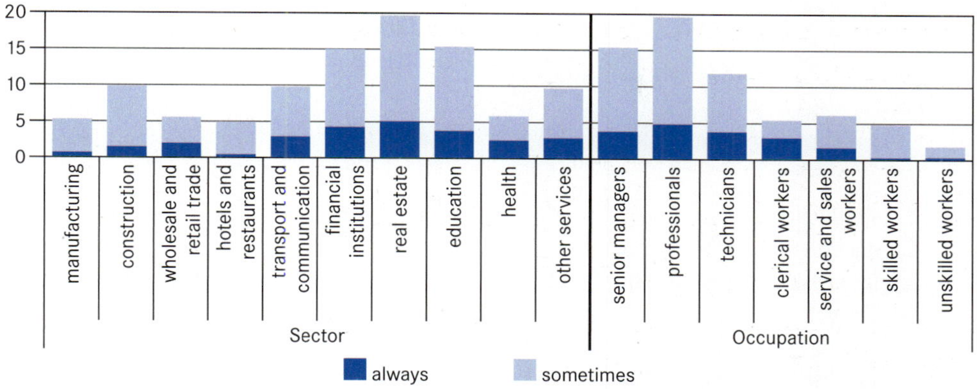

During the study, employers who had introduced teleworking mentioned the benefits to the companies. By 'allowing' their employees to work at home, the study showed that companies save money on office space and other facilities. Apart from money saved, the study also indicated that productivity rises, as teleworkers who are not interrupted by the distractions of office life are often able to get more work done. Last but not least, it appeared that teleworkers are less likely to call in sick than 'normal' office workers.

A large number of teleworkers who were interviewed on this point in the course of the study said that they had more time to pamper themselves if they felt they were getting sick, and they had less stress because they did not have to commute to work.

On the question of commuting, many companies said they were increasingly worried about environmental issues and were looking to reduce their carbon emissions. By introducing teleworking, a company can boast about its smaller carbon footprint. According to the study, this is especially important in countries with poor public transport and long commutes.

What about the managers of teleworkers? According to the study, good managers have to be able to delegate. Many of the managers interviewed said it was important to trust the members of the team to work and to resist the temptation to check up on people or put pressure on them.

This seems to be a good policy, as the study shows that employees working at home actually work more if they are working unsupervised. Many teleworkers said they liked the responsibility of working alone and preferred to be left to get on with things. Knowing that they were trusted made them more committed to getting the job done than if someone were pressurizing them all the time.

It is clear that companies are looking for people who can work independently without a lot of supervision. According to everyone who was interviewed, the ideal teleworker is well organized and has extremely good time-management skills; he/she is also likely to be highly skilled and know the job very well. Last but not least, teleworkers should not mind working alone.

(415 words)

4 THE CHANGING WORLD OF WORK

You are doing an internship at a British company. Your boss has asked you to give a presentation on the world of work in the 21st century and has given you a list of points which you should cover. You have found some ideas in German on the internet and would like to use them in your presentation.

A First, match your notes (1–6) to the German ideas (A–F).

1 *Flexible working hours*
2 *Fitting in with global working hours*
3 *Communication*
4 *Life-long learning*
5 *Part-time work*
6 *Teleworking / Home office*

A Die weltweite Vernetzung von Unternehmen verlangt zunehmend interkulturelle Kompetenzen der Arbeitnehmer.

B Es gibt fast keine Arbeitsplätze mehr ohne Informations- und Kommunikationstechnik. Der Trend zur ständigen Erreichbarkeit nimmt zu.

C In der heutigen Zeit kann sich keiner mehr auf seiner Ausbildung ausruhen. Weiterbildungen prägen immer stärker die Erwerbsbiographien.

D Internationale Kommunikation, längere Service- und Geschäftszeiten, ständige Erreichbarkeit, Schichtarbeit, Arbeitszeitkonten, Abrufarbeit, frei wählbare Gleitzeit oder sogar völlig selbstbestimmte Arbeitszeiten ersetzen zunehmend die 9-bis-17-Uhr-Arbeitsroutine.

E Zwei Menschen teilen sich eine Arbeitsstelle; flexible oder feste Stundenreduzierung, Arbeitszeitansparen durch Zeit- oder Geldguthaben (mehrmonatige Urlaubsphasen, Sabbatjahr).

F Viele arbeiten nicht mehr ortsgebunden. Arbeitnehmer können ganz oder zeitweilig von zuhause aus arbeiten.

B Next, use the information to explain the information orally to your colleagues who cannot speak German.

C Finally, write up your talk in English for the trainee file.

5 DISCUSSING ISSUES IN THE WORKPLACE

A One of your colleagues has collected views from several online forums. (See page 59.) You are going to work in groups of three and discuss some of the points politely. Follow the steps below.

1 In your group, choose an issue you would like to discuss. Then assign roles (A, B or C below) and prepare for, then have a discussion. Try to use phrases from the language box.
Partner A: You agree with what the first person has posted. Make notes and prepare your arguments.
Partner B: You agree with what the second person has posted.
Partner C: You are the moderator. Listen to Partners A and B and take notes. Which of them has presented the best arguments?

2 When you have finished, change roles, choose another issue and have another polite discussion.

1

Availability
CEO: Every employee should have a smartphone. In today's fast-moving world, we can't afford to wait until morning or Monday for a problem to be solved.

Worker: Why should I make myself available 24/7? I don't get paid as much as a boss, so why should I be expected to be on call all the time?

2

Stereotypical roles
Macho Malcolm: Women should stay at home and raise children. They can't do the same jobs that men can do.

Feminist Fran: Men can't do a lot of the jobs that women can do, but nobody ever talks about that. Companies would be better off if there were more female CEOs.

3

Life-long learning
Keen2Learn: Employees should be required to take at least one course every two years. If they don't attend a course, they don't get a pay rise or promotion.

Mike Money: I can't agree with Keen2Learn. I studied for years and got my diplomas, and that's enough. I'm entitled to my pay rises.

4

Intercultural competence
Employer: I'm always looking for employees who have worked abroad for at least six months. I want people who can deal with business partners all over the world.

Employee: Why should I learn foreign languages or find out how people abroad do things? I work here, not abroad.

Asking for somebody's point of view
What do you think?
What's your take on that?
(Name), what's your opinion?
Do you agree with (name)?

Agreeing
I agree.
That's right.
Absolutely.
I see what you mean.

Interrupting
Excuse me.
Can/May I interrupt you?
Can/Could/May I just interrupt here?
I'd like to say something, please.

Giving your opinion
My opinion is ... / In my opinion, ...
If you ask me, ...
As far as I'm concerned, ...
I (don't) think/believe that ...

Disagreeing
Sorry, I don't/can't agree.
I'm afraid that's not right.
What we shouldn't forget is ...
That's a good point, but ...

Asking for clarification or repetition
I'm sorry, I didn't get that.
I'm afraid I don't understand.
What exactly do you mean by that?
Could you say it again / repeat that, please?

B Do one of the following writing tasks.

1 Write a short summary of your discussion. What conclusions did your group reach?
2 Choose one of the issues and write a comment.

E Scenario

Situation: Sie haben die Stelle als Sales and Marketing Assistant bei Fly Bike Werke GmbH in Oldenburg bekommen. Ihre Hauptaufgabe besteht darin, bei der Expansion des Radtour-Geschäftes den Vertriebsleiter, Herrn Ralf Gerland, und seine zuständige Mitarbeiterin für Marketing, Frau Sylvia Dogan, zu unterstützen.

Um das Geschäft mit den Fahrradtouren zu intensivieren, sucht Fly Bike Werke GmbH einen geeigneten Vertriebspartner in Großbritannien. Das neue Konzept von Herrn Gerland sieht vor, dass Fly Bike Werke GmbH deutsche Kundinnen und Kunden für Radtouren in Großbritannien gewinnt. Im Gegenzug soll der neue britische Partner Kundinnen und Kunden für seine Radtouren in Deutschland gewinnen.

1 Herr Richard South von South Riding Tours in York wurde nach Oldenburg eingeladen, um Gespräche über eine mögliche Kooperation mit Fly Bike Werke GmbH zu führen. Während seines Besuches wird Herr South, der leider kein Deutsch spricht, von der/dem Sales and Marketing Assistant der Firma betreut.

Partner A
Sie sind der/die Sales and Marketing Assistant bei Fly Bike Werke GmbH. Sie sollen folgende Themen mit Herrn South erörtern.

- Begrüßen Sie Herrn South, stellen Sie sich vor und fragen Sie ihn, wie sein Flug war.
- Teilen Sie Herrn South mit, dass Sie ihn während seines Besuches betreuen werden.
- Schildern Sie den geplanten Tagesablauf des Besuches.
- Beantworten Sie die Fragen von Herrn South und gehen Sie auf mögliche Wünsche seinerseits angemessen ein.

Partner B
Sie sind Mr Richard South von South Riding Tours, York.

- Reagieren Sie angemessen auf die Informationen, die Sie von Partner A bekommen.
- Stellen Sie Fragen zur Stadt und zur Firma (Größe, Mitarbeiter, Umsatz, Produkte, usw. s. Information auf Seite 182).
- Fragen Sie, wann Sie Gelegenheit bekommen werden, ins Hotel zu fahren.
- Fragen Sie, ob vor Ihrem Rückflug Zeit bleiben wird, etwas von der Stadt zu sehen.

Besuch von Herrn Richard South, 13. Juni

10 Uhr:	Kaffee mit Herrn Gerland und Frau Dogan, danach Präsentation der Firma (Sales and Marketing Assistant)
11 Uhr:	Besichtigung der Firma und des Firmengeländes
12.30 Uhr:	Mittagessen mit Herrn Hans Peters (Geschäftsführer), Herrn Gerland und Frau Dogan
14 Uhr:	Meeting mit Herrn Peters, Herrn Gerland, Frau Dogan
20 Uhr:	Abendessen im Restaurant "Deichgrafen" mit Herrn Ullmann (Firmengesellschafter) und Herrn Peters

Übernachtung im Hotel "Friesischer Hof"
Abflug: 13.45 Uhr, 14. Juni

2 **Während Sie Herrn South die Firma und das Firmengelände zeigen, treffen Sie immer wieder wichtige Mitarbeiter/innen der Firma und stellen sie ihm vor. Stellen Sie anhand der unteren Geschäftskarten Herrn South die folgenden Mitarbeiter/innen vor und erklären Sie ihm ihre Position und wofür sie zuständig sind (s. Organigramm auf S. 186).**

3 **Während des Besuchs von Herrn South ist es auch Ihre Aufgabe, eine kurze Präsentation der Firma vorzubereiten. Schauen Sie sich die Informationen auf Seiten 182–186 an und erstellen Sie eine Präsentation über die Geschichte und die derzeitigen Tätigkeitsfelder der Firma auf Englisch.**

4 **Herr Gerland bittet Sie, einen Text vorzubereiten, der die Firma auf ihrer Webseite in englischer Sprache präsentiert. Schauen Sie sich die Informationen auf Seiten 182–186 an und erstellen Sie einen Text mit den wichtigsten Informationen zur Firma.**

3

Products and services

FOCUS

1 **Which logos do you recognize? Have you ever bought any of these brands? Why/why not? What brands are popular at your school?**

1 18 **2** **Copy the table below and complete it by listening to three friends talk about brands.**

good quality | good value for money | positive feelings | influence of advertising | impress other people | show you have good taste / show that you are cool/special | show that you care about the environment / your appearance

	Nicolas	Bryan	Khanh
Brand(s) he/she likes	...	...	...
Reason(s) for buying brand(s)	...	...	...

3 **Follow these steps to discuss brand awareness.**

1 Work with a partner and interview each other. For which of the products below is the brand important to you? For which products is the brand unimportant?

bicycles | computers | drinks | glasses | fast-food restaurants | furniture | jeans | shoes | stereo systems | travel businesses

Do you look at the brand when you buy ... ?
What about ... ?
I always / don't ever look at the brand when I buy ...
I look for [brand] when I buy ...
I don't care about brands.

2 Now do a class survey. Find out how many care about the brand for each of the items on the list.

3 Work with a partner. Use the phrases below to compare your results to the survey results in file 9 on page 176.

For	*jeans, cars, shoes,*	*60%* / *13 out of 20*		*of*	*the people surveyed* / *our class* / *our group* / *them* / *us*	*thought the brand was important.*
		the brand was	*more* / *less* / *as*	*important for*		*than* / *as* — *it was for ...*

A Advertising products

1 GETTING PRODUCTS TO THE CUSTOMER

What role do the departments in a company play in getting products to the customer? Match the department names to the functions to say what is done where.

customer care | dispatch | logistics | marketing | purchasing | quality control | research and development (R&D) | sales

1 answering customers' questions; writing instruction booklets
2 buying raw materials; ordering packaging
3 checking the products to make sure that they work properly; testing them for safety
4 dealing with documents related to the goods; organizing transport of the goods
5 designing new products; improving products the company already makes
6 filling orders; selling the product
7 doing market research; finding and working with an advertising agency
8 packaging the goods; sending the goods to customers

2 AN ADVERTISING AGENCY

A Work with a partner to brainstorm a list of things that an advertising agency does. Then read the article and check your answers.

1 19

A visit to Randelson Advertising

The loft offices of Randelson Advertising in Manhattan are decorated to inspire creativity. Hundreds of clever print advertisements and colourful works of art are on display.

Larry Niemann, 36, hangs up his telephone, smiles broadly and calls out the name of a major department store. His colleagues in the **Account Services** Department know what this means: Niemann has won the agency a chance at developing an ad campaign for the store. As the account executive, Niemann is the one who will have the contact with the customer as well as coordinate the work between the departments. His next steps will be to meet with the customer and to write a brief for the other departments, describing what the customer needs. 'I enjoy building relationships with customers,' he says. 'I'm a people person.'

You could say that everyone at Randelson Advertising is a 'people person'. They have to be. Only the account services department has daily contact with customers, but everyone here (with the possible exception of computer programmers) works very closely with other colleagues in teams. This is typical of advertising agencies. ▶

Creative Director Randelson and part of her team

Perhaps less typical is the ad campaign idea currently brewing in the **Creative** Department. The proposed television commercial is based on the AIDA model and features two beautiful mermaids looking longingly at a very fat fisherman. They pull him under water, seductively remove his jeans ... and swim away, leaving him in his underwear.

The last shot is of the mermaids, each of them wearing one leg of the fisherman's jeans. The slogan: 'Perfect jeans are no myth.' The idea is unusual, but the customer did not call Randelson to get an unoriginal campaign. They want an interesting and effective ad that makes an impact. 'I'm going to present this idea to the customer tomorrow,' says Creative Director Sophie Randelson, 40, with a twinkle in her eye. 'I think it's brilliant, and I hope they'll think so, too. I don't think the **Production** Department is looking forward to shooting underwater, though.' Randelson founded the agency seven years ago.

The people who work in ad agencies do about two dozen different jobs. Some of these jobs – e.g. graphic artist, buyer or copy editor – also exist in other types of companies but, in advertising, there is something everyone has in common: the goals of advertising effectiveness and customer satisfaction.

The **Strategy** Department is a whirlwind of activity, but Strategist Eva Duda, 27, sits concentrated among the chaos. She is researching the facts needed for creating an advertisement for a fitness centre, and strategizing the best messages and methods to use to reach the health-conscious target audience. Along with account services and creative, her department is considered to be one of the three pillars of the modern advertising agency.

In Randelson's **Media** Department, the buyers purchase ad space in magazines, newspapers, TV shows, cable channels and internet sites, and try to understand the audience for each of these media.

Randelson also has its own **Interactive** Department, where they create the digital components of an advertising campaign, including websites, banner ads and interactive applications. Designer Raul Cornejo, 32, says he loves his job because 'You never stop learning. This year, I'm creating Flash animation, but next year I may have to learn a completely new programming language, if the industry changes.'

Change is the only thing which is constant in the world of advertising. If Randelson is lucky, it will be the one setting the trends in advertising instead of following them. *(577 words)*

B In which department of an advertising agency would you hear each of the following statements? Refer to the words in bold in the text.

1 *The best way to advertise to these customers is with print ads in shopping malls.*

2 *I'd like your channel to run our commercial during the 10 o'clock news.*

3 *Thank you for enquiring about our agency. What product would you like to advertise?*

4 *When the visitor clicks on the customer's logo, he'll be sent to this web page.*

5 *Come on, you guys! Life is too short for boring adverts! We need some fresh ideas!*

6 *Are the models dressed yet? OK, let's start shooting this commercial!*

C How do the departments in an advertising agency work toward the goal of advertising effectiveness? Follow these steps to write a text.

1 First make notes in your exercise books about each department's responsibilities. You do not have to limit yourself to tasks mentioned explicitly in the text; try to 'read between the lines' and think about the jobs people do in each department.

Account services:	*get relevant information from customers; ...*
Creative:	...
Strategy:	...
Media:	...
Production:	...
Interactive:	...

2 Use your notes to write a short text. Describe each department and say which department you think is most important, and why.

> Skills, p. 204

Webcode: FOBNRWT301

3 ANALYSING ADVERTISEMENTS

A Tell your partner about an advertisement you have seen recently. Say what type of advertisement it was, where you saw it and why you remember it.

billboard | brochure | mail shot | full-page ad in a newspaper/magazine | pop-up internet ad | poster | leaflet | small classified ad | TV/radio commercial

clever | disgusting | funny | glamorous | shocking | silly | strange

B Match sentences 1–6 to sentences a–f to explain how advertisers persuade us to buy their products.

1 Advertisers use a 'bad boy' or a 'bad girl' image which makes customers associate the product with actions and lifestyles that are shocking.
2 By asking a rhetorical question about the product, the advertiser forces the customer to answer.
3 Sometimes, the advertiser hints that only intelligent people buy the product.
4 The advertisements show beautiful places, glamorous people and exciting things.
5 The advert indicates that the product belongs to a particular lifestyle.
6 The advert suggests that the product will help customers to escape from their daily routine.

a Customers believe that they will find romance and adventures if they buy the product.
b Customers who dream of that way of life will buy the product.
c The customer is sure that he is intelligent and believes that the product is aimed at him.
d Most people enjoy looking at lovely things, and some of them may also believe that these characteristics will rub off on them if they buy the product.
e People who like to think they are 'rebels' or outsiders buy the product.
f The customer usually answers in a positive way, so convinces herself that the product is good.

C **Describe and analyse the three advertisements below. What is being advertised and who is the target audience? Use ideas from exercise 3B and give reasons for your answers. How effective do you think the adverts are?**

1 A mobile billboard

1 20 **2 A radio commercial**

3 An online advert

1 21

D **What do you know about the AIDA model? Complete Sophie Randelson's analysis of her company's jeans advert with words from the box. There is one word you do not need. Then listen and check your answers.**

banner | campaign | commercial | contact | coordinate | create | effective | featuring | present | print | purchase | research | slogan | space | target audience | trend

Randelson: The ...1 the customer wants to reach is women in their early twenties. We did some ...2 on this group and found out two important facts: first, these women have a hard time finding the 'perfect' jeans; second, mythology and magic are very 'in' right now for this group, and we wanted to follow this ...3. That's how our copywriter came up with the ...4 'Perfect jeans are no myth'.

So, using the AIDA model, we get the audience's **attention** by ...5 other young people: lovely young ladies and a comical young man. We keep their **interest** by telling them a story which promises sex. We ...6 **desire** by showing them the mermaids' desire for the product. We get the consumer to act (= **action**) by giving them the brand name of the product. This is ...7 advertising!

Sophie Randelson, 40, Creative Director at Randelson Advertising

We are not only producing this TV ...8 for the customer; it will only be one part of a larger ad ...9 that will also have ...10 and internet components. Most of the ad ...11 that we will purchase will be ...12 ads on internet sites.

This is a big job, so we have to ...13 the work between our departments. I have to work closely with the account executive, who has the direct ...14 with the customer. He will be there when I ...15 our ideas to the customer. It's important to build relationships in this business.

E **Now use the AIDA model below to analyse the three adverts on page 66 again.**

The AIDA model of advertising

Attention People will decide in the first few seconds if they want to listen to you or not, so you have to really get their attention. A good way to do this is by surprising them, or by asking an engaging question such as 'Have you ever ...?' or 'Can you see ...?'

Interest Once you have their attention, you have to arouse their interest. One way to do this is by demonstrating advantages and benefits of the product. It is best if you can get them actively involved, and leave them wanting more.

Desire The next step is to create a desire in them for the product. You can do this by showing them that it will solve some of their problems or by showing them how much other people want and approve of the product.

Action Now, encourage action by giving them the brand name of the product. You want them to buy your product or at least to get more information. You should make this as easy for them to do as possible.

B Marketing decisions

1 A PRODUCT DEVELOPMENT MEETING

A Ice Duchess Frozen Foods Ltd makes products which are sold in grocery stores. You are doing an internship there and have been invited to a meeting with the people in the photos. Describe what each department is responsible for.

Product Development (PD)

Martin Green

Marketing

Diana Fortnoy

Research and Development (R & D)

Sujata Mishra

Production

Vojta Stivek

The xx department is responsible for ...

a investigation, innovation and improvement of products and processes.

b creating new products.

c organizing the work in the factory and producing the goods efficiently and on time.

d finding out which products may be interesting to customers; developing the strategy for promoting, selling and distributing the products; setting prices and planning product launches.

B Read the e-mail and the product brief and answer the questions.

1 What is the purpose of the meeting on Monday?

2 Why did Martin Green leave question marks on the product brief?

3 What will Diana Fortnoy, Sujata Mishra, Vojta Stivek and you (the intern) have to do before and during the meeting? What will you have to do afterwards? Use the words below to summarize each person's 'to do' lists.

Diana/Sujata/Vojta has to ...	*read ...*	*determine / figure out ...*
They all have to ...	*take notes ...*	*decide (on) ...*
I will have to ...	*carry out ...*	*write up the minutes.*
	find out ...	*think of / come up with ...*

E-MAIL

To:	diana.fortnoy@ice-duchess.co.uk, sujata.mishra@ice-duchess.co.uk, vojta.stivek@ice-duchess.co.uk, intern13@ice-duchess.co.uk
From:	martin.green@ice-duchess.co.uk
Subject:	'Shaped Pizza' meeting on Monday
Attachments:	ShapedPizza_ProductBrief.docx ShapedPizza_Packaging.jpg

Dear Shaped Pizzas team

I've got great news! We've got permission from the Managing Director to develop a new line of novelty pizzas in different shapes. I'm really excited about this, and also excited about developing it with such a great team.

I've scheduled our first team meeting for Monday from 9 a.m. to 11 a.m. According to your online schedules, you are all free then so everybody has to come. No excuses!

Attached is the product brief for the shaped pizza line. Please familiarize yourselves with it before the meeting.

The target group is defined but, as you can see, there are still some decisions we will have to make at the meeting.

Diana, before the meeting, we need you to carry out some market research. Could you please determine the size of the market? I know we will sell all over the UK, but will this product also be marketed abroad? Also, what share of the market are we trying to get? And what about the size of the pizzas? And the price? This product was originally conceived for teens. Do we want to stay with this concept, or do we want to try to market to a wider group?

You can see under the *USPs that we want these pizzas to have unusual shapes, but we have to consider practical aspects, like how they will be shipped and displayed in the supermarkets. Have a look at the Packaging Designer's idea, which I've attached as a jpg. Would something like that be possible? Vojta, what do you think? Can anybody think of any other good, clear USPs?

Sujata, could you please test what shapes are possible from a food-preparation standpoint?

Thanks and see you on Monday!

Best wishes
Martin

PS Our new intern from Germany has volunteered to take the minutes.

* USP = Unique Selling Point (or Proposition)

ShapedPizza_ProductBrief.docx

Product brief

Product: Shaped pizzas
Name: Crazy Shapes
USPs:
fun shapes: heart ? shamrock ? star ? other shapes ?
other USPs ?
Target group / Market:
Sex: both sexes, but females more than males
Age: 14–19
Income / Purchasing power: high
Education: secondary school (parents: higher education)
Shopping habits: large supermarkets evenings and weekends
Market: UK (Ireland ? Europe ? Americas ?)
Size of market: ?
Market share: ?
Size: 600–700 g
Packaging: plastic wrap with sticker label
Price: ?

ShapedPizza_Packaging.jpg 100% (RGB/8)

2 WORKING WITH WORDS

Match words and phrases in boxes A and B to make expressions that fit the definitions.

1 the amount of sales a company might expect
2 the amount that a company sells of its products and services compared with other companies selling the same type of thing
3 a tool used by product developers to describe a product, its special characteristics and its expected market
4 the type of consumer that a product is aimed at
5 something very special which makes a product or service different from other products or services
6 to think of or produce an original product or service

A
to develop
product
size of
market
unique
target

B
selling point
share
market
a new line
brief
group

1 22 3 LISTENING: A TEAM MEETING

A **First look at the product brief on page 69 and copy the lines with question marks into your exercise books or onto your computer. Then listen to three excerpts from the PD team meeting. What information can you add to the product brief?**

B **Listen to the meeting excerpts again and take notes. Then copy the minutes form below and write the minutes of the meeting. What was decided?**

'Shaped Pizza' meeting – Minutes

Date and time:	Monday, 12 Nov. / 09.00–11.00 a.m.
Location:	Room 232
Chairperson:	...
Attendees:	...
Discussion point #1:	...
Decisions or further action:	...
Discussion point #2:	...

Writing minutes in English

When writing minutes in English, it is important to be brief and to the point. The minutes should contain only the most important details about the topics discussed, the decisions made and action points assigned.
Remember to proofread your minutes, checking your English and punctuation. Also make sure you have spelled the names of the chairperson and attendees correctly.

Here are some useful expressions:
The Chairperson drew the attention of the attendees to ...
He/She stated/suggested/recommended/confirmed/explained that ...
Concern was expressed that ...
It was decided/agreed that ...

4 CONFIRMING THE RESULTS OF A MEETING

Martin Green has asked you to send the minutes to the rest of the team. Follow his instructions to write an e-mail. Use the information on writing e-mails on pages 91–92 to help you.

> E-mail layout, pp. 91–92

Please write an e-mail to the team for me.

- *Congratulate everyone on a productive meeting.*
- *Tell them you are attaching the minutes and the new, updated product brief. Ask them to check them for mistakes.*
- *Inform them of the date of the next meeting in about three weeks, and the date of the product launch in about three months.*

Webcode: FOBNRWT302

5 WRITING A PRODUCT BRIEF

You and the other interns have been asked to create a product brief for one of the following Ice Duchess frozen food products.

fish fingers | hamburgers | high-energy snacks | Italian ready meals

Before you write the brief, work with a partner to choose a product and make a mind map around it. Use the tips on making mind maps in the skills file on page 202 to help you.

> Skills, p. 202

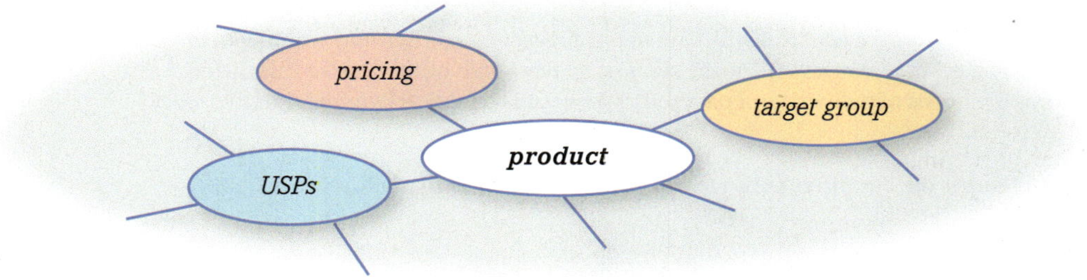

6 ADVERTISING AND PACKAGING YOUR PRODUCT

Work in groups. You are going to produce an advertisement and design the packaging for a new product. Follow the steps below.

1 First, choose one of the Ice Duchess products, either the shaped pizzas discussed at the meeting in exercise 1 or the product for which you wrote the product brief in exercise 5.
2 Decide on your target group and where and how you will advertise the product, then create an effective advert.
3 Now design the packaging (artwork and text) for your product, including the cooking or baking instructions.

EXAMPLE *1 Preheat oven to ... °C.*
2 Remove plastic wrap and ...
3 Bake for ... minutes or until ...

4 When you have completed steps 1–3, present your ideas to the class. Explain why you made the choices you did.
5 Write a short advertising text that can be used online and in print. Remember to include descriptions of the USPs.

7 DEALING WITH ENQUIRIES

A While you are doing your internship at Ice Duchess, your boss asks you to look at enquiries from two customers who are interested in finding out more about the product you worked on in exercise 6. What do the customers require? Make notes on:

> type of customer (commercial, private, service)
> special requests

On the Move Catering Ltd
12 Highland Park Industrial Estate
Edinburgh EH19 45G

AY/TW
12 Februar 20..

Ice Duchess Frozen Foods Ltd
Attn. Customer Enquiries
277–279 Victoria Industrial Estate
London W3 6UU

Dear Sir or Madam

We have seen your company's advertisement in the current edition of Good Food. We are interested in the latest product in your range.

Our company is a leading caterer, supplying to railway companies throughout the whole of Britain and Northern Ireland. Our clients are always interested in new, high-quality products which they can offer to their passengers in their buffet cars and restaurants.

We would like to begin with a trial run with one of our biggest customers and would like to place an initial order for 10,000 items. Please send us a favourable quotation for this order. Please also supply terms of delivery and payment. We would require delivery within two weeks of placing an order.

If your product meets our requirements, we would be in a position to place regular, larger orders.

We look forward to hearing from you in the near future.

Yours faithfully

Aidan Young

Aidan Young
Purchasing Director

E-MAIL

From:	janet_boyd@wecare.com.uk
To:	info@ice-duchess.co.uk
Subject:	Enquiry about your latest product

Dear Sir or Madam

We manage 56 residential and care homes all over England ranging in size from 100 to 650 clients. Some of our clients have diabetes and/or allergies. It goes without saying that we can only serve our clients easily digestible food.

We note from your website that you have developed a new product which may be of interest to us.

Please send us a catalogue and price list, including discounts granted. Terms of payment and delivery would also be appreciated.

If your prices and terms are suitable, we would be in a position to place regular, large orders.

We look forward to your reply with interest.

Best regards

Janet Boyd, Administration

B **Answer the letter or the e-mail, using information from exercises 5 and 6 to do so. You may have to invent some details. See pages 99–105 for help with writing offers.**

> Offers, pp. 99–105

8 MEDIATION

> Skills, p. 211

Eine weitere Anfrage von einem deutschen Kunden ist eingetroffen. Ihr Vorgesetzter bei Ice Duchess spricht kein Deutsch und bittet Sie, ihn über den Inhalt der E-Mail aufzuklären. Machen Sie sich zunächst Notizen über den Kundentyp und seine Wünsche. Schreiben Sie danach eine E-Mail an Ihren Vorgesetzten, in der Sie die Anfrage des deutschen Kunden auf Englisch zusammenfassen.

E-MAIL

From: catering@stadtreha.de
To: info@ice-duchess.co.uk.
Subject: Anfrage über Ihr aktuelles Produkt

Sehr geehrte Damen und Herren,

ich entnehme Ihrer aktuellen Anzeige, dass Sie ein neues Produkt auf den Markt gebracht haben.

Als Menüplaner bin ich verantwortlich für eine große Küche in einem deutschen Rehabilitationszentrum. Ich ziehe in Erwägung, Ihr Produkt zu unserem Mittagsmenüangebot hinzuzunehmen. Könnten Sie mir vielleicht Informationen zukommen lassen, bevor ich eine endgültige Entscheidung treffe?

Um den aktuellen Diätverordnungen zu genügen, wäre es hilfreich, wenn Sie mir eine ausführliche Liste der Inhaltsstoffe und der Zubereitungsarten Ihres Produktes zukommen lassen würden. Unser Grundsatz ist es, unseren Kunden zucker- und fettarme Produkte zu bieten, die keine künstlichen Aromen oder Konservierungsmittel enthalten.

Wenn Ihre Produkte den oben genannten Anforderungen entsprechen, wäre ich in der Lage, regelmäßige monatliche Aufträge zu erteilen.

Bitte teilen Sie mir Ihre Liefer- und Zahlungsbedingungen mit.

Ich freue mich, in Kürze von Ihnen zu hören.

Mit freundlichen Grüßen

Georg Frey
Menüplaner

9 DEALING WITH A VOICEMAIL MESSAGE

Your contract at Ice Duchess finishes at the end of the week. You are in the process of handing over to the next German intern. A customer has left a message on your phone.

1 23

A **Listen to the message and take notes in German for the new intern explaining what the customer would like. Add the caller's contact details and ask the new intern to get in touch with the customer.**

B **The new intern has asked you to help with the phone call. Write the telephone conversation, then role-play it with a partner.**

C Describing products and services

1 LABOUR-SAVING DEVICES

A Read the text about Miele and its products. Then match headings a–e with paragraphs 1–3. Two of the headings are not needed.

a First-rate products and conditions
b New products every year
c Machines do the heavy work
d Minimizing costs
e Long-term planning

1 24

Getting the product right

1 In 1899, when the Miele company was founded, it made machines for farmers to separate cream from milk and make cheese. It then used the same technology to wash clothes and, unwittingly, started a social revolution. At the beginning of the 20th century washing the clothes was a back-breaking and time-consuming job usually performed by women. It often took several days because everything was done by hand and the water used was heated on an open fire. Miele set itself the goal of improving its products year by year and in March 2009, the Vatican newspaper *l'Osservatore Romano* wrote that 'the washing machine did more to liberate women in the 20th century than the pill or the right to work'.

Yesterday ...

2 After its success with washing machines, Miele diversified its range of products, even manufacturing cars and bicycles for a short time, but soon returned to its core business of making the labour-saving devices for which it is known today. Like Marks and Spencer in the UK, Miele was one of the first companies in Germany to introduce medical insurance, a pension scheme and housing for its employees. It believed that contented employees would be loyal to the company and make high-quality goods. Its slogans 'Forever better' and 'Miele – a decision for life' show that the company's goal is to make the best appliances on the market, with a life expectancy of 20 years or more.

3 As a limited partnership, the Miele & Cie. KG is owned by 60 or so shareholders who belong to the families of the two founders, Carl Miele and Reinhard Zinkann. As the Miele company is not publicly owned, it is not under pressure to 'increase shareholder value', i.e. to show a profit every quarter. It is therefore able to plan for longer periods of time than publicly owned companies, which are often forced to borrow capital to buy up competitors and expand production in order to show a profit. Miele only uses the capital it has earned to buy new production facilities and, unlike many other manufacturing companies, it has minimized outsourcing to low-wage countries. It even has its own electronics plant in Gütersloh to develop the electronic controls for its appliances. Although most of its production facilities are no further than a day's trip from its headquarters in Gütersloh, almost two thirds of the company's sales come from exports. *(396 words)*

and today

B Do the following tasks.

> Skills, p. 203

1 Describe Miele's first target group for its products.
2 Explain why there was a market for labour-saving devices in the early 1900s.
3 List the different products Miele has manufactured and marketed over the years, and state which market it has focused on.
4 Find reasons in paragraph 2 for Miele's commercial success.
5 Study paragraph 3 and explain how Miele:
   - is able to operate without needing to show a short-term profit for everything it does.
   - benefits the local economy.
   - benefits the national economy.

2 WORKING WITH WORDS

Match the expressions in box A with a suitable word in box B, and use your answers to complete the text below.

A after-sales | high-quality | labour-saving | same-day | toll-free

B appliances | delivery | devices | hotline | service

Our products are the very best on the market and our customers are prepared to pay top prices for … …[1] like washing machines or dryers. Doing the washing is hard work and today people cannot imagine life without … …[2] to do the work. Most people are in a hurry, so we offer … …[3] if they place their order before 10 a.m. If there is a problem with one of our products customers can call a technician in our … …[4] department 24 hours a day on our … …[5].

3 HOW COMPANIES ADAPT

You are going to prepare a short presentation or report showing how a company has adapted its goods and services over the years with or without success. With a partner, choose one of the companies from the list and follow the steps below.

Adidas | Amazon | Apple Inc | EMI | Grundig | H&M | Nokia | Otto (GmbH & Co KG) | Mayersche Buchhandlung | Vorwerk | own choice of company

1 Research the company you have chosen. Look in particular at how the company has changed its:
   > product range (e.g. best-known product(s), best-selling product(s)).
   > suppliers (e.g. low-wage countries, Fair Trade suppliers, child labour).
   > retail outlets (e.g. shops, supermarkets, mail order, door-to-door sales).
   > target market (e.g. age, spending power, lifestyle).
   > advertising strategies (e.g. billboards, print media, TV, radio, online, mail shots, celebrity endorsement).
   > attitude towards the environment (e.g. sustainability, climate change).
2 Present your findings to the class or write a text summarizing your research and explaining why the company has made changes to its strategies over the years.

4 DEALING WITH A BUSINESS PARTNER'S REQUEST

A **Make a list of as many household appliances as you can think of. Choose two or three and explain what extra work you would have to do if they broke down. Begin like this:**
If the washing machine broke down, I/we would have to ...

B **You work in the customer services department at Miele in Gütersloh and deal with the North American market. Today you receive the following e-mail from a household appliance dealer in the USA. Read the e-mail and complete the sentences below**

E-MAIL

From: "Al Winters, Winters Household Appliances" <al.winter@linkallusa.com>
Subject: Adapter for hot and cold water connection for Miele washing machines
Cc:
Attachment(s):

Dear Sir or Madam:

Here in Tallahassee, Florida, most of my customers only have a cold water supply for their washing machines but, according to the installation guide (see excerpt below), your washing machines need to be connected to both the hot and cold water supplies with a Y-adapter.

Water connection

If the machine is being connected only to a cold water supply, both the hot and cold water intake hoses must be attached to the cold water valve through the use of a Y-adapter (available at a hardware store). Both hoses must be connected to a water source or the machine will not function properly.

Unfortunately, Y-adapters are often out of stock at our local hardware stores, which means the customer has to wait, or buys a washing machine from a different manufacturer.

For this reason I suggest that you make a small change to the design of the washing machines supplied to this market or include a Y-adapter with each machine.

I look forward to your reply with interest.

Sincerely,

Al Winters

Proprietor
Winters Household Appliances

1 The dealer's shop is in ...
2 The owner of the shop is ...
3 Most of the local people connect their washing machines ...
4 A Y-adapter is needed because ...
5 The local hardware stores ...
6 If customers are not prepared to wait for an adapter, they ...
7 Al Winters suggests changing the design or ...

C Now write a reply using the following details.

- kurzfristige Konstruktionsänderung für nordamerikanischen Markt leider nicht möglich
- zuverlässiger örtlicher Lieferant ist ermittelt und kontaktiert worden
- Angabe der Adresse: Green's Household Accessories, 10299 Southside Boulevard, Jacksonville, FL 32256, Tel.: (904) 538-0750
- Lieferung per FedEx innerhalb von 24 Stunden

5 CALLING THE CUSTOMER BACK

A The day after replying to Al Winters' e-mail you receive the message to the right. Prepare yourself for your telephone conversation by making notes on what you wish to say and studying the telephone phrases on page 135.

> **E-MAIL**
>
> I sent you an e-mail on an urgent matter two days ago and have still not received a reply. Please call me today at 01 (850) 874-4091.
>
> Sincerely,
> Al Winters

Group your ideas under the following headings:
Introduction / Apology / Explanation / Solution / Delivery / Polite ending

B With a partner take turns to play the roles of Al Winters and the employee in Customer Services at Miele.

Partner A: Al Winters. Go to file 17 on page 179.
Partner B: You work for Miele. The employee's telephone no. is 00 49 5241 221 88-287.

1 25 **C Listen to the recording of the telephone conversation between Al Winters and the employee in Customer Services at Miele and take notes on the differences between what you hear and your own version of the role-play. Then do the role-play again using the notes you have taken.**

Webcode: FOBNRWT303

6 ENQUIRY ABOUT GOODS AND SERVICES

Die Passstücke für die Waschmaschinen sind inzwischen von Green's Household Accessories in Jacksonville, Florida an Mr Al Winters geliefert worden, und er ist zufrieden. Da Miele mehrere Händler in Florida mit Haushaltsgeräten beliefert, möchten Sie Näheres über Green's Household Accessories erfahren, denn Sie brauchen dort einen zuverlässigen Fachbetrieb für Ersatzteile, Dienstleistungen und Reparaturen aller Art. Verfassen Sie (eigener Name) ein Schreiben (E-Mail oder Brief) folgenden Inhalts an die amerikanische Firma. Benutzen Sie die *Useful phrases* auf Seite 95.

> Enquiries, p. 95

- Ansprechpartner: Mr. Kevin Green, Inhaber *(proprietor)*
- Bitte um kurze Beschreibung seiner Produktpalette
- Welche Dienstleistungen kann er anbieten (z. B. gebührenfreie Hotline, 24-Stunden-Lieferung, Reparaturen, Beratung)?
- Bereit, Ersatzteile vor Ort zu lagern?
- Technisch geschultes (*skilled*) Personal?
- Personal bereit, an Miele-Schulungen (*training courses)* über neue Miele-Produkte teilzunehmen?
- Weitere Angaben nach Wahl
- Angemessene Verabschiedung

7 MEDIATION

> Skills, p. 211

Use the information about the Miele products on the next page to do one or both of the mediation tasks below.

1 Sie sind Praktikant/in bei Miele & Cie KG und sollen nächste Woche am Stand des Unternehmens auf der Fachmesse LivingKitchen in Köln aushelfen. Da man viele englischsprachige Besucher erwartet, bekommen Sie den Auftrag, zwei kurze Flyer mit den wesentlichen Informationen zu den zwei meistverkauften Kaffeemaschinen der Miele-Produktpalette zu erstellen. Schreiben Sie die Flyer in Partnerarbeit mit Hilfe der zwei Beschreibungen und der Language box.

2 Sie haben Standdienst für Miele auf der Fachmesse in Köln. Ein/e englischsprachige/r Messebesucher/in kommt auf Sie zu und bittet um Verkaufsliteratur über Espressomaschinen. Sie nutzen diese Gelegenheit, zwei Espressomaschinen (siehe Beschreibungen) vorzustellen. Übernehmen Sie die beiden unten beschriebenen Rollen in Partnerarbeit mit Hilfe der folgenden Hinweise und der Language box.

Rolle A
Sie (eigener Name)
- Sprechen Sie den/die Besucher/in freundlich auf Deutsch an.
- Bieten Sie Ihre Hilfe auf Englisch an.
- Geben Sie dem/der Besucher/in mehrere Prospekte und erklären Sie, dass zwei der Maschinen ausgestellt (on display) sind.
- Beschreiben Sie die zwei Geräte.
- Bieten Sie dem/der Besucher/in eine Tasse Kaffee an.
- Beantworten Sie die Fragen des/der Besucher/-in.
- Danken Sie dem/der Besucher/in für die Karte.
- Schließen Sie das Gespräch höflich ab.

Rolle B
J. Carter, Home Comfort Ltd, York, UK
- Erklären Sie, dass Sie nur Englisch sprechen.
- Sie suchen Verkaufsliteratur über Espresso- und Kaffeeautomaten.
- Fragen Sie nach den wesentlichen Unterschieden zwischen den zwei Geräten.
- Probieren Sie den Kaffee.
- Fragen Sie nach dem jeweiligen Einzelhandelspreis.
- Stellen Sie weitere Fragen nach Wahl
- Bedanken Sie sich für die Informationen
- Geben Sie dem/der Praktikanten/in Ihre Visitenkarte.

automatisches Spül- und Reinigungsprogramm	*automatic self-cleaning*
beheizte Tassenabstellfläche	*heated cup tray*
Bohnenbehälter	*bean container*
Einbau-Kaffeevollautomat	*fitted coffee machine / countertop coffee machine*
entnehmbares Kapselmagazin	*removable capsule chamber*
gemahlener (Bohnen)Kaffee	*ground coffee*
Geschmacksvariation	*flavour*
höhenverstellbarer Kaffeeauslauf	*adjustable spout*
Kapsel	*capsule*
mehrsprachig	*multilingual*
Milchschaum	*frothy milk*
Pulverkaffee	*instant coffee*
Stand-Kaffeevollautomat	*free-standing coffee machine*
Zubereitung	*preparation*

CM 5200
Modellbezeichnung
Stand-Kaffeevollautomat CM 5200
Genussvorteile
One-Touch-Zubereitung von einfachem und doppeltem Espresso, Kaffee, Cappuccino, Latte Macchiato
Weitere Getränke: Heißwasser, heiße Milch, Milchschaum
Nutzung einer zweiten Kaffeesorte in Form von Pulverkaffee
Bedienkomfort
Mehrsprachiges Klartext-Display
Höhenverstellbarer Kaffeeauslauf für bis zu 13 cm hohe Tassen
Wassertank 1,8 l
Bohnenbehälter für 250 g Kaffeebohnen
Einstellung des Mahlgrades
Beheizte Tassenabstellfläche aus verchromtem Metall
Pflegekomfort
Automatische Spül- und Reinigungsprogramme
Gewicht 9,6 kg

CVA 3650
Modellbezeichnung
Einbau-Kaffeevollautomat CVA 3650
Flexible Verwendung als Einbau-, Stand- oder Unterbaugerät
Genussvorteile
4 Portionsgrößen: Espresso, Kaffee, doppelter Espresso, doppelter Kaffee
Komfortable Zubereitung von Cappuccino, Latte Macchiato, Milchschaum, heißer Milch, Heißwasser
Vorrat von 20 Kapseln in bis zu fünf verschiedenen Geschmacksvariationen
Bedienkomfort
Mehrsprachiges Display
Parallele Zubereitung von Espresso/Kaffee und heißer Milch/Milchschaum
Kaffeeauslauf für bis zu 9 cm hohe Tassen
Wassertank 1,5 l
Entnehmbares Kapselmagazin für 20 Kapseln
Pflegekomfort
Automatische Spül- und Reinigungsprogramme
Gewicht 16,8 kg

8 WRITING A FOLLOW-UP E-MAIL

Nach der Messe werden Angebote per E-Mail an potentielle Großhändler geschickt. Schreiben Sie eine freundliche E-Mail an J. Carter, Head Buyer, Home Comfort Ltd, York, UK (j.carter@homecomfort.co.uk) unter Berücksichtigung folgender Punkte. Benutzen Sie die *Useful phrases* auf Seite 104.

> Offers, p. 104

> Bezug auf Messe
> kurze Beschreibung der zwei Produkte
> Preise laut beigefügter Preisliste
> Lieferbedingungen EXW Gütersloh
> Lieferung ca. 30 Tage nach Auftragseingang
> Probeauftrag anbieten
> Angemessene Verabschiedung

9 DESCRIBING PRODUCT SPECIFICATIONS

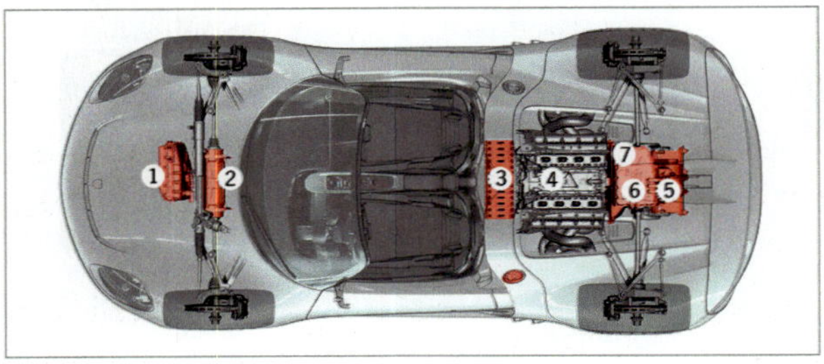

1 Power electronics
2 Electric drive
3 Lithium ion battery
4 V8 high RPM engine
5 Porsche Doppelkupplungsgetriebe (PDK) (= dual clutch transmission)
6 Electric motor
7 Power electronics

1 26 **A In this interview, race car driver Orlando Ricci describes one of his favourite cars: the Porsche 918 Spyder. Listen and correct the six mistakes in the technical highlights below.**

Technical highlights

1 Same chassis as the Carrera GT
2 0–62km/h in 32 sec
3 Top speed: 189 mph
4 Hybrid engine
5 One electric motor, two petrol motors
6 Better V8 petrol engine than the Porsche RS Spyder
7 Four driving modes: E Drive, Hybrid, Sport Hybrid, Rocket Hybrid
8 E-Boost push-to-pass feature for overtaking other cars
9 Mileage: 33 mpg

B What advantages (e.g. speed) are discussed in the interview? Are there any drawbacks to this car? Listen again, if necessary.

10 TECHNOLOGICAL DEVELOPMENTS

You are going to research a modern technological development and present it to the class. Work in groups and follow the steps below.

> Skills, p. 208

1 Agree on the type of technology you would like to present and the area in which it is used. Here are some areas to choose from.

agriculture | communication | computers | energy | medicine | transportation

2 Brainstorm ideas on the following aspects of the type of technology you have chosen and make a mindmap or a list.
   > how/where it can be used
   > how it is marketed and sold
   > environmental aspects
3 Prepare your presentation, including the following points:
   > a comparison of the current technology to what went before
   > a description of what has changed and why
   > an explanation of the advantages and disadvantages associated with the new technology
4 Give your presentation using illustrations or charts where necessary.

D Strategies and solutions

1 GETTING STARTED IN BUSINESS

Ellen Spokes gives seminars to people who would like to set up their own business. She always begins her seminars by asking participants to brainstorm ideas about what they have to do before they set up their company.

- *choose name for company*
- *design logo*
- *get business cards printed*
- *sell in high street shop or over internet only?*
- *look into delivery companies*
- *open bank account*
- *register the business*
- *set prices*
- *write business plan*

In groups, read the points Ellen has collected on the board at her latest seminar. Then copy the mind map into your exercise book and complete it with the points on the left and some of your own ideas.

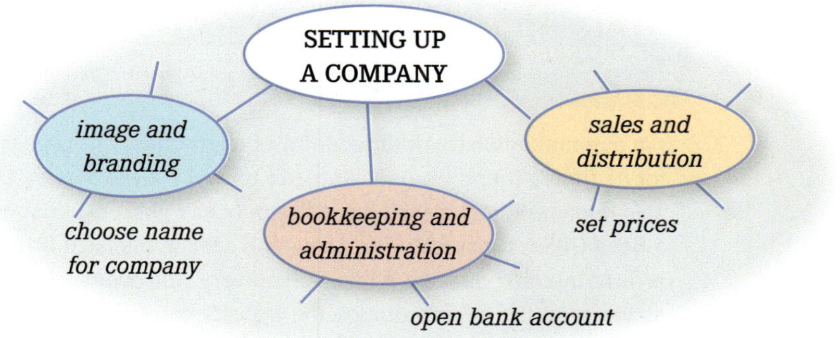

2 ASKING FOR ADVICE

Alex Judd, who participated in one of Ellen's seminars some months ago, is disappointed with the way his business is going. He e-mails Ellen and asks her for advice.

E-MAIL

Dear Ellen

You may remember me from your seminar in June. You said then that you'd be happy to give more advice if anyone needed it. Well, I think I need it now.

Just to remind you, I buy second-hand clothes at low prices in local charity shops or at car boot sales. I mostly buy fashions from the 1960s and 1970s. I clean and repair the clothes, then I advertise them in my eBay store: 'RetroModo'. The old clothes are quite popular, and some items sell for more money than new clothes.

I've been in business for eight months. I've received lots of orders, and I've been really busy. In fact, the business has boomed. The trouble is, I haven't made much profit yet. Lots of money has come in from sales, but I've spent most of it on more stock, so there is very little profit. I've attached some spreadsheets which contain my financial records. Could you take a look at them for me? Maybe you can tell me where I've gone wrong.

Best wishes
Alex

E-MAIL

Hi Alex

Thanks for your e-mail. It was good to hear from you – I was wondering how you were getting on. I am delighted to help if I can.

I have had a good look at your spreadsheets, and yes, there is a problem. It's your price structure. To put it simply, your prices are too low, and you are paying too much for your stock. This often happens with businesses that sell second-hand goods. The idea only works as long as the suppliers don't know what the goods are worth in the wider market-place. Unfortunately for you, the people you buy from have realized that, and they have put their prices up.

I can see two solutions to your problem. The first one is to increase your own prices, so that you make more on each sale. The other solution is to try a new area, e.g. antique jewellery or other fashion accessories.

I hope this helps you. Please e-mail me again if you need any more advice.

All the best
Ellen

A **A German friend who does not speak English is thinking about setting up a similar business. She asks you to explain Alex's problem and the advice Ellen gives him.**

B **What do you think of Alex's business? Would you buy clothes from it? Why (not)?**

In my view, Alex's business idea is ...
What I like / What concerns me about it is this: ...
Personally, I would / would not ...

3 MIXED EXPERIENCES WITH EBAY

A **Read these forum posts from two eBay customers. Describe their experiences, then suggest a solution to Disappointed Donald's problem.**

Apple (12) Amazon eBay Yahoo! News (255)

I'm a mountain biker. Until recently, I bought most of my gear new and paid a lot of money for it. Then a friend introduced me to eBay. I'd always been a bit suspicious, but my friend said it was OK, so I gave it a try. I've only had good experiences. One of my best buys was a used GPS for just €20. The same one sells in the High Street shops for €200. The GPS arrived the next day and it has worked very well ever since. I think eBay is brilliant. As long as you read the information on the website carefully, you shouldn't have any problems.

Sporty Susan

I'm pleased for Sporty Susan, but I've had a couple of bad experiences buying gear on eBay. I ordered a bike helmet from a small company for €45. The seller guaranteed speedy delivery and complete satisfaction or your money back. The helmet arrived within a week, but it was not the same colour as the one in the picture. I used the return label and sent the helmet back to the seller the same day and asked for a replacement or my money back, but so far I haven't heard a thing from the seller.

Disappointed Donald

B **What are your experiences with buying goods online? Were you satisfied with the service or not? Write a post for the forum above describing your experiences. If you have never purchased goods online, explain why you have not done so.**

I occasionally / often ...
In the past, I have ...
In my experience, ...

4 WRITING A COMMENT

> Skills, p. 204

How has the internet changed the way we do business in terms of buying and selling? Describe the changes, focusing on the market, increased competition and distribution, and say if these changes are good or bad. Write from the points of view of both customers and sellers.

5 DEALING WITH POOR SERVICE

The British logistics company, BL-SSD, delivers parcels and packages all over Britain. Despite the claims on the company's website, BL-SDD does not always provide a good service. Look at the website, read the scenario below and do the task that follow.

www.BL-SSD.com/home

Apple (12) ▾ Amazon eBay Yahoo! News (255) ▾

British Logistics – Safe and Speedy Delivery

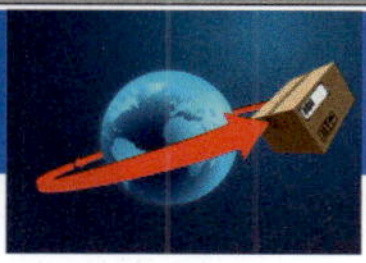

Company policy

✔ BL-SSD guarantees safe and speedy delivery of your parcels and packages, with next day delivery when possible.

Our environmental policy

✔ We use only electrically powered cars.

✔ Delivery personnel are fitted out in uniforms made of organic cotton, designed and produced in Britain.

We aim to please

✔ Our customers come first. We are a friendly, helpful company.

✔ We take very good care of your parcels.

✔ If you have any suggestions as to how we might improve our service, please get in touch. info@BLSSD.com

Scenario

You are doing an internship at a phone shop in the UK. Last week, you bought a second-hand laptop on eBay, and a few days later the seller notified you that the laptop was on its way.

This morning, while you were looking out of your bedroom window, you saw a delivery van with a BL-SSD logo whose driver was walking towards your building carrying a box labelled 'Fragile'. As the delivery man seemed to be taking a long time to ring your doorbell, you went back to the window ... and saw the van driving away.

You ran downstairs. There was no parcel and no 'Sorry, we couldn't deliver' card in your letter box, so you ran after the van. When the driver saw you in his rear-view mirror, he stopped and rolled down the window. You could see that he was sweating heavily in his polyester uniform. 'Did you try to deliver a laptop to me a few minutes ago?' you asked politely, while trying to catch your breath. 'I live on the top floor in number 8, around the corner.'

'You didn't answer the bell,' the delivery man barked as he rolled up the window. 'I left the parcel with your neighbour on the ground floor.' He drove off in a cloud of exhaust fumes.

When you finally got your parcel, you saw that the box had been damaged.

Write a complaint to BL-SSD. Describe what happened and refer to the claims made on the company's website.

> Complaints, p. 127

6 HELPING A CUSTOMER

A During your internship at the phone shop, you often need to help customers choose a smartphone package. Work with a partner. Look together at the customer profiles and the options below and choose the contract which suits each customer best. After that, take on roles, and role-play a situation.

Customer profiles:
> a student who uses internet and texts a lot, but never phones
> a business manager who goes on a lot of business trips
> a freelance journalist
> a working mum who needs to keep in touch with her teenage children

Type of phone	Cost of phone	Cost per month	Download allowance	Calls	Texts	Network
MyPhone	Free	£51.00	1 GB	30 mins. free	20 free	MyPhone UK
BlueHaze	Free	£61.00	unlimited	25 mins. free	unlimited	Blue2
Pear	£335	£40.00	1 GB	10 mins. free	10 free	BuyAPhone
T-Phone	£439	£21.00	500 MB	50 mins. free	250 free	YouCall

GB: gigabyte MB: megabyte

B One of your customers is having trouble loading music onto his new smartphone. Unfortunately, the online instructions which explain how to do this are jumbled up. Put the instructions in the correct order and explain them to the customer.

A After that, connect your smartphone to your computer using the USB cable provided.

B Before you start to upload your music, turn on the 'synchronize files' option on your smartphone.

C Synchronizing will stop automatically when the playlist is uploaded.

D To listen to music on your smartphone, select the playlist you would like to hear and press PLAY.

E Press START to begin to synchronize.

F Now find the music you would like to upload and select the playlists you want to synchronize.

C The following day, you receive phone calls from several customers who have similar problems with the same type of phone. Use the information above to answer the customers' questions.

1 *How do I connect my smartphone to the computer?*

2 *I hooked up my smartphone to my laptop, but my music won't load. What do I do?*

3 *How do I stop the synchronizing process? It seems to be taking forever.*

4 *I don't want all my music on my phone. How do I tell my computer which music to load?*

D You decide to tell the smartphone manufacturer about the poor quality of the online instructions (which are the only instructions they offer for this product). Write a message on the company's contacts page, describing the problem and suggesting a solution.

E Scenario

Situation: Herr Gerland und Herr Peters sind nach ihrem Gespräch mit Herrn South sehr positiv gestimmt und glauben, dass er als Vertriebspartner für Großbritannien gut geeignet wäre. Bevor sie aber eine endgültige Entscheidung treffen, bitten sie Sie, South Riding Tours mit einem anderen Anbieter, GoByCycle Ltd aus London, zu vergleichen.

1 Im Internet finden Sie die folgenden Unternehmensdarstellungen/Produktbeschreibungen. Stellen Sie die wesentlichen Daten tabellarisch auf Deutsch gegenüber.

http://www.gobycycle.com

Apple (12) Amazon eBay Yahoo! News (255)

GoByCycle Ltd

Our 10-day European cycle tours begin at Victoria Coach Station in London, where you will be welcomed by your guide for the tour before boarding the coach to your destination: Belgium or Holland (via Harwich-Hoek van Holland) or Northern France (via Dover-Calais). Your first night will be spent in tents at our cycle centres. Our centre experts will familiarise you with your cycles, all of which are the latest models. You will also have a chance to meet the other members of your group at an evening meal cooked by our centre staff. The next morning you will set off with an experienced guide in groups of 15–20 cyclists, depending on the tour you have chosen. Accommodation each evening is in pre-standing tents on 5-star campsites near to recognised tourist attractions. No putting up tents each evening or taking them down in the morning! Each tent has its own cooking facilities and the campsites all have supermarkets and restaurants so that you can enjoy restaurant service or self-catering as you choose. Your luggage is transferred each day to your next destination in our support bus.

The following tours are available:
- The heart of Holland
- Beaches of Normandy
- Bruges, Ghent and Amsterdam

10 days €530 per person

http://www.south-riding-tours.com

Apple (12) Amazon eBay Yahoo! News (255)

South Riding Tours Ltd

We offer an exclusive service of individual self-guided cycling tours tailored to your specifications on selected routes in the southern UK and northern France. Your benefits when you book with South Riding Tours Ltd:
- flexible weekend, 1- and 2-week tours
- 3*** guesthouse accommodation, incl. bed & breakfast and evening meal
- snack lunches* available
- guesthouse-guesthouse luggage transfer each day
- up-to-date maps included
- fully-guided tours also available
- individual travel to start of tour; travel arrangements can also be booked via South Riding Tours Ltd
- return transfer from destination to start included as necessary
- top of the range cycle hire available or personal cycles can also be used
- Devon, East Anglia, South Coast, Normandy, Brittany, Loire region

(*extra charge may apply)

1 week €540 per person (in double room; single room surcharge €115); cycle hire extra, see charges

2 **Die Geschäftsführung und Herr Gerland sind überzeugt, dass South Riding Tours Ltd der richtige Partner für eine Kooperation ist. In Vorbereitung auf die Kooperation erstellen Sie ein Konzeptpapier, in dem ihre Vorstellung von der Kooperation auf Englisch dargestellt wird. Übertragen Sie die dazu unten aufgeführten Elemente sinngemäß in die englische Sprache.**

Fly Bike Werke GmbH: Konzept für Radtouren in Kooperation mit South Riding Tours Ltd	
Orte in Deutschland	Niedersachsen, Mecklenburg-Vorpommern, Brandenburg, Schleswig-Holstein
Orte in GB	Norfolk Broads (Seengebiet), Cambridge, Ely und Lincoln (Universitäts- und Domstädte)
Art der Touren	selbstgeführte Touren, d. h. Unterkunft und Route sind vorgegeben; Einführung durch Servicepersonal am Anfang. Geführte Touren auch möglich, aber individuelles Reisen bevorzugt
Dauer der Radtouren	flexibel: 3 Tage bis 2 Wochen
Gruppengröße	individuelle Touren möglich; Gruppen von 4 bis 20 Personen
Unterkunft	vorreservierte Gasthäuser bzw. Pensionen; normalerweise 3 Sterne
Verpflegung	Frühstück und Abendessen im Gasthaus
Gepäcktransfer	Gepäcktransfer von Gasthaus zu Gasthaus durch Servicebus oder Gasthäuser (für größere Gruppen) organisiert
An- und Abreise	individuelle An- und Abreise; Bahn- bzw. Flugverbindungen können durch Veranstalter gebucht werden
Leihräder	eigene Fahrräder oder Fly Bike-Leihräder; Reparatur von Leihrädern kostenlos
Extras	Imbiss möglich, gegen Aufpreis, beim Gasthaus zu bezahlen; Karten, Reparaturen und Ersatzteile für eigene Fahrräder vom Servicebus zum Selbstkostenpreis erhältlich
Preise	Preisvorstellung: 85,– € pro Person, pro Tag
Leistungen des jeweiligen Veranstalters	Werbung im eigenen Land für Touren des Partners; Vermittlung von Reservierungen an Partnerveranstalter; Organisation, Durchführung (Servicebus und -personal) und Qualitätskontrolle der Touren im eigenen Land
Form der Kooperation	Vertragliche Vereinbarung zwischen beiden Veranstaltern 15 % Kommission für Vermittlung von Reservierungen an Partnerveranstalter
Vertragsdauer	2 Jahre mit Option auf Verlängerung; Kündigungsfrist: 6 Monate

3 **Nachdem die Vereinbarung zwischen Fly Bike Werke und South Riding Tours Ltd unterzeichnet wurde, müssen die neuen Radtouren im Internet und in den Urlaubsbroschüren von Fly Bike Werke GmbH und South Riding Tours beworben werden.**

Wählen Sie ein Medium aus und erstellen Sie englisches Werbematerial, das Sie Ihren Vorgesetzten, Herrn Gerland und Frau Dogan, zeigen können.

4 Commercial correspondence

FOCUS

1 **Brix Mode GmbH is a company based in Bielefeld, which trades in fashion items. The company does a deal with an Indian supplier in Mumbai and imports 500 fashion tops to Germany. To do so the German company writes a number of e-mails and letters to the Indian company. Put the following extracts in the right order.**

A E-MAIL

As agreed, the goods will be delivered FOB Mumbai by 15 August 20... at the latest. We note that you will arrange for transport and insurance of the goods from Mumbai to your premises in Bielefeld, Germany.

B E-MAIL

As regards the goods requested, we are pleased to submit the following quotation:

100 "Iona" ladies' fashion tops, article no. LFD 322, in S, M and L at US$ 1.50 per unit

C

It has most probably escaped your notice that payment of the above-mentioned invoice was due on receipt of your order.

We look forward to receiving the sum in question in the next few days.

D E-MAIL

I was most impressed by the fashion tops you showed me on your stand at the IGEDO fashion fair last month and would now like more information about your company's products.

E E-MAIL

To: sunil.mittal@jjpd.co.in
Re: Order no. IGTO 32249 for fashion tops dated 10 November 20...

Dear Mr Mittal

The above-mentioned fashion tops arrived at our premises this morning as promised but on examining them we found that they were of poor quality ...

We would welcome your explanation of these discrepancies.

F

The above-mentioned goods are now ready for dispatch and our invoice for €1,125.00 is enclosed for payment. Please remit the invoice amount to our company's account at the Bank of India in Mumbai:

Account number: 6035583131853
Bank code: BKID0006003

G

We now wish to place an order for the following goods:

Quantity	Description	Size	Article No.	Unit Price (€)	Total (€)
250	"Iona" ladies' fashion tops	S	LFD 322-S	1.50	375.00
250	"Iona" ladies' fashion tops	M	LFD 322-M	1.50	375.00
250	"Iona" ladies' fashion tops	L	LFD 322-L	1.50	375.00
				Total	1,125.00

2 **Now label each step of the transaction with a heading from the box.**

acknowledgement | complaint | enquiry | offer | order | payment | reminder

A The layout of letters and emails

1 Business letters

Me2 Mode GmbH 1
Oststr. 44 • 40211 Düsseldorf
Germany

Tel. +49 211 5922876
Fax +49 211 5922870
Email info@Me2-mode.de
www.Me2-mode.de

•
LM/TK 2
05 July 2012 3
•
URGENT 4
•
High End Fashion Ltd 5
99 High Street
NEWCASTLE
NE3 9LM
GROSSBRITANNIEN
•
Attn. Miss Ryan, Import Section 6
•
Dear Miss Ryan 7
•
Complimentary tickets 8
•
As arranged we enclose two tickets for the Body Culture Fashion Show in Düsseldorf next month and look forward to meeting you at our stand. 9
•
Yours sincerely 10
Me2 Mode GmbH

11
•
•
Linda Meier (Mrs)
Managing Director
•
•
Encs 12
•
Me2Mode GmbH, Oststr. 44, 40211 Düsseldorf, Registergericht Düsseldorf, HRB 4421
Geschäftsführerin: Linda Meier

1 Letterhead
2 Reference
3 Date
4 Special marking
5 Inside address
6 Attention line
7 Salutation
8 Subject line
9 Body of the letter
10 Complimentary close
11 Signature
12 Enclosure (Enc), Enclosures (Encs)

Leave a free line for each dot (•).

Business letter layout

There is no standard layout in the English-speaking world, so a typical block form layout used in Europe is shown here. After the letterhead all the sentences are left aligned (*linksbündig*).

1 Letterhead

The letterhead should include the sender's name, postal address, telephone and fax numbers, e-mail address and website address. It often has the company's logo.

2 Reference

Linda Meier (LM) signed the letter and Tina Knopf (TK) typed it. Some companies have different reference systems (e.g. Ref. L/M 07.1000).

3 Date

An all-figure date can be misunderstood. In American English 05/07/12 (or 05-07-12) means May 07, 2012 but in British English it means 05 July 2012. For this reason the month should always be written out and the year should be a four-figure number. The usual order in which a date is written in business letters and forms is: day (in figures) – month (as a word) – year (in figures).

4 Special marking

These include URGENT, PRIVATE AND CONFIDENTIAL, PERSONAL, AIR MAIL, REGISTERED, RECORDED DELIVERY. This line can be seen over the address in a window envelope.

5 Inside address

This is the recipient's address. Always include the country because the same city names can be found in different countries. When writing to a UK address write the town or city in capital letters and the postcode on a separate line under it.

6 Attention (Attn:)

The attention line is under the inside address and close enough to it to be seen in a window envelope. If there is an attention line, the letter may be opened by the company's post department and given to the person named. However, if the inside address starts with someone's name it may only be opened by that person or their secretary.

7 / 10 Salutation / Complimentary close

In most cases the salutation and complimentary close can be written **without** punctuation and they are linked as shown in the table below. In general, it is always better to write to a named person than a company but if this is not possible, start the letter 'Dear Sir or Madam' and use 'Yours faithfully' as the complimentary close.

Salutation	Complimentary close	Formality	Notes
Dear Mrs Brown	Yours sincerely	Formal	The most commonly used form
Dear Sir or Madam	Yours faithfully	Formal	Only used if the name is unknown
Dear Kim Dear Kim and Jim Jim	Regards (Best) Regards Best wishes Yours	Friendly	Used in business if the writers know each other

8 Subject line

This is written in bold letters or underlined.

9 Body of the letter

The first word always starts with a capital letter. The paragraphs are separated by an empty line.

10 Complimentary close
The name of the sender's company is written under the complimentary close.

11 Signature
Signatures are often hard to read, so write the signatory's name and position under the signature. As there is no real English equivalent to *Sachbearbeiter/in*, it is best to name the department where the signatory works (e.g. Sales Department for *Verkaufssachbearbeiter*). Women can add their preferred title in brackets after their name if they wish:

Miss	single, younger woman or girl	Ms	single or married women
Mrs	married woman		

12 Enclosure
It is sometimes enough just to write Enc or Encs but if necessary, details of the enclosure(s) can be listed like this: Enc: Ticket or Encs: Tickets

1 MEDIATION

> Skills, Mediation, p. 221

Sie haben den Auftrag, eine Checkliste der wichtigsten Unterschiede zwischen einem englischen und einem deutschen Geschäftsbrief für deutsche Praktikanten zu erstellen. Nutzen Sie die Infobox und achten Sie insbesondere auf Interpunktion, Groß- und Kleinschreibung und die Reihenfolge der einzelnen Elemente.

2 LOOKING AT LETTERS

A Re-write these German dates in the form *dd* (in figures) – *mm* (as a word) – *yyyy* (in figures) then read them out to your partner.

1	07.05.69	7	01.01.10
2	12.04.71	8	05.11.07
3	20.06.00	9	03.10.90
4	30.09.08	10	24.02.49
5	21.03.89	11	04.07.03
6	31.12.09	12	28.08.12

1	first	14	fourteenth
2	second	15	fifteenth
3	third	16	sixteenth
4	fourth	17	seventeenth
5	fifth	18	eighteenth
6	sixth	19	nineteenth
7	seventh	20	twentieth (pronounced *twen – tee – eth*)
8	eighth	21	twenty-first
9	ninth	22	twenty-second
10	tenth	30	thirtieth (pronounced *thir – tee – eth*)
11	eleventh	31	thirty-first
12	twelfth		
13	thirteenth		

B Find the right complimentary close for these salutations.

1 Dear Ronnie
2 Jim
3 Dear Ms Bush
4 Dear Tina and Tom
5 Dear Sir or Madam

C Use the following information to show the correct layout of a business letter.

Margot Herlitzer, the purchasing director at Fair Fragrance Parfümerie, Ludwigstr. 98, 45239 Essen, Germany, dictates a letter to her secretary, Jessica Degen. The letter is to Ms Charlize Novak, the export sales director at Natural Beauty Products, 4000 East Ocean Boulevard, Long Beach, CA 90803, USA. Frau Herlitzer is writing to Ms Novak about the advertising campaign for Body Flower perfume. The body of the letter is: 'Please find enclosed some photocopies of customers' reactions to the new product. I look forward to your comments with interest.' She encloses the photocopies with the letter. The date is 03/05/20.. .

2 E-mails

To: "Rob Jones" <rob.jones@linkall.com>
Copy: "Bill Hampton, President" <bill.hampton@cherry-sol.com>
1 **Subject:** **"Get the world online" conference in Düsseldorf, Germany**
From: Nina Graham   Attachments: brochure.pdf

2 Dear Rob
(•)
3 Many thanks for speaking at the World Aids Day meeting in South Africa last month. I also hope you had a good trip back home to Ireland and am delighted that you will be coming to Düsseldorf to be a guest speaker at Cherry Solutions Incorporated's annual convention in May.
4 (•)
The theme this year is "Get the world online", and I know how passionately you support internet access for poor countries and the "One laptop per child" charity. Our brochure on this year's
5 programme is attached for your information.
(•)
Please let us know when you would be available and what your fee would be. All travel and hotel expenses will, of course, be paid for by Cherry Solutions Incorporated.
(•)
6 I very much look forward to welcoming you in Düsseldorf in May!
(•)
Best wishes
(•)
Nina
7 Chief Executive Officer
Cherry Solutions Inc.

1 Make sure the subject box shows what the e-mail is about.
2 Use first names if you know the recipient well and sign off with "Best wishes" or "Best regards". Otherwise use "Dear Mr/Mrs/Ms" and sign off with "Yours sincerely"
3 Start the e-mail with a capital letter.
4 Split the e-mail into paragraphs separated by free lines.
5 Refer to any attachments to the e-mail.
6 Finish with a polite phrase.
7 Write your position and the name of your company under your name.

Leave a free line for each dot (•).

3 LOOKING AT E-MAILS

Read the infoboxes about e-mails above and on page 92 and list the similarities and differences between the writing of business e-mails and business letters.

How to write e-mails

More than 90% of businesses use e-mail because it is quick, convenient and cheap. Here are some important things to remember before you hit 'send'.

To:
Subject:
Cc:
Attachment(s):

Salutation
Body
Complimentary close

Subject (Betreff):
This is the same as for a business letter. Begin with a capital letter and keep it short.

Cc: 'carbon copy' (Kopie)

Writing the e-mail
Most mistakes are made here: *E-mails are not always informal.* Like business letters they can be formal or informal but unlike business letters they can be sent to thousands of recipients by mistake.

Salutation / Complimentary close
If you do not know your business partner, use one of the polite forms below. If the relationship becomes more friendly, your business partner will start using informal forms and you should then do the same. Let your business partner take the initiative.

	Salutation	Complimentary close
Polite	Dear Ms Brown Dear Mrs Brown Dear Miss Brown Dear Mr Brown Dear Dr Brown	Regards Best regards Best wishes Yours sincerely
Friendly	Good morning James Dear Kim Dear Kim and Jim	Regards Best regards Best wishes
Informal	Hello Kim Hi Kim Kim	All the best (Atb) Best Cheers

Body of the e-mail
- Start the e-mail with a capital letter.
- Never use text message short forms (CUL8R, etc.).
- If you write back in the spaces between the lines of the original e-mail and/or in a different colour,
  - do not use red
  - do not underline words
  - do not write in **bold letters**
  - do not write in CAPITALS
  - do not use exclamation marks!

  because it sounds as if you are angry or think the reader is stupid.
- Most e-mails are read on-screen, so keep yours as short as possible.

Points of style
Use short forms to be friendly (I've, we'll, he'd etc.) and long forms to be more formal.

Finishing the e-mail
If you know your business partner well, it is enough to sign off with your first name. If you do not, add your position and the name of your company under it.

B Enquiries

Sevda Yildiz is the purchasing director of Brix Mode in Bielefeld. Last month she attended the Igedo fashion fair in Düsseldorf, where she talked to Amanda Lakely of Fair Trade Fashions. She now uses the address on Amanda's business card to write an enquiry.

1 LOOKING AT A LETTER OF ENQUIRY

BRIX Mode GmbH
Feldstraße 42 • 33609 Bielefeld • Germany
Tel +49 521 4827764   Fax +49 521 4824760   info@brixmode.de

SY/GJ
13 October 20..

Ms Amanda Lakely
Sales Director
Fair Trade Fashions
85 Princes Park
GATESHEAD
NE1 9NF
GROSSBRITANNIEN

Dear Ms Lakely

Enquiry about fashion wear and accessories

I was most impressed by the T-shirts you showed me on your stand at the Igedo fashion fair last month and would now like more information about your company's products.

We are a rapidly growing importer and wholesaler of young people's fashions and accessories with excellent business contacts all over Germany and beyond. At present we are particularly interested in importing good quality, stylish Fair Trade clothing at reasonable prices.

Please let us have your latest catalogue and export price list, including all discounts granted. Details of your terms of delivery and payment and your delivery periods would also be appreciated.

We look forward to hearing from you soon.

Yours sincerely
Brix Mode

S. Yildiz

Sevda Yildiz (Ms)
Purchasing Director

Fair Trade Fashions
Amanda Lakely
Sales Director
85 Princes Park, GATESHEAD NE1 9NF, England
Tel.: +44 191 4982686
Fax: +44 191 4982680
amanda.lakely@fair-trade-fashion.co.uk

Brix Mode GmbH • Bielefeld, Registergericht Bielefeld, HRB 82071, Geschäftsführerin: Karla Wenz

Fair Trade T-shirt

Igedo fashion fair, Düsseldorf

A Read Sevda's letter and match the sentences halves.

1 Sevda Yildiz is the
2 Amanda Lakely is the
3 Brix Mode is
4 Fair Trade Fashions is
5 Sevda met Amanda
6 Amanda showed Sevda
7 Sevda's company imports
8 Sevda would like Amanda to send her a
9 Sevda needs to know how long
10 The Managing Director of Brix Mode

a clothes and accessories for young people.
b at the Igedo fashion fair.
c catalogue and a price list.
d it will take to deliver the goods.
e Purchasing Director of Brix Mode.
f in Bielefeld.
g some T-shirts.
h in Gateshead, England.
i is Karla Wenz.
j Sales Director of Fair Trade Fashions.

B Match the German translations below with points 1–6 in the box.

Beschreibung Ihrer Gesellschaft | Grund für Ihre Anfrage | Angemessene Verabschiedung | Ihr Bedarf | Liefer- und Zahlungsbedingungen | Lieferung | Muster/Probe(n) | Preisangebot | Preisliste | Herkunft der Anschrift | Rabatte | Referenzen | Verkaufsunterlagen | Vertreterbesuch

Structure of an enquiry

An enquiry covers some or all of the following points:

1 Source of address
2 Description of your company
3 Reason for your enquiry
4 Your requirements:
> quotation
> sales material
> price list
> discounts
> samples
> terms of delivery and payment
> delivery
> representative's visit
5 References
6 Suitable ending

C Find words in the letter to replace the words in italics.

1 *Please tell me more* about your products.
2 My company is *importing more and more young people's clothes all the time.*
3 We have customers both in Germany and *in other countries.*
4 We are only prepared to buy clothing *if it doesn't cost too much.*
5 Please give us details of *any reductions in price you are prepared to make.*
6 We would also like to know *how long it will take to deliver the goods.*

2 LOOKING AT AN E-MAIL ENQUIRY

Sevda Yildiz now contacts a Chinese supplier and requests a quotation for T-shirts.

E-MAIL

To: "Chen Yu Lan" <chen.yu.lan@632trading.cn>
Subject: Enquiry about fashion wear

Dear Ms Chen Yu Lan

We note from your company's website that you sell a wide range of stylish fashion wear. Our company is a major German wholesaler of adults' and children's clothing with many long-standing customers all over Europe. As there is considerable demand for T-shirts at the moment, we would welcome a quotation for the following articles:

1000 men's T-shirts in black, dark blue and grey in S, M, L, XL and XXL
1000 ladies' T-shirts in white, black and pink in XS, S, M, L and XL

Please also let us know if you are able to provide samples. Delivery would need to be made within 6 weeks DDP our premises.

References are available on request.

We look forward to your early reply with interest.

Yours sincerely

Sevda Yildiz (Ms)

Brix Mode
Bielefeld
Germany
www.brixmode.de
Telephone: +49 521 4827764
Fax: +49 521 4827760

632 Trading Company reagiert auf Sevdas Anfrage nicht, so dass Sevda Sie bittet, Frau Chen Yu Lan in China anzurufen. Übernehmen Sie die zwei Rollen mit Hilfe der folgenden Hinweise und der Useful phrases unten und auf der Seite 135 (Telephoning).

Partner A ist Chen Yu Lan. Sie haben keine E-Mail erhalten und fragen nach weiteren Infos, damit Sie entsprechend per E-Mail antworten können. **Partner B** (eigener Name) arbeitet bei Brix Mode. Wenn Sie hören, dass Sevdas E-Mail nicht angekommen ist, geben Sie die Details aus der E-Mail weiter.

Source of address	Quelle der Anschrift
I was most impressed by the … (*product[s]*) you showed me on your stand at the … (*name of trade fair/exhibition*).	Ich war von den … (*Produkte*), die Sie mir auf Ihrem Stand auf der … (*Name der Handelsmesse/ Ausstellung*) zeigten, höchst beeindruckt.
We have seen your company's advertisement in the current edition of … (*name of publication*) and are most interested in your products.	Wir haben Ihre Anzeige in der aktuellen Ausgabe von … (*Name der Veröffentlichung*) gesehen und interessieren uns sehr für Ihre Produkte.
We note from your company's website that you sell a wide range of … (*product*).	Wir entnehmen der Homepage Ihres Unternehmens, dass Sie eine breites Sortiment von … (*Produkt*) anbieten.

You have been recommended to us by... (*name of the person/company*), who tells us that you have brought out ... (e.g. a new line of costume jewellery).	Sie wurden uns von ... (*Name der Person/Firma*) empfohlen, der/die uns mitgeteilt hat, dass Sie ... (z. B. eine neue Produktlinie im Bereich Modeschmuck) auf den Markt gebracht haben.
Description of your company	**Beschreibung Ihres Unternehmens**
We are a rapidly growing/leading importer and wholesaler of ... (*goods/services*) with excellent business contacts all over ... (*place*) and beyond.	Wir sind ein schnell wachsender/führender Importeur und Großhändler für ... (*Waren/Dienstleistungen*) mit hervorragenden Geschäftskontakten in ganz ... (*Ort*) und darüber hinaus.
Our company is a major/well-established [German] wholesaler of ... (*goods/services*, e.g. camping equipment) both at home and abroad.	Unsere Firma ist ein bedeutender/etablierter [deutscher] Großhändler von (*Waren/Dienstleistungen*, z. B. Campingausrüstung) im In- und Ausland.
We have many long-standing customers all over Europe.	Wir haben viele langjährige Kunden in ganz Europa.
Reason for your enquiry	**Grund für Ihre Anfrage**
At present we are particularly interested in ... (*goods/services*, e.g. environmentally friendly technology) at reasonable prices, as goods of this nature are in great demand at present.	Gegenwärtig gilt unser besonderes Interesse ... (*Waren/Dienstleistungen*, z. B. umweltfreundlicher Technik) zu angemessenen Preisen, da eine große Nachfrage nach Waren dieser Art zurzeit besteht.
As we are extending our range at present, we are particularly interested in ... (*product*).	Da wir gegenwärtig unser Sortiment erweitern, sind wir besonders an ... (*Produkt*) interessiert.
Your requirements:	**Ihr Bedarf:**
Quotation Please send us a favourable quotation for these items / for ... (*product*). We would welcome a quotation for ...	**(Preis)angebot** Bitte schicken Sie uns ein günstiges (Preis)angebot für diese Artikel / für ... (*Produkt*). Wir hätten gerne ein (Preis)angebot für ...
Sales material We would therefore/also be grateful if you would let us have a comprehensive catalogue on your entire range. Please let us have your latest catalogue ...	**Verkaufsmaterial** Wir wären Ihnen deshalb/auch dankbar, wenn Sie uns einen umfassenden Katalog über Ihre gesamte Produktpalette schicken würden. Bitte lassen Sie uns Ihren aktuellen Katalog /... zukommen.
Current price list ... and export price list	**aktuelle Preisliste** ... und Exportpreisliste
Discounts ... including all discounts granted	**Rabatte** ... einschl. aller gewährten Rabatte
Samples Please also let us know if you are able to provide samples.	**Muster/Proben** Bitte teilen Sie uns auch mit, ob Sie Muster/Proben zur Verfügung stellen können.
Terms of delivery and payment ... including details of your terms of delivery and payment. Details of your terms of delivery and payment would also be appreciated. Delivery would need to be made DDP (*destination*) our premises. We would require delivery ... (e.g. within 6 weeks / by the end of the month).	**Liefer- und Zahlungsbedingen** ... einschl. Einzelheiten über Ihre Liefer- und Zahlungbedingen. Einzelheiten über Ihre Liefer- und Zahlungsbedingen würden wir ebenfalls begrüßen. Die Lieferung müsste DDP unsere Geschäftsräume erfolgen. Die Lieferung hätten wir gerne... (z. B. innerhalb 6 Wochen / bis Ende des Monats).

Representative's visit	Vertreterbesuch
We would be grateful if a representative could call on us.	Wir wären dankbar, wenn uns ein/e Außendienstmitarbeiter/in besuchen könnte.
References	**Referenzen**
References are available on request.	Referenzen sind auf Wunsch erhältlich.
Suitable ending	**Angemessene Verabschiedung**
If your products meet our requirements, we will be in a position to place a substantial order.	Wenn Ihre Produkte unseren Anforderungen entsprechen, werden wir in der Lage sein, einen größeren Auftrag zu erteilen.
We look forward to hearing from you soon / in the near future. We look forward to your early reply with interest.	Wir freuen uns, bald / in Kürze von Ihnen zu hören. Wir sehen Ihrer baldigen Antwort mit Interesse entgegen.

3 WRITING ENQUIRIES

A Use the useful phrases to write a letter enquiry.

Sie sind Einkaufsleiter/in bei der FreiLuft Rhein GmbH, Richthofenstr. 100, 53117 Bonn, Fax-Nr. 0049 228 422390, E-Mail: vorname.nachname@flr.de. In der aktuellen Ausgabe von *Camper's World* lesen Sie folgende Anzeige über umweltfreundliche Campingausrüstung, die zurzeit sehr gefragt ist.

MORE TOP-QUALITY APEX PRODUCTS
BUY NOW WHILE STOCKS LAST!

Description
Our great new environmentally friendly range of portable camping equipment is lightweight and folds flat for easy storage and transportation. It's great for picnics, parties, camping, sporting events and even trade shows. Use it outdoors or indoors – anywhere!

Foldable camping chair

Details
Lightweight design for easy transportation
Folds into a compact size for simple storage
Long-lasting and robust aluminium frames
Perfect for camping, barbeques, picnics or any outdoor event

Prices
Available on request

Contact
Emma Wade, Export Sales Director, Apex Leisure Ltd, 62 Commercial Road, Nottingham NO4 3FL, England, Fax: 0044 115 910635, E-Mail: emma@apex-leisure.co.uk.

Aufgabe
Verfassen Sie eine Anfrage an die englische Firma unter Berücksichtigung folgender Punkte:
> Bezug auf Anzeige
> Beschreibung Ihrer Firma
> Ihr besonderes Interesse gilt umweltfreundlicher Technik zu vernünftigen Preisen.
> Bitte um Zusendung eines aktuellen Katalogs und Exportpreisliste
> Bitte um Angabe von Liefer- und Zahlungsbedingungen einschl. aller Rabatte
> Aussicht auf regelmäßige Aufträge, wenn die Ware Ihren Kunden zusagt.

B Use the useful phrases to write an e-mail enquiry.

Sie (eigener Name) sind Sachbearbeiter/in bei Bijou Bianca Modische Accessoires GmbH, Bahrenfelder Chaussee 1, 22761 Hamburg, Fax-Nr. 0049 40 533422, E-Mail: vorname.nachname@bbma.de. Ihre Firma ist einführender Importeur und Großhändler von Modeschmuck in Deutschland mit vielen langjährigen Kunden und ist gegenwärtig dabei, ihr Sortiment zu erweitern. Heute erhalten Sie folgende E-Mail von einer Kollegin aus der Bijou Bianca Filiale in London.

E-MAIL

Mail from: brenda.parker@bbma.co.uk
Subject: Fantastic new costume jewellery by Daisy Chain
Cc:
Attachments:

Hi <Ihr Vorname>

Just seen a fabulous new line of jewellery! I'm sure you'll love it. It's called "Daisy" and I've fallen in love with the earrings and bracelets. Here's the link, so you can see what I mean:

www.daisy-chain.co.uk
Contact:
Ms Aisha Iqbal, Export Director, 35 Nightingale Park Road, Manchester M50 3BB, England
Fax: 0044161 4882219, e-mail: aisha.iqbal@daisy-chain.co.uk

Talk to you soon.

Brenda

Aufgabe
Verfassen Sie eine entsprechende Anfrage an die englische Firma unter Berücksichtigung folgender Punkte:
- Bezug auf Empfehlung
- Beschreibung Ihrer Firma
- Grund für Ihre Anfrage
- Sie sind an der neuen Serie von "Daisy" Ohrringen und Armreifen besonders interessiert.
- Bitte um Zusendung eines günstigen Preisangebots unter Angabe von Liefer- und Zahlungsbedingungen einschl. aller Rabatte
- Sie möchten auch einen umfassenden Farbkatalog über die gesamte Produktpalette der Firma.
- Aussicht auf einen größeren Auftrag, wenn die Ware Ihren Anforderungen entspricht.

C Offers

Sevda Yildiz is the Purchasing Director of Brix Mode in Bielefeld. Last month she went to the Igedo fashion fair in Düsseldorf and today she gets a phone call from one of the companies she visited there.

1 LISTENING TO A TELEPHONE OFFER

2 2

A Listen to the dialogue and complete the sentences below.

1 Sevda is phoned by a company in ...
2 The caller is responsible for ...
3 The caller knows that Sevda's company is interested in ...
4 The caller's company can deliver the goods to ...
5 Delivery would not take long because ...
6 The caller first quotes a price of ...
7 He finally quotes a price of ...
8 The caller promises to send Sevda ...

B Schreiben Sie ein kurzes Memo auf Deutsch über dieses Telefongespräch. Das Memo ist von Sevda Yildiz an Frau Silke Meyer, Leiterin Marketing.

Wählen Sie zuerst Stichwörter auf Englisch aus (z. B. Pehr Lindquist, responsible for exports usw.) und fertigen Sie damit Ihr Memo an. Verwenden Sie den Vordruck auf Seite 180 (File 20).

2 LOOKING AT AN OFFER SENT BY E-MAIL

A Pehr Lindquist sends the following offer to Sevda. Read the e-mail and match the sentence halves on the next page.

E-MAIL

To:	"Sevda Yildiz" <Sevda.yildiz@brixmode.de>
Date:	29 October 20..
Subject:	Quotation for T-shirts
Attachments:	Patrik K collection.pdf, Patrik K price list.pdf

Dear Sevda

As agreed in our pleasant telephone conversation of this morning, I'm pleased to let you have details of our offer in writing and enclose our current illustrated catalogue and price list for your information.

We are a major distributor of fashion wear with an excellent reputation throughout Europe, and will be pleased to supply you with 100 ladies' and 100 men's T-shirts at €4 each. Delivery will be made CIP Dortmund airport within 7 days after receipt of order.

Our terms of payment for an initial order are CWO or, with favourable references, 10 days 3%, 30 days net. If regular orders are placed with our company, open account terms may be granted.

We look forward to receiving your order.

Pehr Lindquist
Export Sales Director

CIP stands for 'carriage and insurance paid to ...'.
It is one of the 11 Incoterms (international commercial terms). See page 187 for more details.
CWO stands for 'cash with order'.
It is a term of payment. See page 192 for more details.

1 We were very pleased
2 Our company has
3 We enclose our
4 Delivery would be made
5 As you are a new customer, our
6 If you can give us favourable references,
7 Open account terms may be granted

a terms of payment would be cash with order.
b we will grant you 10 days + 3%, 30 days net.
c company's latest catalogue and price list.
d if regular orders are placed with our company.
e to receive your enquiry.
f CIP German airport.
g an excellent reputation throughout Europe.

B **Match the German translations with points 1–8 in the box below.**

Anlage(n) | Beschreibung Ihrer Firma / Waren / Dienstleistungen | Bezug auf Anfrage | Angemessene Verabschiedung | Geschäftsbedingungen und Rabatte | Lieferung | Preis | Verkaufsmaterial

Structure of an offer

An offer covers some or all of the following points:

1 Reference to an enquiry
2 Description of your company / goods / services
3 Sales material
4 Price
5 Terms and discounts
6 Delivery
7 Suitable ending
8 * Enclosure(s) / Attachment(s)

* Letters have enclosures and e-mails have attachments.

3 LEAVING A MESSAGE

Do the following role-play.

Sevda Yildiz möchte modische Damen- und Herrentops in Deutschland vertreiben. Also ruft sie Sunil Mittal, den Exportleiter der indischen Firma J.P. Designs Incorporated in Neu Delhi, an, um ein Angebot einzuholen. Da er nicht im Büro ist, spricht sie mit seinem/er persönlichen Assistenten/in Frau Yamini (Herrn Rajiv) Rawat. Übernehmen Sie die zwei Rollen in Partnerarbeit mit Hilfe der folgenden Hinweise und der *Useful phrases* auf den Seiten 135 *(Telephoning)* und 95 *(Enquiries)*. Tauschen Sie anschließend die Rollen und führen Sie das Gespräch ein zweites Mal durch.

Partner A:
Yamini/Rajiv Rawat, Assistent/in von Herrn Mittal, J.P. Design, Neu Delhi, Indien
- Vorstellung (Firmenname, Begrüßung)
- Herr Mittal ist außer Haus. Sie sind sein/e Assistent/in.
- Nachricht hinterlassen?
- Sie bitten gelegentlich, dass ein Wort (z. B. *Igedo*) buchstabiert wird.
- Sie bitten um Angabe der benötigten Größen.
- Weitere Angaben?
- Bis wann *(How soon)*?
- Sie bitten den/die Anrufer/in, seinen/ihren Namen noch einmal zu buchstabieren.
- Höflicher Schluss

Partner B: Go to file 12 on page 178.

4 LOOKING AT AN OFFER SENT BY LETTER

A In the meantime the Indian supplier which Sevda called in Exercise 3 contacts Brix Mode with an offer. Read the offer and find out how J. P. Designs:

1. describes itself
2. gives references
3. refers to sales material
4. offers certain products to Brix Mode
5. informs about their terms of delivery
6. informs about their delivery periods
7. informs about the possible terms of payment
8. tries to win Sevda Yildiz as a possible customer

J.P. Designs Incorporated
44 Mandir Marg • NEW DELHI 110 001 • INDIA

SM/AK
25 October 20..

Ms Sevda Yildiz
Purchasing Director
Brix Mode GmbH
Feldstraße 42
33609 Bielefeld
Germany

Dear Ms Yildiz

Your enquiry dated 14 October 20.. about fashion tops

We were delighted to receive your enquiry about our fashion wear and feel sure we can supply you with all the goods you need. Our company manufactures a wide range of high-quality products and already has many satisfied customers throughout Western Europe and North America.

To download our latest comprehensive catalogue and export price list, please visit our website at www.jpdesigns.in.

As regards the goods requested, we are pleased to submit the following quotation:

100 'Iona' ladies' fashion tops, article no. LFD 322, in XS, S, M, L and XL at US$1.50 (EUR 1,16) per unit
100 'Roshan' men's fashion tops, article no. MFT49, in S, M, L, XL and XXL at US$1.00 (EUR 0,78) per unit

Our prices are quoted FOB Mumbai or Calcutta and delivery is made within approx. 30 days after receipt of order while stocks last. Our usual terms of payment are letter of credit or CWO by PayPal or Western Union bank transfer. Regular customers may be granted preferential terms.

We feel sure that a trial order will convince you of the quality of our products and look forward to doing business with you.

Yours sincerely
J.P. Designs Incorporated

Sunil Mittal
Export Sales Director

The Incoterm FOB stands for 'free on board ...'. See page 188 for more details.

5 UNDERSTANDING INCOTERMS

> Full Incoterms diagram, p. 189

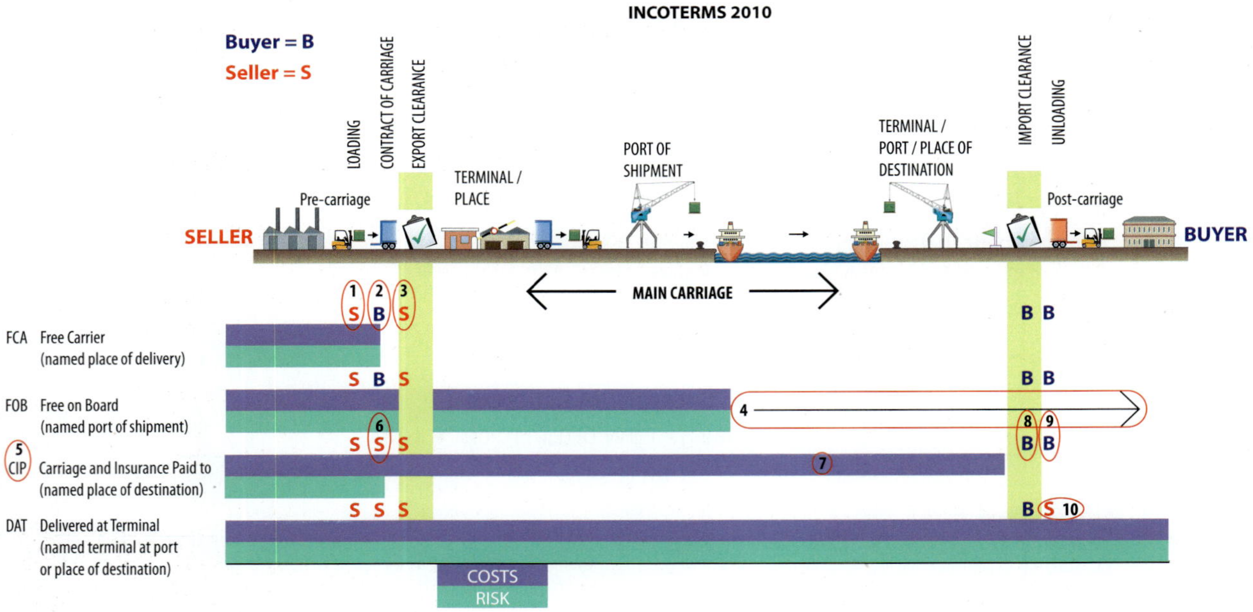

1 The seller (S) loads the goods.
2 The buyer (B) arranges for transport.
3 The seller (S) gets customs clearance for the goods.
4 The buyer (B) pays for the main carriage.
5 Insurance (I) for the main carriage is included in CIP.
6 The seller (S) arranges for transport.
7 The seller (S) pays for the main carriage.
8 The buyer (B) pays import duty.
9 The buyer (B) pays for unloading.
10 The seller (S) pays for unloading.

A Use the diagram to answer the following questions.

1 Who pays for loading with FOB delivery?
2 Who pays for unloading with FOB delivery?
3 Who pays for the main carriage with DAT delivery?
4 Who pays customs duty with DAT delivery?
5 Who bears the risk when the goods are on board the ship with FOB delivery?
6 Who bears the risk when the goods are on board the ship with CIP delivery?

B Look at the diagrams on page 189 for two minutes only and then answer the following questions.

1 How many Incoterms are there?
2 How many Incoterms are there for any mode or modes of transport?
3 How many Incoterms are there for sea and waterway transport?
4 How many Incoterms begin with the letter E?
5 How many begin with the letter F?
6 What does DAT stand for?
7 Which Incoterm is best for the seller?
8 Which Incoterm is best for the buyer?

C Refer to the definitions on pages 187–188 and the diagram on page 189 to recommend suitable Incoterms. Include the destination with the Incoterm, e.g. CPT Hamburg.

1 A German exporter in Dresden is only prepared to pack the goods, load them on board the carrier's vehicle at his premises and provide any documents needed.
2 An American importer requires the goods he has bought in Berlin to be transported and insured all the way to Dallas/Fort Worth International Airport in Texas, USA.
3 An Italian company in Naples buys some heavy road construction machinery from a German company in Duisburg. The buyer requires the exporter to bear all the costs and risks for the goods to their destination, including unloading the machinery at the terminal in Naples.
4 A British tractor manufacturer in Yorkshire, Northern England receives an order for 200 vehicles from an African buyer in Accra, Ghana. It is decided to send the goods by sea from the Port of Dover to the Port of Tema near Accra. The British manufacturer is only prepared to transport the goods to Dover and load them on board a ship.
5 An Argentinian beef exporter in Buenos Aires, Argentina sends a consignment of meat by ship from the Port of Buenos Aires to the Port of Hamburg. The exporter bears the transport costs to the port of destination and also pays for the meat to be insured while it is on board the ship.

Transport

Note: 'To ship' means to transport. The word does not only refer to transport by ship.

> Heavy and/or bulky goods are usually shipped by rail or ship.

> Light loads or perishable *(leicht verderblich)* goods are normally shipped by air over long distances.

> The motorway networks of industrialized countries make it possible to ship goods door-to-door by road.

> Multi-modal transport is used for goods in containers, because they can be easily loaded onto trains, lorries, ships and planes.

by rail

by road

by ship

by air

6 DECIDING ON A MEANS OF TRANSPORT

A Recommend suitable means of transport in the following cases. Give reasons for your answer.

1 a cargo of wood from South America to Europe
2 fresh flowers from Africa to Europe
3 vegetables from the Netherlands to the Ruhr Area
4 coal from a coal mine to a power station in the same country
5 oil from Saudi Arabia to a terminal in Europe
6 furniture from a furniture manufacturer to a warehouse 200 km away

B Now, from your own experience, think of two or three more examples of how goods are shipped.

7 COMPARING OFFERS

A Copy the table below into your exercise book or onto your computer and fill it in to compare the Swedish and Indian offers on page 99 and 101.

Name of supplier	*Patrik K, Sweden*	*J.P. Designs Incorporated, India*
Products	…	…
Price		
Delivery period	…	…
Terms of delivery	…	…
Distance between place of delivery and our premises		
Customs duty to be paid	…	…
Terms of payment	…	…

B Brix Mode finds out that after adding customs duty, other taxes and transport costs, the final price for clothes imported from India is approximately 40% higher. Calculate the final price of the Indian company's ladies' and men's tops for Brix Mode.

C Which of the two offers should Brix Mode choose in the following situations? Explain your answer.

1 Brix Mode needs 250 men's and women's tops as soon as possible for an important customer.
2 The company wants to give away a free men's top with every ladies' top bought to encourage men to buy more fashion tops.
3 The company wishes to collect the goods from the place of delivery with its own lorry.
4 The company cannot provide references but wants a guarantee that it will receive the goods after it has paid.

Reference to enquiry	**Bezug auf Anfrage**
As agreed in our pleasant telephone conversation of this morning / of today, …	Wie heute (Morgen) in unserem netten Telefonat vereinbart, …
We were delighted to receive your enquiry dated … about our … (e.g. fashion wear).	Wir waren sehr erfreut, Ihre Anfrage vom … über unser(e) … (z. B. Modebekleidung) zu erhalten.
Many thanks for the above-mentioned enquiry / your enquiry dated …	Wir danken für die oben genannte Anfrage / Ihre Anfrage vom …
… and feel sure we can supply you with all the goods you need.	… und sind sicher, dass wir Ihnen die Waren liefern können, die Sie benötigen.
Description of your company/goods/ services	**Beschreibung Ihrer Firma/Waren/ Dienstleistungen**
We are a major distributor of … (e.g. fashion wear, GPS devices) …	Wir sind ein bedeutender Großhändler für … (z. B. Modebekleidung, GPS-Geräte) …
… with an excellent reputation throughout Europe.	… mit einem hervorragenden Ruf in ganz Europa.
Our company manufactures a wide range of high-quality products …	Unsere Firma stellt eine breite Palette hochwertiger Produkte her …

... and already has many satisfied customers throughout ... (e.g. Western Europe).	... und hat bereits viele zufriedene Kunden überall in ... (z. B. Westeuropa).
Sales material	**Verkaufsmaterial**
We enclose our current catalogue and price list for your information.	Wir fügen unseren aktuellen Katalog und die Preisliste zu Ihrer Information bei.
To download our latest comprehensive catalogue and export price list, please visit our website at www.jpdesigns.in.	Um unseren aktuellen Katalog und die Exportpreisliste herunterzuladen, besuchen Sie unsere Homepage unter www.jpdesigns.in.
Samples are available on request.	Muster sind auf Wunsch erhältlich.
Price	**Preis**
As regards the goods requested, we are pleased to submit the following quotation:	Was die gewünschten Waren betrifft, freuen wir uns, Ihnen folgendes Angebot zu unterbreiten:
... and will be pleased to supply you with 100 ladies' and 100 men's T-shirts at €4 each ...	... und liefern Ihnen gerne 100 Damen- und 100 Herren-T-shirts zu je 4 € ...
... at US$ 10 per unit.	... zu 10 US$ pro Stück.
Terms and discounts	**Geschäftsbedingungen und Rabatte**
Our prices are quoted FOB Calcutta.	Unsere Preise verstehen sich FOB Kalkutta.
Delivery will be made ...	Die Lieferung erfolgt ...
CIP Frankfurt Airport	CIP Flughafen Frankfurt
DDP your (*buyer's*) premises	DDP Ihre Geschäftsräume
Wholesalers are granted a trade discount of ... %.	Großhändlern wird ein Handelsrabatt von ... % eingeräumt.
A quantity discount of ...% is granted on orders for 10 or more ... (e.g. machines, items).	Bei Abnahme von 10 oder mehr ... (z. B. Geräten, Artikeln) wird ein Mengenrabatt von ... % gewährt.
Our terms of payment for an initial order are CWO.	Unsere Zahlungsbedingungen für einen Erstauftrag sind Kasse bei Auftragserteilung.
Our usual terms of payment are letter of credit or CWO by PayPal or Western Union bank transfer ...	Unsere üblichen Zahlungsbedingungen sind per Akkreditiv oder Kasse bei Auftragserteilung per Überweisung durch PayPal oder Western Union ...
... or, with favourable references, 10 days 2%, 30 days net.	... oder bei günstigen Referenzen 2% Skonto bei Zahlung innerhalb von 10 Tagen, netto bei Zahlung innerhalb von 30 Tagen.
If regular orders are placed with our company, open account terms may be granted.	Wenn unserer Firma regelmäßige Aufträge erteilt werden, kann ein offenes Zahlungsziel gewährt werden.
Delivery	**Lieferung**
Delivery is made within approx. 30 days after receipt of order ...	Die Lieferung erfolgt innerhalb von ca. 30 Tagen nach Auftragseingang ...
... while stocks last.	... solange der Vorrat reicht.
Suitable ending	**Angemessene Verabschiedung**
We hope our offer is to your liking.	Wir hoffen, dass unser Angebot Ihnen zusagt.
We look forward to receiving your order.	Wir freuen uns, Ihren Auftrag zu erhalten.
We feel sure that a trial order will convince you of the quality of our products and look forward to doing business with you.	Wir sind sicher, dass ein Probeauftrag Sie von der Qualität unserer Produkte überzeugen wird und freuen uns, mit Ihnen eine Geschäftsbeziehung aufzunehmen.

Enclosure(s)	Anlage(n)
Catalogue Price list	Katalog Preisliste

8 WRITING OFFERS

A Look at the e-mail and then use the useful phrases to write an offer.

Sie sind Sachbearbeiter/-in in der Verkaufsabteilung der Firma World Navigator GmbH (Querstraße 20, 44866 Bochum, E-Mail info@worldnavigator.de). Ihre Firma ist ein bedeutender Großhändler für GPS-Geräte mit einem ausgezeichneten Ruf in ganz Europa.

Heute erhalten Sie eine Anfrage per E-Mail aus Irland.

E-MAIL

Mail from:	aileen.oreilly@whitefriar.ie
Subject:	Enquiry about handheld GPS devices
Cc:	
Attachment(s):	

Dear Ms Schmitt

You have been recommended to us by a business partner of ours, Mr Conrad Holstein, who tells us that you are able to supply GPS devices at competitive prices.

As we are extending our range at present, please send us a favourable quotation for an average priced and a high-end product, including all discounts granted and details of your terms of delivery and payment. We would require delivery within 6 weeks after placing our order.

If your products meet our requirements, we will be in a position to place a substantial order.

We look forward to your early reply with interest.

Yours sincerely

Aileen O'Reilly (Mrs)
Purchasing Director
Whitefriar Trekking Ltd
31 Wicklow Street
DUBLIN 8
Ireland

Tel. 00353 1 874 9826
Fax 00353 1 874 9827

Schreiben Sie ein Angebot mit heutigem Datum als Antwort auf die Anfrage unter Berücksichtigung der Checkliste *(Structure of an offer)* auf Seite 100 und folgender Punkte:

> Hinweis auf die Homepage Ihrer Firma (www.worldnavigator.de) mit downloadbarem Gesamtkatalog und Exportpreisliste

> Angebot für folgende Produkte:
- GPS-Gerät vom Typ „eTreck" mit Touchscreen, Artikel-Nr. eT49 zum Preis von 250 € pro Stück
- GPS-Handgerät vom Typ „Xpedition", Artikel-Nr. XP1 zum Preis von 100 € pro Stück
- Mengenrabatt von 10 % bei Abnahme von 10 oder mehr Geräten
- Lieferung DAT Geschäftsräume des irischen Kunden innerhalb 14 Tagen nach Auftragseingang

B Look at the letter and then use the useful phrases to write an offer.

Sie sind Sachbearbeiter/-in in der Verkaufsabteilung der Firma Dadias Sportbekleidung GmbH. Ihre Gesellschaft stellt eine breite Palette hochwertiger Artikel her und hat bereits viele zufriedene Kunden überall in Westeuropa.

Heute erhalten Sie eine Anfrage aus den Vereinigten Arabischen Emiraten.

Sand and Sun Sports
P.O. Box 259288
DUBAI
UNITED ARAB EMIRATES
Tel. 00971 4 3577700
Fax 00971 4 3577701
Website: www.sandsunsports.ae
E-mail: sandsun@eim.ae

JD/SS
10 March 20...

Mr Markus Wangemann
Sales Department
Dadias Sportbekleidung GmbH
Dadias Str. 37
91074 Herzogenaurach
Germany

Dear Mr Wangemann

Enquiry

We have seen your company's advertisement in the current edition of Sports International and are most interested in your products. Our company is a leading wholesaler of sports goods with excellent contacts all over the Middle East and beyond.

At present we are particularly interested in football shirts and would therefore be grateful if you would let us have your latest catalogue and export price list, including all discounts granted and details of your terms of delivery and payment. Please also let us know if you are able to provide samples.

If your products meet our requirements, we will be in a position to place a substantial order.

We look forward to your early reply with interest.

Yours sincerely
Sun and Sand Sports

J Dickinson

July Dickinson
Purchasing Department

Schreiben Sie ein Angebot als Antwort auf die Anfrage unter Berücksichtigung folgender Punkte:

- Sie fügen einen aktuellen Katalog mit Preisliste bei.
- Muster sind auf Wunsch erhältlich.
- Alle Preise verstehen sich CIP Flughafen Dubai.
- Großhandelsrabatt von 20 %
- Zahlungsbedingungen bei Erstauftrag sind Kasse bei Auftragserteilung (CWO).
- Lieferung erfolgt innerhalb von ca. 30 Tagen nach Auftragseingang.

Webcode: FOBNRWT401

D Orders and acknowledgements

Sevda is preparing for a trade fair and needs material for advertising banners.

1 LOOKING AT AN ORDER

A Study the following order and complete the sentences on the next page.

BRIX Mode GmbH
Feldstraße 42 • 33609 Bielefeld • Germany
Tel +49 521 4827764 Fax +49 521 4824760 info@brixmode.de

SY/GJ
04 July 20..

TAYA Canvas Company Limited
110 Huaning Road
200245 SHANGHAI
CHINA

Attn. Mr Andy Zhao, Export Sales Director

Dear Mr Zhao

Order no. BK42 for banner material

Many thanks for your offer dated 28 June 20.. .

We now wish to place an order for the following goods:

Quantity	Description	Article No.	Unit Price ($)	Total ($)
10 rolls	Frontlit banner material	FL136	50.00	500.00
20 rolls	Backlit banner material	BL284	40.00	800.00
			Total price	**1,300.00**

Delivery: FOB Shanghai within 30 days after receipt of order
Packing: Container
Payment: 30% in advance, 70% after completion by transfer to your a/c at the Bank of China

Transport and insurance of the goods from Shanghai to Bielefeld via the Port of Rotterdam will be arranged by us.

We look forward to receiving your confirmation of order and advice of dispatch in the near future.

Yours sincerely
Brix Mode GmbH

S. Yildiz

Sevda Yildiz (Ms)
Purchasing Director

> The Incoterm FOB stands for 'free on board ...'.
> See page 188 for more details.
> a/c = account

Brix Mode GmbH • Bielefeld, Registergericht Bielefeld, HRB 82071, Geschäftsführerin: Karla Wenz

1 The TAYA Canvas Company is in ...
2 Andy Zhao sent Sevda an offer on ...
3 All the prices are in ...
4 10 rolls of FL136 cost ...
5 One roll of BL284 costs ...
6 The TAYA Canvas Company has a bank account at ...
7 The goods will be sent in a ...
8 The goods will be sent to Europe by ship to ...

Port of Shanghai

B Match the German translations with points 1–8 in the box below.

Angaben über die bestellten Waren / Dienstleistungen | Angemessene Verabschiedung | Anlage(n) | Bestätigung / Versandanzeige | Bezug auf Angebot | Internationale Handelsklausel | Liefertermin/-zeit | Lieferung | Preise und Rabatte | Verpackung | Versand | Versicherung | Zahlung

Structure of an order

An order covers some or all of the following points:

1 Reference to offer
2 Details of goods/services ordered
3 Price(s) and discount(s)
4 Delivery
  > Incoterm
  > delivery date/period
  > transport and packing
  > insurance
5 Payment
6 Acknowledgement / Advice of dispatch
7 Suitable ending
8 Enclosure(s)/Attachment(s)

C Lesen Sie folgende Bestellung aufmerksam durch und entscheiden Sie, ob die Aussagen falsch oder richtig sind. Berichtigen Sie die falschen Aussagen. Schlagen Sie unbekannte Wörter im Vokabelverzeichnis nach.

Quantity	Description	Article No.	List Price	Total
100	HQ printer	HQ3000	€60.00	€6,000.00
250	Quickchip laptop	QC99	€100.00	€25,000.00
			- 30% trade discount	-€9,300.00
			Subtotal	€21,700.00
			+ 19% VAT*	€4,123.00
			Total price	**€25,823.00**
Delivery:	CIF Rotterdam by 30 June 20..			
Packing:	Sturdy cartons			
Payment:	2% 10 days, 30 days net after receipt of invoice			
				*Value added tax = *Mehrwertsteuer*

1 Ein Drucker kostet normalerweise 60,00 €.
2 Es wird ein Rabatt in Höhe von 19 % in Abzug gebracht.
3 Der Endpreis der Bestellung beträgt 21.700 €.
4 Der Lieferort befindet sich in den Niederlanden.

5 Der Verkäufer wird die Kosten für den Transport von Rotterdam zu den Geschäftsräumen des Käufers übernehmen.
6 Der Käufer möchte, dass die Lieferung bis spätestens 30. Juni erfolgt.
7 Der Käufer erhält einen Rabatt in Höhe von 10 %, wenn er innerhalb von zwei Tagen zahlt.
8 Der Käufer hat ein Zahlungsziel von 30 Tagen, nachdem er die Rechnung erhalten hat.
9 Die Drucker und Laptops werden in leichte Kartons verpackt.

D When writing prices in English, follow the instructions to the right. Study the examples in the two orders on pages 108 and 109, and then write out the following prices in figures.

1 a hundred dollars
2 five thousand dollars
3 ten pounds and fifty pence
4 twenty thousand pounds and seventy-five cents
5 eighty-two dollars and sixty-seven cents
6 thirty pence
7 nine euros and ninety-nine cents
8 a million euros

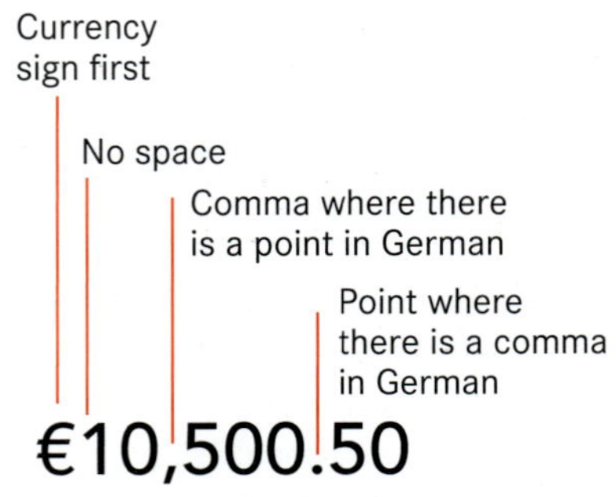

Writing prices

Reference to offer	**Bezug auf Angebot**
Many thanks for your offer dated ...	Vielen Dank für Ihr Angebot vom ...
Having seen your offer on the internet and spoken to you on the telephone, ...	Nachdem wir Ihr Angebot im Internet gesehen und mit Ihnen gesprochen haben, ...
We have seen your offer for ... on the internet.	Wir haben Ihr Angebot über ... im Internet gesehen.
Details of goods/services ordered	**Einzelheiten über bestellte Waren/ Dienstleistungen**
We now wish to place an order / a trial order for the following goods: ...	Wir möchten einen Auftrag / Probeauftrag über folgende Waren erteilen: ...
[*Headings*] Quantity / Description / Size / Catalogue No.	[*Überschriften*] Menge / Beschreibung / Größe / Katalog-Nr.
Price(s) and discount(s)	**Preis(e) und Rabatt(e)**
[*Headings*] Unit Price / List Price / Catalogue Price / Total	[*Überschriften*] Stückpreis / Listenpreis / Katalogpreis / Gesamt
Subtotal / Total price	Zwischensumme / Gesamtpreis
19% VAT [value added tax]	19 % USt [Umsatzsteuer / Mehrwertsteuer]
Delivery	**Lieferung**
Incoterm FOB Shanghai / CIF Rotterdam / DDP (*destination*) / our premises	**Incoterm (siehe Seite 193)** frei an Bord (FOB) Shanghai / Kosten, Versicherung Fracht (CIF) Rotterdam / geliefert verzollt zu unseren Geschäftsräumen (DDP ...)
Delivery date/period ... within 10 days after receipt of order ... by 30 June 20..	**Liefertermin/-zeit** ... innerhalb von 10 Tagen nach Auftragserhalt ... bis zum 30. Juni 20..

Transport Transport and insurance of the goods from ... to ... via ... ... will be arranged by us/you.	**Versand** Versand und Versicherung der Ware von ... nach ... über ... wird von uns/Ihnen übernommen.
Packing container in sturdy cartons	**Verpackung** Container in robusten Kartons
Insurance Insurance will be arranged by us/you.	**Versicherung** Die Versicherung wird von uns/Ihnen übernommen.
Payment	**Zahlung**
30% in advance, 70% after completion	30 % im Voraus, 70 % bei Fertigstellung
by transfer to our a/c at ... (*name of bank*)	per Überweisung auf unser Konto bei ... (*Geldinstitut*)
by bank transfer	per Banküberweisung
2% 10 days, 30 days net after receipt of invoice	2 % Skonto bei Zahlung innerhalb von 10 Tagen, netto bei Zahlung innerhalb von 30 Tagen nach Rechnungserhalt
Acknowledgement / advice of dispatch	**Auftragsbestätigung / Versandanzeige**
We look forward to receiving your advice of dispatch.	Wir freuen uns auf den Erhalt Ihrer Versandanzeige.
Please send us your confirmation of order and advice of dispatch in the near future.	Bitte schicken Sie uns Ihre Auftragsbestätigung und Versandanzeige in den nächsten Tagen zu.
Suitable ending	**Angemessene Verabschiedung**
We trust the goods will arrive punctually and in good condition ...	Wir vertrauen darauf, dass die Ware pünktlich und in gutem Zustand ankommt ...
... and will place further/regular orders if they sell well.	... und werden weitere/regelmäßige Aufträge erteilen, wenn sie sich gut verkauft.
Enclosure(s)	**Anlage(n)**
order form	Bestellformular

2 WRITING ORDERS

A Use the useful phrases to write a letter order based on the following details.

Sie (eigener Name) sind Einkaufsleiter/in bei der Firma TT Autobeschriftung GmbH, Tempelstr. 99, 47918 Tönisvorst, Fax-Nr. 0049 2151 450277, E-Mail: vorname.nachname@tt-auto.de. Ihre Firma vertreibt selbstklebende Autobeschriftungsfolien (*film*) und Zierstreifen (*tape*). Sie finden folgendes Angebot auf einer chinesischen Website und rufen bei der Firma an.

Aufgabe

Erteilen Sie der chinesischen Firma einen Probeauftrag unter Berücksichtigung folgender Punkte:

- Bezug auf Angebot im Internet und Telefongespräch
- Sie bestellen mit Auftrags-Nr. VF247 je 100 Rollen *Go faster tape*, 0.08 mm x 1.07 m zu 7,50 $ pro Rolle, Katalog-Nr. VF8107 und *Self-adhesive film*, 0.10 mm x 1.27 m zu 9,00 $ pro Rolle, Katalog-Nr. SAF10127.
- Lieferung im Container CIF Rotterdam innerhalb von 50 Tagen nach Auftragserhalt
- Zahlungsbedingungen: 30 % im Voraus, 70 % bei Erhalt per Banküberweisung

- > Bitte um Auftragsbestätigung und Versandanzeige
- > Hoffnung auf pünktliche Lieferung der Ware in gutem Zustand
- > Aussicht auf weitere Aufträge, wenn die Ware sich gut verkauft

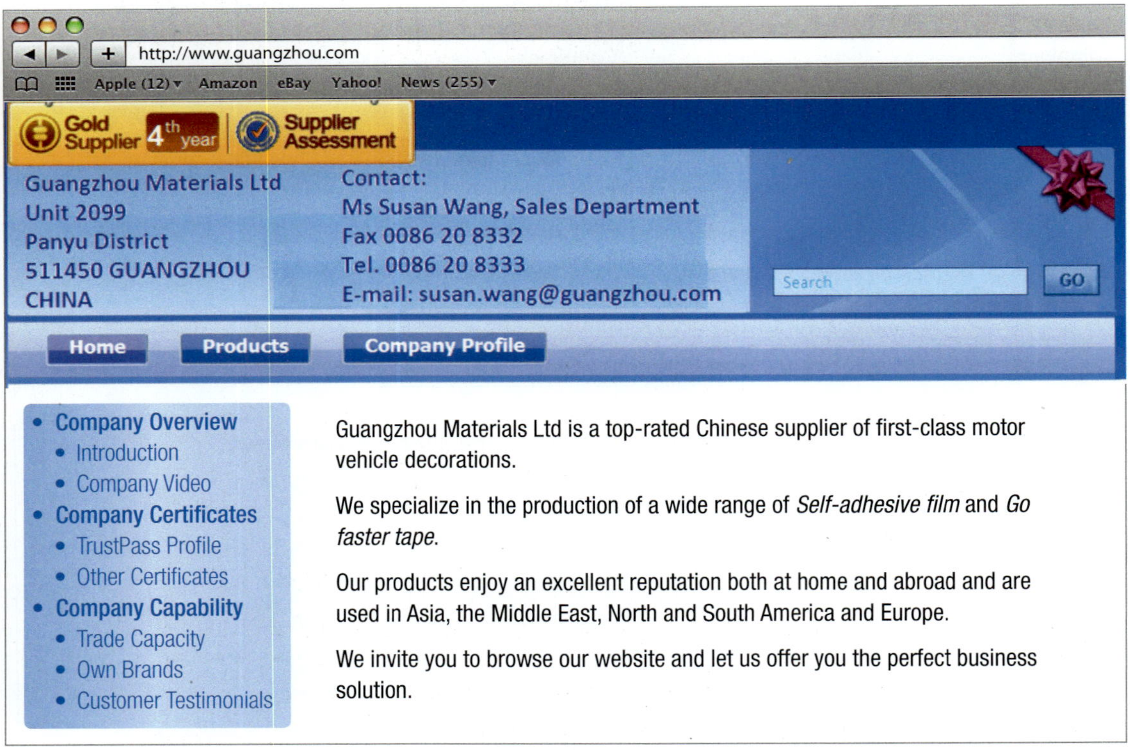

B Use the useful phrases to write an e-mail order based on the following details.

Sie sind Sevda Yildiz bei Brix Mode in Bielefeld (siehe Seite 93).

Aufgabe
Verfassen Sie mit heutigem Datum eine Bestellung an die schwedische Firma (Patrik K, Exportleiter, Björnbo 53, 11825 Stockholm, Schweden, Fax-Nr. 0046 8 609 4988, E-Mail: pehr.lindquist@patrikk.com) unter Berücksichtigung folgender Punkte:

- > Bezug auf Angebot vom ... (vor ca. einer Woche)
- > Mit Auftrags-Nr. TS826 bestellen Sie 1.000 Damen Seidenschals (*lady's silk scarf / ladies' silk scarves*) vom Typ „Sunrise", Stückpreis 10 €, Artikel-Nr. HB49.
- > Bringen Sie einen Mengenrabatt von 3 % in Abzug.
- > Errechnen Sie den Endpreis.
- > Lieferung CIP Flughafen Düsseldorf innerhalb von 7 Tagen nach Auftragserhalt
- > Zahlung: per Banküberweisung, 2 % Skonto bei Zahlung innerhalb von 10 Tagen, netto bei Zahlung innerhalb von 30 Tagen
- > Bitte um Auftragsbestätigung
- > Hoffnung, dass die Ware pünktlich und wohlbehalten ankommt
- > Aussicht auf regelmäßige Aufträge, wenn sie sich gut verkauft

3 ACKNOWLEDGING ORDERS

A Study the Chinese company's reply to Sevda's letter and answer the questions below.

E-MAIL

To: sevda.yildiz@brixmode.de
Subject: Your order no. BK42 dated 04 July 20.. for banner material
Attachments: SuperFlat.pdf

Dear Ms Yildiz

Many thanks for the above-mentioned order. We are pleased to confirm the details as listed below:

Quantity	Article	Size	Article No.	List Price	Total
10 rolls	Frontlit banner material	5m wide	FL136	$50.00	$500.00
20 rolls	Backlit banner material	4m wide	BL284	$40.00	$800.00
				Total price	**$1,300.00**

As agreed, the goods will be packed in a container and delivered FOB Shanghai by 15 August 20.. at the latest. We note that you will arrange for transport and insurance of the goods from the Port of Shanghai to the Port of Rotterdam and then to your premises in Bielefeld, Germany.

Payment of 30% of the total amount is now due. Please therefore transfer $390 to our account at the Bank of China. We expect to complete your order in approx. 20 days' time and will inform you as soon as the goods are ready. Payment of the remaining 70% will then be due. As soon as the total amount has been received, the goods will be transported to the Port of Shanghai for shipment and we will send you our advice of dispatch.

We would also like to take this opportunity to draw your attention to our new SuperFlat display material. It is suitable for high resolution posters and is supplied in 50m x 3.20m rolls. A pdf file on the new product is enclosed for your information.

If you have any queries about your order or wish to receive a quotation for our new SuperFlat display material, please do not hesitate to contact us.

Thank you for placing your order with the TAYA Canvas Company.

Yours sincerely

Andy Zhou
Export Sales Director

1 How will the goods be transported from Shanghai to Rotterdam?
2 What does FOB stand for?
3 Where is the German buyer's firm located?
4 What are the terms of payment?
5 Who will pay for transport of the goods from Shanghai to Germany?
6 Why has the Chinese company enclosed a pdf file with its acknowledgement?

B **Match the German translations with points 1–9 in the box below.**

Ablehnung des Auftrags | Angebot von Ersatzware | Angemessene Verabschiedung | Anlage(n) | Auftragsbestätigung | Bezug auf Auftrag | Bezug auf neue Produkte / Dienstleistungen | Bitte um Bestätigung | Datum und Art der Lieferung | Liefer- und Zahlungsbedingungen | Preise und Rabatte | Versandanzeige

Structure of an acknowledgement

An acknowledgement covers some or all of the following points:

1 Reference to order
2 Confirmation of order or
   > offer of substitutes
   > rejection of order
3 Price(s) and discount(s)
4 Terms of delivery and payment
5 Date and mode of delivery
   > advice of dispatch
6 Request for confirmation
7 Reference to new product(s)/services
8 Suitable ending
9 Enclosure(s)/Attachments

Reference to order	**Bezug auf Auftrag**
Many thanks for the above-mentioned order.	Vielen Dank für den oben erwähnten Auftrag.
Confirmation of order	**Auftragsbestätigung**
We are pleased to confirm the details as listed below:	Wir bestätigen gern die Einzelheiten wie folgt:
Offer of substitutes Unfortunately, the article you require is currently out of stock. Might we therefore suggest supplying ... (*substitute*) instead? Please refer to the enclosed brochure/document for more details. The list price of this article is ... . Under the circumstances we are prepared to offer it at ... (*price/Incoterm*) Alternatively, we can supply it at ... (*price/ Incoterm*).	**Angebot von Ersatzware** Leider ist der von Ihnen benötigte Artikel nicht vorrätig. Dürfen wir deshalb stattdessen ... (*Ersatz*) vorschlagen? Weitere Einzelheiten können der beigefügten Broschüre/Datei entnommen werden. Der Preis dieses Artikels beträgt ... . Unter den Umständen sind wir bereit, ihn zum Preis von ... (*Preis/Incoterm*) anzubieten. Als Alternative können wir ihn zum Preis von ... (*Preis/Incoterm*) anbieten.
Rejection of order We are unfortunately unable to fill/execute/ complete your order.	**Ablehnung des Auftrags** Leider können wir Ihren Auftrag nicht ausführen.
Price(s) and discount(s)	**Preis(e) und Rabatt(e)**
[*Headings*] Unit Price / List Price / Catalogue Price	[*Überschriften*] Stückpreis/Listenpreis/ Katalogpreis
[*Headings*] Total / Sub-total / Total Price	[*Überschriften*] Gesamt / Zwischensumme / Gesamtpreis
quantity discount	Mengenrabatt
Terms of delivery and payment	**Liefer- und Zahlungsbedingungen**
As agreed, the goods will be delivered FOB Shanghai.	Wie vereinbart wird die Ware FOB Shanghai geliefert.

Payment of 30% of the invoice / total amount is now due.	30 % des Rechnungsbetrags/ Gesamtbetrags sind jetzt fällig.
Please therefore transfer $390 to our account at the Bank of China.	Bitte überweisen Sie deshalb 390 $ auf unser Konto bei der Bank of China.
Payment of the remaining 70% will then be due.	Die verbleibenden 70 % des Rechnungsbetrags werden dann fällig sein.
Our terms of payment for an initial order are ... (e.g. CWO [cash with order]).	Unsere Zahlungsbedingungen für einen Erstauftrag lauten ... (z. B. Kasse bei Auftragserteilung (CWO)).
Date and mode of delivery	**Datum und Art der Lieferung**
The goods will be delivered by ... (*date*, e.g. 15 August 20..) at the latest.	Die Ware wird bis spätestens ... (*Datum*, z. B. 15. August 20..) geliefert.
We expect to complete your order in approx. 20 days' time and will inform you as soon as the goods are ready.	Wir rechnen mit der Erledigung Ihres Auftrages in ca. 20 Tagen und werden Sie benachrichtigen, sobald die Ware fertig ist.
The goods will be packed in a container.	Die Ware wird in einen Container verpackt.
We note that you will arrange for transport and insurance of the goods from ... to your premises.	Wir nehmen zur Kenntnis, dass Sie Versand und Versicherung der Ware von ... bis zu Ihren Geschäftsräumen übernehmen werden.
Delivery will be made within approx. 30 days after receipt of order / by the end of the month.	Die Lieferung erfolgt innerhalb von ca. 30 Tagen nach Auftragserhalt / bis Ende des Monats.
Advice of dispatch As soon as the total invoice amount has been received, ... the goods will be transported to the Port of ... (*city*) for shipment. ... we will send you our advice of dispatch.	**Versandanzeige** Sobald der volle Rechnungsbetrag eingegangen ist, ... wird die Ware zum Hafen ... (*Stadt*) zur Verladung transportiert. ... werden wir Ihnen die Versandanzeige zuschicken.
Request for confirmation	**Bitte um Bestätigung**
Please let us know which offer you prefer.	Bitte lassen Sie uns wissen, welches Angebot Sie bevorzugen.
Reference to new product(s)/services	**Bezug auf neue(s) Produkt(e)/ Dienstleistungen**
We would also like to take this opportunity to draw your attention to ...	Bei dieser Gelegenheit möchten wir Ihre Aufmerksamkeit auch auf ... lenken.
... which is currently on offer.	... das derzeit im Angebot ist.
A pdf file/document / A brochure on the new product is enclosed for your information.	Zu Ihrer Information ist eine pdf-Datei/ Broschüre beigefügt.
Suitable ending	**Angemessene Verabschiedung**
If you have any questions/queries about your order / the (new) product ...	Sollten Sie weitere Fragen/Rückfragen zu Ihrem Auftrag / zum (neuen) Produkt haben, ...
If you wish to receive a quotation for our new ... (product), ...	Wenn Sie ein Angebot über unser neues ... (Produkt) erhalten möchten, ...
... (please) do not hesitate to contact us / to get in touch with us.	... (bitte) zögern Sie nicht, sich mit uns in Verbindung zu setzen.
Thank you for placing your order with ... (*name of company*).	Vielen Dank für Ihren Auftrag.

4 WRITING AN ACKNOWLEDGEMENT

Use the useful phrases to write an e-mail acknowledgement based on the following details.

Sie (eigener Name) arbeiten in der Exportabteilung bei Brix Mode (siehe Seite 93). Sie erhalten aus der Online-Verkaufsabteilung folgende Information zu einer Internet-Bestellung.

Brix Mode GmbH - ONLINE SALES ORDER

Order no:	**42BK**
Priority	**NORMAL**
Order date:	[5 days ago]
Item:	**Sunrise lady's silk scarf**
Article no:	**HB49**
Quantity:	**20**
Customer company:	**High End Fashion Ltd**
Customer name:	**Jill Ryan**
Customer title:	**Ms**
Customer position:	**Import Department**
Customer address:	**99 High Street**
Customer address 2:	
Customer city:	**NEWCASTLE**
Customer postcode:	**NE3 9 LM**
Customer country:	**England**
Customer e-mail:	**jill.ryan@highend.co.uk**
Customer fax:	**0044 191 407877**

Aufgabe

Verfassen Sie eine Auftragsbestätigung an die englische Firma mit Hilfe der Einzelheiten der Online-Bestellung und unter Berücksichtigung folgender Punkte:

- Bezug auf Bestellung
- Darstellung der einzelnen Positionen der Bestellung (Artikel, Menge usw.)
- Mengenrabatt von 5 % wird gewährt.
- Errechnen Sie den Endpreis.
- Lieferung CIP Flughafen Newcastle bis ... *(Datum in 10 Tagen angeben)*
- Zahlung: Kasse bei Auftragserteilung per Banküberweisung
- Versandanzeige wird nach Erhalt des Rechnungsbetrags verschickt
- Bezug auf neues Produkt und beigefügte Broschüre/Datei: Damenstrickjacke *(lady's cardigan)* „Flair“
- Bitte um Mitteilung, falls weitere Informationen über Bestellung oder Angebot über neues Produkt erwünscht

Webcode: FOBNRWT402

E Payments and reminders

1 LOOKING AT A REQUEST FOR PAYMENT

A Fair Trade Fashions in the UK requests payment from Brix Mode in Bielefeld for a consignment of goods. Read the letter and choose the right answers to complete the sentences.

Fair Trade Fashions

85 Princes Park
GATESHEAD
NE1 9NF
GREAT BRITAIN

JM/TT
10 December 20..

Brix Mode
Feldstraße 42
33609 Bielefeld
GERMANY

Attn. Ms Sevda Yildiz, Purchasing Director

Dear Ms Yildiz

Your order no. FWA 4226 dated 05 December 20.. for fashion wear and accessories

The above-mentioned goods are now ready for dispatch and our invoice for £10,500.00 is enclosed for payment. Please remit the invoice amount to our company's account at NatWest Bank plc in Gateshead:

IBAN: GB38NWBK57002167984202
BIC: NWBKGB2LXXX

The goods will be shipped as soon as payment has been received.

For your information we are also enclosing a brochure on our company's latest collection, 'Spring Surprises.' Should you require further information, please do not hesitate to contact us.

Thank you for choosing to place your order with Fair Trade Fashions.

Yours sincerely
Fair Trade Fashions

Joanne Miles

Joanne Miles
Accounts Section

Enc

1 Sevda Yildiz
   a works in Germany.
   b works in England.
   c works in Turkey.

2 Joanne Miles
   a now has to pay £10,500.00.
   b has not yet received £10,500.00.
   c has just spent £10,500.00.

3 Brix Mode has
   a received the goods.
   b paid for the goods.
   c ordered the goods.

4 The German company
   a ordered the goods on 10 December.
   b ordered the goods on 05 December.
   c received the goods on 05 December.

5 The goods are
   a on their way.
   b waiting to be sent.
   c already with the buyer.

6 The brochure is about
   a new fashion wear.
   b the fashion wear ordered.
   c all the company's products.

B Match the German translations with points 1–5 in the box below.

Weitere Informationen | Anlage(n) | Bezug auf Rechnung für Waren oder Dienstleistungen | Angemessene Verabschiedung | Zahlung

Structure of a request for payment

A request for payment covers some or all of the following points:

1 Reference to invoice for goods or services
2 Payment
3 Further information
4 Suitable ending
5 Enclosure(s)

C Use words in the letter from Fair Trade Fashions to fill in the gaps.

I work in the ...1 department of my company, which means we buy goods. We normally get an e-mail when the goods are ready for ...2 and sometimes we have to pay the ...3 before the supplier will ...4 the goods. If this happens, we ...5 the amount to the supplier's bank ...6. We need two things for this – the supplier's ...7, which is a very long number and also his ...8, to make sure the money goes to the right bank.

2 LOOKING AT A COMMERCIAL INVOICE

Study the commercial invoice on the next page and then answer the following questions.

1 What is the name of (a) the buyer and (b) the seller?
2 How do we know that the goods will be transported by ship?
3 How much of the invoice amount must the buyer pay first?
4 What must the buyer do before the goods can be shipped?
5 What currency is the invoice in?

达亚帆布(上海)有限公司
TA YA CANVAS (SHANGHAI) COMPANY LIMITED

上海市闵行经济技术开发区华宁路 110 号 邮编 : 200245
NO. 110, HUANING ROAD, MINHANG ECONOMIC & TECHNOLOGICAL DEVELOPING ZONE,
SHANGHAI, P.R. CHINA. P.C.: 200245
TEL: (86-21) 6463 2409 FAX: (86-21) 6463 2157

COMMERCIAL INVOICE

Invoice No. TYSH910
21 March 20..

To:
Brix Mode GmbH
Feldstraße 42, 33609 Bielefeld
Registergericht Bielefeld HRB 14446
Tel: +49 521 482 77 64
Fax: +49 521 482 77 60

Quantity	Width	Length	Description	Area (m^2)	Unit Price (USD)	Total (USD)
55 rolls	3.20 m	50 m	Matte white banner material, 450 g	8,800	1.51	13,288.00
20 rolls	1.37 m	50 m	Matte white banner material, 510 g	1,370	1.61	2,205.70
					Total	**15,493.70**

Fifteen thousand four hundred and ninety-three United States dollars and seventy cents only

Terms of payment: 30% deposit, 70% balance to be paid before shipment
Delivery: FOB Shanghai, 4 weeks after receipt of deposit
Packing: Seaworthy container
Name of bank: Bank of China (Shanghai) Ltd
Account number: 031-355-8-313199-4
Swift code (BIC): BKCHSHHH

Terms of payment and reminders

The terms of payment for new or unreliable customers are usually payment in advance, CWO (cash with order) or letter of credit (*Akkreditiv*), because in each case the seller can be sure of being paid.

Regular and/or trusted customers are given better terms pf payment, e.g.
> open account terms
> 10 days 2%, 30 days net
> 30/60/90 days net
> 1/3 with order, 1/3 on delivery, 1/3 within 30 days after delivery

In most cases, a reminder is therefore sent to a regular and/or trusted customer. The first reminder is a polite reference to the unpaid invoice and a request to pay soon. The second reminder is more forceful. It asks for an explanation and is an urgent request for payment. The third reminder (or final demand) sets a deadline and describes the consequences of non-payment. It is normally addressed to a senior executive and marked 'Confidential'.

3 LOOKING AT A REMINDER

A Read the reminder below and describe the problem. Explain what will happen if the problem is not resolved.

26 June 20..

Attn. Ms Margery Ingram, Export Sales Director

Dear Ms Ingram

Invoice no. BT9854 for £8,525.75 dated 18 May 20..

We wish to point out that payment of the above-mentioned invoice was expected on 18 June 20.. .

The invoice is therefore 8 days overdue.

We would very much welcome an explanation as to why payment has not been made but, whatever the case may be, we would urgently request you to pay within the next 7 days, after which time we will stop all further deliveries to your company.

If payment has already been made, please disregard this letter.

Yours sincerely

B Match the German translations with points 1–7 in the box below.

Angemessene Verabschiedung | Anlage(n) | Bezug auf frühere Mahnung(en) | Bezug auf überfällige Rechnung | Bitte um eine Erklärung | Bitte um Zahlung einschließlich Fristsetzung | Folgen bei Nichtzahlung

Structure of a reminder

A reminder covers some or all of the following points:

1 Reference to overdue invoice/account
2 Reference to previous reminder(s)
3 Request for explanation
4 Request for payment including deadline
5 Consequences of non-payment
6 Suitable ending
7 Enclosure(s)

Reference to overdue invoice/account	**Bezug auf überfällige Rechnung**
We wish to point out that payment of the above-mentioned invoice was expected on ...	Wir möchten darauf hinweisen, dass die Bezahlung der oben genannten Rechnung am ... erwartet wurde.
We are sorry to note that our invoice for ...is now ... days/weeks overdue ... despite our letter dated ... / our telephone call on ...	Wir bedauern festzustellen, dass unsere Rechnung über ... nun ...Tage/Wochen überfällig ist... trotz unseres Schreibens vom ... / Telefonats am...
We wish to draw your attention to the fact that that our sales agreement provides for payment within 30 days at the latest.	Wir möchten Sie darauf aufmerksam machen, dass unsere Verkaufsvereinbarung eine Zahlung innerhalb von spätestens 30 Tagen vorsieht.
Reference to previous reminder(s)	**Bezug auf frühere Mahnung(en)**
We refer to our two previous letters (see enclosures), dated ... and ... with regard to the above-mentioned invoice, which is still overdue.	Wir beziehen uns auf unsere zwei vorhergehenden Briefe (siehe Anlagen) vom ... und ... bezüglich der oben genannten Rechnung, die noch offen steht.
As we have received neither an explanation nor a remittance ...	Da wir weder eine Erklärung noch eine Überweisung erhalten haben, ...
Request for explanation	**Bitte um eine Erklärung**
We would therefore welcome an explanation as to why payment is delayed.	Wir würden deshalb eine Erklärung für den Zahlungsverzug begrüßen.
Request for payment including deadline	**Bitte um Zahlung einschl. Fristsetzung**
Whatever the case may be ...	Wie dem auch sei, ...
We must therefore request that you pay by 30 November 20.. at the latest.	Wir müssen Sie deshalb bitten, bis spätestens 30. November 20... zu zahlen.
We must insist that you remit the amount in question without delay.	Wir müssen darauf bestehen, dass der betreffende Betrag unverzüglich überwiesen wird.
We are setting you a final deadline for payment of 7 days.	Wir setzen Ihnen eine letzte Zahlungsfrist von sieben Tagen.
Consequences of non-payment	**Folgen der Nichtzahlung**
If payment is not made by 03 October 20.., we will stop all further deliveries and take the necessary steps to recover the sum owing.	Sollte die Zahlung bis zum 3. Oktober nicht geleistet werden, werden wir alle weiteren Lieferungen einstellen und die notwendigen Schritte einleiten, um den fälligen Betrag zu erhalten.
Should you fail to pay this invoice, we will have no choice but to discontinue our business relationship with your company.	Wenn Sie es versäumen, unsere Rechnung zu begleichen, haben wir keine andere Wahl, als unsere Geschäftsbeziehungen zu Ihrem Unternehmen einzustellen.
Suitable ending	**Angemessene Verabschiedung**
We look forward to receiving the sum in question in the next few days.	Wir würden uns freuen, die betreffende Summe in den nächsten Tagen zu erhalten.
Prompt payment is all that is needed to settle this matter.	Diese Angelegenheit kann durch eine umgehende Überweisung Ihrerseits geregelt werden.
If payment has already been made, please disregard this letter/fax/e-mail.	Sollte die Zahlung bereits erfolgt sein, betrachten Sie diesen Brief / dieses Fax / diese E-Mail bitte als gegenstandslos.

4 WRITING REMINDERS

A Use the useful phrases to write a reminder in the form of a letter/fax/e-mail based on the following details.

Situation

(Fortsetzung Aufgabe 8A *Offers* auf Seite 106)
Sie (eigener Name) sind Sachbearbeiter/in in der Buchhaltung der Firma World Navigator GmbH in Bochum. Ihre Firma hat eine Lieferung GPS-Geräte mit Rechnung-Nr. GPSIR-92 über 6.300,00 € (Datum vor fünf Wochen) an die Firma Whitefriar Trekking Ltd in Dublin, Irland geliefert. Auf Grund der guten Referenzen der irischen Firma waren die Zahlungsbedingungen 10 Tage 2 %, 30 Tage netto. Da zwei Tage nach Fälligkeit der Rechnung kein Geld auf Ihr Firmenkonto eingegangen war, haben Sie die irische Firma angerufen und von der Einkaufsleiterin erfahren, dass die Zahlung unterwegs sei. Es sind inzwischen drei weitere Tage verstrichen, ohne dass die Rechnung bezahlt wurde.

Aufgabe

Verfassen Sie mit heutigem Datum eine Mahnung an die irische Firma unter Berücksichtigung folgender Punkte:

> Ihr Ansprechpartner ist Mrs Aileen O'Reilly, Einkaufsleiterin.
> Bezug auf Rechnung (Kopie beigefügt/angehängt)
> Bezug auf Telefonat von vor 3 Tagen
> Laut Kaufvertrag beträgt die Zahlungsfrist 30 Tage.
> Die Rechnung ist nunmehr 5 Tage überfällig.
> Sie bitten um eine Erklärung und unverzügliche Überweisung des fälligen Betrags.
> Bei Nichtzahlung Einstellung der Geschäftsbeziehungen
> Angemessene Verabschiedung

B Use the useful phrases to write a reminder in the form of a letter/fax/e-mail based on the following details.

Situation

Sie (eigener Name) arbeiten in der Buchhaltung der Firma Sportbedarf Reimann GmbH in Köln. Vor sechs Wochen hat Ihre Firma Skiausrüstung an die schottische Firma Winter Gear Ltd in Aviemore geliefert und anschließend eine Rechnung geschickt. Bis heute haben Sie weder eine Erklärung noch eine Überweisung erhalten.

Aufgabe

Verfassen Sie eine Mahnung (Brief, Fax oder E-Mail) an die schottische Firma unter Berücksichtigung folgender Einzelheiten:

> Ansprechpartner: Ms Sheena Murray, Einkaufsleiterin
> Behandlungsvermerk: Vertraulich
> Bezug auf Rechnung Nr. NM319 über 5.875,00 € vom ... (Datum vor 6 Wochen)
> Sie haben weder eine Erklärung noch eine Überweisung erhalten.
> Setzen Sie eine letzte Zahlungsfrist von 14 Tagen.
> Bei Nichtzahlung Stornierung künftiger Lieferungen
> Bitte, dieses Schreiben als gegenstandslos zu betrachten, wenn Zahlung bereits erfolgt ist
> Angemessene Verabschiedung

Webcode:
FOBNRWT403

F Complaints

1 LISTENING TO A TELEPHONE COMPLAINT

Sevda Yildiz, the purchasing director at Brix Mode GmbH in Bielefeld, is dissatisfied with a consignment of goods from Patrik K, a Swedish fashion company in Stockholm, so she phones Pehr Lindquist, the export sales director.

2 3

A Listen to the phone call and complete the sentences below with the information you hear.

1 Sevda has just received a consignment of ...
2 The order number is ...
3 The terms of delivery were ...
4 Sevda received the consignment with a delay of ...
5 Some of the goods are the wrong ... and others are ...
6 Some of the boxes are labelled Patrik K and others are labelled ...
7 Sevda will get the right goods in ...
8 Sevda wants the goods to be in stock in time for ...

2 3

B Listen to the phone call again and, with a partner, put the pictures in the right order and use them to explain what happened. Begin like this: *The goods arrived in Germany ...*

2 LOOKING AT A COMPLAINT ABOUT A DELAY IN DELIVERY

A Jana Lorenz works in the purchasing department at Brix Mode GmbH in Bielefeld. Five weeks ago her company ordered a consignment of ladies' shoes from a Chinese supplier in Shanghai and was promised delivery within 30 days after receipt of order. The goods are now four days late, so she contacts the supplier. Read her email and match the sentence halves.

E-MAIL

To:	chen-yu-lan@632tradingchina.cn
Subject:	Delay in delivery of order no. LTS36B dated 13 February 20..
Cc:	sevda.yildiz@brixmode.de

Dear Ms Chen Yu Lan

On 13 February 20.. we placed the above-mentioned order for ladies' T-shirts for delivery by 16 March.

The consignment is now four days overdue.

We would welcome your explanation of the delay, but must be sure that the consignment will reach our premises by 30 March at the latest, as several customers are now threatening to cancel their orders and look elsewhere.

We trust that we will hear from you in the very near future. Prompt delivery is all that is needed to settle this matter.

Yours sincerely

Jana Lorenz

1	Brix Mode placed its order on	a	the delay.
2	The deadline for delivery was	b	as soon as possible.
3	This email was written on	c	cancel their orders.
4	So far the supplier has not explained	d	20 March.
5	Some German customers might	e	16 March.
6	Brix Mode wants the goods	f	13 February.

B Match the German translations with points 1–5 in the box below.

Angemessene Verabschiedung | Bezug auf Verzögerung | Bitte um Erklärung | Bitte um Lieferung innerhalb einer bestimmten Frist | Folgen einer weiteren Verzögerung

Structure of a complaint about delay in delivery

A complaint about delay in delivery covers some or all of the following points:

1 Reference to delay
2 Request for explanation
3 Request for delivery by a given time
4 Consequences of further delay
5 Suitable ending

C Match these possible complaints with the solutions and then make sentences with the words. Start like this: *If you get the wrong goods, you can ...* **There is sometimes more than one solution.**

SEND BACK THE EXTRA GOODS AT THE BUYER'S EXPENSE

POOR QUALITY

SEND BACK THE GOODS AT THE BUYER'S EXPENSE

WRONG GOODS

WRONG SIZE/COLOUR

TOO FEW GOODS

KEEP THE EXTRA GOODS AT A REDUCED PRICE

TOO MANY GOODS

KEEP THE GOODS AT A DISCOUNT

GOODS ARE DAMAGED

HAVE THE GOODS NEEDED SENT BY EXPRESS DELIVERY

Reference to delay	Bezug auf Verzögerung
On 1 November we placed an order with you for the above-mentioned items to be delivered within three weeks.	Am 1. November erteilten wir Ihnen einen Auftrag für die oben erwähnten Positionen, die innerhalb von drei Wochen geliefert werden sollten.
It was agreed that delivery was to be made within three weeks.	Es wurde vereinbart, dass die Lieferung innerhalb von drei Wochen erfolgen sollte.
Our order is now five days overdue.	Unser Auftrag ist jetzt fünf Tage überfällig.
Request for explanation	**Bitte um Erklärung**
We would welcome an explanation of the delay.	Wir würden eine Erklärung der Verzögerung begrüßen.
So far we have not been given a reason for the delay.	Bisher haben wir noch keine Begründung für die Verzögerung erhalten.
Please let us know why the goods have been delayed.	Bitte lassen Sie uns wissen, warum die Waren verspätet angekommen sind.
Request for delivery by a particular time	**Bitte um Lieferung innerhalb einer bestimmten Frist**
Please let us know immediately when we will be able to take delivery of the goods.	Bitte teilen Sie uns sofort mit, wann wir mit der Lieferung der Waren rechnen können.
We must be certain that the consignment will reach our premises by 17 January at the latest.	Wir müssen sicher sein, dass die Sendung unsere Geschäftsräume spätestens bis zum 17. Januar erreicht.
Please ensure that we receive the goods within seven days.	Bitte stellen Sie sicher, dass wir die Waren innerhalb von sieben Tagen erhalten.
Consequences of further delay	**Folgen einer weiteren Verzögerung**
If this deadline is not kept we will be obliged to cancel this and all future orders ...	Wenn dieser Termin nicht eingehalten wird, sehen wir uns genötigt, diesen und alle weiteren Aufträge zu stornieren ...
... as several customers are threatening to cancel their orders and look elsewhere.	... da einige unserer Kunden drohen, ihre Bestellungen zu stornieren und sich anderweitig zu orientieren.
... since some of our customers have now cancelled their orders.	... da einige unserer Kunden ihre Aufträge jetzt storniert haben.
Suitable ending	**Angemessene Verabschiedung**
Prompt delivery is all that is needed to settle this matter.	Diese Angelegenheit kann durch eine umgehende Lieferung Ihrerseits geregelt werden.
We trust that we will be hearing from you in the very near future.	Wir vertrauen darauf, dass wir von Ihnen in Kürze hören.

3 WRITING AN E-MAIL COMPLAINT

Use the useful phrases to write an e-mail complaint based on the following details.

Situation

Sven Neumann ist Einkaufsleiter bei Intertrade Großhandel GmbH in Dortmund. Da eine Lieferung Haushaltsporzellan (*household crockery*) überfällig ist, mahnt er sie beim chinesischen Lieferanten, Man Sang Trading Limited in Hongkong, an.

Aufgabe

Schreiben Sie Svens E-Mail an Mr John Zheng (j.zheng@mansang.org) in der Exportabteilung unter Berücksichtigung folgender Punkte:

> Ware wurde vor 3 Wochen am ... mit Auftrag-Nr. HHC/46 bestellt.
> Lieferung ist inzwischen 7 Tage überfällig.
> Grund für Verspätung?
> Ihre Kunden drohen inzwischen, ihre Aufträge zu stornieren und die Ware von einem anderen Lieferanten zu beziehen.
> Letzte Frist für Lieferung: heute in 5 Tagen (*genauen Termin angeben!*)

4 LOOKING AT A LETTER OF COMPLAINT

A Read Sevda's complaint to an Indian supplier and say if the statements on the next page are true or false. Correct the false statements.

BRIX Mode GmbH
Feldstraße 42 • 33609 Bielefeld • Germany
Tel +49 521 4827764 Fax +49 521 4824760 info@brixmode.de

SY/AK
10 January 20..

Mr Sunil Mittal
Export Sales Director
J.P. Designs Incorporated
44 Mandir Marg
NEW DELHI
110 001
INDIEN

Dear Mr Mittal

Order no. IGTO 32249 for fashion tops dated 10 November 20..

The above-mentioned fashion tops arrived at our premises this morning as promised but on examining them we found that they were of poor quality. The sample tops sent to us were brightly coloured and wider with long sleeves and a low neck. The tops we have received are darker coloured, narrower and have short sleeves and a high neck.

We would welcome your explanation of these discrepancies.

Whatever the case may be, you will appreciate that we cannot sell these articles at the usual price and will only keep them if you reduce the price considerably.

We look forward to receiving your comments on this matter.

Yours sincerely
Brix Mode GmbH

S. Yildiz

Sevda Yildiz
Purchasing Director

Brix Mode GmbH • Bielefeld, Registergericht Bielefeld, HRB 82071, Geschäftsführerin: Karla Wenz

1 Die Tops sind mit Verspätung angekommen.
2 Die Muster waren besser als die gelieferte Ware.
3 Sevda möchte schmalere Tops.
4 Brix Mode möchte ärmellose Tops.
5 Sevda erwartet, dass die Indische Firma erklärt, was schief gegangen ist.
6 Brix Mode wird ihr Bestes tun, die Tops zum normalen Preis zu verkaufen.

B **Match the German translations with points 1–7 in the box below.**

Bitte um Erklärung | Bezug auf Waren | Angemessene Verabschiedung | Darstellung des Problems | Bitte um Ergreifung geeigneter Maßnahmen | Anlage(n) | Folgen für Käufer und Verkäufer

Structure of a complaint

A complaint covers some or all of the following points:

1 Reference to goods
2 Description of problem
3 Request for explanation
4 Consequences for the buyer and seller
5 Request for action
6 Suitable ending
7 Enclosure(s)/attachment(s)

Reference to goods	**Bezug auf Waren**
The above-mentioned goods were delivered to us today, seven days later than expected.	Die oben erwähnten Waren wurden uns heute – sieben Tage nach dem vereinbarten Termin – geliefert.
We have just taken delivery of the above-mentioned consignment/goods/articles.	Wir haben soeben die oben erwähnte(n) Sendung/Waren/Artikel erhalten.
We regret to inform you that we are dissatisfied with it/them.	Leider müssen wir Ihnen mitteilen, dass wir damit unzufrieden sind.
Description of problem	**Darstellung des Problems**
On examining the goods we found that ...	Bei Prüfung der Waren stellten wir fest, dass ...
... the contents were wet, (obviously) due to poor packing/rough handling in transit.	... der Inhalt war nass (offensichtlich) wegen mangelhafter Verpackung / unsachgemäßer Behandlung während des Transports.
... they are the wrong colour/size/shape, because they are ... instead of ... (as ordered).	... sie haben die falsche Farbe/Größe/Form, denn sie sind ... statt ... (laut Bestellung).
... (e.g. six) of the ... (e.g. 30) articles/tents/wardrobes ordered are (badly) damaged/dirty/discoloured.	... (z. B. sechs) der insgesamt ... (z. B. 30) bestellten (Artikel/Zelte/Schränke) sind (stark) beschädigt/verschmutzt/verfärbt.
... the quality and colour were not up to sample.	... Qualität und Farbe entsprechen nicht dem Muster.
We believe this was caused by rough handling in transit.	Wir glauben, dies wurde durch unsachgemäße Behandlung während des Transports verursacht.
We enclose photographs of these items for your information.	Wir fügen Fotos dieser Artikel zu Ihrer Information bei.
We are of the opinion that this is the result of poor packing (see photographs enclosed).	Wir sind der Meinung, dass dies das Ergebnis schlechter Verpackung ist (siehe beiliegende Fotos).

Request for explanation	Bitte um Erklärung
We would welcome your explanation of the damage.	Wir würden Ihre Erklärung des Schadens begrüßen.
Please explain why our order was so poorly executed.	Bitte erklären Sie, warum unser Auftrag so schlecht ausgeführt wurde.
Consequences for the buyer and seller	**Folgen für Käufer und Verkäufer**
Whatever the case may be, ...	Wie dem auch sei, ...
You will appreciate that ...	Sie werden dafür Verständnis haben, dass ...
... we cannot sell these articles at the normal price.	... wir diese Artikel nicht zum normalen Preis verkaufen können.
... we can only keep them if the price is reduced by 25%.	... wir sie nur behalten können, wenn der Preis um 25 % reduziert wird.
If they do not arrive here by ... (e.g. 30 June) we will have to obtain them elsewhere.	Wenn sie bis ... (z. B. 30. Juni) nicht hier ankommen, werden wir sie woanders beziehen müssen.
Request for action	**Bitte um Ergreifung geeigneter Maßnahmen**
Whatever the case may be, we need ... urgently.	In jedem Fall benötigen wir ... dringend.
We must also/therefore ask you to send us replacements (for the damaged goods) by return, as these goods are needed urgently.	Wir müssen Sie auch/deshalb bitten, Ersatz (für die beschädigten Waren) zu schicken, da diese Waren dringend benötigt werden.
We would also point out that ...	Wir möchten Sie (auch) darauf hinweisen, dass ...
... we are only prepared keep the substandard items if a considerable reduction in price is granted.	... wir nur bereit sind, die minderwertige Ware zu behalten, wenn ein erheblicher Preisnachlass gewährt wird.
Suitable ending	**Angemessene Verabschiedung**
We look forward to receiving your comments on this matter without delay.	Wir erwarten Ihre unverzügliche Stellungnahme zu dieser Angelegenheit.
We feel sure you will appreciate that our future business relationship will depend on how this matter is dealt with.	Sie werden sicherlich dafür Verständnis haben, dass die Fortsetzung unserer Geschäftsbeziehung von der Regelung dieser Angelegenheit abhängig ist.
We trust you will deal with this matter without delay.	Wir vertrauen darauf, dass Sie sich unverzüglich mit dieser Angelegenheit befassen werden.
We expect to hear from you in the very near future.	Wir erwarten, in Kürze von Ihnen zu hören.
Enclosure(s)	**Anlage(n)**
Photograph(s)	Foto(s)

5 WRITING COMPLAINTS

A Use the useful phrases to write a complaint based on the following details.

Situation

(Fortsetzung von Aufgabe 3A *Enquiries* auf Seite 97)
Sie (eigener Name) sind Einkaufsleiter/in bei der FreiLuft Rhein GmbH in Bonn. Ihre Firma hatte mit Auftrag-Nr. EVCE3000 vom ... (*Datum vor vier Wochen*) 50 Zelte vom Typ Klondike beim britischen Lieferanten Apex Leisure Ltd bestellt. Die Sendung ist heute angekommen und weist verschiedene Mängel auf.

Tent

Aufgabe

Verfassen Sie mit heutigem Datum eine Beschwerde (Brief, E-Mail oder Fax) an die englische Firma unter Berücksichtigung folgender Punkte:

- Ihre Ansprechpartnerin ist Ms Emma Wade, Exportleiterin.
- Bezug auf Bestellung
- Statt orangefarbener Zelte sind graue geliefert worden.
- Sechs der insgesamt 50 bestellten Zelte sind schmutzig, wahrscheinlich infolge mangelhafter Verpackung (siehe Fotos).
- Bitte um Erklärung, warum Ihr Auftrag so schlecht ausgeführt wurde
- Ware kann zum normalen Preis nicht verkauft werden.
- Sie sind bereit, die Zelte zu behalten, wenn der Preis um 20% reduziert wird.
- Bitte um baldige Stellungnahme
- Angemessene Verabschiedung

B Use the useful phrases to write a complaint based on the following details.

Situation

Die Firma „Jeans On The Rocks" GmbH in Essen (Sachsenstr. 27, 45128 Essen, Fax-Nr. 0049 201 9766507) hat heute von der chinesischen Firma Shenzhen Fashion Factory (Foreign Economic Building, 2 Yuan Dun Dong Street, Shenzhen, China 518000, Fax-Nr. 0086 10 544 8128, E-Mail: jjw@shenzhen.fashion.ch) eine Sendung Jeansjacken erhalten, die Anlass zu Beanstandungen gibt.

Jeans jacket

Aufgabe

Verfassen Sie mit heutigem Datum für die Einkaufsleiterin Ihrer Firma, Frau Mareike Sperling (E-Mail: mareike.sperling@jotr-essen.de), eine Mängelrüge (Brief, E-Mail oder Fax) an die Exportleiterin der chinesischen Firma, Ms Juanjuan Wan. Berücksichtigen Sie folgende Punkte:

- Heutiges Datum
- Bezug auf Lieferung (Auftrag Nr. JJ106/CH von vor 14 Tagen)
- Inhalt bei Ankunft nass wegen mangelhafter Verpackung
- Farbe und Qualität weichen erheblich von dem Muster ab (Fotos beigefügt).
- Bitte um umgehenden Ersatz, da Jeansjacken dringend benötigt werden
- Ohne beträchtliche Ermäßigung keine Bereitschaft, die minderwertige Ware zu behalten
- Bitte um Stellungnahme
- Fortsetzung der Geschäftsbeziehung von der Regelung der Beschwerde abhängig
- Angemessene Verabschiedung

G Scenario

Situation: Die neue Kooperation mit South Riding Tours für Radtouren in Deutschland und Großbritannien hat nun begonnen. Sie helfen Frau Dogan, die Touren zu organisieren und die Zusammenarbeit zu koordinieren.

1 **Frau Dogan leitet folgende Email von Richard South an Sie weiter. Verfassen Sie eine entsprechende Antwort an Richard South nach ihren Angaben.**

E-MAIL

Von: Sylvia Dogan
An: Sales & Marketing Assistant
Datum: 14. December
Betreff: WG: Extra capacity

Hallo,

ich habe diese Mail gerade von Richard South bekommen. Kannst du bitte eine Antwort verfassen?

1. Gratulation, dass der Verkauf so gut läuft.
2. 10–15 % mehr verkaufte Touren als vereinbart ist kein Problem; wir haben genügend Reserven, da der Verkauf in Deutschland ganz normal läuft.
3. Umstieg auf Zelte bzw. Zeltplätze kommt nicht in Frage; kurzfristige Investition in geeignetes Material und Wartungspersonal (zur Pflege) wäre zu hoch. Diese Vertriebsschiene müssten wir längerfristig planen und mit der Geschäftsführung abstimmen.
4. Wenn er mehr als 15% des vereinbarten Volumens verkaufen kann, müssen wir höherwertige Hotels buchen; alles andere (Leihräder, Servicebus, usw.) ist kein Problem. Spätbucher müssen allerdings mit einem Zuschlag von 10–15% auf den Endpreis rechnen. Vielleicht könnte er seine Werbung jetzt darauf ausrichten? ("While stocks last...")
5. Er soll uns über die Verkaufszahlen auf dem Laufenden halten.

Liebe Grüße
Sylvia

From: Richard South, South Riding Tours Ltd
To: Sylvia Dogan, Fly Bike Werke GmbH
Date: 14 December
Re: Extra capacity

Dear Sylvia

How are you this morning? Well, I hope.

The good news is that we already have enquiries from customers in Britain for 60–70% of the capacity of tours in Germany that we agreed on back in July. We already have confirmed bookings for 30%, but experience shows that most bookings take place in January and February. If the current interest in tours in N Germany continues, we should be able to sell 25–30% more holidays than we had budgeted for.

The problem is, do you have the capacity (personnel and accommodation) to meet the extra demand? We could imagine using campsites as a cheaper option if the demand continues to rise.

Please let me know what you suggest.
Best regards
Richard

2 Neun Monate sind vergangen, und die erste Saison der Touren in Deutschland und Großbritannien ist sehr erfolgreich verlaufen. Trotzdem gibt es Probleme mit einer Unterkunft. Daher hat Frau Dogan Sie gebeten, einen Beschwerdebrief an Richard South zu verfassen.

E-MAIL

Von:	Sylvia Dogan
An:	Sales & Marketing Assistant
Datum:	12. September
Betreff:	Beschwerden über "Manor House Bed & Breakfast", Ely

Hallo,

könntest du bitte einen Brief an Richard South schreiben? Es gibt einige Beschwerden von unseren Kunden über das "Manor House Bed & Breakfast" in Ely (siehe angehängte Dateien).

- Besitzer extrem unfreundlich und wenig hilfsbereit
- Zimmer sehr kalt und klein
- Kein warmes Wasser nach 21 Uhr
- Abendessen fast ungenießbar (siehe angehängte Fotos!)
- keine Möglichkeit, einen Imbiss zu bekommen
- Gepäcktransfer, der vom Hotel organisiert werden sollte, hat mehrmals nicht funktioniert

Richard soll das "Manor House" selbst ansehen und ggf. von seiner Hotelliste für die nächste Saison streichen. Er soll eine Lösung für die Kundebeschwerden finden. Betone, dass die meisten Kunden mit dem Rest der Tour sehr zufrieden waren.

Schöne Grüße
Sylvia

3 Fly Bike Werke GmbH hat auch eine Beschwerde von Richard South bekommen. Frau Dogan bittet Sie, eine entsprechende Antwort auf diese E-Mail zu verfassen.

E-MAIL

From:	Richard South, South Riding Tours Ltd
To:	Sylvia Dogan, Fly Bike Werke GmbH
Date:	15 September
Re:	Complaint about unfair treatment

Dear Sylvia

I have just received a worrying complaint (attached) from one of our customers who was on the "Mecklenburgische Seenplatte" Tour.

It seems that they were doing the tour at the same time as a large group of German guests (who had apparently booked through Fly Bike Werke GmbH). They had the feeling that the German guests were always given preferential treatment: whenever they arrived at a guesthouse, all the best rooms were taken, the same applied to the tables in the restaurant and at breakfast, etc. In one case, there were no spaces left for them to park their bikes.

I hope that some hoteliers do not feel that British cyclists are second-class citizens, otherwise the bad word-of-mouth propaganda may damage our reputation and affect our sales for next year.

Please let me know what you suggest.
Best regards
Richard

5

Communication at work

FOCUS

1 **Match the pictures with four of the expressions in the box.**

e-mail | Facebook | face-to-face meeting | fax | internet chat | letter | MMS | phone call | postcard | SMS | teleconference | telegram | Twitter | video conference | voicemail

1

2

3

4

2 **Sometimes you want a response straight away (real-time communication) and sometimes it is better to get a response later (delayed communication). Use the word spiders to sort the expressions in the box into two groups.**

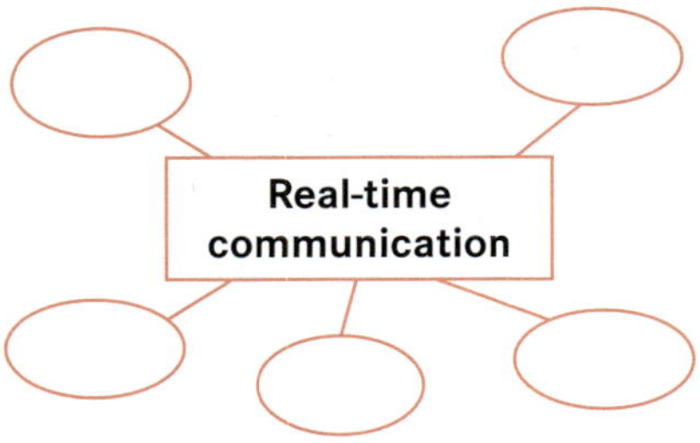

3 **Explain which form(s) of communication you would use in the following cases:**

- someone is in danger
- someone has won a big prize in a competition
- you wish to advertise a product or service to as many people as possible
- you want someone who is not in their office to call you back
- two teenagers want to send each other a photo
- 10 people at different places want to discuss something
- 10 people at different places want to look at something and discuss it
- you want to remind a customer to pay an overdue invoice
- you want to send someone an internet link

4 **Think of two or three more examples of your own and explain why you would want real-time or delayed communication.**

A Telephoning and voicemail

Nina Wittstock is the chief executive officer of Top Act Event Management AG in Düsseldorf. Today she is trying to contact a celebrity speaker for a three-day sales conference in Düsseldorf for Cherry Solutions Incorporated, a major American software developer.

1 MAKING CONTACT BY TELEPHONE

2 4

A Use words from the box to complete the dialogue and then listen to the recording to check your answers.

calling | hold | message | number | speak to | this is | unavailable | urgent

VOICE: Thank you for calling Rob Heldof's press office. If you wish to contact his fan club, press 1. If you wish to leave a ... 1, press 2. If you wish to make a donation to a Rob Heldof charity, press 3. For all other calls, please press zero and ... 2 the line.
NINA: I hate these automatic systems! Come on! This is important.
ZOE: Good afternoon and thank you for calling Rob Heldof's press office. How can I help?
NINA: Hello, ... 3 Nina Wittstock from Top Act Event Management in Germany. I'd like to ... ... 4 Rob about the conference in May.
ZOE: Well, I'm very sorry, Ms Wittstock, but Rob is ... 5 at the moment. He's actually at his castle in Ireland and it's quite hard to reach him there.
NINA: I see. Well it's very ... 6.
ZOE: Can I take a message?
NINA: No thanks. I'll try him on his mobile.
ZOE: Well, I wish you good luck! Have you got his ... 7?
NINA: Yes, I've got it, thanks.
ZOE: Good. Please let me know if there's anything else I can do for you.
NINA: OK, I will.
ZOE: Thanks for ... 8. Goodbye, Ms Wittstock.
NINA: Bye.

2 5

B Now Nina calls Rob on his mobile. Listen to the dialogue and fill in the missing words.

ROB: Hello?
NINA: Hello Rob. It's Nina ... 1! How are you?
ROB: Fine thanks, and you?
NINA: Fine. Is this a ... 2 time to call you, Rob?
ROB: It's fine. I'm out in the countryside taking a ... .
NINA: Sorry, I didn't quite ... 3 that.
ROB: I'm taking a walk in the countryside.
NINA: Oh I see! You're taking a walk in the countryside. That sounds great! Anyway, I just wanted to ... 4 that everything was all right for the conference.
ROB: I'm sorry but I didn't quite catch that, Nina. You're ... 5 up.
NINA: This must be a bad ... 6.
ROB: OK, it's a bit better now. Go ... 7.

NINA: As I was saying, I just wanted to check that everything was all right for the conference.
ROB: This is no good, Nina! I'm ... [8] I can't hear you! Call ... on the landline. Did you ... [9] that?
NINA: Call who?
ROB: Zoe! Call Zoe on the landline. OK?
NINA: Well, actually, I've just called Zoe and ...
ROB: That's right! Call Zoe!
NINA: OK! ... [10] do that.
ROB: Nice talking to you, Nina! Bye.
NINA: Bye.

C Find two expressions in the dialogues for each of the following headings.

You answer the phone → You say who you are → You say why you're calling → You offer to help the other person → You finish the phone call

D Match the meanings on the left with the expressions from the dialogues on the right.

1 wait
2 Hurry up!
3 not able to come to the phone
4 I can't hear every word clearly
5 very important
6 Are you free to talk?
7 I didn't hear what you said
8 I understand
9 Please do what you wanted to do
10 Did you hear what I said?

a urgent
b Did you get that?
c I didn't catch that
d Go ahead
e unavailable
f hold the line
g I see
h You're breaking up
i Come on!
j Is this a good time to call you?

2 LEAVING A MESSAGE

2 6

Nina tells her PA, Helena Sawicki, to phone for her. Helena gets Zoe's voicemail and leaves a message. Listen to the recording and complete the sentences below.

1 Helena phones ...
2 If she wants to be contacted she must ...
3 Helena's number is ...
4 Nina's number is ...

3 LISTENING TO A PHONE CALL

2 7

Helena gets an interesting phone call from Zoe, Rob Heldof's PA. Listen to the recording and complete the sentences.

1 Zoe calls because ...
2 Rob wants a list of the ...
3 Lily was ...
4 Katie is ...
5 Rob will be coming to Germany by ...
6 Someone from Top Act will meet Rob at ...
7 Helena will pass on the information to Nina by ...
8 Zoe promises to...

Saying telephone numbers

0 is 'oh' or 'zero'.
00 is 'double oh' or 'zero, zero'.

Say each number separately:
0172 is 'oh-one-seven-two' or 'zero-one-seven-two'.
+ 49 is 'plus four-nine'.

4 MEDIATION

Sie sind Helena Sawicki. Benutzen Sie die Inhalte des Telefongesprächs und folgende Stichpunkte, um eine entsprechende E-Mail an Nina Wittstock (nina.wittstock@top-act.de) zu verfassen.

- Bezug auf Anruf von Rob Heldofs persönlicher Assistentin
- Rob Heldofs Wünsche
- Was Nina berücksichtigen soll, wenn Rob Heldof kommt.
- Einzelheiten seiner Anreise nach Deutschland

Spelling words on the phone

D is capital 'd' or upper-case 'd'.
d is small 'd' or lower-case 'd'.
Use the spelling alphabet to spell difficult words like 'Xavier':
That's capital 'x' for X-ray, 'a' for alpha, 'v' for Victor, 'i' for India, 'e' for echo and 'r' for Romeo.

The spelling alphabet

A	Alpha	N	November
B	Bravo	O	Oscar
C	Charlie	P	Papa
D	Delta	Q	Quebec
E	Echo	R	Romeo
F	Foxtrot	S	Sierra
G	Golf	T	Tango
H	Hotel	U	Uniform
I	India	V	Victor
J	Juliet	W	Whisky
K	Kilo	X	X-ray
L	Lima	Y	Yankee
M	Mike	Z	Zulu

Answering the phone
Top Act Limited. Good morning. How can I help?
What can I do for you?
Hello?
Speaking.
Saying who you are
It's Nina Wittstock from ...
It's Nina calling.
Saying why you're calling
Can I speak to ..., please? / Am I speaking to ...?
I'd like to speak to ... about ...
I just wanted to (check that ...).
I'd like to know ... (if/what/...).
I'm just calling to ask you ... (if/what/about/...).
Could you tell me ... (if/what/...)
Reacting to what you hear
I see. (anything)
That's great/marvellous! (good thing)
Oh dear! (bad thing)
Oh really! (surprise)
Apologizing
I'm (very) sorry but ...
I'm afraid I can't ...

Poor connection
I'm sorry but you're breaking up.
This must be a bad connection.
Did you get that?
Person is not available
... is unavailable at the moment.
... is out of the office.
Promising action
I'll ... / I'll do that.
We'll get back to you as soon as possible.
Offering help
Can I take a message?
Is there anything else I can help you with?
Please let me know if there's anything else I can do for you.
Finishing the call
Thanks for calling.
Nice talking to you.
Talk to you soon.
Bye.
Goodbye,
Have a nice day.

5 MAKING TELEPHONE CALLS

A With a partner use the language box on page 135 to write or act out the following dialogue.

A Helena Sawicki, Nina Wittstocks persönliche Assistentin	B Lily Boyd, Rob Heldofs Freundin
1 Melden Sie sich wie gewohnt auf Englisch. →	2 Stellen Sie sich kurz vor. Sie möchten mit Nina Wittstock sprechen.
← 3 Frau Wittstock ist leider nicht zu sprechen. →	4 Es ist dringend.
← 5 Möchte Frau Boyd eine Nachricht hinterlassen? →	6 Ja. Warum haben Sie noch kein Flugticket für die Konferenz in Düsseldorf erhalten?
← 7 Sie versprechen, die Nachricht weiterzuleiten, wünschen ihr einen schönen Tag und schließen das Gespräch höflich ab. →	8 Sie schließen das Gespräch ab.

B With a partner use the table of useful phrases to act out the following dialogue.

Partner A

You are DJ 60 Cent, a famous American rapper. Today you get a call from Top Act Event Management in Düsseldorf on your mobile phone. Follow the steps below to play your role. (Partner B has steps 2, 4, 6 and 8.)

1 Answer your mobile phone.
3 Say you're the person she wants and ask what you can do for her.
5 Say you have received it and will sign and send it back.
7 Finish the call.

Partner B

Go to file 21 on page 180.

C Follow the instructions to leave a voicemail message.

Sie sind Nina Wittstock. Top Act Event Management AG hat den amerikanischen Rapper DJ 60 Cent für einen Auftritt in Düsseldorf engagiert. Er hat gebeten, dass man ihm telefonisch mitteilt, um wie viel Uhr sein Auftritt ist. Da er nicht ans Telefon geht, hinterlassen Sie ihm eine Nachricht folgenden Inhalts:

> Sie geben Ihren Namen, den Ihrer Firma und Ihre Handy-Nr. (+49 176 ...) an.
> Er wollte wissen, wann er am Samstagabend auftritt (*when you're on*).
> Er tritt nach *Ethnoscream* um ca. 23 Uhr auf.
> Er möge Sie informieren, wenn Sie sonst noch etwas für ihn tun können.
> Sie wünschen ihm einen schönen Tag.

B Making appointments

Helena Sawicki works for Top Act Event Management AG. She is personal assistant to Nina Wittstock, the company's chief executive officer (CEO). Top Act has the task of organizing a three-day international sales conference in Düsseldorf for Cherry Solutions Incorporated, a major American software developer. Rob Heldof, a famous rock star, is to speak at the meeting. Today Helena phones Zoe, Rob's personal assistant, to make an appointment for a press conference when he arrives in Düsseldorf.

1 ARRANGING AN APPOINTMENT

2 8

Use the diaries on the following page to select the correct words in the telephone dialogue below. Then listen to the recording to check your answers.

ZOE: Good morning and thank you for calling Rob Heldof's press office. How can I help?

HELENA: Hello, it's Helena Sawicki in Germany. Is that Zoe?

ZOE: Yes, it is. Nice to talk to you again, Helena.

HELENA: Nice to talk to you too, Zoe. I'm just calling to ask you about holding a press conference with Rob Heldof when he comes here in May. Nina Wittstock wants one either before or after his speech on Thursday *afternoon/evening* [1] and she'd also like him to go on a breakfast *TV/radio* [2] show the next day.

ZOE: Oh right. Just let me look at his diary. I have it here on my phone. OK, go ahead.

HELENA: When does Rob arrive in Düsseldorf on the first?

ZOE: He arrives in the *morning/afternoon* [3] but he'll have jet lag.

HELENA: Oh I see. How about a press conference at six o'clock in the evening *after/before* [4] his speech?

ZOE: He's going *shopping/sightseeing* [5] with Katie in the afternoon. That'll take about three hours at least. What about 11 o'clock after the conference?

HELENA: I'm afraid that won't work out because he's having a *meeting/meal* [6] then. How about Friday morning at about 10 a.m.?

ZOE: I'm not sure. He wants to buy some new sunglasses for Rio. And then his flight is at *12.00/1.30* [7].

HELENA: I see. OK. Let's look at Thursday again. What about after his *dinner/speech* [8] at about 9.30 p.m.?

ZOE: Yes, he's free then but let's make it ten o'clock to give him a bit more time.

HELENA: Great!

ZOE: I'll check with him and get back to you.

HELENA: That's marvellous. Oh, and please ask him if he wants to go on the breakfast show on *Thursday/Friday* [9] morning.

ZOE: What time would that be?

HELENA: It starts at 6.30 a.m. but how about *eight/nine* [10] o'clock?

ZOE: Mmm, I'm not sure. I'll ask him and get back to you as soon as possible. Talk to you soon. Bye.

HELENA: Bye.

Terminkalender Nina Wittstock

Donnerstag, 01. Mai
09:00
10:00
11:00
12:00
13:00
14:00
15:00
16:00
17:00
18:00 Pressekonferenz mit Rob?
19:00 Pressekonferenz mit Rob?
20:00 Vortrag Rob H.
21:00 Pressekonferenz mit Rob?
22:00 Pressekonferenz mit Rob?
23:00 Ethnoscream
23:30 Restaurant Steigenberger Park-Hotel
00:00

Freitag, 02. Mai
07:00 Chat, chat, chat breakfast TV (bis 09:00 Uhr) + Rob um 08:00?
08:00
09:00 Pressekonferenz mit Rob?
10:00 Pressekonferenz mit Rob?
11:00 Frühstück Peter Raffay
12:00
13:00
14:00
15:00 Tennis
16:00
17:00
18:00
19:00
20:00
21:00 Boxkampf ESPRIT Arena Düsseldorf
00:00 Empfang VIP Lounge

Rob Heldof's diary on Zoe Kline's smartphone

Thursday	01/05/20... ▶
Time	**Appointments**
09:00 am	9.05 am Arrive DUS
10:00 am	
11:00 am	
12:00 am	
01:00 pm	
02:00 pm	
03:00 pm	
04:00 pm	Shopping with Katie
05:00 pm	Shopping with Katie
06:00 pm	Shopping with Katie
07:00 pm	Shopping with Katie
08:00 pm	Speech
09:00 pm	
10:00 pm	
11:00 pm	Dinner at hotel restaurant
00:00 pm	
Priority	**To do**
High	**Read through speech for DUS**
Low	**Check weather in DUS**
Don't forget	
Jet lag!!!	

Friday	02/05/20... ▶
Time	**Appointments**
07:00 am	
08:00 am	
09:00 am	
10:00 am	Buy sunglasses!
11:00 pm	
12:00 pm	
01:00 pm	1.30 pm DUS Fly to Rio (21 hrs!!!)
02:00 pm	
03:00 pm	
04:00 pm	
05:00 pm	
06:00 pm	
07:00 pm	
08:00 pm	
09:00 pm	
10:00 pm	
Priority	**To do**
High	**Buy sunglasses**
Low	**Check weather in Rio**
Don't forget	

2 CHANGING AN APPOINTMENT

2 9

Nina Wittstock phones Rob Heldof at the airport. Listen to the phone call and then say if the following statements are true or false. Correct the false statements.

1. Rob arrives at Düsseldorf Airport in the afternoon.
2. Rob's girlfriend isn't with him.
3. Rob's girlfriend is ill.
4. Rob is ill.
5. Rob is free this afternoon.
6. Nina wants to have the press conference earlier.
7. Nina wants to have the press conference at 8 p.m.
8. The conference will be in a TV studio.
9. Britt Elsner will e-mail Rob later.
10. Nina is tired and wants to get some sleep now.

Suggesting a meeting

I'd like to make an appointment at ... (time) on ... (day).
What about ... (e.g. having lunch, meeting at the airport)?
Would you/he/she be able to (e.g. talk on our show tomorrow)?
Would it be possible to meet ... (e.g. while you're/he's/she's here / in town)?

Suggesting a time

How about ... (e.g. meeting at 2 p.m.)?
It'll take about ... (e.g. three hours)
How about ... (e.g. 9.30) at ... (e.g. the hotel reception / the airport)?
Would you/he/she be available ... (e.g. tomorrow morning at seven)?
Do you / Does he/she have time to meet later today / tomorrow?

Checking availability

Just let me look at my/his/her diary.
What time would that be?
I'm not sure. I'll check. / I'll get back to you.

Declining

I'm afraid that won't work out because ... (e.g. he's having a meal / he's going shopping).
That time's bad for me/him/her, I'm afraid.
How about 9.30 instead?

Accepting

Yes, I'm/he's/she's free then.
I've/He's/ She's got nothing/something on this afternoon / that day / then.
Let's make it ... (e.g. 2.15 p.m.). That will give me/him/her a bit more time.

Finishing the conversation

Great! Thank you very much.
That's marvellous!
I really appreciate it.
I/We look forward to seeing you/him/her then.

3 MAKING APPOINTMENTS

A With a partner, role-play this situation.

Partner A

Sie sind Britt Elsner. Sie moderieren jeden Freitag von 5:30 - 9:00 Uhr eine Sendung im Frühstücksfernsehen. Um 16:00 Uhr am Donnerstag rufen Sie Rob Heldof an, um ihn zu Ihrer Show einzuladen. Sie möchten, dass er um 7:25 Uhr als erster vor drei anderen Gästen erscheint. Die anderen Gäste sind der berühmte deutsche Rapper Mr Smarty, Natascha Merck, das berühmte deutsche Model, und ein katholischer Priester aus Düsseldorf namens Pfarrer Hubert. Da Sie möchten, dass Rob mindestens eine halbe Stunde bleibt, ist der späteste Zeitpunkt für seine Ankunft 8:30 Uhr. Das Thema lautet: Geld für gute Zwecke spenden *(Giving money to charity)*.

Partner B

Go to file 14 on page 178.

B With a partner, role-play this situation.

Partner A

You are Father Hubert. You have just been on a TV chat show together with Rob Heldof. It's 10.30 a.m. after the show. You phone Rob to ask him to autograph a T-shirt that you want to auction for charity (suggest a charity, e.g. SOS Kinderdorf).

Suggest meeting him

> at his hotel in Düsseldorf
> somewhere in Düsseldorf city centre (e.g. at [Calvin Klein] boutique with designer sunglasses)
> at Düsseldorf Airport this afternoon.

Partner B

Go to file 24 on page 181.

C With a partner, role-play this situation.

Partner A

You are Natasha Merck, the famous German model. A week after the TV talk show where you met Rob Heldof, you are in Rio de Janeiro on a photo shoot for a famous fashion designer.

You are modelling summer fashions. You have Rob's business card and this morning you phone him on his mobile to arrange to meet. You want to talk about a boycott of real fur in fur coats (you know Rob is a vegetarian).

Partner B

Go to file 10 on page 177.

Terminkalender Natasha Merck

Donnerstag 08 Mai	Freitag 09 Mai
07:00	07:00 *Arpoador Fitness Studio*
08:00	08:00 *Arpoador Fitness Studio*
09:00 *Arpoador Fitness Studio*	09:00
10:00 *Arpoador Fitness Studio*	10:00
11:00 *Arpoador Fitness Studio*	11:00
12:00	12:00
13:00	13:00
14:00 *Schminken*	14:00
15:00	15:00
16:00	16:00
17:00	17:00
18:00 *Rob – Passeio Público?*	18:00 *Schminken*
19:00	19:00 *Fotoshooting Ipanema*
20:00	20:00 *Fotoshooting Ipanema*
21:00 *Fotoshooting Ipanema*	21:00 *Fotoshooting Ipanema*
22:00 *Fotoshooting Ipanema*	22:00 *Fotoshooting Ipanema*
23:00 *Fotoshooting Ipanema*	23:00 *Dinner at Zero Zero night club*
00:00	00:00 *Dinner at Zero Zero night club*

C Travel arrangements

Rob Heldof, the famous rock star, has invited Nina Wittstock, the chief executive officer of Top Act Event Management AG in Düsseldorf, to spend the weekend at his castle near Cork in Ireland. It's Sunday evening and Nina needs some help with a last-minute booking, so she phones Zoe, Rob Heldof's PA. Zoe is staying a few minutes away in the gatehouse.

1 ARRANGING TRAVEL TO LONDON

2 10

A Listen to the dialogue and say if the following statements are true or false. Correct the false statements.

1 When Zoe answers the phone she is already in bed.
2 Nina has just received an e-mail from Germany.
3 Nina is invited to lunch the next day.
4 The invitation is from Bill Hampton, one of the directors of Cherry Solutions Incorporated.
5 Nina has to fly from Ireland to London.
6 Nina can choose to land at any of the five airports Zoe names.
7 Nina's flight can be booked online.
8 She will definitely be able to travel from the airport to her appointment by underground train.
9 If Nina takes the Tube, she'll go by bus.
10 Zoe brings Nina a laptop.

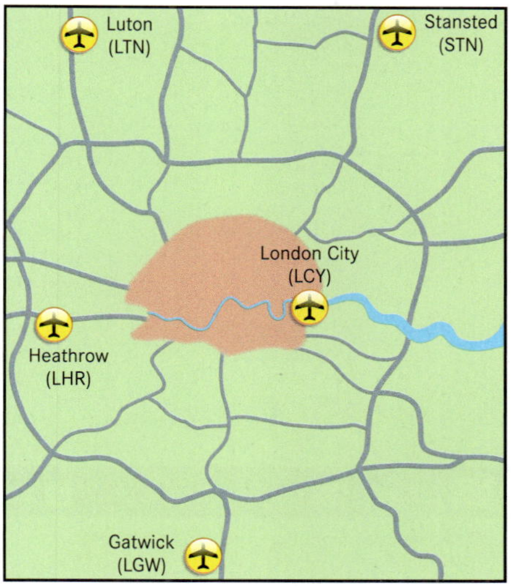

B Listen to the dialogue again and complete Zoe's notes.

Check transport links for Nina Wittstock!

Nina

Invited to ... ¹ at the Savoy ... ² in Central ... ³ at ... ⁴ o'clock tomorrow.

Invitation from ... ... ⁵, President of ... ⁶ Solutions Incorporated.

N. can fly from Cork to ... ⁷, ... ⁸ or ... ⁹ Airport.

No flights to Luton Airport or ... ... ¹⁰ Airport.

Tube link from ... ¹¹ Airport to central London.

Can go from other airports to central London by ... ¹², ... ¹³, fast ... ¹⁴ or ... ¹⁵.

2 LOOKING AT FLIGHT INFORMATION

This is the information that Zoe gets about flights to London. Study the list of flight times from Cork to London and choose the right ending for the sentences below.

Home | Departure | Arrival

AERFORT CHORCAÍ
CORK AIRPORT

London, United Kingdom

Carrier	Departs	Arrives	Via	Duration
EI/BA	ORK 6:10	LGW 11:55	AMS	5 hrs 45 min
EI/KL	ORK 6:10	LHR 10:50	AMS	4 hrs 40 min
EI/BA	ORK 6:10	LHR 11:00	AMS	4 hrs 50 min
EI/BA	ORK 6:10	LHR 12:05	AMS	5 hrs 55 min
EI/KL	ORK 6:10	LHR 13:50	AMS	7 hrs 40 min
EI/LH	ORK 6:10	LHR 14:15	AMS	8 hrs 05 min
EI/BD	ORK 6:10	LHR 14:15	AMS	8 hrs 05 min
KL	ORK 6:10	LHR 10:50	AMS	4 hrs 40 min
KL	ORK 6:10	LHR 13:50	AMS	7 hrs 40 min
EI	ORK 7:30	LHR 9:00		1 hrs 30 min
FR	ORK 8:10	STN 9:25		1 hrs 15 min
EI/AF	ORK 10:50	LHR 16:25	CDG	5 hrs 35 min
EI/BA	ORK 10:50	LHR 17:25	CDG	6 hrs 35 min
EI/AF	ORK 10:50	LHR 18:15	CDG	7 hrs 25 min
EI/BA	ORK 10:50	LHR 18:25	CDG	7 hrs 35 min
EI/AF	ORK 10:50	LHR 19:20	CDG	8 hrs 30 min
EI/BA	ORK 10:50	LHR 19:35	CDG	8 hrs 45 min
EI	ORK 11:50	LHR 13:05		1 hrs 15 min
FR	ORK 12:55	LGW 14:20		1 hrs 25 min
EI	ORK 16:00	LHR 17:15		1 hrs 15 min
EI	ORK 20:00	LHR 21:15		1 hrs 15 min
FR	ORK 21:45	STM 23:05		1 hrs 20 min

17.06.20... Show ✓ Nonstop Flights ✓ Direct Flights ✓ Connecting Flights

Notes: *ORK = Cork, AMS = Amsterdam, CDG = Charles de Gaulle (Paris)*

1 Carrier means
   a someone who carries your luggage.
   b a shopping bag.
   c an airline.

2 Duration means
   a how much earlier you have to arrive at the airport.
   b how long the trip will take.
   c the time difference between Cork and London.

3 There are flights from Cork to
   a three airports near London.
   b two airports near London.
   c one airport near London.

4 Most of the flights to London are
   a direct flights.
   b via the Netherlands.
   c via France.

5 The earliest arrival time in London is
   a 6.10 a.m.
   b 9.00 a.m.
   c 10.50 a.m.

6 The shortest flights are
   a only to London Heathrow (LHR).
   b to London Heathrow or London Gatwick (LGW).
   c to London Heathrow or London Stansted (STD).

3 AT THE AIRPORT

Early the next day, Nina is nearly at the airport when she receives a call on her mobile from Jennifer Hicks, Bill Hampton's personal assistant. Do the role-play below using the useful phrases on page 135.

A Nina Wittstock

B Jennifer Hicks, persönliche Assistentin von Bill Hampton, Cherry Solutions Incorporated, USA

1 Melden Sie sich auf Deutsch.

2 Sagen Sie, dass Sie leider nur Englisch sprechen und stellen Sie sich vor. Sie möchten mit Nina Wittstock sprechen.

3 Führen Sie das Gespräch auf Englisch fort. Bestätigen Sie, dass Sie Nina Wittstock sind und fragen Sie, was Sie für die Anruferin tun können.

4 Sie wollen nur sicher sein, dass Nina tatsächlich auf dem Weg zum Mittagessen in London ist.

5 Sie bestätigen, dass Sie unterwegs sind und rechtzeitig ankommen werden.

6 Sie reagieren sehr positiv auf Ninas Nachricht und erklären, dass Mr Hampton Nina näher kennen lernen möchte, denn er hätte evtl. einen Auftrag für sie.

7 Sie freuen sich sehr auf das Gespräch mit Herrn Hampton und schließen das Gespräch höflich ab.

8 Schließen Sie das Gespräch höflich ab.

4 LOOKING AT THE UNDERGROUND TIMETABLE

> Grammar Summary, *if*-sentences, p. 220

Use the information in the journey planner and the words in brackets to complete the sentences. Use *if*-sentences type 1 (*if* + present, *will/won't* + infinitive).

At 9.30 a.m. on Monday morning Nina uses her netbook to go online at Heathrow Airport. She wants to see if it would be a good idea to go to the restaurant by public transport.

1 If Nina (leave) Heathrow airport at 09.52, she (arrive) at Charing Cross Underground Station at ...

2 She (have to) leave at ... or ... if she (not want) to walk much.

Journey Planner

Choose your route/s from the options below

Journey Summary

Departing: Monday 17 June 20.. at: 10:00
From: London Heathrow Airport; Harrow Road / London Road
To: Charing Cross Unterground Station

Route	Depart	Arrive	Duration	Interchanges
1	09:52	11:16	**01:24**	
2	09:57	11:19	**01:22**	
3	10:01	11:19	**01:18**	
4	10:02	11:25	**01:23**	
5	10:04	11:25	**01:21**	

3 Her journey (take) the least time if she (leave) at ...
4 If she (want) to leave before 10 a.m., she (have to) walk from a bus stop to an ...
5 If she (leave) Heathrow Airport at ... or ... she (arrive) at Charing Cross Station at 11.25.

5 MEDIATION

> Skills, p. 211

Ihr Chef zieht nach England, um in der Filiale in London zu arbeiten. Er hat diese Informationen über die öffentlichen Verkehrsmittel gefunden und bittet Sie, die wesentlichen Inhalte der Webseite auf Deutsch zusammenzufassen.

Transport for London
Using contactless payment cards on buses

You can now pay for your bus travel using contactless credit, debit or charge cards, as well as cash.

If you have a credit, debit or charge card that has been issued in the UK and displays the contactless payment symbol (pictured on the right), you should be able to use it on buses to pay for single journeys. You just need to touch your card flat on the yellow card reader as you board a bus.

Not all contactless payment cards carry this symbol. Your card issuer should have told you if your card can be used for contactless transactions when it was issued to you.

Why use contactless payment cards?
It's cheaper than paying cash. For example, you'll only be charged a single fare of £1.35 instead of £2.30.

It's secure: Your card is protected by your card issuer against fraudulent use in just the same way as when using your contactless payment card at any other retailer.

It's quick and easy, because there's no need to enter a PIN number.

6 BOOKING A MINICAB

2 11

Nina checks her mobile and finds a text from Zoe. Listen to the telephone conversation between Nina and the minicab company and make a note of:

- the fare for a one-way trip to central London
- how long the trip will take
- where Nina is now
- how long Nina will have to wait for the minicab to arrive
- what other information she gives the minicab company

Webcode: FOBNRWT501

D Hotel reservations

Nina Wittstock, the chief executive officer of Top Act Event Management AG in Düsseldorf is invited by Rob Heldof to see him play unplugged at the Edinburgh Festival in August. He will be there with his band for a week. She asks Helena Sawicki, her personal assistant, to book her a room.

1 ENQUIRING ABOUT HOTELS ONLINE

Helena Sawicki findet die Webseite VisitScotland.com im Internet und sucht nach einer passenden Unterkunft für Nina Wittstock. Beantworten Sie folgende Fragen zu ihren Internetrecherchen.

1 Auf welche der sieben Schaltflächen unter dem Titelbalken klickt Helena Sawicki, um nach einer Unterkunft zu suchen?
2 Welche sind die Pflichtfelder in der Maske? Erklären Sie ihre Bedeutung.
3 Welche Unterbringungsmöglichkeiten werden auf der Website angeboten?
4 Was versteht man unter *half board* und *full board*?
5 Was ist das Ergebnis der von Helena durchgeführten Suche?
6 Was muss Helena laut Website machen, um eine passende Unterkunft zu finden?
7 Welche andere Möglichkeit steht Helena zur Verfügung, falls sie keine Internetbuchung durchführen kann?

Booking accommodation

Meals

B&B means bed and breakfast.
Half board means breakfast and an evening meal.
Full board means three meals a day.
All inclusive normally means that there are no extra charges, e.g. for drinks, snacks or entertainment.
Self-catering means you cook your own meals.

Breakfast

A *continental breakfast* is usually only coffee and bread rolls with butter and jam. (Note: *jam* = Marmelade. English *marmalade* is *Orangenmarmelade*.)
A *full English breakfast* is a large breakfast, usually with cereal (e.g. cornflakes, porridge, muesli), cooked bacon, sausages and eggs, baked beans, toast, and tea or coffee.

Rooms

Single rooms can have a normal size bed, a *queen-size* (large bed) or a *king-size* (very large) bed.
Double rooms can have a *double bed* (one big bed) or *twin beds* (two single beds).
A *family room* sleeps three or four people.
An *en suite* bathroom or *en suite facilities* means that the room has a bathroom connected to it (with a shower and/or bathtub (*Badewanne*).
A *serviced apartment* means that you have a fully furnished flat with a cleaner.

Facilities/Amenities

Car park / bar / restaurant / wellness centre / spa / sauna / swimming pool / gym (*Fitnessraum*) / wifi, wireless internet (*WLAN*)
Sometimes there is a charge (*Gebühr*) or a surcharge (*Aufpreis*) for a service.
A *guest house* has fewer facilities than a hotel and many only offer bed and breakfast.

Payment

The price (or *rate*) for a room is usually per person per night.
Payment is normally by *credit card*.
If you book through an agency, there can be a *booking fee*.
Sometimes a deposit (*Anzahlung*) must be paid to secure the room.

2 MAKING A HOTEL RESERVATION BY TELEPHONE

Helena phones the hotline to book a room for Nina Wittstock.

2 12

A Listen to the dialogue and decide which of the following three summaries is correct.

1 Helena phones the hotline on the VisitScotland.com website because she needs a room in Edinburgh for a few days to visit the International Festival starting on 19 August. She intends to travel by car and finally decides to book a room in a four-star hotel for £130 a night. She pays the whole amount immediately by credit card.

2 Helena phones the hotline on the VisitScotland.com website and books a room in Edinburgh for Nina Wittstock for three nights from 17–20 August. The room is in a 4-star guest house called Clifford House, which is about 20 minutes from the centre. It costs £165 a night. She pays a deposit of £10 to secure the room by credit card.

3 Helena phones the hotline on the VisitScotland.com website but as she is unable to book a hotel room in Edinburgh for Nina Wittstock from 17–20 August, she books a room for a later date at a four-star guest house called Clifford House about 20 minutes away from the centre on foot. She pays the booking fee and deposit by credit card.

B Listen to the dialogue and complete the statements.

1 Helena first waits because ...
2 She wants a room for ...
3 The agent first offers her ...
4 He says it's a bad idea to ...
5 He next offers her a room in ...
6 The distance to the city centre is ...
7 Helena agrees to pay ...
8 The agent will send her ...

C Listen to the dialogue again and explain the meaning of each number as it occurs.

1 0
2 3
3 165
4 24
5 3
6 4
7 130
8 20

Hotel / Booking Agent

Greeting the caller

Park Hotel, good morning. How may I help?
Welcome to ... (name of hotel / booking agency).
You're through to ... (first name of agent).

Offering a room

I can offer you a ... (type of room, e.g. single, double room) for that date / those dates.
We've (only) got a ... for that date / those dates.

Caller

Saying what you need

Hello / Good morning, I'd like to book a ... (single/double/twin room) from ... to ..., please.
It's for ... night(s) beginning ... (date of arrival).
It's just for me / one person.
It's for two/three etc. people.

Accepting

I'll take it. / We'll take it.
That's great! / That's fine.

Hotel / Booking Agent

Offering alternatives

I'm afraid we're booked up for those dates.
How about ... (e.g. a day later / a self-catering apartment / a guest house)?
Could you come ... (e.g. a day/week) later?

Caller

Leaving the booking open

Thanks for the information. I'll get back to you. / I'll let you know.

Rejecting

Well, if that's all you've got, I'll leave it.

Finishing the call

Hotel / Booking Agent	Caller
Thanks for calling. Bye.	*Thanks very much. Bye.*
We look forward to seeing you ... (e.g. in May).	*Have you got nothing at all for those dates?*
I'm sorry we couldn't help you, sir/madam.	*Could you let me know if there's a cancellation?*
Please try again in a few days. There might be a cancellation.	*Could you recommend another hotel / guest house?*

Follow-up questions

Hotel / Booking Agent	Caller
Could you just spell your name for me, please?	*How far is it from ... (e.g. the city centre)?*
Could I have ... (e.g. your name / e-mail address / credit card number), please?	*What facilities has it got? / Has it got a ... (e.g. car park, restaurant, bar, spa, wifi [WLAN])?*
Would you just let me have the security number on the back (of your credit card), please?	*Can I book a conference room for ... (number) people for ... (number) day(s)?*

D With a partner write or act out the following telephone booking.

Partner A

You are Michael/Michaela Lorenz (m.lorenz@oekopur.com). Make a telephone booking at Hotel Vanadisvägen in Stockholm. Include the following details:

Dates:	3rd-6th of next month
Rooms:	4 single rooms
Meals:	Half board - charge?
Conference room:	For 4 people for the 4th and 5th - charge?
Internet:	Needed
Payment:	Visa
Questions:	Shower or bathtub? Other facilities?

Partner B

Look at file 3 on page 174.

★★★
Hotel Vanadisvägen

Luntmakargatan 22
11351 Stockholm
Sweden
Tel. +46 08 162294

Facilities

TV in all rooms
Wifi
All rooms en suite
Underfloor heating
Sauna
Conference rooms

B&B from €100 per person per night
Check out our special mid-week offers!

3 COMPARING HOTELS

Top Act Event Management AG empfängt Gäste aus Australien. Peter Jones and Sylvia Jason haben eine Besprechung mit Nina Wittstock, möchten aber auch den Karneval in Düsseldorf erleben und brauchen dafür ein geeignetes Hotel. Helena Sawicki hat den Auftrag, ihnen bei der Hotelbuchung zu helfen und hat folgende Angebote im Internet gefunden. Sie ruft Oliver Carter, Peter Jones Assistent, an, um die Details zu besprechen.

A Übernehmen Sie die zwei Rollen (Rolle A auf Seite 149, Rolle B auf Seite 179 (File 16)) in Partnerarbeit mit Hilfe der folgenden Hinweise und der Useful phrases auf der Seite 135.

Rolle A
Helena Sawicki

- Fragen Sie nach den An- und Abreiseterminen der Gäste.
- Fragen Sie, was für ein Hotel sie möchten.
- Sie finden die zwei abgebildeten Hotels im Internet. Beschreiben Sie ihre Lage.
- Erklären Sie, was die Hotels pro Nacht und insgesamt kosten würden.
- Beantworten Sie die Fragen.
- Sie helfen gerne und sind auch jederzeit bereit, ihm/ihr wieder zu helfen.

Hotel International Düsseldorf ★★★★ €86,70

5,9 km: Flughafen
1,1 km: Stadtzentrum

Anzahl Zimmer	Zimmertyp	Beschreibung
2xDOUBLE	Doppelzimmer	Doppelzimmer mit Frühstück Frübucher-Rate

Hotelausstattung		Zimmerausstattung	
▪ WLAN	▪ Bar	▪ Schreibtisch	▪ Minibar
▪ Büroservice	▪ Haustiere erlaubt	▪ Telefon	▪ Badezimmer/Dusche
▪ Restaurant	▪ Wäscheservice	▪ Bademantel	▪ Radio
▪ Aufzug	▪ FeeRequiredParking	▪ Internet	▪ Nichtraucherzimmer
▪ Vegetarische Küche		▪ Klimaanlage	▪ Behindertengerechtes Zimmer
		▪ Kabel-TV	

Hotel Mon Dieu ★★★ €57,00

6,8 km: Flughafen
0,6 km: Stadtzentrum

Anzahl Zimmer	Zimmertyp	Beschreibung
2xDOUBLE	Doppelzimmer	Doppelzimmer ohne Frühstück Bestpreis

Hotelausstattung		Zimmerausstattung	
▪ WLAN	▪ Weckruf	▪ Schreibtisch	▪ Badezimmer/Dusche
▪ Aufzug		▪ Internet	▪ Pay-TV
		▪ Kabel-TV	▪ Telefon
		▪ Satelliten-TV	▪ Haartrockner

B **Sie sind Helena und erhalten folgende E-Mail von Oliver Carter. Fassen Sie die Einzelheiten des entsprechenden Hotels in einer E-Mail an Oliver zusammen. Ihre E-Mail sollte informell und freundlich sein und folgende Punkte enthalten:**

> Termine
> Hotelkategorie
> Lage
> Verpflegung
> Zimmerausstattung
> Bezahlung
> Weitere Angaben nach Wahl

E-MAIL

To: "Helena Sawicki, Top Act Event Management AG" <helena.sawicki@top-act.de>
From: "Oliver Carter" <olivercarter@powerevents.au>
Subject: Hotel in Düsseldorf

Hey Helena

Thanks for your help on the phone earlier. I've spoken to Peter and Sylvia and they would like to take the cheaper one. Can you e-mail me details please?

Thanks and talk to you soon.

Oliver

Webcode: FOBNRWT502

E Welcoming a visitor

Helena Sawicki is personal assistant to Nina Wittstock, the chief executive officer of Top Act Event Management AG in Düsseldorf. Today Helena gets a visitor from Ireland.

1 INFORMING SOMEONE ABOUT A DELAY

Read the e-mails and complete the sentences below.

1 Zoe Kline is on her way to ...
2 She's late because ...
3 Zoe works for ...
4 Helena has not met Zoe ...
5 Zoe's plane finally lands in Düsseldorf at ...

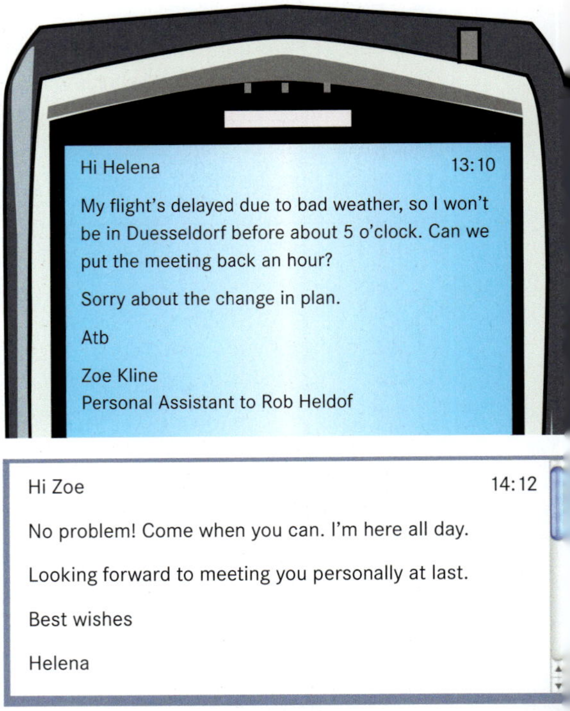

2 MAKING SMALL TALK

2 13

Guess which words are missing in the dialogue and then listen to the recording to check your answers.

HELENA: Hello, you must be Zoe Kline! I'm Helena Sawicki. ... [1] to Düsseldorf! It's so nice to ... [2] you at last!

ZOE: Hello Helena. It's nice to meet you, too. I'm so ... [3] I'm late. I hope I haven't ... [4] your plans for this afternoon!

HELENA: Not at all. Did you have a good ... [5]?

ZOE: Apart from the delay it was fine.

HELENA: Good. Now, can I get you ... [6] before the meeting – tea, coffee, mineral water?

ZOE: I'd ... [7] a cup of coffee!

HELENA: Black or white? Sugar?

ZOE: Black, no sugar, please.

HELENA: Here ... ... [8].

ZOE: Thanks.

HELENA: Now here's the ... [9] for the meeting. We've made a few changes but nothing big. And here's the ... [10] for the next two days.

ZOE: Thanks.

HELENA: Now just let me give you my ... ... [11], in case you need to phone me on my mobile.

ZOE: Thanks. And here's ... [12].

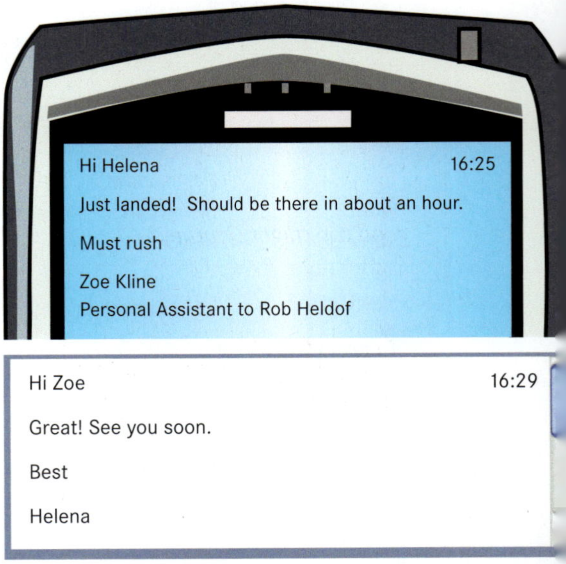

Meeting and greeting

First meeting

- Introduce yourself clearly using your first name and surname and the name of your company if appropriate.
- Use 'Nice to meet you' or 'Pleased to meet you' to greet your guest.
- Shake hands.
- Break the ice with a polite question (see below for examples).
- If the visitor is clearly older and/or more important than you, use his/her surname (e.g. Can I take your coat, Mrs Baker?). Otherwise use first names.
- Have your business card ready to give to the visitor.

Meeting your visitor again a short time later

- Don't shake hands again. You only do this after a long break.
- Listen carefully to see if your visitor is using first names now (e.g. Hi, Nina) and or is still formal (Good morning, Mrs Wittstock) and do the same.
- Make some small talk before getting down to business (see below for examples).

3 MEDIATION

Skills, Mediation, p. 211

Es findet demnächst eine Infoveranstaltung an Ihrer Schule zum Thema Auslandspraktika statt. Vor der Veranstaltung solle ein kurzer Knigge erstellt werden, um Praktikanten/innen auf ihre Arbeit in einem englischsprachigen Büro vorzubereiten. Sie sollen den Teil über die Begrüßung von englischsprachigen Gästen und den Gebrauch von Vor- und Nachnamen schreiben. Benutzen Sie die Informationen in der Infobox, um einen kurzen Text oder eine Präsentation über die wichtigsten Inhalte zu erstellen.

Host	***Guest***
Speaking to someone for the first time (e.g. in reception, at an airport)	
You must be ... (e.g. Emma Brown) from ... (company e.g. Global Solutions) /	*Yes, that's right.*
Introductions	
Hello, Ms Brown. I'm ... (first name, e.g. Tom) ... (surname, e.g. Schmidt) from ... (company).	
This is my colleague, Silke Rademacher. She's in ... (department, e.g. Marketing).	
Nice/Pleased to meet you.	*Nice/Pleased to meet you (too).*
Making the visitor feel at home / Small talk	
Welcome to ... (e.g. Germany / Düsseldorf / Top Act Event Management). Did you have a good trip/flight/journey?	*Yes, it was fine thanks. / It was a bit bumpy. / There was some turbulence./ We were half an hour late.*
Is your hotel all right?	*Yes, it's fine. Very comfortable / convenient / easy to find / near the centre.*
Can I get you something to drink? / Can I get you anything – tea, coffee or mineral water? / Would you like tea, coffee or mineral water?	*Yes, please. / A cup of coffee, please. / I'd love a cup of tea. / No, thank you very much.* * *I ate on the plane / on the way here.*
Is this your first visit to ... (e.g. Essen)?	*Yes, it is actually. / No, it isn't actually. I've been here once / twice / a few times before.* **

Host	*Guest*
Giving information	
We've booked you in at ... (name of hotel, e.g. the Park Hotel). Here's a card with the details.	*Oh, thanks. / Great!*
Here's a copy of ... (e.g. the agenda of the meeting / the programme for today).	*Thanks a lot.*
Here's a folder with everything you need.	*Thanks for that.*
Here's my business card, in case you need to contact me.	*Thanks. Here's mine.*

* *Never just answer with the word 'no'! Native speakers of English find this very impolite.*
** *Here the host could say 'I see'. This is almost always a good answer.*

4 INTRODUCING YOURSELF

With a partner, use the useful phrases to practise introductions.

Partner A: Use the business cards on this page.
Partner B: Use the business cards in file 5 on page 175.

Role A (with Jonathan Sykes)

Soyang
Europe GmbH
www.soyang.webwasher-dev.de

SOYANG
EUROPE GMBH

Dr. Alexander Mieberg
Managing Director

Soyang Europe GmbH
Hammer Landstraße 1a
41460 Neuss
Germany

Tel.: +49 (2131) 51...
Mobil: +49 (160) 96...
Fax: +49 (2131) 51...
E-Mail: koch@soyang.eu

Role B (with Amanda Lakely)

BRIX Mode GmbH

Sevda Yildiz
Einkaufsleiterin / Purchasing Director

Feldstraße 42
33609 Bielefeld
Germany

Tel.: +49 521 4827764-32
Mobil: +49 179 2049512
Sevda.yildiz@brixmode.de

5 MAKING SMALL TALK

Now make small talk with your partner.

Partner A: Use the business cards above and the background information below.
Partner B: Use the background information in file 5 on page 175.

Role A

You are Dr. Alexander Mieberg.

> You introduce yourself to your visitor.
> You ask about the flight.
> You offer your visitor something to drink.
> You ask about the hotel in Neuss (Holiday Inn).
> You exchange business cards.

Role B

You are Sevda Yildiz.

> You introduce yourself to your visitor.
> You ask about the flight.
> You offer your visitor something to drink.
> You tell your visitor that you have booked her a hotel in Düsseldorf (Parkhotel).
> You give her a card with the address of the hotel.
> You exchange business cards.

F Meetings

1 LOOKING AT DIFFERENT TYPES OF MEETING

A What different types of meeting can you see here? Label the pictures (a – d) with words from the box.

conference call | face-to-face meeting | teleconference | video conference

B What type(s) of meeting would be suitable in each of the following situations?

> discussions between North Sea oil workers and Head Office on land
> firing an employee
> job interview
> technical presentations
> weekly international team meetings

2 PREPARING FOR A CONFERENCE

Top Act Event Management AG is having its regular quarterly video conference with its European branches in two weeks' time and Helena Sawicki has been given the task of drawing up the agenda. She writes an e-mail to all the participants to ask for their suggestions and comments.

Look at the e-mail and match the definitions below (1-10) with the highlighted words.

E-MAIL

To:
Subject: Draft agenda for quarterly video conference at 10 a.m. CET on 10 June 20..
Cc: Nina Wittstock
Attachment(s): draft_agenda.video_conference2.pdf

Dear All

I hope you're all well.

The draft agenda for our quarterly video conference is attached. As some participants were not available in calendar week 23, it is now scheduled for calendar week 24.

I would now like you to make suggestions as regards changes and additions to the topics listed. I will then amend the agenda and circulate it to all participants in advance.

As always, the minutes of the meeting will be e-mailed to you after the conference.

I very much hope you will all be able to attend the meeting.

Best regards
Helena Sawicki
PA to Nina Wittstock
Top Act Event Management AG

1 a big piece of paper on the wall which shows the days, weeks and months of the year
2 a list of the points to be discussed at a meeting
3 a record of all the things said or decided at a meeting
4 fixed for a certain date
5 free; able to come to the meeting
6 points to be discussed
7 send to all of the people in a group
8 the first version of a document
9 the people who go to a meeting
10 to be present at a meeting

3 UNDERSTANDING AN AGENDA

Study the agenda on the next page and explain:

1 how long the conference will last.
2 how many different matters will certainly be discussed.
2 how many people are expected to be present at the conference.
3 who cannot be at the meeting.
4 how often conferences like this take place.
5 why CET (Central European Time) is used to state the time of the meeting.
6 when it will be possible to talk about something which is not on the agenda.

Top Act Event Management AG, Königsallee 550, 40212 Düsseldorf, Germany

DRAFT AGENDA

QUARTERLY VIDEO CONFERENCE No. 2, 20..

Date: 10 June 20...
Time: 10 a.m. – 1 p.m. CET
Attendees: Nina Wittstock, CEO Top Act Event Management
Betina Høch, Sales Director, Top Act, Denmark
Simon Osborne, General Manager, Top Act, UK
Lars Ehnbom, Marketing Manager, Top Act, Sweden
Helena Sawicki, PA to Ms Wittstock
Absentees: Chantal Bachelot, General Manager, Top Act, France
Minutes: Helena Sawicki

Topics
1 Presentation: Danish sales figures for second quarter (Betina Høch)
2 Expansion of UK branch (Simon Osborne)
3 Customer feedback
4 Recruiting new staff
5 Any other business (AOB)

Telefonnotiz

Datum: *27. Mai 20..*

Telefonat mit: ____________________

Firma: ____________________

Grund für Anruf

____

____

____

____

____

Tipp: Schreiben Sie zuerst nur die englischen Wörter auf. Übertragen Sie erst danach Ihre Notizen ins Deutsche.

4 AMENDING THE AGENDA

Helena Sawicki now gets feedback from the people she has e-mailed.

2 14

A There is a message on Helena's answerphone so she phones the caller back. Listen to the telephone call and complete the memo below.

B Helena also receives the e-mails below. Use the information from the telephone call and the e-mails to update the agenda for the conference.

1 E-MAIL

Mail from: Simon Osborne
Subject: Re: Draft agenda for quarterly video conference at 10 a.m. CET on 10 June 20..
Cc:
Attachment(s):

H Helena

I've just seen your draft agenda and would like you to make a small change for me. The UK branch hasn't actually expanded at all over the last quarter. In fact, it's shrunk so can we change point 2 to Key UK accounts? I think that will look a bit better.

Many thanks.

S.

2 E-MAIL

Mail from: Chantal Bachelot
Subject: Re: Draft agenda for quarterly video conference at 10 a.m. CET on 10 June 20..
Cc:
Attachment(s):

Dear Helena

Many thanks for your e-mail. The good news is that I can attend the conference because I'm back at work now and feeling a lot better.

Best regards

Chantal

5 DRAWING UP AN AGENDA

A **Nina has a meeting with the Irish band Tina and the Heartbreakers (Tina O'Connell, Sammy Slow, Jess Stone, Ginger Brown, Justin Time) and their manager, Rocky Fabian, in Düsseldorf to talk about their tour of Germany. Use Nina's notes to write the agenda in English.**

- 09:00 – 11:00 Uhr im großen Konferenzraum
- Präsentation des neuen Videoclips
- Besprechung der Veranstaltungsorte (venues)
- Vorverkaufszahlen (advance ticket sales)
- Tourbus oder Hotels?
- Anfrage für Auftritt in Prag
- Sonstiges
- Protokoll: Helena
- Hartmut Bonraths Frau hat ihr Baby bekommen, also kann er nicht teilnehmen.

B **Now write a short, friendly e-mail to Rocky with the agenda as an attachment. Give him your phone number and offer your help if he needs it.**

6 PRESENTING INFORMATION

> Skills, p. 209

During the meeting Nina would like to present the sales figures for the tour in English and compare them with sales from the year before to find out where to advertise the tour. Make a diagram using the figures in the box and then prepare a short presentation about the figures and where more advertising could be useful. Use the useful phrases on page 209.

Vorverkauf als Prozentsatz der insgesamt verfügbaren Tickets

Bevorstehende Tournee in NRW
Bielefeld 60%
Dortmund 75%
Düsseldorf 45%
Köln 30%

Tournee in NRW letztes Jahr
Bielefeld 40%
Dortmund 65%
Düsseldorf 85%
Köln 90%

7 CHECKING THE MINUTES OF A MEETING

2 15

Helena writes the minutes from Nina's meeting with Tina and the Heartbreakers. Read Helena's minutes and then listen to the extracts from the meeting and find the mistakes.

MINUTES

Title:	Tina and the Heartbreakers' European Tour
Time and date:	09 – 11 a.m. 28 November 20...
Place:	Conference room
Attendees:	Nina Wittstock, Tina O'Connell, Sammy Slow, Jess Stone, Ginger Brown, Justin Time Rocky Fabian (Manager), Helena Sawicki
Absentees:	Hartmut Bonrath
Minutes:	Helena Sawicki

Topic 1 Video clip
The video clip was well received. Rocky Fabian thought Tina looked good in black. Tina said she wanted to be in black next time, too.

Topic 2 Venues
Rocky said the band only wanted to play in big cities for no less than 1,000 people. Nina suggested making the tickets more expensive for small crowds and Tina added that a fair maximum price for a ticket was €15.

Topic 3 Advance ticket sales
After Helena's presentation it was agreed that more advertising is needed for Düsseldorf and Cologne.

Topic 4 Accommodation: Tour bus or hotel
The band members all preferred a tour bus.

Topic 5 Prague
It was decided that the band would perform in Prague after the tour.

AOB
Rocky and the band only want afternoon meetings in future.

Wie man ein englisches Protokoll schreibt

Im Englischen wird ein Protokoll nicht nur in der Gegenwart geschrieben. Im Allgemeinen erfolgt die Berichterstattung unter Anwendung der Regeln der indirekten Rede (siehe Grammatikanhang Seite 217). Es empfiehlt sich, mit einer Reihe von einleitenden Verben zu arbeiten, z. B. *added / went on to say / thought / it was agreed / suggested + ing*. Eine Aussage kann auch mit *according to* eingeleitet werden. *According to* ist zeitlos, z. B.
– According to Rocky the band *is/was/will* be tired.

8 WRITING THE MINUTES OF A MEETING

> Grammar Summary, reported speech, p. 217

At another meeting (2 December, 15.00–16.00 in Nina's office) Nina, Rocky and Helena discuss the concert in Prague. Hartmuth Bonrath was unable to come. Use Helena's notes below to write the minutes.

TOP 1 Auftritt in Prag
– Rocky nur einverstanden, wenn Auftritt mindestens eine Woche nach Deutschland-Tournee stattfindet, sonst zu viel Stress für die Band. Einige Mitglieder seien jetzt schon sehr müde und brauchen Ruhe.

TOP 2 Unterkunft in Prag
– Rocky besteht auf einem Fünf-Sterne Hotel in der Stadtmitte mit Pool zum Relaxen.

TOP 3 Ticket-Preise
– Laut Rocky sollen die Tickets 80 € – 100 € kosten.

Sonstiges
–

Webcode: FOBNRWT503

G Scenario

Situation: Nach dem Abschluss der aktuellen Radtourensaison wollen sich Herr South und die Geschäftsführer von Fly Bike Werke GmbH treffen, um die Absatzzahlen für die letzte Saison zu analysieren und ihre Pläne für die kommende Saison abzustimmen. Herr South lädt die Mitarbeiter von Fly Bike Werke GmbH ein, sich mit ihm in Cambridge zu treffen, dem Ausgangspunkt für viele Touren in Großbritannien.

1 Frau Lily Allen, die Leiterin der Marketingabteilung von South Riding Tours Ltd, ruft den/die Sales and Marketing Assistenten/in von Fly Bike Werke GmbH an, um die Details des geplanten Treffens zu besprechen. Frau Allen spricht leider kein Deutsch. Spielen Sie die Rollen mit einem Partner / einer Partnerin durch.

Partner A: Frau Allen
Sie organisieren das Treffen und buchen Flüge und Hotelzimmer. Sie haben folgende Informationen für die Fly Bike Werke GmbH:

- Das Treffen soll am Freitag, den 29. September oder Freitag, den 6. Oktober in Cambridge stattfinden.
- Herr South lädt die Gäste für Donnerstag zum Abendessen im Hotel ein und bietet die Möglichkeit einer Stadtbesichtigung am Samstag an. Die Gäste werden am Flughafen, wahrscheinlich London-Stansted, abgeholt.
- Rückflug Samstag Abend oder Sonntag möglich.
- Tagesordnung für das Treffen wird nächste Woche an die Fly Bike Werke GmbH geschickt.
- Eine Aufstellung der Verkaufszahlen der letzte Saison in Deutschland wird dazu benötigt.

Sie benötigen folgende Informationen der Fly Bike Werke GmbH:

- welche Mitarbeiter/-innen von Fly Bike Werke GmbH werden am Treffen teilnehmen?
- welcher der beiden Terminvorschläge (Freitag, 29. September oder Freitag, 6. Oktober) passt?
- Gibt es Sonderwünsche?

Partner B: Sales and Marketing Assistant
Sie sind der/die Sales and Marketing Assistant von Fly Bike Werke GmbH. Sie können South Riding Tours Ltd folgende Informationen geben:

- Teilnehmer: Herr Ullmann, Herr Peters, Herr Gerland, Frau Dogan, Sie (als Belohnung für Ihre gute Arbeit!)
- Terminvorschlag der Fly Bike Werke: Freitag, 6. Oktober, da Herr Ullmann am 29. September anderweitig beschäftigt ist.
- Alle Teilnehmer möchten am Samstagabend zurückfliegen
- Herr Ullmann ist Vegetarier

Sie haben folgende Fragen an South Riding Tours:

- Wie sollen Sie vom Flughafen nach Cambridge kommen?
- Wann können Sie mit der Tagesordnung für das Treffen rechnen?
- Welche Unterlagen werden für das Treffen noch benötigt?

2 **Ein paar Tage später schreibt Ihnen Lily Allen folgende Email als Bestätigung der Reisepläne. Informieren Sie die anderen Teilnehmer Ihrer Firma über deren Inhalt:**

E-MAIL

Meeting in Cambridge, Friday 6 October

Location: Hotel Intercontinental, 21 Parkway West, Cambridge CB3 2QU
Attending: Richard South, Lily Allen (Marketing Manager), Martin Corman (Tour Manager, Europe); Jan Ullmann, Hans Peters, Ralf Gerland, Sylvia Dogan, Sales and Marketing Assistant (Fly Bike Werke GmbH)
Meeting place: seminar room "Cambridge Blue", 9.30 a.m. to 5.30 p.m.
Agenda: attached

Additional information
Outward flight: AB 728, Hamburg-Stansted, 5 October, 2.45 p.m.
Minibus from Stansted airport to hotel in Cambridge is arranged.
Evening meal in "Mary's Plaice", Thursday 5 October, 7.30 p.m.
Friday evening: free
Guided tour of Cambridge: 10 a.m. to 4 p.m., Saturday 7 October; pub lunch
Return flight: AB 729, Stansted-Hamburg, 7 October, 8.15 p.m.

Agenda for Cambridge meeting

9.30 a.m. Greeting and introduction (Richard South)
9.45 a.m. Presentation sales figures UK (Lily Allen)
10.30 a.m. Coffee
10.45 a.m. Discussion sales figures UK
11.30 a.m. Presentation sales figures Germany (Ralf Gerland)
12.15 a.m. Discussion sales figures Germany
1.00 p.m. Lunch (in hotel restaurant)
2.30 p.m. Presentation of new routes in UK and Germany (Richard South, Sylvia Dogan)
3.00 p.m. Sales estimates for coming year
4.00 p.m. Discussion of new sales strategies
5.00 p.m. AOB (any other business)

3 **Benutzen Sie diese Details aus der englischen Agenda, um eine vollständige deutsche Tagesordnung für die Teilnehmer aus Ihrer Firma zu erstellen.**

4 **Herr Gerland wird die Verkaufszahlen für die Touren in Deutschland für die abgelaufene Saison beim Meeting präsentieren. Dafür sollen Sie ihm die folgenden Zahlen als klar verständliche Grafiken in englischer Sprache aufbereiten.**

Region I (Norddeutschland)	Gäste insgesamt	aus UK	%	aus D	%
Niedersachsen	1.490	257	17,25	1.233	82,75
Schleswig-Holstein	952	76	8,00	876	92,00
Berlin-Brandenburg	1.908	312	16,35	1.596	83,65
Mecklenburg-Vorpommern	2.217	396	17,86	1.821	82,14
Nordrhein-Westfalen	2.830	446	15,76	2.384	84,24
Gesamt	9.397	1487	15,82	7.910	84,18

Umsatz pro Region (%)	
Verkaufsregion	%
Region I (Norddeutschland)	23,3
Region II (Südwestdeutschland)	20,9
Region III (Bayern, Baden-Württemberg)	39,1
Region IV (Ostdeutschland)	16,7

Fly Bike Werke GmbH Radtouren in Deutschland	
Herkunftsland der Gäste	%
Großbritannien	13,63
Deutschland	80,37
Niederlande	4,61
Andere	1,39

5 **Notieren Sie nun auf Englisch einige Kommentare für Herrn Gerland, die wichtige Eckdaten herausstellen.**

6

Dealing with conflicts at work

FOCUS

1 **What conflicts might you find in the workplace? How different do you think these conflicts are to the ones you find at school?**

2 **How can people deal with conflicts at work?**

3 **Describe and analyse the cartoons below. What do they say about the difficulties of conflict resolution?**

The cartoon shows ...
... filing cabinet / paper shredder / boxing gloves
The man appears / men appear to be ...
I think the cartoonist wants to say ...
The point of the cartoon seems to be that ...
I agree with the cartoonist, but ...
The cartoon has the effect of ...

Conflict resolution in the workplace

*'We'll save a fortune in employment tribunals'**

* Arbeitsgericht

A Problems in the workplace

1 DEALING WITH BULLYING

Dan Griffiths from Cardiff, Wales, works in the sales department of a company that makes office furniture. He is having a difficult time at work because of his supervisor. Dan meets his friend Marcus O'Reilly and they discuss Dan's problem.

2 16

A Listen to the conversation and make notes on the following:

1 the kind of problem that is reported
2 how the supervisor is trying to get Dan into trouble
3 what happened when Dan tried to talk to her about things
4 what Dan is considering
5 Marcus's advice
6 what happened to another colleague who complained

B How would you translate the German expressions below? Use your translation to complete these sentences that Dan says. Then listen again and check.

1	jmdm das Leben zur Hölle machen	*Mrs Patterson, that's her name. She's ...*
2	inkompetent	*She says that I'm ...*
3	jdn unter vier Augen sprechen	*I tried to ...*
4	jmdn beschuldigen	*She's ... for the whole thing.*
5	die Kündigung einreichen	*I'm going to ...*
6	für jdn Partei ergreifen	*He isn't going to ... against my supervisor.*
7	zusammenhalten	*You know what management is like, they all ...*
8	eine dienstliche Beschwerde einreichen	*If I ..., it won't help.*

C You are Dan. Write an e-mail to Mrs Patterson's manager explaining the situation.

D In response to your e-mail, Mrs Patterson's manager invites you and Mrs Patterson to a formal meeting to talk things over.

Work in groups of three. You are going to role-play the discussion.

> Skills, p. 210

Partner A: Dan. Go to file 18 on page 179.
Partner B: Mrs Patterson. Go to file 22 on page 181.
Partner C: Mrs Patterson's manager. Go to file 26 on page 182.

2 STRATEGIES FOR DEALING WITH HARASSMENT

Sie absolvieren ein Praktikum. Ein Kollege, der kein Deutsch spricht, hat das Gefühl, dass er am Arbeitsplatz gemobbt wird. Er fragt Sie, was er tun sollte. Erklären Sie mit Hilfe der Wortliste die Strategien aus dem Text.

> Skills, p. 211

Mögliche Strategien gegen Mobbing:

Selbstbewusstsein zeigen: Lassen Sie sich durch Vorwürfe von Kollegen oder Chefs nicht beeindrucken und rechtfertigen Sie sich vor allem nicht.

Mögliche Eigenanteile identifizieren: Überprüfen Sie, ob Sie selbst einen Anlass für das Mobbing-Geschehen gegeben haben könnten, z.B. durch Überschreitung von Kompetenzen.

Gespräch mit dem Kollegen: Sprechen Sie den Verbreiter von Gerüchten etc. konkret an (am besten unter vier Augen) u. bitten Sie ihn/sie, dies zukünftig zu unterlassen. Drohen Sie hierbei aber bitte nicht. Befindet sich der Konflikt schon im fortgeschrittenen Stadium, hat solch ein Gespräch allerdings oft keinen Sinn mehr und ein entsprechender Gesprächswunsch wird eher als Schwäche ausgelegt.

Führen Sie ein Mobbing-Tagebuch: Halten Sie die Mobbing-Vorfälle mit Datum, Akteuren, Zeugen fest. Das macht den Kopf frei und bringt Sie aus der passiven Haltung heraus.

Tagesprotokoll über Arbeitsleistungen führen: Da man begonnen hat, Ihre Arbeitsleistungen schlecht zu machen, sollten Sie diese ab jetzt genau dokumentieren. Das gleiche gilt für den ständigen Wechsel von Aufgaben.

Vermeiden Sie Isolation: Halten Sie den Kontakt zu Kollegen und nehmen Sie weiter an betrieblichen Feiern usw. teil. Lassen Sie sich nicht provozieren und isolieren!

http://www.strategien-gegen-mobbing.de/mobbing-beratung-koeln-nrw-06-anti-mobbing-strategien.html

Akteure	*people involved*
Arbeitsleistungen	*work performance*
drohen	*to threaten*
Eigenanteile	*own contributions*
etw. unterlassen	*to refrain from doing sth.*
Kompetenzen überschreiten	*to exceed one's authority*
provozieren	*to provoke*
sich vor etw beeindrucken lassen	*to let yourself be affected by sth.*
sich rechtfertigen	*to explain oneself; to justify one's actions*
Verbreiter von Gerüchten	*person spreading rumours*
Vorwürfe	*accusations*
Zeugen	*witnesses*

3 A HELPLINE

Complete the advertising poster with words from the box.

blame | bullying | complaint | counsellor | embarrassing | fault | sexual | victims

Workplace harassment

This is a situation many people have to face at some point in their working lives. It may take the form of physical …[1], unwanted …[2] interest or just …[3] comments.

The …[4] often …[5] themselves for the situation, but the important thing to remember is that it isn't your …[6].

Don't put up with the problem; if necessary, make an official …[7] or talk to someone you can trust. Your company may even have a …[8] who is there to deal with problems like yours.

If you need further advice, phone our helpline on 081 121212.

2 17

4 LISTENING: A CALL TO A HELPLINE

A **Listen to three excerpts from a call to a helpline. Describe the problem and the counsellor's suggestion on how to deal with it.**

B **Which of the suggestions in the text *Mögliche Strategien gegen Mobbing* are mentioned? Do you agree (or not) with the advice?**

C **Match the sentence halves to make complete sentences that the counsellor uses. Then decide which sentences are used to:**

> calm the caller
> interact actively with the caller
> give advice

1 Take it easy and try to tell me …
2 If you ever feel afraid or if he threatens you physically, …
3 Can you …
4 Could it be that …
5 Stay confident and don't give your colleague …
6 Please don't …
7 If I understand you correctly, …
8 Keep a record …

a explain?
b your colleague thinks you work too hard?
c what's troubling you.
d of your performance at work.
e your colleague is making things difficult for you.
f tell someone.
g the satisfaction of seeing that you're worried.
h worry.

Webcode: FOBNRWT601

5 SOLVING OTHER PROBLEMS AT WORK

A You have just started working in an office and are not sure how to deal with some difficult situations there. Work with a partner and take turns asking and giving advice about the situations below. Try to use phrases from the box.

Your boss has invited you to his/her home for a candlelight dinner.
Your colleague has asked you to take a packet of printing paper home for him.
You have found out that your company has been breaking some environmental laws.
You have seen the boss of the canteen taking left-over food to a shelter for homeless people.
You think that a new colleague has told a few lies on his CV.

Asking for advice
Can you help me / suggest what I should do?
Could you give me some advice?
What do you think I should do?
I don't know what to do/think.
Is there any place I can go for help?

Reporting what someone said
She said that ... (e.g. if I went to dinner with her, I would get a promotion next year)
He told me (that) ... (e.g. if I helped him, he would help me)
Another colleague informed me (that) ... (e.g. she had also seen/heard ...)

Interacting and checking your understanding
Can you explain?
What happened exactly?
If I understand you correctly, ...
I see.
Could it be that ...?

Giving advice
If my boss invited me ... , I would/might/could ... because ...
Why don't you ...?
If I were you, I would(n't) ...
How do you feel about the situation?
Sorry, but is it really any of your business?

B Everyone is talking about the latest items of news in the InHouse Magazine. Do the tasks below.

1 Read the headlines and, in groups, work out strategies to deal with the problems described.
2 Make notes and use them to write a recommendation in the form of a letter to the editor of the magazine.

Racist remarks overheard in the canteen

Thief at work! Valuables are missing from several lockers

Reaching the glass ceiling – Women in all departments complain about being passed over for promotion again

6 WRITING A COMMENT

Lehrjahre sind keine Herrenjahre

Sie sind Auszubildende/r in einem kleinen deutschen Unternehmen. Am Ende des Tages müssen Sie immer alle Mülleimer im Büro leeren. Als Sie Ihrem Vorgesetzten erklären, dass Sie nicht der Ansicht sind, diese Aufgaben erledigen zu müssen, konfrontiert er Sie mit dem obigen Spruch.

> Skills, p. 204

Verfassen Sie eine Stellungnahme, in der Sie den Spruch auf Englisch erklären und formulieren Sie, ob Sie diesem zustimmen oder nicht. Begründen Sie Ihre Meinung.

B Unfair policies and practices

1 DEALING WITH A COMPLAINT

A **Have you ever been disappointed with a product or service? What did you do about it? Tell your partner about the experience.**

B **Read this protest letter and tell your partner what happened to David Mitchell when he shopped at MyTunes.de.**

Dear Sir or Madam

Complaint about MyTunes.de one-device policy

I am writing to express my disapproval of MyTunes.de policy of selling music downloads which are only playable on one device. I have already written an e-mail to you but have received no reply.

As consumers of music, we have always been able to play CDs on as many CD players as we choose, and the same principle should hold for music downloads.

What makes MyTunes.de's policy even worse is that the consumers are not informed about it before they make their purchase. If the customers knew that they would only be able to play their purchase on one device, they would have the chance to download it to their MP3 players or to whichever device they use most. As for me, I downloaded my purchase onto my desktop computer, which I rarely use to listen to music.

I would like to buy items from MyTunes.de in the future, but I will not do so again until this unfair policy is corrected. I like MyTunes.de products, and the prices are very good, but this is a matter of principle for me.

Yours faithfully

David Mitchell

David Mitchell
(e-mail: d-mitchell@gmx.com)

Bitte per E-Mail antworten:

- *Wir haben seine E-Mail nie bekommen.*
- *Wir bedauern, dass er von der MyTunes.de-One-Device-Policy enttäuscht ist.*
- *Ihm zufolge werden Kunden nicht über die One-Device-Policy informiert, aber die Infos können auf dem Link zu unseren Kaufbedingungen unten auf unserer Homepage nachgelesen werden.*
- *Senden Sie ihm einen Gutscheincode für Gratis-Downloads und sagen Sie ihm, wir hoffen, dass er weiterhin MyTunes.de benutzt.*

C **You work at MyTunes.de. Your boss has asked you to reply to David Mitchell and has given you some notes in German. Use the notes to write the reply in English.**

2 MISLEADING ADVERTISING

A How many times have you bought a product online because the advertisement made it sound great? How many times did the product live up to the claims of the advert?

B Before you read the article below, study the headline and skim the text to answer these questions:

1 What is the ASA, when was it founded and what does it do?
2 Who is the latest target of the organization and why is the ASA focussing on this group?

2 18

Crackdown on misleading ads

By James Hall, Consumer Affairs Editor, The Telegraph

27 Oct 2012

The British Advertising Standards Authority (ASA), which looks into businesses that run misleading internet adverts, has announced that it will target small online businesses that make exaggerated claims in their internet ads. Guy Parker, the ASA's chief executive, said that the organization receives "thousands" of complaints from consumers about online ads offering misleading information.

The move follows growing concerns that online "banner ads" can carry misleading information. For example, Unbiased.co.uk, an organization that represents independent financial advisers, said recently that ads for "independent financial advisers" often take unsuspecting browsers to sites that are not independent and only recommend financial products from limited sources. Mr Parker also gave the example of ads for items such as nappies that contain misleading information about the product's quality.

The clampdown follows changes last year which broadened the ASA's remit to regulate online marketing in the same way that it regulates TV or radio advertising. The change brought adverts on websites and on social networking sites like Facebook and Twitter under the ASA's sphere of control for the first time.

Mr Parker said: "One of the challenges of regulating online advertising is that anyone can advertise. Putting up your own website costs almost nothing and you can set up a small business in your back room and you can be up and running in a day. Many of the advertisers haven't got a clue about the ASA and about the advertising codes, and we have to make sure that we do all we can to educate them and get them up to speed so they at least get the basics." He said that the watchdog has the power to ban ads it believes are misleading.

"We have got good plans for targeting small businesses and sole traders," Mr Parker went on. "We've had talks with the people who run search engines and we might ask them to help to develop a strategy to help stamp out misleading adverts. Many of the online companies use Google ads to try and lead customers to their websites. So that might be a good point at which we can reach advertisers and say "don't forget about us, there are things you do need to know," he said.

Mr Parker said that 90% of the problems are business owners "getting carried away" and making exaggerated claims. "Online advertising takes up roughly a third of our work, and 90% of the complaints are about 'misleading' adverts," he said. "It is not the ASA's job to conduct an investigation into, for example, the absorbing capacity of nappies," he explained. "It is much more about saying to the advertiser 'Do you know you are not allowed to say that?' And then we close down the advert."

The ASA was launched 50 years ago. In its first year it received 100 complaints while last year it received 32,000 complaints.

(476 words)

Adapted from
http://www.telegraph.co.uk/technology/news/9634413/Ad-watchdog-to-launch-crackdown-on-misleading-internet-ads.html

C Do the following tasks. Use your own words as often as possible. Skills, p. 203

1 Say where misleading advertising sometimes appears online and give two specific examples of 'bad behaviour' on the part of advertisers.
2 Compare and contrast the media which the organization has been concerned with in the past with the new media it is looking into. Say what makes the new media more attractive to advertisers and why it might also lead to advertisers making false claims.
3 Reading between the lines, does it appear to the ASA that every company consciously tries to mislead consumers? Support your answer with evidence from the text.

3 UNFAIR COMPETITION

A Apart from misleading advertising, what kinds of commercial practices could come under the heading 'unfair competition'? Brainstorm some ideas.

B Die Wettbewerbszentrale in Bad Homburg kümmert sich um unlautere Geschäftspraktiken sowohl Verbrauchern als auch Wettbewerbern gegenüber. Sie absolvieren ein Praktikum in der Beschwerdeabteilung. Ihr Vorgesetzter hat Sie gebeten, eine englische Version für die unten stehende Website der Organisation anzulegen.

http://www.wettbewerbszentrale.de/de/beschwerdestelle/hinweise/

Apple (12) Amazon eBay Yahoo! News (255)

Hinweise zur Beschwerdestelle

Wir empfehlen eine postalische Beschwerde, weil nur so sichergestellt ist, dass uns insbesondere die Originale der Werbemaßnahmen vorliegen oder wir Ausdrucke der Webseiten von dem Tag erhalten, an dem Sie den Wettbewerbsverstoß festgestellt haben.
Um die schnelle und effektive Verfolgung von Wettbewerbsverstößen zu gewährleisten, halten wir uns bei der Bearbeitung an folgende Vorgaben. Erläuterungen finden Sie unter den jeweiligen Hyperlinks:

- Jeder kann sich bei der Wettbewerbszentrale über einen Wettbewerbsverstoß beschweren. Anonyme Beschwerden werden von uns jedoch nicht bearbeitet!
- Wenn der Wettbewerbsverstoß nicht durch Dokumente belegt werden kann, benötigen wir für die Rechtsverfolgung eine eidesstattliche Versicherung.
- Je nach Art des Wettbewerbsverstoßes müssen uns (ggf. neben der Beschwerde-E-Mail oder dem Ausfüllen des Beschwerdeformulars) weitere Informationen postalisch zur Verfügung gestellt werden.
- Wir versichern Ihnen die vertrauliche Behandlung Ihrer personenbezogenen Daten (Datenschutzhinweis).

Beschwerdestelle	*complaints office*
eidesstattliche Versicherung	*affidavit (a written statement that can be used as evidence in court)*
personenbezogene Daten	*personal data*
vertraulich behandeln	*to treat sth as confidential*
Wettbewerbsverstoß	*violation of competition laws*
Wettbewerbszentrale	*Centre for Protection against Unfair Competition*

4 WRITING A COMMENT

What role should a government play in protecting consumers from misleading advertisers, and companies from unfair competition? Write a comment.

Webcode: FOBNRWT602

C Labour disputes

1 STRIKES IN THE NEWS

Look at the headlines and describe the kinds of 'bargaining' tools strikers use to get what they want.

Patients waiting as hospital workers work to rule

Sit-in at car plant

Strike! Last attempt to stop closure

Go-slow at job centre as staff protest against layoffs

Brrrr! It'll be a cold winter as miners threaten strike

Just in time for the holiday season – ground staff on go-slow

2 SUCCESSFUL STRIKING

Read the newspaper article about a successful strike. What do the following numbers and expressions refer to?

one-day | half | two-thirds | 5 % | 3.6 % | 1.5bn | 24 % | 3,500

2 19

Lufthansa ends strike, agrees to arbitration

From our business correspondent Bel Cunnison

Passengers get off the ground as cabin crew go back to work

Lufthansa could give a huge sigh of relief this morning as strikers returned to work after the one-day strike which forced the airline to ground almost half of its flights yesterday. The airline has agreed to arbitration in an effort to settle the dispute over wages and conditions. The strike was called by the UFO union (Unabhängige Flugbegleiter Organisation), which represents around two-thirds of Lufthansa's 19,000 cabin crew. It is calling for a 5% pay rise and job security for its members, who have not had an increase in salary in three years. The union has furthermore demanded that the airline stop using flight attendants on temporary contracts. These staff members are employed by a separate agency and often work longer hours on an irregular basis. Earlier this year, the union went to court to try to stop Lufthansa hiring temporary workers, but lost the case.

Passengers affected by the recent strike

Going some way towards finding an agreement

During the latest talks, however, the airline has offered permanent contracts to some of the temporary flight attendants working out of Berlin. Commenting on this move, Lufthansa's Chief Executive Christoph Franz said: "We hope this step will help the UFO to join us in constructive talks to come up with a competitive pay structure for cabin crew."

The airline is also offering to stop the use of temporary staff, and has proposed that short-term contracts will soon become a thing of the past.

While the UFO welcomes these concessions, it points out that Lufthansa remains unwilling to offer more than a 3.6% pay rise in return for longer hours.

The rising cost of fuel and competition from budget airlines has forced Lufthansa to initiate a 1.5bn euro cost-cutting programme. The airline posted a 24% drop in second-quarter earnings compared with last year. Earlier this year, Lufthansa said it would have to axe 3,500 office jobs.

Other airlines come to the aid of passengers

As the strike hit Germany's six main airports, other airlines flew larger planes on the German routes, helping passengers at airports affected by the strike to get to their destinations.

Though many travellers said they could understand the position of the strikers, the majority were irritated by the disruption.

(377 words)

B Do the following tasks in English.

1 Erklären Sie, warum das Bordpersonal von Lufthansa gestreikt hat.
2 Beschreiben Sie die Angebote, die die Gewerkschaft überzeugt haben, den Streik zu beenden.
3 Lufthansa ist auf eine Forderung der streikenden Mitarbeiter nicht eingegangen. Beschreiben Sie die Forderung und erklären Sie, weshalb Lufthansa ungern einwilligen könnte.
4 Erklären Sie, warum Lufthansa versucht, die Kosten zu reduzieren.
5 Beschreiben Sie die Situation für die Fluggäste und erklären Sie, wie die anderen Fluggesellschaften versucht haben, das Ausmaß der Störung auf einem Minimum zu halten.

3 WORKING WITH WORDS

Match the verbs on the left to the words on the right to make expressions to talk about striking. Which expressions can you use to describe actions by a) strikers and their union b) employers, companies, etc. c) both parties?

1	to agree to	a	a competitive pay structure
2	to settle	b	a cost-cutting programme
3	to call	c	a dispute
4	to go	d	arbitration
5	to offer	e	a strike
6	to join	f	concessions
7	to come up with	g	in constructive talks
8	to welcome	h	jobs
9	to initiate	i	permanent contracts
10	to axe	j	to court

4 AN EMPLOYEE'S POINT OF VIEW

A Sie arbeiten als Praktikant/in bei einer in Großbritannien niedergelassenen Economy-Airline, bei der die Bedingungen für die Angestellten nicht ideal sind. Ihre britische Vorgesetzte hat den folgenden Beitrag in einem Forum gesehen. Sie spricht kein Deutsch und bittet Sie, zu erklären, was Amelia R. geschrieben hat.

Ich stimme dem streikenden Bordpersonal von Lufthansa voll und ganz zu. Die Firma versucht Kosten zu reduzieren, und wie üblich leiden die Angestellten. Ich arbeite für eine Economy-Airline, und unsere Bedingungen sind noch schlimmer. Unser Dienstplan wird wöchentlich erstellt, und manchmal wird angeordnet, dass wir zuhause bleiben, wenn ein Flug nicht voll ausgelastet ist und gestrichen wird. Wir werden nach Stundensatz bezahlt, also ist es schwierig, meine Finanzen zu organisieren, und es ist nahezu unmöglich, mein Leben zu planen. Wir haben befristete Verträge und sind immer besorgt, dass unsere Verträge nicht verlängert oder erneuert werden, also haben viele von uns zu viel Angst, in den Streik zu treten. Ich kann meinen Kollegen bei Lufthansa nur das Beste wünschen. Amelia R.

B Work in groups. Talk about employees in similar situations, e.g. working in discount supermarkets or doing temporary work. Make notes and write a comment. Look at the situation from the point of view of an employee and suggest how things might be improved.

5 A PANEL DISCUSSION

A You are going to take part in the panel discussion announced below. Before you start, brainstorm some of the topics and questions that are likely to come up. Make a list on the board.

10.30 *As far as I'm concerned ... with Chris Mahoney*

Strikes: Who wins, who loses?
They've been in the news once again: striking post office workers, teachers, transport workers. Although cabin crew got what they wanted, the latest strike at Britain's airports disrupted travelling. Join Chris Mahoney and guests this evening.

How can strikers ensure that the man in the street will support them?
What does a strike do to the economy?
Why do workers always go on strike just before/over the holidays? Is that fair to travellers?

B Now, work in groups of five. Decide who is going to be the moderator and distribute the other roles below. Put your points across in a serious manner and respond politely to the other participants. The useful phrases on page 59 will help you.

Partner A: The moderator. Go to file 8 on page 176.
Partner B: A CEO. Go to file 15 on page 179.
Partner C: An employee. Go to file 23 on page 181.
Partner D: A member of the audience. Go to file 6 on page 175.
Partner E: A union representative. Go to file 27 on page 182.

> Phrases, p. 59
> Skills, p. 210

C Two days after the panel discussion, the newspaper review of the programme appeared in the local press. The reviewer was critical about a lot of what was said on air. Write as the character you played and justify what you said. If you were the moderator, describe why the programme was a success.

D Scenario

Situation: Während der darauffolgenden Radtoursaison häufen sich seitens vieler deutscher Kunden, die Radtouren in Großbritannien gebucht haben, Beschwerden über die Qualität der Leihräder, die von South Riding Tours Ltd zur Verfügung gestellt wurden. Die Beschwerden werden individuell an South Riding Tours Ltd weitergeleitet, wo sie meistens zur Zufriedenheit der Kunden bearbeitet werden. Trotzdem sind Herr Gerland und Frau Dogan der Meinung, dass dies ein grundsätzliches Problem darstellt. Dieses soll mit South Riding Tours diskutiert und gelöst werden.

1 Herr Gerland bittet Sie, einen formellen Brief in englischer Sprache an Herrn South von South Riding Tours anhand unten stehender Angaben zu formulieren.

Notizen für Brief an Richard South:
- *mit Zusammenarbeit in der abgelaufenen Saison grundsätzlich zufrieden*
- *Situation und die hiermit verbundenen Probleme schildern*
- *Fly Bike Werke GmbH ernsthaft beunruhigt, weil ...*
  - *unzufriedene Kunden = weniger Kunden für Fahrradtouren, sowohl in GB als in D*
  - *schlecht für Image von FBW GmbH, gerade als "Fahrrad"-Firma*
  - *mögliche negative Auswirkungen auf das Kerngeschäft Fahrräder*
- *um Stellungnahme bzw. Lösungsvorschläge bitten*

2 Vier Tage später bekommt Herr Gerland folgende Antwort von Richard South. Er bittet Sie, den Inhalt des Briefes auf Deutsch für die Geschäftsführung und Frau Dogan zusammenzufassen.

Dear Ralf

Thank you for your letter of 18 September in which you raise a number of points about the standard of the hire bikes that we use for our tours in UK. I am very sorry that you feel this is a serious problem.

According to our records, there were only 12 individual complaints about our bikes during the whole season. Admittedly, most of these complaints came from German customers, who are less likely to transport their own bikes to use in UK. On the other hand, our British customers seem to be very happy with the quality of the bikes we use.

The complaints have been dealt with individually, usually resulting in either a refund of part of the cost or a voucher that can be used when booking for next year. There have been no further complaints from these customers.

We have been running our UK tours for several years now. While some of the equipment is no longer brand new, we check the cycles regularly and replace any that are no longer up to standard. I am sure you will appreciate that it would be too expensive – and we consider it unnecessary – to replace all our bikes with new models for next season.

I would like to assure you that we are monitoring the situation and that we always do our best to keep our German customers satisfied.

Yours sincerely
Richard
Richard South
Managing Director

3 **Nach der Lektüre des Briefes ist Herr Gerland überzeugt, dass Richard South die Bedenken von Fly Bike Werke nicht ernst genug nimmt, und er informiert ihn per E-Mail, dass er das Thema beim gemeinsamen jährlichen Treffen (diesmal in Oldenburg) auf die Tagesordnung setzen möchte.**

Arbeiten Sie in Vierergruppen. Die zwei Firmen beraten zuerst getrennt und stecken ihre Position zu dem Thema untereinander ab.

Partner A und B: Sie sind Richard South und Lily Allen von South Riding Tours Ltd. Sie sehen keine Notwendigkeit, das Thema ausführlich zu diskutieren.
- Formulieren Sie noch einmal Ihre Argumente zu dieser Frage.
- Überlegen Sie trotzdem, wie Sie die Bedenken von Fly Bike Werke GmbH entkräften können.

Partner C und D: Sie sind Ralf Gerland und Sylvia Dogan von Fly Bike Werke GmbH. Sie sind überzeugt, dass South Riding Tours Ltd die möglichen Auswirkungen von schlecht gewarteten Leihrädern auf das Geschäft unterschätzt.
- Formulieren Sie noch einmal Ihre Argumente zu dieser Frage.
- Überlegen Sie, wie Sie South Riding Tours Ltd veranlassen können, das Problem ernst zu nehmen.

4 **Beim jährlichen Herbsttreffen der beiden Firmen in Oldenburg wird das Problem nun in der Gesprächsrunde auf Englisch diskutiert. Arbeiten Sie wieder in Vierergruppen: Jede Seite (die Gäste aus England zuerst!) sollte zunächst ihre Position darlegen. Danach sollten Sie versuchen, Lösungsvorschläge zu machen und einen Konsens zu finden, der für beide Seiten zufriedenstellend ist.**

Appendix

Files

FILE 1 Topic 1, Part E, Exercise 3, p. 27

Partner A
You *(your own name)*

- Answer the phone with the words 'Ja, hallo?'
- Confirm that you are ... (*own name*).
- Say you will be happy to answer Ms Chandler's questions.
- Give your own answers to her questions.
- Ask your own question(s).
- Thank Ms Chandler for calling.

FILE 2 Topic 2, Part C, Exercise 7, p. 53

Partner A
Unemployed teenager

- You went to a vocational training college and did a commercial course with foreign languages.
- You have written 50 job applications and found nothing.
- You have been to three job fairs without finding a job.
- The only money you get is from your parents.
- You have little or no social life.
- You can't buy new clothes and you can't go on holiday with your friends.
- All you want is a job: you don't care what sort of company it is.

FILE 3 Topic 5, Part D, Exercise 2D, p. 148

Partner B

You are the booking clerk at Hotel Vanadisvägen in Stockholm, Sweden. You take a telephone booking from Michael/Michaela Lorenz. Pass on the following details:

Dates:	Available
Rooms:	Available
Meals:	Half board costs €30 per person per day.
Conference room:	Only large conference room (20 seats) available. €50 per day.
Internet:	Free wifi throughout the hotel
Payment:	All major credit cards accepted
Questions:	All rooms are en suite rooms with a shower
	Free parking (underground car park)
	Special discount of 10% if the booking is made today

FILE 4 Topic 2, Part B, Exercise 5, p. 40

Partner A

You believe the following things:
- Firing your workers would be unfair. They helped build the company!
- Firing them would be unwise. Quality would suffer. Excellent customer service must be the top priority and your full-timers do it best.
- People in poorer countries work for 'slave wages'. You don't want to support this.
- Overseas companies have cultures that are different from yours. This would create problems with communication and productivity.

FILE 5 Topic 5, Part E, Exercises 4 and 5, p. 152

Role A (with Dr. Alexander Mieberg)

Background

You are Jonathan Sykes.
- You have just flown over to Düsseldorf from the UK.
- You had a bad flight with a lot of turbulence.
- You would like a cup of tea – white, no sugar.
- You are happy with your hotel in Neuss. It is very comfortable.
- You exchange business cards.

Role B (With Sevda Yildiz)

Background

You are Amanda Lakely.
- You have just flown from Paris to Düsseldorf at the last minute to attend the Igedo fashion fair.
- Your flight was half an hour late but otherwise it was fine.
- You would like a glass of mineral water.
- You thank Sevda for booking you a hotel. You had no time to book a hotel yourself.
- You exchange business cards.

FILE 6 Topic 6, Part C, Exercise 5B, p. 170

Partner D

You are a member of the audience. You can understand strikers even though you've been affected twice by striking airport ground staff. Once, you and your family were stranded abroad; the second time, you were on your way to an important business meeting.

FILE 7 Topic 1, Part E, Exercise 3, p. 27

Partner B
Ms Angela Chandler, Recruitment Director, Travel and Tourism Services UK

- Place a call to (Partner A's first name and surname).
- Explain that you have received A's application and are interested but have a few questions.
- Ask if A has ever been to the UK.
- Ask if A has ever done work like this before.
- Ask if A finds it easy to get on with people.
- Ask how A's friends and teachers would describe him/her.
- Ask about A's plans for the future.
- Ask if A has any questions.
- Finish the telephone conversation politely.

FILE 8 Topic 6, Part C, Exercise 5B, p. 170

Partner A
Chris Mahoney – moderator

Before you start, choose five to six questions (or topics) from the list on the board and make notes. Think of more questions to ask, if necessary.
During the discussion, direct each question first at the person who is most likely to have the answer.
Respond appropriately to the answers and guide the discussion carefully.
Make sure that everyone has a fair chance to speak.

FILE 9 Topic 3, Focus, Exercise 3, p. 62

Percentage of 13- to 20-year-olds
who think the brand is important, by product

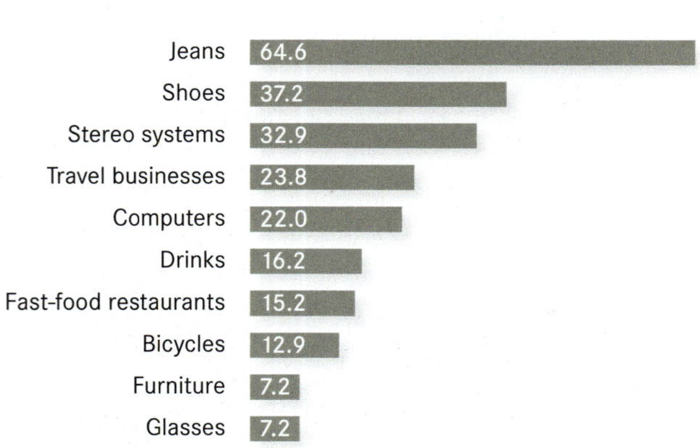

Source: Youngcom!
© Handelsblatt-Grafik

FILE 10 Topic 5, Part B, Exercise 3C, p. 140

Partner B

You are Rob Heldof. It is 10 a.m. You're staying at the Hotel Santa Teresa in Rio with Katie (your girlfriend) when your mobile rings. It is Natasha Merck, the famous German model. She is in Rio, too. You are surprised and ask what brings her to Rio. She explains and suggests some times to meet. Use Rob's diary below to make an appointment.

Rob Heldof's diary

Thursday	08/05/20...
Time	**Appointments**
09:00 am	9.05 am Arrive DUS
10:00 am	SLEEP!
11:00 am	SLEEP!
12:00 am	SLEEP!
01:00 pm	
02:00 pm	Shopping with Katie
03:00 pm	Shopping with Katie
04:00 pm	Shopping with Katie
05:00 pm	
06:00 pm	Talk about new album with agent
07:00 pm	Skype call to Mum in Ireland
08:00 pm	
09:00 pm	Dinner at Zero Zero night club
10:00 pm	Dinner at Zero Zero night club
11:00 pm	Dinner at Zero Zero night club
00:00 pm	
Priority High Low	**To do**
Don't forget	
ACT POSITIVE!	

Rob Heldof's diary

Friday	09/05/20...
Time	**Appointments**
09:00 am	SLEEP!
10:00 am	SLEEP!
11:00 am	SLEEP!
12:00 am	
01:00 pm	Rehearsal with Brazilian band
02:00 pm	Rehearsal with Brazilian band
01:00 pm	Rehearsal with Brazilian band
02:00 pm	
03:00 pm	Visit to Corcorvado
04:00 pm	Visit to Corcorvado
05:00 pm	Visit to Corcorvado
06:00 pm	
07:00 pm	Guest appearance on
08:00 pm	Show do Milhão
09:00 pm	(Who Wants to be a Millionaire?)
10:00 pm	
Priority High Low	**To do**
Don't forget	
THINK POSITIVE!	

FILE 11 Topic 2, Part B, Exercise 5, p. 40

Partner B

You believe that the only way the company can survive is to outsource your customer service department.
All your competitors are saving money this way.
You also believe global outsourcing makes the world a fairer place. Why should workers here have such luxury when workers in poorer countries have it so hard?
You argue from the perspective of the workers overseas. They need work, and they deserve it just as much as people here.

FILE 12 Topic 4, Part C, Exercise 3, p. 100

Rolle B
Sevda Yildiz, Brixmode, Deutschland

- Vorstellung (Firmenname, Begrüßung)
- Bitte um Gespräch mit Herrn Mittal
- Ihre Nachricht:
  - Sie haben Herrn Mittal letzten Monat auf der Igedo-Modemesse in Düsseldorf kennen gelernt.
  - Interesse an modischen Damen- und Herrentops
  - Alle Größen
  - Preise, Liefer- und Zahlungsbedingungen und Lieferzeiten?
  - Alle Angaben möglichst bald
- Höflicher Schluss

FILE 13 Topic 2, Part C, Exercise 7, p. 53

Partner C
Owner of a clothes manufacturing company

- There is intense competition in your field.
- You have to keep prices low or go out of business.
- Your goods are produced in Bangladesh because the prices there are lowest.
- Your company gives work to poor people.
- There are safety checks at the factories in Bangladesh once a year.
- Your Bangladeshi agent has checked your factories and taken photographs of all the safety precautions (fire extinguishers, emergency exits, etc.).
- You intend to travel to Bangladesh soon and see for yourself.
- If you don't use the factories in Bangladesh, another western manufacturer will.

FILE 14 Topic 5, Part B, Exercise 3A, p. 140

Partner B

Sie sind Rob Heldof. Es ist 16:00 Uhr am Donnerstagnachmittag. Sie sind gerade aufgewacht und haben noch Jetlag. Sie erhalten einen Anruf von Britt Elsner, der berühmten deutschen Talkshow-Moderatorin. Sie möchte, dass Sie morgen in ihrer Sendung im Frühstücksfernsehen erscheinen, also holen Sie Ihren Kalender und schauen sich Freitag, 02. Mai an. Ihr erster Terminvorschlag ist für Sie zu früh. Fragen Sie auch, wer sonst noch in der Sendung ist. Besprechen Sie ihre Vorschläge für ein paar Minuten, dann vereinbaren Sie mit ihr einen viel späteren Zeitpunkt in der Sendung. Akzeptieren Sie nicht gleich Britt Elsners ersten oder zweiten Vorschlag!

FILE 15 Topic 6, Part C, Exercise 5B, p. 170

Partner B

You are the CEO of a manufacturing company which might have to shut down very soon. The economy is very bad at the moment and no one is buying your goods. The only way you can hope to stay open is to lay off some workers and keep the company going until the economic situation improves.

FILE 16 Topic 5, Part D, Exercise 3A, p. 148

Rolle B
Oliver Carter

- 09.–13.02.20..
- Sie möchten ein Drei- oder Vier-Sterne- Hotel in zentraler Lage, damit sie den Karnevalszug *(procession)* besser sehen können.
- Sie finden die Lage gut und fragen, was sie kosten.
- Fragen Sie nach der Verpflegung und Zimmerausstattung.
- Weitere Fragen nach Wahl
- Sie werden sich mit Peter Jones unterhalten und sich wieder melden.
- Sie bedanken sich für die Hilfe.

FILE 17 Topic 3, Part C, Exercise 4B, p. 77

Partner A
Al Winters

- You thought Miele had forgotten you.
- It's eight o'clock in the morning and you haven't opened your store or checked your e-mail yet.
- You need to get a pen to write down the details.
- You ask about delivery.
- You ask for a phone number for Miele.

FILE 18 Topic 6, Part A, Exercise 1D, p. 161

Partner A

You are Dan.

- You believe that Mrs Patterson is harassing you and you have always done your best at work.
- Use the notes you prepared for task A to respond to any questions or statements from Mrs Patterson and Mrs Patterson's supervisor.
- Remember to remain polite throughout the discussion.

FILE 19 Topic 2, Part C, Exercise 7, p. 53

Partner B

Public relations manager of a big supermarket chain

- A green image is a must.
- Pollution is still a big problem.
- It is your duty to tell the public that your company takes pollution seriously.
- Your company only uses suppliers who treat their employees fairly.
- You regularly visit your overseas suppliers to check their standards.
- At Head Office in Germany you save energy, recycle paper, have online meetings instead of travelling long distances, have solar panels on the roof to save energy and use gas-powered vehicles.
- Your company supports charities all over the world.

FILE 20 Topic 4, Part C, Exercise 1B, p. 99

Memo

An: ...

Von: ...

Datum: ...

Betreff: ...

FILE 21 Topic 5, Part A, Exercise 5B, p. 136

Partner B

You are Nina Wittstock, the CEO of Top Act Event Management. Today you phone a famous American rapper called DJ 60 Cent. Follow the steps below to play your role. (Partner A has steps 1, 3, 5 and 7.)

2 Say who you are and ask to speak to DJ 60 Cent.

4 Ask if he has received the contract.

6 React with enthusiasm and say it was nice talking to him.

8 Finish the call.

FILE 22 Topic 6, Part A, Exercise 1D, p. 161

Partner B

You are Mrs Patterson.

- You are sorry that you embarrassed Dan in front of his colleagues, but you still think he is lazy and incompetent.
- You think that he doesn't listen and doesn't follow instructions.
- You believe that he does't respect authority.
- You expect your manager to support you in all your decisions.

FILE 23 Topic 6, Part C, Exercise 5B, p. 170

Partner C

You are an employee who is currently on strike. Prices are rising all around, but you and your fellow strikers have not had a pay rise for five years. Some months ago, your union agreed to take a cut in pay in order to help the company survive. Things have not improved and now there are talks of layoffs.

FILE 24 Topic 5, Part B, Exercise 3B, p. 140

Partner B

You are Rob Heldof. It is 10.30 a.m. and you have already checked out of your hotel in Düsseldorf. Your flight to Rio leaves Düsseldorf Airport at 1.30 p.m. and you have to check in by 11.30 a.m. You have just bought a pair of designer sunglasses at a shop in Düsseldorf and you and your girlfriend Katie are about to go to the airport by car. You get a phone call from Father Hubert, who wants you to autograph a T-shirt for charity. Explain why you cannot meet where he suggests and agree to meet him in the airport's VIP Lounge at about 11 a.m.

FILE 25 Topic 2, Part B, Exercise 5, p. 40

Partner C

You believe that it is necessary to cut costs.
You want to keep the customer service department in-house.
Your plan:

- Let the full-time employees go.
- Offer the same workers freelance work, without benefits like health insurance, etc.
- Offer them more flexibility, e.g. work part-time or from home.
- If some do not accept the offer, find other local freelancers.

FILE 26 Topic 6, Part A, Exercise 1D, p. 161

Partner C

You are Mrs Patterson's manager and boss.
- You believe that Dan tries his best.
- You think Mrs Patterson is expecting too much from him.
- Ask Dan if he thinks Mrs Patterson is giving him too much responsibility.
- Try to persuade Mrs Patterson to be less strict with Dan.

FILE 27 Topic 6, Part C, Exercise 5B, p. 170

Partner E

You are a union representative. You believe that a strike is the final option. You always try to reach agreement through discussion and negotiation first, but if a company isn't willing to make concessions, you will call a strike.

FILE 28 Scenarios, Information: Fly Bike Werke Gmbh

Die Fly Bike Werke GmbH

1 Unternehmensportrait

Jan Ullmann und Björn Ries, die Gesellschafter der Fly Bike Werke GmbH, sind seit frühester Jugend befreundet und hatten immer ein gemeinsames Hobby, das Radrennfahren. Die Väter der beiden Amateur-Rennfahrer waren schon frühzeitig im Fahrradmarkt ambitioniert. Dirk Ries, Vater von Björn Ries, betrieb in Oldenburg einen Fahrradeinzelhandel, wobei Rennräder für den Amateurbereich einen Schwerpunkt in seinem Sortiment darstellten. Klaus Ullmann, Vater von Jan Ullmann, produzierte in Oldenburg Standardfahrradrahmen aus Stahl für die Fahrradindustrie. Die Erfahrungen, die Jan Ullmann als Hobbysportler gesammelt hatte, ließen sich gut mit dem Knowhow seines Vaters kombinieren. Die Geschäftsidee, eigene Freizeit-Sporträder aus Stahl zu entwickeln, erschien ihm so vielversprechend, dass er 1982 die Fly Bike Werke GmbH (als so genannte Ein-Mann-GmbH) gründete. Die Aufgaben eines Geschäftsführers übertrug er an den ebenfalls radsportbegeisterten Hans Peters.
Der Zwang zu modernen Fertigungsmethoden und die damit verbundenen Investitionen erhöhten den Kapitalbedarf zum Ende des ausgehenden Jahrhunderts erheblich. Da traf es sich gut, dass Jan Ullmann seinen alten Freund Björn Ries bei einem Radrennen traf und von seinen Sorgen erzählte. Der aufgrund eines erfolgreichen Berufslebens vermögende Björn Ries war spontan bereit, sich an der Fly Bike Werke GmbH zu beteiligen, und trat Anfang 2001 als weiterer Gesellschafter in die GmbH ein.

Modellunternehmen Fly Bike Werke GmbH		
Rechtsform und Unternehmensgröße, Handelsregistereintrag	Gesellschaft mit beschränkter Haftung (GmbH) Kleine Kapitalgesellschaft gem. § 267 HGB Oldenburg HRB 2134	
Gesellschafter und Geschäftsanteile	Herr Jan Ullmann 200.000,00 €	Herr Björn Ries 100.000,00 €
Geschäftsführer	Herr Hans Peters	
Geschäftsjahr	Kalenderjahr (01. 01. bis 31. 12.)	
Umsatz Berichtsjahr	Ca. 6,9 Mio. €	
Kontakt	Post- und Lieferadresse: Rostocker Str. 334, 26121 Oldenburg Telefon: 0441 885-0 Telefax: 0441 885-9211 Internet: www.flybike.de E-Mail: mail@flybike.de	
Absatzprogramm	Produktionsprogramm	Fahrräder: City-Räder, Mountainbikes, Rennräder, Jugendräder, Trekkingräder
	Handelswaren	Fahrradbekleidung, Fahrradzubehör, Fahrradanhänger
	Dienstleistungen	Vermittlung von Fahrradreisen
Stoffe, Vorprodukte, Fremdbauteile (Beispiele)	Rohstoffe	Rohre und Bleche aus Stahl und Aluminium
	Hilfsstoffe	Farben und Grundierungen, Schrauben und Kleinteile
	Betriebsstoffe	Strom, Gas, Wasser, Heizöl, Schmierstoffe
	Vorprodukte, Fremdbauteile	Räder, Beleuchtung, Sättel, Spezialrahmen, Federgabeln
Fertigungstypen und Fertigungsarten	Fließ- bzw. Gruppenfertigung Werkstattfertigung (Rennräder-Profi) Serienfertigung Einzelfertigung (Rennräder-Profi)	
Technische Anlagen und Maschinen (Beispiele)	Universalroboter, Rohrschneideanlage, Rahmenrichtmaschine, Schleifmaschine, Schweißmaschine, Montagebänder, Verpackungsanlage, Lackierautomaten	
Mitarbeiter	1 Geschäftsführer, 37 Arbeitnehmer	
Kunden	Großhändler, Filialisten, Cash-and-Carry-Märkte im Inland, Großhändler im Ausland	
Lieferanten	Industriebetriebe und Spezialgroßhändler im In- und Ausland	
Verbände	Oldenburgische Industrie- und Handelskammer, Oldenburg (Pflichtmitgliedschaft); NORDMETALL e. V., Hamburg, Geschäftsstelle Oldenburg, Bezirksgruppe Nordwest (Arbeitgeberverband)	

2 Absatzprogramm, Kunden, Preise

Das **Produktionsprogramm** umfasst zurzeit zwölf verschiedene Fahrradmodelle. Das Produktionsprogramm wird durch Handelswaren und Dienstleistungen zum **Absatzprogramm** erweitert.

City-Rad Modell 102 Surf

Rennrad Modell 401 Renn Fast

Mountainbike Modell 302 Constitution

Kinderrad Modell 502 Cool

Produktionsprogramm			
Modell	**Artikel-Nr.**	**Modell-Name**	**unverbindl. Preis**
City-Räder	101	City *Glide*	245,00 €
	102	City *Surf*	274,40 €
Trekkingräder	201	Trekking *Light*	299,25 €
	202	Trekking *Free*	350,00 €
	203	Trekking *Nature*	437,50 €
Mountainbikes	301	Mountain *Dispo*	393,75 €
	302	Mountain *Constitution*	598,50 €
	303	Mountain *Unlimited*	997,50 €
Rennräder	401	Renn *Fast*	1.260,00 €
	402	Renn *Superfast*	2.205,00 €
Kinderräder	501	Kinder *Twist*	196,88 €
	502	Kinder *Cool*	262,50 €

Handelswaren und Dienstleistungsangebote der Fly Bike Werke		
Handelswaren	Textilien aus Goretex (x = Größen S, M, L, XL, XXL)	701 x Shirts *STEFF superfast* 702 x Shorts *STEFF superfast* 703 x Jacketts *STEFF superfast*
	Fahrradanhänger	601 Modell *Kelly* 602 Modell *Mini* 603 Modell *Max* 604 Modell Kids 605 Modell *Sven*
Dienstleistungen	Vermittlung von Radtouren/Reisen (Veranstalter: UIT und Rebbel)	901 Brandenburg und Mecklenburg-Vorpommern (Alleestraßen) 902 Rheinland-Pfalz (Mosel/Saar) 903 Niedersachsen (Nordsee) 904 Südtirol (Pässetour, Teilnahme an Dolomiti Open) 905 Toskana (Kultur, Tour und Mee(h)r) 906 Schweiz (Pässetour)

Kunden der Fly Bike Werke	
Einzelhandel	Umsatzstarke Fachhandelsunternehmen mit eigenen Filialen und abgegrenzten Vertriebsgebieten in Deutschland
Großhandel national	Fahrradgroßhandelsunternehmen, die den Fahrradeinzelhandel in Deutschland beliefern
Großhandel Europa	Je ein Großhändler in Belgien, in den Niederlanden, in Österreich und der Schweiz, die dort landesweit den Fahrradeinzelhandel beliefern
Private-Label-Kunden	Eine Kaufhauskette und ein Cash-and-Carry-Konzern, die Fahrräder unter eigenem Markennamen (Private Label) vertreiben

Die Preise der Fahrräder werden von der Fly Bike Werke GmbH in Preislisten als unverbindliche Preisempfehlungen angegeben (zuzüglich Umsatzsteuer). Auf diese Preise erhalten die Wiederverkäufer (Kunden der Fly Bike Werke) Preisnachlässe in Form von **Rabatten**, **Boni** und **Skonto**. Auftragsfertigungen werden kundenindividuell kalkuliert.

Preisnachlässe	
Rabattstaffel	
Stückzahl	Rabatt
1–10	27,5 %
11–50	29,0 %
51–100	30,0 %
101–250	31,0 %
251–500	32,0 %
> 500	33,0 %
Boni (Jahresboni bezogen auf den Zielverkaufspreis der Gesamtmenge)	
Abnahme von mdst. 1.000 Fahrrädern	1 %
Abnahme von mdst. 5.000 Fahrrädern	2 %
Skonto	
2 % bei Zahlung innerhalb von 8 Tagen	

3 Leistungserstellung

Die Fly Bike Werke GmbH produziert die meisten Fahrradrahmen und Fahrradgabeln selbst.
Der voll gefederte Y-Rahmen des Modells Unlimited wird zurzeit fremdbezogen. Dies gilt auch für die Federgabeln der Modelle Constitution und Unlimited, die von einem amerikanischen Lieferanten bezogen werden. Alle übrigen Teile werden ebenfalls fremdbezogen. Mit den Lieferanten sind hinsichtlich der technischen Spezifikationen der Bauteile und Baugruppen feste Vereinbarungen getroffen worden. Ein Hersteller liefert immer eine komplette Baugruppe (Komponentengruppe), der eine von der Fly Bike Werke GmbH vergebene Set-Nr. (Komponentennummer) zugeordnet wird.
Ein Fahrrad besteht bei Vollausstattung aus bis zu über 1000 Einzelteilen. Der Fly Bike Werke GmbH ist es in Zusammenarbeit mit ihren Lieferanten gelungen, die notwendigen Teile in Baugruppen so zusammenzufassen, dass die Baugruppe (Komponente) komplett von einem Lieferanten zur Verfügung gestellt werden kann. Der Weltmarktführer für Fahrradteile, Tamino Inc., liefert z. B. für das Modell Dispo alle Teile für die Komponenten „Räder und Schaltung", „Antrieb" und „Bremsen". Das positive Image bestimmter Teilehersteller wird bei den Endverbrauchern auf das Fertigprodukt Fahrrad übertragen. Zu diesen Teileherstellern zählen z. B.

- Tamino Inc., Japan: (Ketten-)Schaltungen, Antriebe, Bremsen
- Dax AG, Deutschland: (Naben-)Schaltungen, Antriebe, Bremsen
- Sella SA, Italien: Sättel
- Shokk Ltd., USA: Federgabeln

4 Organigramm

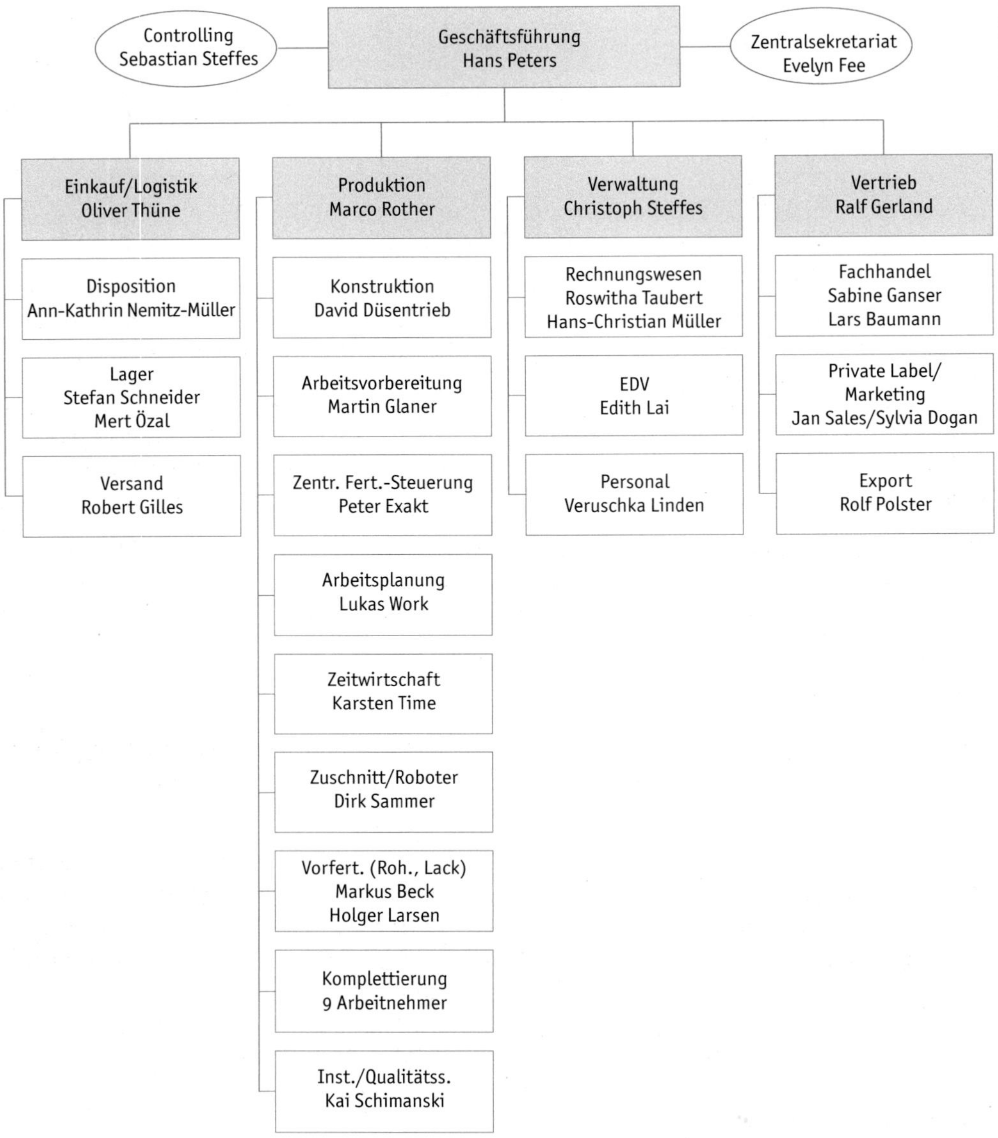

Sicherheitsbeauftragter: Peter Exakt
Umweltbeauftragter: Oliver Thüne
Qualitätsbeauftragter: Kai Schimanski
Datenschutzbeauftragter: Christoph Steffes
Betriebsratsmitglieder: Sabine Ganser, Thomas Preis, Saskia Engel
technischer Auszubildender: Ralf Schumacher
kfm. Auszubildende: Bettina Lotto

Glossary of business terms

TYPES OF BUSINESS ORGANIZATION

In the **EU**, there are two basic types of company, the **private limited company** (GB: Ltd; German: *GmbH*) and the **public limited company** (GB: plc; German: AG). In the **USA** and **Canada** there are three types of company, as follows:

Incorporated company (Inc.) There is no exact equivalent of an incorporated company in the EU. 'Incorporated' simply means 'registered as a company'. It does not say anything about ownership or liability, or capitalization.

Close corporation (Corp.) This is the North American equivalent of the British Ltd and German *GmbH*. Close corporations have a small number of shareholders (here: *Gesellschafter/in*) and do not offer their shares on the stock market (*Börse*).

Open corporation (Corp.) The North American equivalent of the British PLC and German *AG*. Open corporations usually have numerous shareholders (here: *Aktienbesitzer/in*), often other corporations, and sell their shares on the stock market.

In **South Africa**, **Australia** and **New Zealand** the equivalents of the British Ltd and plc are **limited proprietary company** (Pty Ltd) and **proprietary company** (Pty).

TERMS OF DELIVERY

Incoterms 2010

As trade becomes more and more global, goods travel further and further, crossing geographical, cultural and language barriers on their way. For this reason is essential that importers and exporters agree to use the same terms of reference.

In 1936 the International Chamber of Commerce in Paris invented a set of International Commercial Terms (Incoterms) to define importers' and exporters' rights and obligations, such as transport costs, risk, insurance, customs duty, documentation, loading and unloading. Since then the Incoterms have been revised eight times to keep up with developments in the field of international trade and translated into many different languages. The last revision was in 2010. There are now eleven Incoterms, seven of which can be used for any mode or combined modes of transport, e.g. truck, train, ship or rail. The other four are used for ship or inland waterway transport only.

Rules for any mode or modes of transport

1
EXW (EX WORKS)
Ab Werk
The seller makes the goods available at his premises. The buyer bears all the costs and risks of transporting the goods to their destination.

2
FCA (FREE CARRIER)
Frei Frachtführer
The seller loads the goods on board the first carrier's vehicle. The buyer bears all the costs and risks of transporting the goods to their destination.

3
CPT (CARRIAGE PAID TO)
Frachtfrei bis
The seller bears all the costs and risks until the goods are handed over to the first carrier. He pays the transport costs, without insurance, for the main carriage to the named destination. The buyer insures the goods for the main carriage and bears all other costs.

4
CIP (COST AND INSURANCE PAID TO)
Frachtfrei versichert bis
The seller bears all the costs and risks until the goods are handed over to the first carrier. He pays the transport costs, including insurance, for the main carriage to the named destination. The buyer bears all other costs.

5
DAP (DELIVERED AT PLACE)
Geliefert benannter Ort
The seller bears all the costs and risks until the goods have reached their destination. The buyer is responsible for import duties and unloading the goods.

6
DAT (DELIVERED AT TERMINAL)
Geliefert Terminal
The seller bears all the costs and risks until the goods have reached the terminal and is also responsible for unloading them. The buyer bears all other costs.

7
DDP (DELIVERED DUTY PAID)
Geliefert Zoll bezahlt
The seller bears all the costs and risks until the goods have reached their destination, including import duties. The buyer is responsible for unloading the goods.

Rules for sea and inland waterway transport

8
FAS (FREE ALONGSIDE SHIP)
Frei Längsseite Schiff
The seller delivers the goods alongside the ship at the port of shipment. The buyer bears all the costs and risks of transporting the goods to their destination.

9
FOB (FREE ON BOARD)
Frei an Bord
The seller delivers the goods on board the ship at the port of shipment. The buyer bears all the costs and risks of transporting the goods to their destination.

10
CFR (COST AND FREIGHT)
Kosten und Fracht
The seller delivers the goods on board the ship at the port of shipment. He pays the transport costs, without insurance, for the main carriage to the port of destination. The buyer insures the goods for the main carriage and bears all other costs.

11
CIF (COST, INSURANCE AND FREIGHT (... named port of destination))
Kosten, Versicherung und Fracht
The seller bears all the costs and risks until the goods are delivered on board the ship at the port of shipment. He pays the transport costs, including insurance, to the named port of destination. The buyer bears all other costs.

INCOTERMS 2010

RULES FOR ANY MODE OR MODES OF TRANSPORT

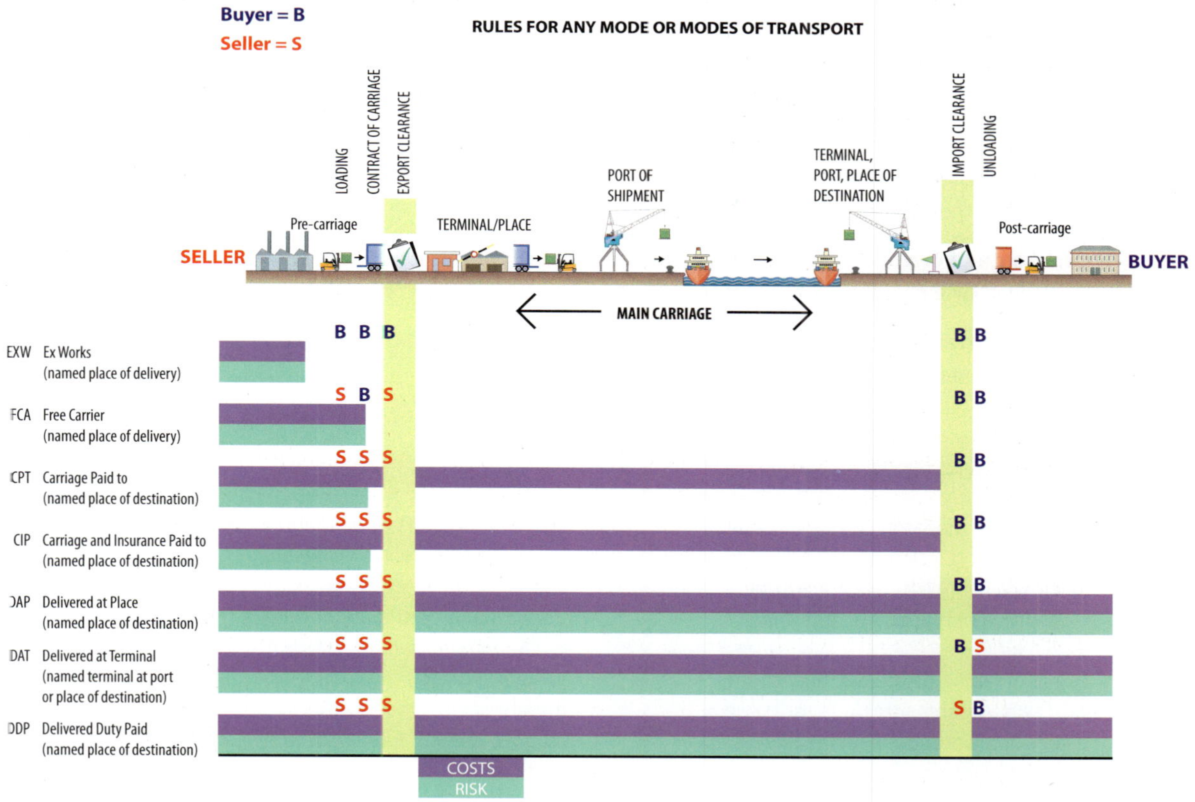

INCOTERMS 2010

RULES FOR SEA AND INLAND WATERWAY TRANSPORT

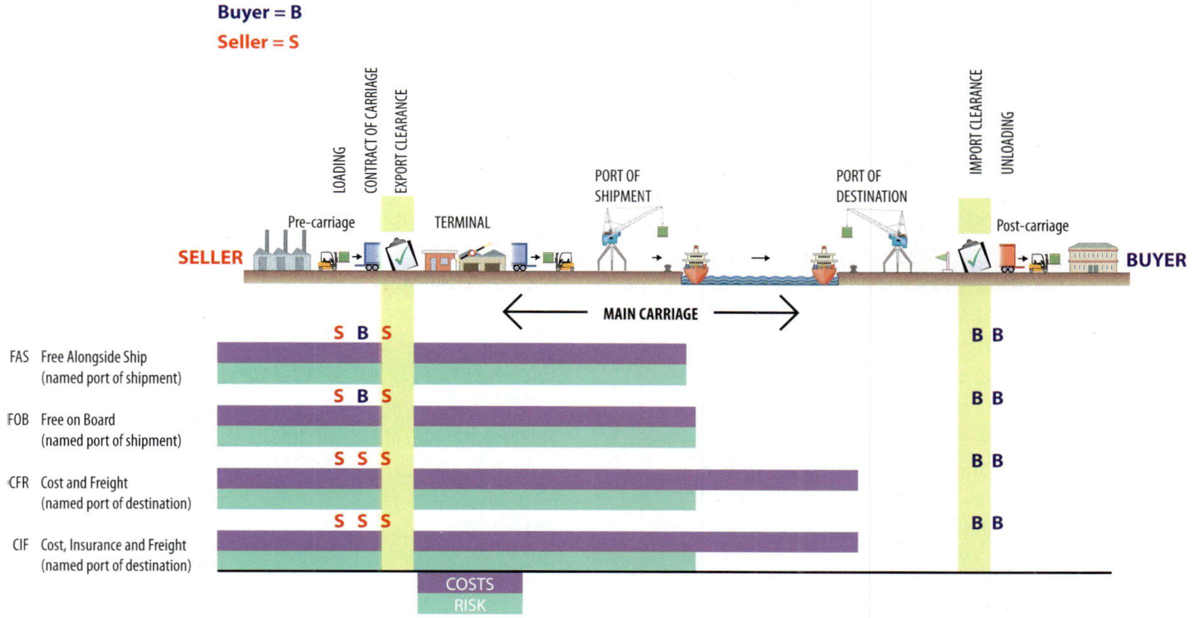

SHIPPING DOCUMENTS

Air waybill (AWB) The airline issues the air waybill to the consignor/exporter of the goods. It is a receipt for the goods and a contract of carriage. It is not a document of title (see Document of title). A copy accompanies the goods to their destination.

Bill of lading (B/L, plural Bs/L) The shipping company issues the bill of lading to the consignor/exporter of the goods. It is a document of title, a receipt for the goods and a contract of carriage. It is described as 'clean' if the goods are in apparent good order and 'foul' if they are not. A copy accompanies the goods to their destination.

Certificate of origin A certificate of origin shows which country the goods are from. It is issued by a chamber of commerce in the exporter's country.

Combined transport waybill This document is used for multi-modal transport, e.g. a container sent by road-sea-road.

English → German

advice of dispatch *Versandanzeige*
airfreight *Luftfracht*
air waybill (AWB) *Luftfrachtbrief*
approval: on approval *zur Ansicht, auf Probe*
bill of lading (B/L) *Seefrachtbrief, Konnossement*
bonded warehouse *Zollverschlusslager*
cargo *Ladung, Fracht*
cargo liner *Frachtschiff*
cargo space *Frachtraum*
certificate of origin (C/O) *Ursprungszeugnis*
chamber of (industry and commerce *(Industrie- und) Handelskammer*
combined transport waybill *kombinierter Warenbegleitschein*
commercial invoice *Handelsrechnung*
consignment note [road or rail] *Frachtbrief [Straßen- oder Bahn-]*
consignee *Empfänger/in*
consignor *Absender/in, Versender/in*
consular invoice *Konsularrechnung, Konsultatsfaktura*
contract of carriage *Beförderungsvertrag*
customs clearance *Zollabfertigung*
customs declaration *Zollinhaltserklärung*
customs invoice *Zollrechnung, Zollfaktura*
dangerous goods certificate *Gefahrgutbescheinigung*
delivery note *Lieferschein*
destination; port of destination *Bestimmungsort; Bestimmungshafen*
export licence *Exportlizenz*
forwarder's certificate of receipt (FCR) *Spediteurübernahmebescheinigung*
freight *Fracht*
freight rates *Frachttarife*
import licence *Einfuhrgenehmigung*
to take out insurance *eine Versicherung abschließen*
insurance certificate (IC) *Versicherungsschein, -police*
to insure goods against a risk *Ware gegen ein Risiko versichern*
to issue *ausstellen, ausfertigen*
loss; total or partial loss *Verlust; Gesamt- oder Teilverlust*
packing list *Packliste*
pro forma invoice (P/I) *Proforma-Rechnung*
rail consignment note *Bahnfrachtbrief*
receipt *Erhalt; Empfangsbescheinigung*
ro-ro (roll on-roll off) ferry/vessel *von Straßenfahrzeugen befahrbare/s Fähre/Schiff*
shipping note (S/N) *Schiffszettel, Warenbegleitschein*
single administrative document *Einheitspapier*
warehouse *Lager*
waybill (WB) *Frachtbrief*

Commercial invoice This document is a request for payment. It contains details of the goods, the sum to be paid, the terms of delivery and payment and the buyer and seller's addresses.

Consignment note This document is for road or rail transport. It is issued to the consignor/exporter of the goods by the railway or haulage company. It is a receipt for the goods and a contract of carriage. It is not a document of title. A copy accompanies the goods to their destination.

Document of title The holder of a document of title owns the goods described in it. A document of title can be bought or sold without moving the goods from one place to another. It is often used in international trade. A bill of lading is a document of title to a consignment of goods transported by sea.

Insurance certificate This is an extract from the insurance policy. It contains details of the insurer and the insured, the goods insured and the sum for which they are insured. It includes details of the risks covered, the time for which they are covered and any geographical restrictions, e.g. the route to be taken by the ship or plane.

Packing list The packing list is put both inside the container with the goods and on the outside of the container. It lists the goods in the container.

Pro-forma invoice This document shows how much the goods will or would cost. It is not a request for payment. It contains details of the goods, the price, the terms of delivery and payment and the buyer and seller's addresses. It is normally used for a quotation, for payment in advance, for goods sent on approval or to open a letter of credit (Akkreditiv).

Shipping note (S/N) A document signed by the ship's chief officer when goods are taken on board.

Shipping documents This is all the documentation used when exporting goods (commercial invoice, bill of lading, insurance certificate, certificate of origin, etc).

Single administrative document This is a single document describing a consignment of goods issued by the customs authorities. It makes importing and exporting goods within the EU easier. It contains copies for the importer and exporter, the importer's and exporter's customs authorities and for transit through other countries.

PACKAGING

Here is a list of the most common types of packaging used when transporting goods.

German → English

Ballen *bale*
Beutel *bag (small)*
Dose *can; tin*
Fass *barrel*
Flasche *bottle*
Karton *carton*
Kasten *box*
Kiste *box; crate*
Korb *basket*
Laderost *pallet*
Luftpolstertasche *bubble envelope*
Paket *carton; packet*
Pallette *pallet*
Rolle *roll*
Sack *sack*
Schachtel *box*
Seecontainer *sea container*
Tasche *bag (big); pouch (small)*
Tonne *barrel; drum*
Tube *tube*
Umschlag *envelope*

TERMS OF PAYMENT

payment in advance	*Vorauszahlung/Vorkasse*
cash with order (CWO)	*Barzahlung bei Auftragserteilung*
payment by irrevocable and confirmed documentary (letter of) credit	*Zahlung durch unwiderrufliches und bestätigtes Dokumentenakkreditiv*
documents against payment (D/P) / cash against documents (CAD)	*Kasse gegen Dokumente*
cash on delivery (COD)	*gegen Nachnahme*
30% with order, 70% on completion	*30% bei Auftragserteilung, 70% bei Fertigstellung*
⅓ with order, ⅓ on delivery, ⅓ within 30 days after delivery	*⅓ bei Auftragserteilung, ⅓ bei Lieferung, ⅓ innerhalb von 30 Tagen nach Lieferung*
payment within 30/60/90 days from date of invoice	*Zahlung innerhalb von 30/60/90 Tagen nach Rechnungsdatum*
10 days 2%, 30 days net	*Zahlung innerhalb 10 Tagen abzüglich 2 % Skonto oder innerhalb 30 Tagen netto*
payment on receipt of goods	*Zahlung bei Erhalt der Waren*
payment on receipt of invoice	*Zahlung bei Rechnungserhalt*
documents against (three months') acceptance (D/A)	*Dokumente gegen (Dreimonats)akzept*
open account terms with monthly / quarterly settlement	*offenes Zahlungsziel mit monatlicher/ vierteljährlicher Abrechnung*

This diagram shows how attractive the different terms of payment are for the importer and exporter.

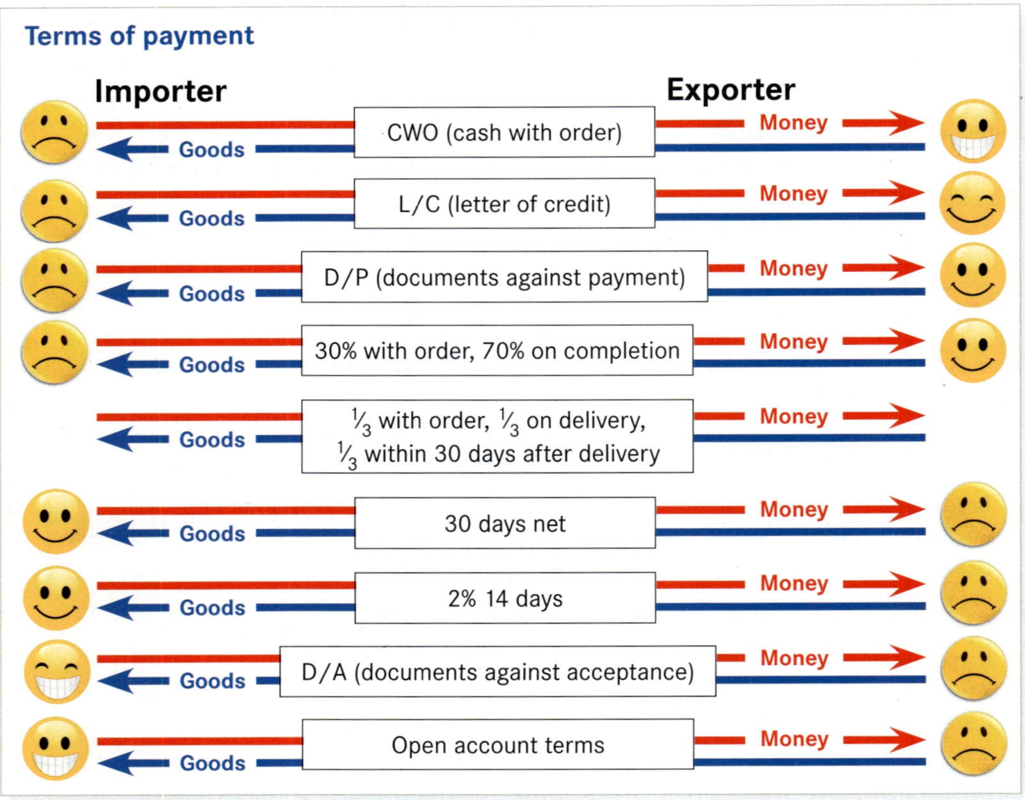

Methods of payment in foreign trade

The most common methods of payment are:

Bank transfer *(Überweisung)* Since the creation of the Single Euro Payments Area (SEPA) in 2008 it has been possible to make international bank transfers electronically between the banks of member states as quickly and cheaply as for domestic transfers. To make an international transfer it is necessary to know the payee's Bank Identifier Code (BIC) and International Bank Account Number (IBAN).

Bill of exchange (B/E) *(Wechsel/Tratte)* A bill of exchange (draft) is a promise by the buyer to pay the seller a sum of money on an agreed date. It is an instrument of payment used in international trade, e.g with a letter of credit or documentary collection.

Cheque *(Scheck)* Cheques (AE: checks) are widely used in North America. They are still used in the United Kingdom, Ireland, and France but losing popularity in favour of electronic means of payment.

Documentary collection *(Dokumenteninkasso)* In this case there is no guarantee of payment. The seller's bank forwards the shipping documents to the buyer's bank and pays the seller when it has received the money from the buyer's bank. With documents against payment (D/P), the buyer's bank gives the buyer the shipping documents if the buyer pays for them immediately. With documents against acceptance (D/A), the buyer's bank gives the buyer the shipping documents if the buyer promises to pay for them later (e.g. 30, 60 or 90 days later). In both cases the seller waits longer for payment than with a documentary credit.

Documentary credit *(Dokumentenakkreditiv)* Payment by confirmed and irrevocable documentary credit is the safest method of payment in international trade. In simple terms, the buyer's bank promises to pay the seller's bank if the seller gives his bank the shipping documents for the goods. The buyer's bank stipulates exactly which documents the seller must give to his bank (e.g. the transport document [bill of lading or air waybill or consignment note], the commercial invoice, the certificate of origin, the insurance certificate etc.). The seller gives these documents to his bank. The bank checks them and, if they are correct, pays the seller. The seller's bank now sells the documents to the buyer's bank. The buyer's bank sells the documents to the buyer. The buyer uses them to collect the goods at the port / airport / terminal.

A letter of credit can be *confirmed* and *irrevocable*. If it is *confirmed*, the seller's bank promises to pay the seller as long as the seller gives it documents stipulated by the buyer's bank. If the documentary credit is *irrevocable*, none of the details of the credit can be changed, e.g. the name of the ship, the route, the quantity of goods etc.

See also the diagram on page 194: A documentary credit step by step.

Draft *(Tratte)* (→ Bill of exchange)

PayPal This is an online payment system which can be used in and between many countries all over the world. In China PayPal can only be used for domestic payments.

SWIFT The Society for Worldwide Interbank Financial Telecommunication (SWIFT) is an international network used to transfer funds all over the world. It has data centres in the United States, the Netherlands and Switzerland.

A documentary credit step by step

1 The buyer and seller agree to pay by documentary credit.
2 The buyer instructs his bank to open a documentary credit in the exporter's favour.
3 The buyer's bank opens the documentary credit and instructs the seller's bank to inform the seller which documents are needed.
4 The seller's bank tells the seller which documents he needs.
5 The seller ships the goods.
6 The seller presents the documents stipulated in the documentary credit to his bank.
7 The seller's bank checks the documents and, if they are as stipulated, pays the seller as agreed.
8 The seller's bank sells the documents to the buyer's bank.
9 The buyer's bank sells the documents to the buyer.
10 The buyer uses the documents to collect the goods.

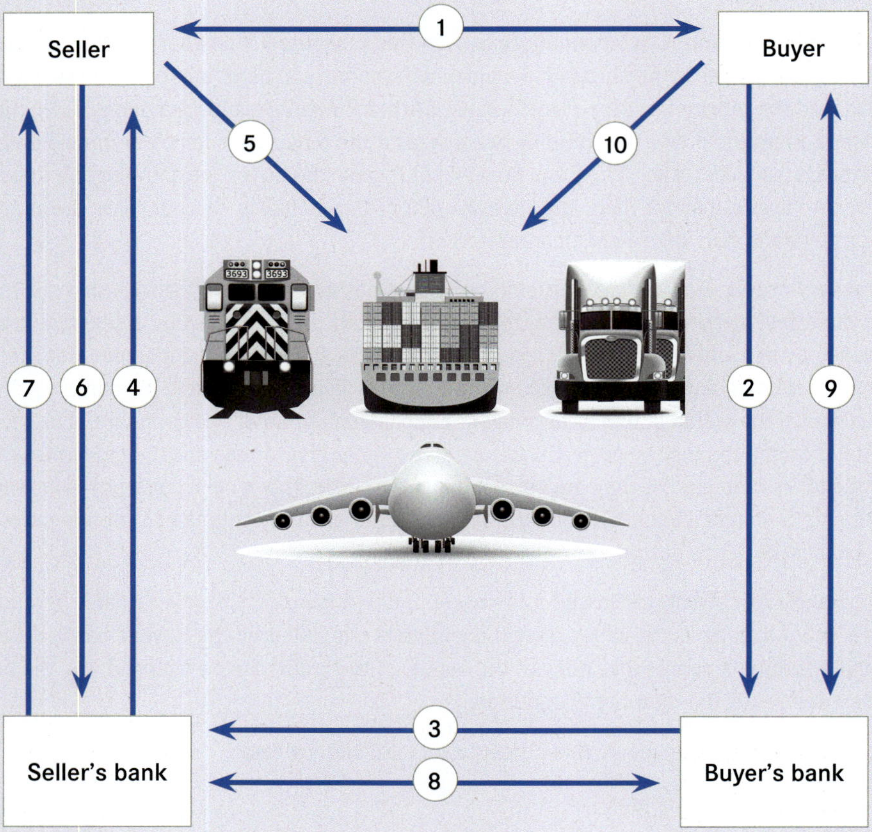

COMMON ABBREVIATIONS

English → German

a/c account *Konto*
a.m. *vormittags* (→ **p.m.**)
AOB any other business *Sonstiges, Verschiedenes [Tagesordnung]*
approx. approximate(ly) *ungefähr*
asap as soon as possible *so bald wie möglich*
attn attention *zu Händen (von) (z. Hd.)*
Ave. *(BE)* **Av.** *(AE)* Avenue *Allee*
AWB air waybill *Luftfrachtbrief*
B/E bill of exchange *Wechsel*
B/L bill of lading *Seefrachtbrief, Konnossement*
bn billion *Milliarde USA*
Bros brothers *Gebrüder*
BST British Summer Time *britische Sommerzeit*
CAD cash against documents *Zahlung gegen Dokumente*
cc carbon copy *Kopie, Durchschrift*
CC Chamber of Commerce *Handelskammer*
CEO Chief Executive Officer *Vorstandsvorsitzende/r*
cf. *vergleiche (vgl.)*
c/o care of *bei [Adresse], zu Händen (von)*
C/O certificate of origin *Ursprungszeugnis*
COD cash on delivery *Zahlung bei Lieferung*
cr credit *Haben; Kredit* (→ **deb**)
CWO cash with order *Zahlung bei Auftragserteilung/Bestellung*
D/A documents against acceptance *Dokumente gegen Wechselakzept*
deb debit *Soll, Debet* (→ **cr**)
dep. departure *Abreise, Abfahrt, Abflug*
Dept department *Abteilung*
D/P documents against payment *Dokumente gegen Zahlung*
Enc(s) enclosure(s) *Anlage(n)*
E&OE errors and omissions excepted *Irrtümer und Auslassungen vorbehalten*
est. established; estimated *gegründet; geschätzt*
ETA estimated time of arrival *voraussichtliche Ankunftzeit*
excl. excluding *ausschließlich, ohne*
ft foot, feet [length] *Fuß [30,48 cm]*
FYI(O) for your information (only) *(nur) zu Ihrer Information*
gal(s). gallon(s) *Gallone(n) [GB: 4,546 l, USA:3,785 l]*
GDP gross domestic product *Bruttoinlandsprodukt*
GMT Greenwich Mean Time *Greenwicher Zeit*
GNP gross national product *Bruttosozialprodukt*
HGV heavy goods vehicle *(Schwer-) Lastfahrzeug*
h.p. horsepower *Pferdestärke(n) (PS) [Kfz]*
IC insurance certificate *Versicherungsschein*
i.e. *das heißt (d. h.)*
incl. including *einschließlich, mit*
IOU I Owe You *Schuldanerkenntnis, Schuldschein*
K thousand *tausend*
lb(s) pound(s) [weight] *Pfund [0,454 kg]*
L/C (plural: Ls/C) letter of credit *Akkreditiv*
m million(s) *Million(en)*
max maximum *Höchst-*
MD Managing Director *Geschäftsführer*
min. minimum *Mindest-*
misc miscellaneous *Verschiedenes*
mpg miles per gallon *Meilen pro Gallone*
mph miles per hour *Meilen pro Stunde*
n/a non-applicable; not available *nicht zutreffend; nicht verfügbar*
no. (nos) number(s) *Nummer(n), Nr.*
oz ounce(s) [weight] *Unze(n) [28,35 g]*
p.a. per annum *pro Jahr*
PA personal assistant
P/A power of attorney *Vertretungsvollmacht*
pd paid *bezahlt*
pls please *bitte*
p.m. nachmittags (→ **a.m.**)
PO Box post office box *Postfach*
pp on behalf of *im Auftrag (i. A.)*

P&P postage and packing *Porto und Verpackung*

PS postscript *Postskriptum, Nachsatz*

PTO please turn over *bitte wenden (b.w.)*

qtly quarterly *vierteljährlich*

Rd Road *Straße (Str.)*

R&D research and development *Forschung und Entwicklung*

ref. reference *Bezug,Bezugszeichen*

reg(d). registered *eingetragen; eingeschrieben [Post]*

rep representative *Vertreter/in*

ro-ro roll-on roll-off *von Straßenfahrzeugen befahrbar [Schiff]*

RRP recommended retail price *unverbindliche Preisempfehlung*

sae stamped addressed envelope *frankierter und adressierter Rückumschlag*

S/N shipping note(s) *Schiffszettel, Warenbegleitschein(e)*

sq square *Quadrat(-)*

Sq. Square *Platz*

St Street *Straße*

SWIFT Society for Worldwide Interbank Financial Telecommunication *Gesellschaft für internationalen Bankverkehr*

TM trademark *(eingetragenes) Warenzeichen*

VAT value added tax *Mehrwertsteuer (MwSt.)*

via by way of [named place] *über [Ortsangabe]*

vol. volume *Volumen; Band [Buch]*

wk(s) week(s) *Woche(n)*

yd(s) yard(s) [length] *Yard(s) [91,4 cm]*

Skills

REZEPTION

Lesen schwieriger Texte

Texte werden zu unterschiedlichen Zwecken gelesen. Manchmal braucht man nur zu wissen, worum es geht, dann reicht in der Regel ein aufmerksames Überfliegen des Textes. Oft müssen gezielt Informationen herausgesucht werden, dann kommt es darauf an, die richtigen Schlüsselwörter zu finden. Will man sich gründlich mit einem Text auseinandersetzen, um z. B. Fragen zu beantworten oder einen Aufsatz dazu zu schreiben, ist gründliches, möglicherweise zweimaliges Lesen erforderlich.

Grobverständnis: Sich einen schnellen Überblick über einen Text verschaffen

Manchmal werden Sie im Buch aufgefordert, einen Text schnell zu lesen, um das Thema grob zu erfassen.

1. Schritt: Suchen Sie nach Anhaltspunkten, die Ihnen Aufschluss über den Textinhalt geben: Titel und Zwischenüberschriften, fett gedruckte Wörter, Bilder und Bildunterschriften.

2. Schritt: Sind Sie noch unsicher, lesen Sie die ersten und letzten Sätze jedes Absatzes. Bleiben Sie nicht an Einzelwörtern, schwierigen Zitaten usw. hängen.

Suche nach Einzelinformationen im Text

Bei vielen Textverständnisfragen oder Aufgaben vom Typ *True or false* geht es darum, schnell bestimmte Informationen im Text zu finden und nicht jedes Mal den ganzen Text neu zu lesen.

1. Schritt: Suchen Sie den Text nach Schlüsselbegriffen für die gesuchten Informationen ab. Geht es etwa um die Meinung des Autors zu einem bestimmten Thema, halten Sie nach Wörtern wie *think, believe, opinion* usw. Ausschau. Geht es um Informationen zu einem Thema, rufen Sie sich ein paar Schlüsselbegriffe in Erinnerung, nach denen Sie Ausschau halten. Manchmal hilft es, sich den gesuchten Begriff als gedrucktes Wort vor dem geistigen Auge vorzustellen.

2. Schritt: Gehen Sie falls nötig mit dem Finger die Zeilen entlang, während Sie suchen. Wenn Sie sich wie oben beschrieben vorbereitet haben, springen Ihnen die gesuchten Begriffe sofort ins Auge.

Detailverständnis: Gründliches Lesen

Lesen Sie nicht einfach drauflos. Ein paar einfache Schritte helfen Ihnen, den Text besser zu verstehen, ohne sich in Details zu verlieren.

1. Schritt: Der erste Schritt sollte darin bestehen, sich einen groben Überblick vom Textinhalt zu verschaffen (siehe oben). So werden Sie unklare Stellen besser in den Gesamtzusammenhang einordnen können. Es ist hilfreich, sich die wichtigsten Stichwörter kurz zu notieren. Zu dem Text *Fringe benefits then and now* auf S. 17 etwa könnten Sie nach kurzem Überfliegen aufschreiben: *The text is about how benefits given to employees have changed over the years.*

2. Schritt: Machen Sie sich die Struktur des Textes bewusst. Wo ist die Einleitung? Welcher Teil enthält die Hauptinformationen, und wie sind sie aufgebaut (Zwischenüberschriften, Absätze usw.)? Achten Sie auf Strukturwörter wie *only, but while, that's why, while, however* usw., mit denen der Verfasser seine Argumentation gliedert.

3. Schritt: Lesen Sie den Text nun aufmerksam. Notieren Sie sich Schlüsselstellen, z. B: *Fringe benefits include child care, flexible working hours, etc; in the past only the boss got many benefits; no benefits aimed at women before, etc.* Schlagen Sie Wörter beim ersten Lesen nur nach, wenn die Bedeutung des ganzen Satzes an ihnen hängt. Oft lässt sich die wesentliche Bedeutung durch den Kontext erschließen.

4. Schritt: Notieren Sie sich den Textinhalt in strukturierter Form, etwa einer Mind Map oder einer Liste (Themen, pro/kontra). Fügen Sie auch Formulierungen hinzu, die Ihnen später helfen, sich in eigenen Worten über den Textinhalt zu äußern. Schlagen Sie jetzt das notwendige Vokabular nach.

> Note Making S. 202, Mind Mapping S. 202

Umgang mit neuen Vokabeln

Fragen Sie sich bei neuen Vokabeln immer, ob sie für das Verständnis des Zusammenhangs unbedingt notwendig sind. Nachschlagen kostet Zeit und hilft oft nicht beim Verständnis des wirklich Wichtigen.

Erschließen der Bedeutung aus dem Kontext

> Ein Wort, das unbekannt scheint, kann z. B. mit einem anderen, Ihnen bekannten Wort verwandt sein (Ableitungen wie *aggressor* von *aggressive*). Oder das Wort hat einen bekannten Wortstamm und ein angehängtes Wortteil, mit dessen Hilfe Sie die Bedeutung erkennen können (*formal* – ***in**formal, clockwise* – ***anti**clockwise, change* – *change**able**, stupid* – *stupid**ity***). Manche Wörter haben Ähnlichkeiten mit einem deutschen Wort (vgl. etwa *initial* und „Initialen", *potential* und „potenziell").

> Sind Sie sich immer noch nicht sicher, kann der Satzzusammenhang Aufschluss geben. Machen Sie sich zunächst die Wortart bewusst: Suchen Sie nach einem Substantiv? Wofür steht das gesuchte Substantiv wahrscheinlich – für ein Gebäude? Eine Person? Handelt es sich um ein Adjektiv, das die Situation näher beschreibt oder jemanden charakterisiert?
Schauen Sie sich den folgenden Absatz an und versuchen Sie die Bedeutung der fett gedruckten Wörter aus dem Zusammenhang zu erschließen:
*Business is bad at the moment and we don't expect it to **rally** for at least a year. All the signals are very **inauspicious**, I'm afraid.*
Auch wenn man *rally* und *inauspicious* nicht kennt, kann man aus dem Kontext erschließen, dass *rally* ein Verb ist, das eine positive Entwicklung beschreibt und *inauspicious* ein Adjektiv mit negativer Bedeutung ist.

Umgang mit dem einsprachigen Wörterbuch

Machen Sie sich mit Ihrem Wörterbuch vertraut, so dass Sie die Symbole, Abkürzungen und die Lautschrift verstehen und die Hilfen, die vorne und hinten im Wörterbuch oder auf Zusatzseiten angeboten werden, nutzen können. Auf der folgenden Seite sehen Sie ein Beispiel eines typischen Wörterbucheintrags.

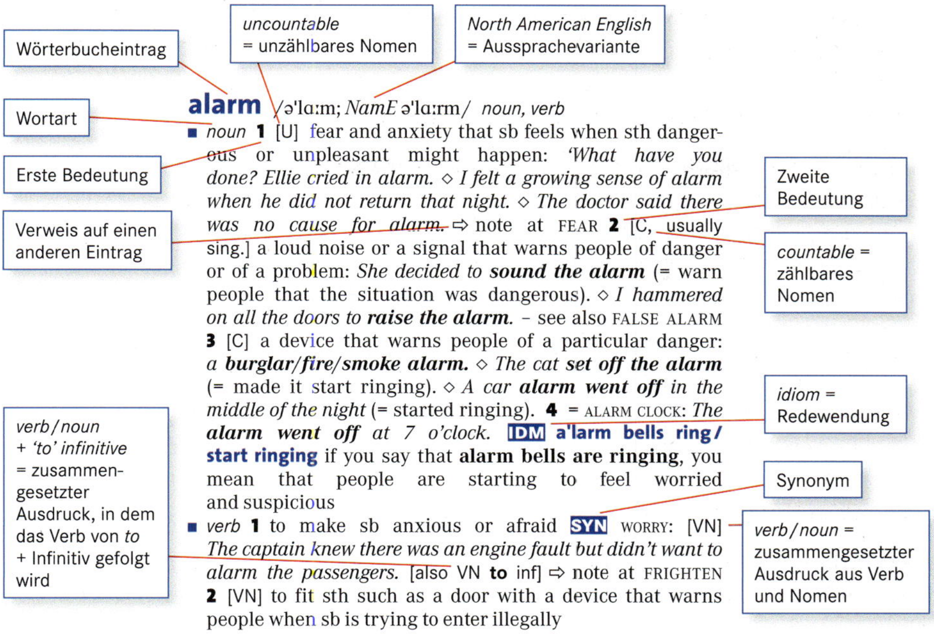

alarm /əˈlɑːm; *NAmE* əˈlɑːrm/ *noun, verb*

■ *noun* **1** [U] fear and anxiety that sb feels when sth dangerous or unpleasant might happen: *'What have you done?' Ellie cried in alarm.* ◇ *I felt a growing sense of alarm when he did not return that night.* ◇ *The doctor said there was no cause for alarm.* ⇨ note at FEAR **2** [C, usually sing.] a loud noise or a signal that warns people of danger or of a problem: *She decided to* ***sound the alarm*** (= warn people that the situation was dangerous). ◇ *I hammered on all the doors to* ***raise the alarm.*** – see also FALSE ALARM **3** [C] a device that warns people of a particular danger: *a* ***burglar/fire/smoke alarm.*** ◇ *The cat* ***set off the alarm*** (= made it start ringing). ◇ *A car* ***alarm went off*** *in the middle of the night* (= started ringing). **4** = ALARM CLOCK: *The* ***alarm went off*** *at 7 o'clock.* **IDM** **a'larm bells ring/start ringing** if you say that **alarm bells are ringing**, you mean that people are starting to feel worried and suspicious

■ *verb* **1** to make sb anxious or afraid **SYN** WORRY: [VN] *The captain knew there was an engine fault but didn't want to alarm the passengers.* [also VN **to** inf] ⇨ note at FRIGHTEN **2** [VN] to fit sth such as a door with a device that warns people when sb is trying to enter illegally

- Notieren Sie sich alle Wörter, deren Bedeutung Sie suchen, und schlagen Sie dann alle hintereinander nach.
- Lesen Sie nicht den gesamten Eintrag, sondern beschränken Sie sich auf die Verwendung Ihres Stichworts in der gesuchten Wortart (z. B. Sie suchen *alarm* als Verb, also ignorieren Sie den ersten Teil des oben stehenden Eintrags). Den entsprechenden Abschnitt mit allen zusammengesetzten Ausdrücken und den Beispielsätzen, die Ihnen helfen zu unterscheiden, in welchen Zusammenhängen welche Bedeutung zutrifft, müssen Sie dann allerdings gründlich lesen.
- Schauen Sie sich auch die Einträge in der unmittelbaren Umgebung Ihres Stichworts an, um eine Vorstellung von dem Wortfeld zu bekommen.
- Notieren Sie sich die passende Bedeutung, damit Sie sie nicht wieder vergessen.

Lernen neuer Vokabeln

Es gibt verschiedene Möglichkeiten, Vokabeln zu lernen – suchen Sie sich die, die Ihnen am besten liegt. Eines gilt jedoch für alle Methoden: Wörter prägen sich am besten ein, wenn man nicht nur das Stichwort aufschreibt, sondern auch noch dazugehörige Ausdrücke, Synonyme, Gegenteile, verwandte Wörter und Verwendungsbeispiele, evtl. auch Aussprachehinweise. Besonders wichtig sind zusammengesetzte Ausdrücke. Dazu gehören auch *phrasal verbs* (*set about, put off* usw.). Der Eintrag für das Stichwort *pay* könnte z. B. so aussehen:

pay (noun)	–	*Bezahlung, Gehalt, Lohn*
payslip	–	*Gehaltsabrechnung*
pay day	–	*Zahltag*
pay-off	–	*Abfindung*
pay (verb)	–	*zahlen*
pay for sth	–	*etw bezahlen*
pay off	–	*auszahlen*
pay as you go (phone)	–	*Prepaid(-Handy)*

Natürlich brauchen Sie nicht gleich komplette Wörterbucheinträge aufzuschreiben. Überlegen Sie sich jedoch, welche Ableitungen Ihnen zu dem neuen Wort schon bekannt sein könnten oder in welchem zusammengesetzten Ausdruck es Ihnen begegnet ist. Lassen Sie Platz für spätere Hinzufügungen, so dass die Einträge nach und nach „wachsen".

Karteikarten: Sie benötigen Karteikarten und einen Karteikasten mit mehreren Abteilungen. Schreiben Sie das englische Wort mit den dazugehörigen Ergänzungen auf eine Seite einer Karteikarte und die deutschen Bedeutungen auf die Rückseite. Sobald Sie ein Wort wissen, wandert es von der ersten in die zweite Abteilung des Karteikastens. Die Wörter in der zweiten Abteilung schauen Sie sich in größeren Abständen nochmal an, um diejenigen, die Sie wissen, dann in die dritte Abteilung fürs Langzeitgedächtnis abzulegen. Was Sie nicht wissen, kommt zurück in die erste Abteilung, die Sie sich möglichst oft anschauen sollten.

Vokabelheft: Wenn Sie im Unterricht neue Vokabeln mitschreiben wollen, bietet sich ein Vokabelheft an. Benutzen Sie ein zweispaltiges Heft, damit Sie eine Spalte leicht bedecken können. Gestalten Sie das Lernen weniger schematisch, indem Sie die Seiten, die Sie lernen wollen, zufällig auswählen und ab und zu mal Deutsch-Englisch statt Englisch-Deutsch lernen.

Wortfamilien: Fertigen Sie Listen mit Wortfamilien an, um sich zusammen mit einem neuen Wort auch noch seine Ableitungen einzuprägen (*approve - approval - approving - disapprove - disapproval*).

Wortfelder: Die beste Methode, Wortfelder, also zusammenhängende Wortgruppen zu einem Thema zu lernen, sind Mind Maps, also grafisch angelegte Wortnetze. Diese Methode ist gut geeignet, um den Themenwortschatz für eine Klassenarbeit zu lernen. Um den Schlüsselbegriff herum werden einzelne Oberbegriffe für die wichtigsten Aspekte des Themas angeordnet. Um jeden Oberbegriff werden nun die dazugehörigen Vokabeln herumgeschrieben.

> Mind Mapping S. 202

Vokabeltrainer: Wer gerne am Computer lernt, findet problemlos einen geeigneten Vokabeltrainer im Handel. Solche Software enthält meistens vielerlei Übungen, die das Vokabellernen unterhaltsam und spielerisch gestalten. Achten Sie darauf, dass es sich um eine Software handelt, die auf Ihre Schulart abgestimmt ist. Es gibt auch zahlreiche kostenlose Online-Vokabeltrainer im Internet.

Das Hörverständnis üben

Um gesprochenes Englisch zu verstehen, z. B. in Unterhaltungen, Telefongesprächen, Vorstellungsgesprächen, im Fernsehen u. a., sollten Sie sich gut auf die jeweilige Situation vorbereiten. Oft beeinträchtigen der Akzent, Hintergrundgeräusche und andere Störungen das Verständnis so, dass man sich auf das Wichtigste konzentrieren muss. Eignen Sie sich die unten beschriebene Methode an, wenn Sie die Hörverständnisaufgaben in *Focus on Business* bearbeiten. Damit lassen sich Barrieren bei schwierigen Hörtexten leicht abbauen.

Vor dem Hören

- Lesen Sie die gesamte Aufgabenstellung sorgfältig durch. Nutzen Sie alle Hilfen, die Ihnen zur Verfügung stehen - Abbildungen, Überschriften usw.
- Schreiben Sie wenn möglich **Schlüsselbegriffe** auf und rufen Sie sich, wenn genug Zeit ist, kurz wichtige Wortfelder zum Thema in Erinnerung.

Während des Hörens

- Hören Sie sich den gesamten Hörtext zunächst in Ruhe an, um zu verstehen, worum es geht. Machen Sie in dieser Phase keine Notizen.
- Achten Sie bei einem zweiten Hören nur auf die für die Aufgabe wichtigen Informationen. Konzentrieren Sie sich nicht auf einzelne Wörter und Ausdrücke, die Sie nicht verstehen.

- Achten Sie auf Ausdrücke, die den logischen Gedankengang verdeutlichen, z. B. *however, in my view, in conclusion* usw. Sie helfen Ihnen, den roten Faden nicht zu verlieren.
- Notieren Sie Informationen nur **stichpunktartig**, nie in ganzen Sätzen. Dabei kann ein Raster sehr hilfreich sein. In diesem Beispiel handelt es sich um den Wandel der Geschlechterrollen in unserer Gesellschaft:

	changed role	*reasons*	*consequences*
men			
women			

- Verwenden Sie Zeichen, Abkürzungen und Wortverkürzungen, um beim Notieren Zeit zu sparen:

Zeichen	
=	*the same as*
≠	*not the same as*
+	*and*

Abkürzungen	
e.g.	*for example*
km	*kilometres*
w., w/o	*with, without*

Wortverkürzungen	
govt	*government*
impt	*important*
kids	*children*

Nach dem Hören

- Formulieren Sie Ihre Stichpunkte so schnell wie möglich aus – vielleicht können Sie später Ihre Aufzeichnungen nicht mehr lesen oder Ihre Wortverkürzungen nicht mehr verstehen.
- Versuchen Sie, alle Fragen zu beantworten. Wenn Sie einige Informationen nicht verstanden haben, stellen Sie eine begründete Vermutung an.

Suche nach Informationen im Internet

Das Internet bietet riesige Ressourcen für die Recherche, z. B. für Aufsätze oder Präsentationen, aber es ist wichtig zu wissen, wo und wie man am besten sucht.

1. Schritt: Notieren Sie, wonach Sie genau suchen, und halten Sie passende Suchbegriffe fest. Ohne eine solche Vorgabe, die so spezifisch wie möglich sein sollte, gerät man vom Suchen leicht ins Surfen.

2. Schritt: Überlegen Sie sich, wo Sie mit der Suche beginnen sollten. Es ist sinnvoll, sich mit der Zeit einen Grundstock an englischsprachigen Ressourcen zusammenzustellen, z. B. *online encyclopedias* (etwa www.encyclopedia.com), *online dictionaries* (z. B. www.leo.org), *facts and figures about different countries* (etwa https://www.cia.gov/library/publications/the-world-factbook/), *news sites* (z. B. www.bbc.co.uk), *science and technology sites* (etwa www.howstuffworks.com).

3. Schritt: Suchen Sie sich die beste Suchmaschine und geben Sie möglichst spezifische Suchbegriffe ein. Machen Sie sich mit allen Suchfunktionen vertraut. Schränken Sie die Sprache der angezeigten Ergebnisseiten auf Englisch ein.

4. Schritt: Achten Sie darauf, nur verlässliche Quellen zu benutzen. Im Durchschnitt ist das Internet nicht sehr zuverlässig, da jeder Nutzer beliebige Informationen einstellen kann. Prüfen Sie immer, wer für die jeweiligen Inhalte verantwortlich ist, und verlassen Sie sich nicht auf die nächstbeste Information.

5. Schritt: Bevor Sie einzelne Artikel Satz für Satz lesen, überfliegen Sie sie. Sind nur einzelne Abschnitte für Ihr Thema relevant, suchen Sie sich diese heraus und ignorieren Sie die übrigen Teile.

> Grobverständnis S. 197

6. Schritt: Anstatt ganze Textabschnitte in Ihr Dokument herüberzukopieren, machen Sie sich gezielt Notizen. Speichern Sie die Seite unter Ihren Favoriten, wenn Sie später noch einmal darauf zurückkommen oder Materialien bzw. Zitate von der Seite verwenden möchten.

> Note Making S. 202

PRODUKTION

Note Making

Es ist sinnvoll, sich beim Lesen und Hören eines Textes Notizen zu machen. So können Sie später leichter auf die Informationen zurückgreifen.

Beim Lesen

Auf den ersten Blick scheint es ziemlich leicht, sich beim Lesen eines Textes Notizen zu machen. Trotzdem fällt es vielen schwer, sich wirklich kurze, sinnvolle Stichpunkte zu notieren. Oft führt die Sorge, etwas Wichtiges auszulassen, dazu, dass ganze Sätze des Originaltextes abgeschrieben werden. Damit verliert man nicht nur Zeit, sondern es wird später auch schwierig, seinen Text in eigenen Worten zu formulieren.

Hier einige Tipps, damit Sie diese Falle umgehen:

- Geben Sie Ihren Notizen eine Überschrift, die Ihr Thema klar umreißt, z. B. *Effects of genetic engineering on the environment.*
- Gehen Sie den Text durch und filtern Sie die wesentlichen Unterthemen heraus, die Sie als Überschriften verwenden können. Denken Sie daran, unter den Überschriften genug Platz für Ihre Stichpunkte zu lassen. > Detailverständnis S. 197
- Halten Sie Ausschau nach Signalen wie Hervorhebungen, Wiederholungen und bedeutungstragenden Adjektiven wie *huge, incredible, devastating* usw. Diese zeigen, was der Verfasser für wichtig hält.
- Notieren Sie nur Stichwörter, nicht ganze Sätze.
- Verdeutlichen Sie den logischen Aufbau der Informationen, z. B. indem Sie bestimmte Punkte in einer Liste untereinanderschreiben, Themen durch Leerzeilen voneinander abheben oder die wichtigsten Begriffe unterstreichen.
- Kontrollieren Sie, ob Sie alle notwendigen Informationen zusammengetragen haben. Vergessen Sie nicht, dass sie oft über den gesamten Text verstreut sind.

Beim Hören

In diesem Fall ist es schwieriger Notizen zu machen, da man oft sehr schnell schreiben muss. Man muss sich auf das Wesentliche konzentrieren und sollte Abkürzungen verwenden, damit man den Faden nicht verliert.

> Das Hörverständnis üben S. 200

Mind Mapping

Eine Mind Map ist eine sinnvolle Methode, Begriffe und Angaben übersichtlich in einem Netz um einen Oberbegriff herum anzuordnen. Sie eignet sich z. B. zum Vokabellernen, zum Brainstorming, zum Ideensammeln und zur Vorbereitung eines Aufsatzes oder einer Präsentation.

> Umgang mit unbekannten Vokabeln S. 198

Materialien: Ein großes Blatt (z.B. DIN A3), farbige Stifte.

1. Schritt: Schreiben Sie den Oberbegriff (wenn es um Wortfelder geht) bzw. das Thema (wenn es um eine Ideensammlung geht) deutlich und groß in die Mitte.

2. Schritt: Schreiben Sie die wichtigsten Begriffe zum Thema um den Oberbegriff herum; sie sollten durch starke „Äste" mit dem Oberbegriff verbunden sein.

3. Schritt: Fügen Sie nach demselben Prinzip weitere Wörter und Ideen zu den einzelnen Unterthemen hinzu. Je spezieller, desto kleiner die Verzweigungen, d.h. der Weg vom Thema nach außen führt vom Allgemeinen zum Speziellen. Sie können jederzeit und überall neue Ideen hinzufügen.

4. Schritt: Heben Sie wichtige Begriffe durch farbige Markierungen und Symbole hervor.

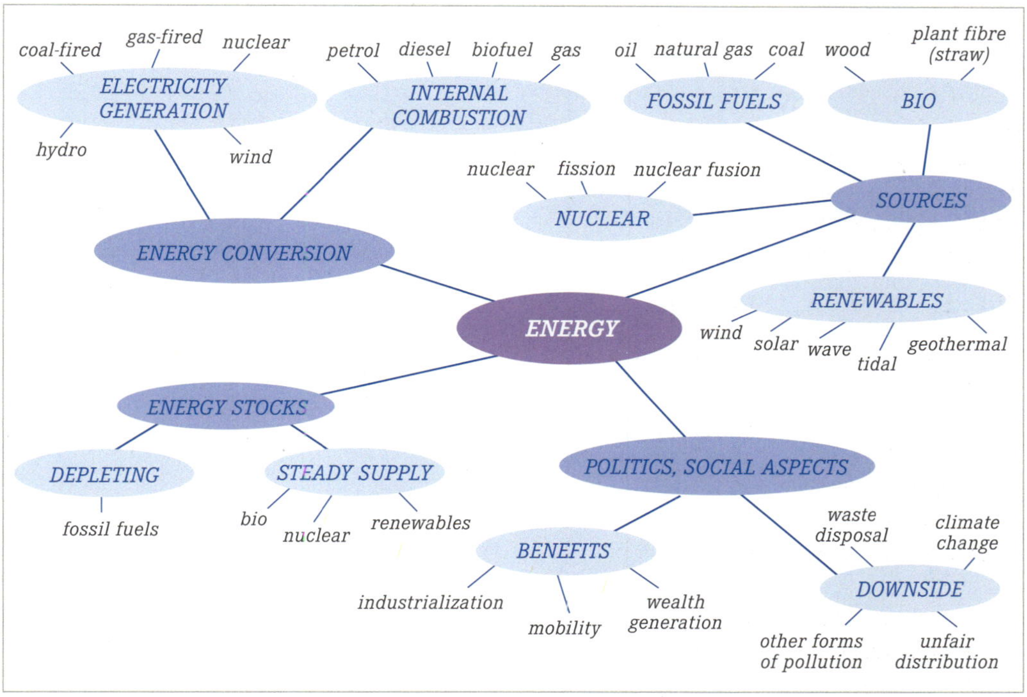

Fragen zum Text beantworten

> Lesen schwieriger Texte S. 197

Bevor Sie mit dem Schreiben beginnen, vergewissern Sie sich, dass Sie den gesamten Text verstanden haben. (Nicht jedes Wort ist wichtig – überlegen Sie sich, ob Sie die Bedeutung des Satzes auch verstehen, ohne jedes Wort zu kennen.) Lesen Sie die Aufgabenstellung immer genau, um zu verstehen, worauf es bei der Beantwortung genau ankommt – ein häufiger Fehler ist das „Vorbeischreiben" an der Frage. Achten Sie auch darauf, keine Informationen zu „verpulvern", die Sie möglicherweise für die Beantwortung einer anderen Frage benötigen.

- Wenn Sie im Buch nichts anstreichen dürfen, machen Sie sich Notizen in Form von Stichpunkten und Listen, anstatt ganze Sätze aus dem Text herauszuschreiben. In der Klassenarbeit bzw. Prüfung sollten Sie die wichtigsten Passagen im Text markieren. Am besten markieren Sie alles, was für eine Textverständnisfrage wichtig ist, mit einer bestimmten Farbe, und nehmen dann eine andere Farbe für die nächste Textverständnisfrage.
- Verwenden Sie in der Antwort die Zeitform der Fragestellung.

- Verwenden Sie so viele Synonyme und Umschreibungen der Begriffe und Formulierungen aus dem Text wie möglich, z. B. *recently - in recent years; violent crime - crime involving violence; think - believe; to a great extent - greatly; when she was a child - in her childhood* usw.
- Suchen Sie Signale im Text wie Hervorhebungen, Wiederholungen und bedeutungstragende Adjektive und Adverbien wie *absolutely, unbelievably, amazing*. Dies sind Signale dafür, was der Verfasser für wichtig hält.
- Versuchen Sie nicht, Ihre eigene Meinung einzubringen, wenn dies nicht in der Fragestellung gefordert ist.

Formulierungen für das Schreiben über den Text

- *According to the author, ...*
- *The article goes on to say that ...*
- *The text says that ...*
- *The author makes the point that ...*

Aus dem Text zitieren

Wenn Sie wirklich einmal eine wichtige Aussage aus dem Text zitieren möchten, um einen Punkt zu unterstreichen, so tun Sie dies nicht, indem Sie einfach die Formulierung des Textes übernehmen, sondern zeigen Sie, dass Sie bewusst zitieren und dies auch sprachlich deutlich machen können. Zitieren Sie in Ihrer Antwort höchstens einmal aus dem Text.

Zitate in die Antwort einbauen

- *To quote the author, ...*
- *According to the article, the high cost makes hosting these events 'a liability rather than an asset'.*
- *David Lambert criticizes people who give the 'feel-good-factor' as a reason for hosting events, and poses the question: 'Does bankruptcy feel good?'*

Eine Stellungnahme (*comment*) schreiben

Bei einer Stellungnahme geht es darum, Ihre Meinung zu einem bestimmten Thema darzulegen. Wichtig ist, dass Ihre Meinung begründet und mit Beispielen belegt ist.

1. Schritt: Machen Sie sich genau bewusst, worüber Sie schreiben sollen. Lesen Sie die Aufgabenstellung mehrmals durch.

2. Schritt: Machen Sie sich Notizen. Ordnen Sie Ihre Stichwörter übersichtlich an, z. B. in einer Mind Map, einer Liste oder einer Übersicht. > Note Making S. 202, Mind Mapping S. 202

3. Schritt: Schreiben Sie einen Einleitungssatz, der sich auf die Aufgabenstellung beziehen sollte.

4. Schritt: Behandeln Sie jedes Argument in einem Absatz. Handelt es sich um ein Pro-/Kontra-Thema, können Sie erst die Pro- und dann die Kontra-Argumente anführen. Verdeutlichen Sie Ihre Argumentation durch die Verwendung von Strukturwörtern; hierzu siehe die Liste auf der hinteren Umschlagklappe dieses Buches (*Language for writing*). > Einen Text sinnvoll gliedern S. 207

5. Schritt: Bringen Sie Ihre Argumentation in einem prägnanten Schlusssatz auf den Punkt.

Eine Stellungnahme einleiten

- *In the following I shall deal with the problem/subject/issue of ...*
- *I would like to discuss ...*
- *I intend to present arguments in favour of ... and against ...*

Eine Stellungnahme abschließen

- *All in all, I think it can be said that ...*
- *In conclusion, I would like to say that ...*
- *I would like to conclude by saying that ...*

Einen Text zusammenfassen

Die Fähigkeit, einen gelesenen Text zusammenzufassen, ist nicht nur wichtig, um den Text richtig zu verstehen, sondern sie hilft auch bei anderen Situationen, in denen Sie Informationen aus einem Text auf das Wesentliche reduzieren müssen. Zu solchen Situationen gehören z. B. die Beantwortung von Textverständnisfragen oder eine Mediation.

> Fragen zum Text beantworten S. 203, Mediation S. 211

1. Schritt: Lesen Sie den Text so oft wie möglich, bis Sie sicher sind, alles verstanden zu haben.

> Detailverständnis S. 220, Umgang mit unbekannten Vokabeln S. 221

2. Schritt: Fassen Sie in ein oder zwei einleitenden Sätzen zusammen, worum es in dem Text geht, z. B.: *The text is an extract from a radio phone-in show which is looking at people's attitudes to the EU.*

3. Schritt: Machen Sie sich bewusst, welche Informationen für den Leser wichtig sind, indem Sie *Wh*-Fragen beantworten: *Who? What? When? Where? Why?*, z. B.:
- *Who: Dr Peter Brown from Manchester University*
- *What: has been doing research into corruption in the EU*

4. Schritt: Machen Sie sich Notizen in Form von Stichwörtern. > Note Making S. 202

5. Schritt: Schreiben Sie Ihren Text. Beachten Sie dabei folgende Punkte:
- Lassen Sie Unwesentliches weg. Dazu gehören etwa Beispiele, Aufzählungen, Namen, Zitate usw.
- Verwenden Sie so weit wie möglich Ihre eigenen Worte.
- Vermeiden Sie es, zu dem Text Stellung zu nehmen. Dies gehört in der Regel nicht zur Aufgabenstellung.
- Denken Sie daran, Zitate in indirekte Rede umzuwandeln. > Reported speech S. 217

6. Schritt: Kontrollieren Sie Ihren Text auf Fehler und vergewissern Sie sich, dass Sie alle wichtigen Aspekte des Textes berücksichtigt haben.

Einen Bericht schreiben

Ein Bericht fasst die Hauptinformationen einer Präsentation, einer Sitzung, eines Geschäftsvorhabens oder über ein wichtiges Ereignis wie einen Streik, einen Unfall oder die Folgen einer Naturkatastrophe zusammen.

- Ein Bericht ist die **objektive Darstellung** eines Vorgangs oder einer Situation. Daher enthalten Berichte oft Antworten auf folgende Fragen:
  - ***What*** *event took place? /* ***What*** *situation came about?*
  - ***Where*** *and* ***when*** *did it take place?*
  - ***Who*** *was involved in the event or situation?*
  - ***Why*** *and* ***how*** *did the event take place or the situation arise?*
- Berichte haben einen **förmlicheren Stil**. Eine objektive Haltung wird durch den Gebrauch des **Passivs**, insbesondere des **unpersönlichen Passivs** *(It was suggested that ..., The sales department was reported to have ...)* und durch eine wertfreie Darstellungsweise zum Ausdruck gebracht. > Impersonal passive S. 220
- Beginnen Sie immer mit einer knappen Einleitung, in der Sie das **Ziel** Ihres Berichts aufzeigen.
- Lassen Sie alles Unwesentliche weg! Beziehen Sie nur so viele Informationen ein, wie der Leser braucht, um zu verstehen, was Sie ihm sagen wollen.
- Verwenden Sie Überschriften, um Ihren Bericht klar zu strukturieren.

Einen Aufsatz schreiben

Im Laufe der Oberstufe, in der Abschlussprüfung und auch später, z. B. im Studium, werden Sie immer wieder Aufsätze zu unterschiedlichsten Themen schreiben müssen. Es ist sinnvoll, sich von Anfang an einige Regeln zu eigen zu machen, um das Vorgehen möglichst zu automatisieren und sich gleich auf den Inhalt konzentrieren zu können. Dies ist besonders wichtig, wenn es – wie in der Abschlussprüfung – auf die Zeit ankommt.

1. Schritt: Verschaffen Sie sich Klarheit über Ihr Thema. Welche Aspekte gehören dazu, welche nicht?

2. Schritt: Machen Sie ein Brainstorming, indem Sie alle Ideen aufschreiben, die Ihnen zum Thema in den Kopf kommen. Wichtig: Die Ideen sollten Sie gleich in eine Struktur bringen, um nicht in einem Wust von ungeordnetem Gekritzel zu enden. Zur Strukturierung eignen sich z. B. Listen oder Mind Maps. > Note Making S. 202, Mind Mapping S. 202

3. Schritt: Überlegen Sie sich einen Aufbau für Ihren Text. Dies kann z. B. in Form einer Mind Map geschehen. Eine andere Möglichkeit ist eine Übersicht (*outline*) wie die folgende:

Should old towns be closed to private vehicles?

Einleitung: Umreißen des Themas
Hauptteil: Ausführung zum Thema, z. B.:

1. *Disadvantages for business*
  1.1 *Job losses*
    1.1.1 *retail trade*
    1.1.2 *fewer tourists*
      1.1.2.1 *less money for tourist attractions*
      1.1.2.2 *job losses in cafés, etc.*
  1.2 *What about town centre residents, delivery vehicles, etc.?*
2. *Advantages, positive effects on town and people*
...
Schluss: Zusammenfassung, Fazit

4. Schritt: Schreiben Sie Ihren Text. Lassen Sie Platz für Korrekturen, Änderungen oder Ergänzungen. Wichtig: Verdeutlichen Sie Ihre Argumentation durch die Verwendung von Strukturwörtern; hierzu siehe die Liste auf der hinteren Umschlagklappe dieses Buches (*Language for writing*) und den Abschnitt auf der nächsten Seite „Einen Text sinnvoll gliedern".

5. Schritt: Überprüfen Sie Ihren Entwurf auf:
- **Rechtschreibfehler** (z. B. gleichlautende Wörter wie *there/their*, *meet/meat* usw.)
- **Grammatikfehler** (z. B. Gebrauch der Zeitformen; *-ly*-Endung für Adverbien)
- **Wortwahl** (z. B. Wiederholungen; *False friends* wie „aktuell" ≠ *actual*, „eventuell" ≠ *eventual*, „spenden" ≠ *spend*)
- **Satzbau** (z. B. unvollständige Antworten, die mit *Because* beginnen)
- **Gedankenführung** (z. B. Klarheit des Ausdrucks; Verwendung von Strukturwörtern wie *However, On the other hand, In addition, As a result* usw.)

Einen Text sinnvoll gliedern

Wann immer es darum geht, einen zusammenhängenden Text zu schreiben, sei es eine Antwort auf eine Frage zum Text, einen Aufsatz, eine Zusammenfassung o. Ä., ist es ganz wichtig, die Gedanken in einen logischen Zusammenhang zu bringen, damit der Leser den Faden nicht verliert. Dies alles gilt ebenso für mündliche Präsentationen, nur werden Sie dabei Ihre Materialien nicht Wort für Wort ablesen, sondern frei sprechen. Daher ist es wichtig, Formulierungen für die Gliederung auch mündlich parat zu haben.

Die wichtigsten Strukturwörter finden Sie auf der hinteren Umschlagklappe dieses Buches (*Language for writing*). Im Folgenden sehen Sie einige Beispiele, wie man diese Formulierungen in einen Text einbauen kann.

Argumente gliedern

> *In his text 'The world's changing energy supplies' Knapp discusses many aspects of energy and the environment. Firstly, he states that ... Secondly / Then he goes on to say that ... Another point he makes is that ... Finally, ...*

Eine Begründung anführen

> *Due to / Because of / As a result of all the discussions about renewable sources of energy ...*

> *Renewable energy has been talked about a lot. Therefore, the public ...*

> *Renewable energy has been talked about a lot, so the public ...*

Aspekte ergänzen

> *Brian Knapp states that many renewable sources of energy include high development costs. In addition, / Moreover, he points out that these energy forms still only offer a small amount of the world's rising energy requirements.*

> *In addition to / Besides / As well as mentioning the high development costs of many renewable forms of energy, Knapp points out that these energy forms still only offer a small amount of the world's rising energy requirements.*

Einen Gegensatz ausdrücken

> *Although the demand for cheap energy is continuing to rise, our current main sources of energy – fossil fuels – are running out.*

> *In spite of the rising demand for cheap energy, our current main sources of energy are running out.*

> *While/Whereas the demand for cheap energy is continuing to rise, our current main sources of energy are running out.*

> *Our current main sources of energy are running out. However, / But nevertheless, the demand for cheap energy is continuing to rise.*

> *On the one hand, our current main sources of energy are running out; on the other hand, the demand for cheap energy is continuing to rise.*

Beispiele anführen

> *The writer is of the opinion that nuclear fusion is a safe energy source compared with other energy sources, for example / for instance / such as / e.g. ...*

Ein Fazit ziehen

> *As a consequence, / All in all, / Consequently, Brian Knapp thinks that ...*

> *To sum up, / To conclude, I would like to say that ...*

Diese Strukturwörter (*connectors*) sollten Sie sich so zu eigen machen, dass Sie sie möglichst in jedem Text verwenden. Dadurch gewöhnen Sie sich eine genaue und logische Ausdrucksweise an. Achten Sie auch beim Lesen von Texten auf Strukturwörter; so können Sie der Gedankenführung leichter folgen.

Die Arbeitsergebnisse präsentieren

Die Fähigkeit, wirkungsvoll vor einem Publikum zu referieren, ist wichtig im Berufsleben und zunehmend auch in der Schule. Dabei kommt es nicht nur auf den Inhalt an, sondern auch darauf, wie anschaulich Sie den Inhalt „verpacken“, d.h. dass Sie Ihren Vortrag leicht nachvollziehbar gliedern, abwechslungsreich gestalten und lebendig illustrieren.

Vor der Präsentation

1. Schritt: Bereiten Sie Ihr Thema gründlich vor und machen Sie sich dabei schon Notizen auf Englisch.

2. Schritt: Prüfen Sie Ihre Stichpunkte sprachlich und vergewissern Sie sich, dass Sie alles richtig aussprechen (anhand der Lautschrift in einem Wörterbuch oder der Aussprachebeispiele in gängigen Online-Wörterbüchern oder auf Wörterbuch-CD-ROMs).

3. Schritt: Überlegen Sie sich, wie Sie Ihren Vortrag interessanter und lebendiger machen können (Anschauungsmaterial, Audiobeispiele, Anekdoten usw.).

4. Schritt: Organisieren Sie alle Hilfsmittel, die Sie benötigen (OHP, Flipchart usw.).

5. Schritt: Üben Sie die Präsentation, am besten vor Zuhörern.

Während der Präsentation

1. Schritt: Steigen Sie nicht gleich mitten ins Thema ein, sondern geben Sie einen Überblick über Ihre Präsentation.

2. Schritt: Machen Sie es den Zuhörern leicht, indem Sie sich klar ausdrücken, kurze Sätze benutzen und langsam sprechen.

3. Schritt: Die Zuhörer bleiben am ehesten interessiert, wenn Sie Ihre Präsentation so abwechslungsreich wie möglich gestalten: Ziehen Sie zwischendurch Anschauungsmaterial (OHP, Beamer usw.) heran und teilen Sie Handouts aus. Wenn Sie Folien benutzen, halten Sie sie klar und übersichtlich, anstatt sie mit Grafiken zu überladen.

4. Schritt: Achten Sie auf Ihre Körpersprache: Wenden Sie sich dem Publikum zu, halten Sie Blickkontakt mit den Zuhörern, sprechen Sie langsam und deutlich und benutzen Sie Gesten, um den Inhalt zu verdeutlichen.

5. Schritt: Fassen Sie zum Schluss das Wichtigste zusammen. Bedanken Sie sich bei den Zuhörern für ihre Aufmerksamkeit und ermuntern Sie sie, Fragen zu stellen.

Interpretation von Grafiken, Diagrammen und Tabellen

Wie im Falle von Cartoons ist es auch bei Grafiken, Diagrammen und Tabellen sinnvoll, einen Grundstock an Formulierungen zur Beschreibung und Interpretation parat zu haben. Halten Sie die folgenden Schritte ein, um Ihre Antwort sinnvoll zu gliedern:

1. Schritt: **Beschreibung der Vorlage.** Hier geht es nicht darum, alle Details aufzuzählen, sondern zu beschreiben, worum es in der Vorlage geht und welche Daten dargestellt werden.

2. Schritt: **Zusammenfassung der dargestellten Tendenzen, Entwicklungen bzw. Größen.** Welche Schlussfolgerungen ergeben sich aus den Daten? Kann man zusammenfassend ein Ergebnis oder Fazit formulieren?

Typen von Diagrammen

Tabelle (*table*)

	USA	UK
1995	495	105
2005	718	85

Kurvendiagramm (*graph, line graph*)

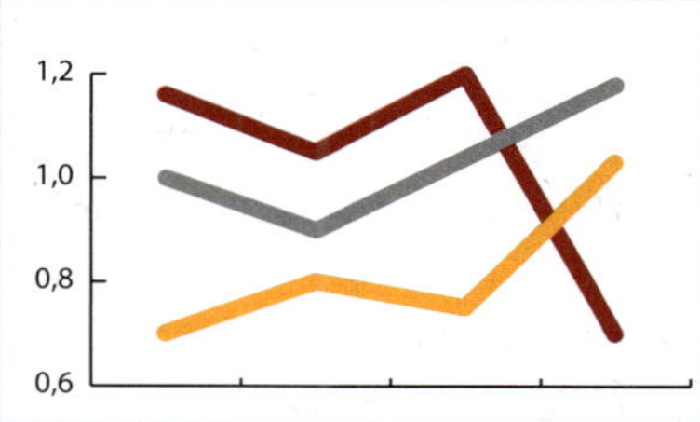

Balkendiagramm (*bar chart*)

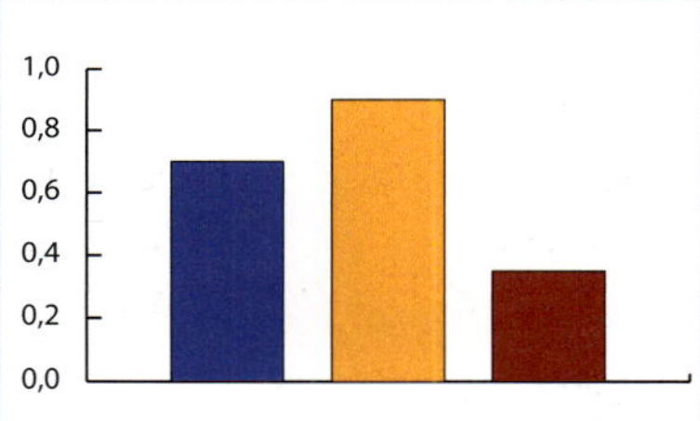

Kreis-/Tortendiagramm (*pie chart*)

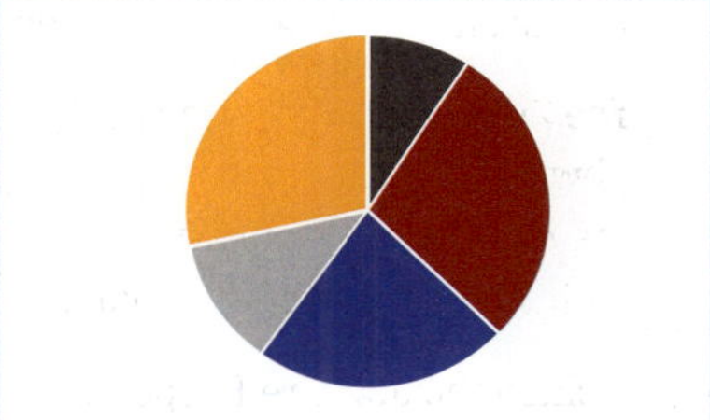

Sprechen über Zahlen und Mengenangaben (*values, amounts*)

- > *more / less than ...*
- > *no less than ...*
- > *eighty-five per cent (said that ...)*
- > *On the other hand, almost ...*

Sprechen über Proportionen (*proportions, shares, percentages*)

- > *(over) half of ...*
- > *more / less than one third / quarter of ...*
- > *the (vast) majority of ...*
- > *a mere third of ...*

Sprechen über Entwicklungen (*developments*) und Tendenzen (*tendencies*)

- > *a huge / sharp increase / decrease*
- > *a small / slight raise / dip*
- > *levels out, remains constant*
- > *drastically, gradually, sharply, steadily*
- > *rises / increases / hits a maximum*
- > *drops / decreases / falls / plunges*
- > *over a period of ...*
- > *between 2000 and 2008*

INTERAKTION

Gruppengespräche und Diskussionen führen

Ob es um Gruppengespräche, Diskussionen oder Rollenspiele geht: Machen Sie das Beste daraus, indem Sie die folgenden Punkte beherzigen.

> Lernen Sie die Formulierungen auf der hinteren Umschlagklappe dieses Buches (*Language for discussion*). Klappen Sie diese während des Unterrichts aus. Die Formulierungen helfen Ihnen, sich klar und logisch auszudrücken.
> Bereiten Sie sich inhaltlich vor, indem Sie sich einzelne Aspekte des Themas noch einmal in Stichworten ins Gedächtnis rufen und Schlüsselbegriffe auf Englisch notieren.
> Legen Sie sich, wenn genügend Zeit ist, ein paar Fragen/Antworten zum Thema zurecht.
> Bleiben Sie immer ruhig und denken Sie nach, bevor Sie sprechen.
> Bleiben Sie beim Thema und schweifen Sie nicht ab.
> Gehen Sie auf Ihre Gesprächspartner ein und halten Sie Blickkontakt.
> Beteiligen Sie sich und hören Sie nicht bloß still zu: Gruppenarbeit ist eine hervorragende Gelegenheit zum freien Sprechen.

Melden Sie sich auch immer mal wieder spontan zu Wort und lassen Sie Ausdrücke einfließen, die Interesse, Überraschung, Skepsis usw. äußern - so etwas macht das Gespräch gleich viel lebendiger:

Sich zu Wort melden	
> *Can I just say that ... ?*	> *Well, if you ask me ...*
Jemand anderen ins Gespräch einbringen	
> *What do you think, Sven / Svenja?*	
Verständnis, Erstaunen usw. ausdrücken	
Ach so. / Ah ja.	*I see. / Right. / Oh, right.*
Oh je!	*Oh dear!*
Echt?	*Really?*
Gut. / Okay.	*Fine.*
Alles klar.	*OK then.*
Das ist doch wohl nicht dein Ernst!	*You're kidding!*

Ein Interview führen

Ein Interview ist eine Unterhaltung zwischen Ebenbürtigen, das heißt der Person, die Fragen stellt (*the interviewer*) und der, die sie beantwortet (*the interviewee*). Es ist kein Verhör. Die Wendungen unten werden Ihnen helfen, nicht in diese Falle zu tappen.

1. Schritt: Beginnen Sie, indem Sie sich bei dem zu Befragenden dafür bedanken, dass er/sie sich die Zeit genommen hat, Ihre Fragen beantworten zu wollen.

2. Schritt: Machen Sie sich im Voraus ein Konzept zur Reihenfolge Ihrer Fragen, aber bleiben Sie flexibel. Seien Sie darauf vorbereitet, Fragen zu vertauschen oder wegzulassen, je nach den Antworten des Befragten. Wenn Sie zu unnachgiebig sind, könnte sich Ihr Interview in ein Quiz verwandeln!

3. Schritt: Seien Sie niemals aggressiv oder aufdringlich. Wenn der Befragte eine Frage nicht beantworten möchte, bringen Sie Ihre Frage anders zum Ausdruck. Wenn er/sie immer noch nicht bereit ist zu antworten, fahren Sie fort.

4. Schritt: Beenden Sie das Interview mit einer positiven Anmerkung, beispielsweise indem Sie sagen, wie interessant Sie es fanden. Vergessen Sie nicht, sich bei dem Befragten nochmals dafür zu bedanken, dass er/sie sich die Zeit genommen hat.

Interviewer

> *May I start/end by asking you your views on ...?*
> *Can/May I go on to ask you about ...?*
> *Do you mind if we turn to ... now?*

> *I (quite) see what you mean.*
> *That's interesting. I didn't know / wasn't aware that ...*
> *Yes, I was just about to turn to the question of ...*
> *It's funny/interesting you say that because I wanted to ask you ...*

> *So what you are getting at is ...*
> *Am I correct/right in thinking that ...?*

> *Tell me more.*
> *Yes, but I'm sure you'd agree that ...*

> *Sorry to break in / interrupt you, but ...*
> *If I may just go back (for a moment) to ...*

Interviewee

> *What I mean is ...*
> *What I'm getting at / trying to say is ...*
> *In other words, ...*

> *Take ... for instance. In my opinion/view, ...*
> *To give you an example of this / of what I'm getting at, ...*

> *From my point of view, the fact is that ...*
> *It seems to me that ...*

MEDIATION

Mediation

Im Gegensatz zur Übersetzung ist bei der Mediation nicht jedes Wort des Originaltextes wichtig. Schriftliche Mediation bedeutet das sinngemäße Übertragen von Texten in eine andere Sprache für jemanden, der das Original nicht versteht. Wichtig bei einer Mediation ist immer die Konzentration auf das Wesentliche, im Unterschied zur Übersetzung. Einzelheiten sind bei einer Mediation ebenso zweitrangig wie stilistische Feinheiten.

1. Schritt: Lesen Sie genau, **für welche Situation** Sie den Text zusammenfassen müssen und **für wen**. Meist bestimmt die jeweilige Situation, worauf es ankommt.

2. Schritt: Lesen Sie den gesamten Text durch, ohne sich dabei auf Einzelwörter zu konzentrieren. Ignorieren Sie unbekannte Vokabeln wenn möglich, oft sind sie für das Verständnis des Hauptinhalts nicht wesentlich.

3. Schritt: Lesen Sie nochmals, worauf es in der Aufgabenstellung ankommt und in welcher Form die Lösung abgefasst sein soll. Wenn es einzelne Fragen gibt, markieren Sie die für die jeweiligen Fragen wichtigen Textpassagen in unterschiedlichen Farben.

4. Schritt: Fassen Sie die Hauptpunkte des Textes zusammen. Drücken Sie sich klar und verständlich aus; vereinfachen Sie die Sprache des Originals, indem Sie sich darauf konzentrieren, **was** gesagt wird, nicht **wie** es gesagt wird.

5. Schritt: Lesen Sie Ihren Text nochmals durch und vergewissern Sie sich, dass der Inhalt des Originals angemessen und verständlich ausgedrückt ist.

Grammar summary

THE SIMPLE PRESENT

1 I **go** to meetings twice a week.
2 We **live** in Bavaria.
3 Mr Brown **teaches** us English every day.
4 I **don't like** conference calls.
5 **Does** he **like** travelling?

> Man gebraucht das **simple present** für regelmäßige, sich wiederholende Ereignisse oder Handlungen (1, 3) und für Dauerzustände (2, 4, 5).

> Mit Ausnahme der 3. Person Singular (*he, she, it*) hat das **simple present** dieselbe Form wie der Infinitiv (1, 2).
⚠ Die **3. Person Singular** endet auf *-(e)s* (3).

> Ist **kein Hilfsverb** im Satz vorhanden, werden **Verneinung** und **Fragen** mit der entsprechenden Form von *to do* gebildet (4, 5).

Das **simple present** wird häufig mit den folgenden **Zeitangaben** benutzt:

> *always, never, often, rarely, seldom, sometimes*
> *generally, mostly, normally, regularly, usually*
> *every day/week/month/..., every morning/afternoon/...*
> *on Mondays/Tuesdays/..., on weekdays*
> *in (the) summer/winter/...*
> *at Christmas/Easter, at weekends*

THE PRESENT PROGRESSIVE

1 I**'m calling** to say that Ben's ill.
2 He**'s working** from home today.
3 The computer **isn't working**.
4 **Are** you **eating** lunch?

> Man benutzt das **present progressive** (auch **present continuous** genannt) für Vorgänge oder Handlungen, die im Moment des Sprechens oder Schreibens passieren und noch nicht abgeschlossen sind (1, 3, 4).

> Es wird auch für vorübergehende Situationen gebraucht (2).

> Das **present progressive** wird mit dem Präsens von *to be* und der *-ing*-Form des Vollverbs gebildet.

> Da beim **present progressive** immer ein Hilfsverb vorhanden ist, wird die **Verneinung** mit *not/n't* gebildet (3).

> Fragen werden durch Umstellung gebildet (4).

Das **present progressive** wird oft mit den folgenden **Zeitangaben** benutzt:

at the moment, at present, now, this week/month, currently

⚠ Diese Verben bilden normalerweise **keine progressive-Form**:

be, believe, doubt, feel (meinen), *hate, hear, imagine, know, like/dislike, love, mean, notice, prefer, realize, recognize, remember, see* (begreifen), *seem, suppose, think* (meinen), *understand, want, wish*

THE SIMPLE PAST

1 We **wanted** to go to the USA last year.
2 She **went** on a business trip to London.
3 Jasmin **did not enjoy** her holiday in Rimini last summer.
4 Where **did** you **go** last year?

> Man benutzt das **simple past**, um über Vergangenes zu berichten.
> Das **simple past** wird auch gebraucht, wenn man sagen will, **wann** etwas geschehen ist (1, 3, 4).
> Bei **regelmäßigen** Verben wird das **simple past** durch das Anhängen von *-ed* an den Infinitiv gebildet (1).
⚠ Die unregelmäßigen Verben haben eine Sonderform (2), die man sich merken - auswendig lernen! - muss.
> Irregular Verbs (S. 283)
> Ist **kein Hilfsverb** im Satz vorhanden, bildet man die **Verneinung** und **Fragen** mit *did/didn't* (3, 4).

Das **simple past** wird häufig mit den folgenden **Zeitangaben** benutzt:

> *yesterday, the day before yesterday, the week/month/... before last*
> *last night/week/month/summer/December/Easter/...*
> *two/three/... hours/days/years/... ago*
> *in 2005/in the 20th century ...*
> *at that time, in those days*

THE PAST PROGRESSIVE

1 The boss **was talking** to Heather **during the presentation**.
2 The businessmen **were exchanging** business cards when a fire alarm (suddenly) **rang**.
3 I **wasn't doing** anything particular when he **arrived**.
4 **Were** you **having** breakfast when I **phoned**?

> Wenn man ausdrücken möchte, dass eine Handlung zu einem bestimmten Zeitpunkt oder während eines bestimmten Zeitraumes in der Vergangenheit **im Gange** war, benutzt man das **past progressive** (auch **past continuous** genannt) (1).
> Das **past progressive** wird auch benutzt, um zu verdeutlichen, dass eine Handlung im Gange war, als ein neues Ereignis (plötzlich) eintrat (2-4).
> Man bildet das **past progressive** mit *was/were* und der *-ing*-Form des Vollverbs (1).
> Die **Verneinung** wird mit *was not/wasn't* bzw. *were not/weren't* gebildet (3).
> **Fragen** bildet man durch Umstellung (4).
⚠ Einige Verben haben normalerweise **keine progressive-Form** (siehe die Liste unter **present progressive**).

THE PRESENT PERFECT

1 I**'ve bought** a new computer.
2 I **haven't seen** the new office yet.
3 How long **have** you **had** a laptop?
4 We**'ve had** snow **for** two weeks.
5 She**'s had** a cold **since** December.

> Wenn man ausdrücken will, dass etwas geschehen ist, ohne dass der genaue Zeitpunkt des Ereignisses wichtig ist, wird das **present perfect** benutzt (1, 2).
> Man gebraucht das **present perfect** auch, um zu sagen, seit wann oder wie lange ein Zustand oder eine Handlung schon andauert (3–5). Dafür wird sehr oft *for* bzw. *since* verwendet. (Im Deutschen steht dafür „seit" plus Gegenwart.)
> Das **present perfect** wird mit *have/has* und der 3. Form des Vollverbs gebildet (1, 4, 5).
⚠ Die unregelmäßigen Verben haben eine Sonderform (1, 2), die man auswendig lernen muss.

> Irregular verbs (S. 283)

> Die **Verneinung** wird durch das Einfügen von *not/n't* nach *have/has* gebildet (2).
> **Fragen** bildet man durch Umstellung (3).

Das **present perfect** wird oft mit den folgenden Zeitangaben benutzt:

> *already, still (not), (not) yet*
> *(not) ever, just, lately, never, recently*
> *so far this week/month/..., till/until now*

THE PRESENT PERFECT PROGRESSIVE

1 I**'ve been learning** English since I was ten.
2 They**'ve not been speaking** to each other lately.
3 **Has** he **been planning** the meeting for long?

> Das **present perfect progressive** (auch **present perfect continuous** genannt) benutzt man für Handlungen und Vorgänge, die in der Vergangenheit begonnen haben und zum Zeitpunkt des Sprechens bzw. Schreibens noch nicht beendet sind.
> Das **present perfect progressive** wird mit *have/has been* und der *-ing*-Form des Vollverbs gebildet (1).
> Die **Verneinung** bildet man durch das Einfügen von *not/n't* unmittelbar nach *have/has* (2).
> **Fragen** werden durch Umstellung gebildet (3).
⚠ Einige Verben haben normalerweise **keine progressive-Form** (siehe die Liste unter **present progressive**, S. 212).

THE PAST PERFECT

1 Laura couldn't pay. She **had forgotten** her purse.
2 Nina **had** already **left** the coffee bar by the time I arrived.
3 When I visited John in hospital, he **had been** there for ten days.

> Mit Hilfe des **past perfect** drückt man aus, dass zwei Handlungen oder Vorgänge in der Vergangenheit aufeinander folgten (1, 2). Die Handlung, die zeitlich voranging, steht im **past perfect**.
> Das **past perfect** wird auch verwendet, um auszudrücken, dass ein Zustand vor einem Zeitpunkt der Vergangenheit begann und zu diesem Zeitpunkt noch andauerte (3).

⚠ Wenn zwei oder mehrere kurze Handlungen in der Vergangenheit direkt aufeinander folgen, wird für alle Handlungen das **simple past** verwendet:
*The cat **ran** out when Joanne **opened** the door.*

THE PAST PERFECT PROGRESSIVE

1 Rod **had been preparing** for his interview for three weeks when he got another job offer.
2 When I found Mary, I could see that she **had been crying**.

> Das **past perfect progressive** (auch **past perfect continuous** genannt) wird verwendet, wenn man ausdrücken will, dass eine Handlung oder ein Vorgang vor einem Zeitpunkt in der Vergangenheit begonnen hatte und bis (oder fast bis) zu diesem Zeitpunkt andauerte.

THE FUTURE

A will

1 In the future people **will use** public transport more often.
2 We can only hope that everyone **will accept** this shift in attitudes.
3 You've forgotten your purse? Don't worry. **I'll lend** you some money.
4 Ms Smith **will not be** at the meeting this afternoon.
5 I **won't come** either.
6 **Will** he **get** the job?

> Das **will future** benutzt man, um Vorhersagen zu machen (1) oder Vermutungen über die Zukunft zu äußern (2).
> Man benutzt es auch, wenn man sich spontan zu etwas entschließt, Angebote oder Versprechen macht (3).
> Das **will future** wird mit *will* + Infinitiv des Vollverbs gebildet. Es hat für alle Personen die gleiche Form (1–3).
> Die **Verneinung** bildet man durch das Einfügen von *not* unmittelbar nach *will* (4). Im gesprochenen Englisch sagt man häufig *won't* (5).
> **Fragen** werden durch Umstellung gebildet (6).

Das **will future** kommt häufig mit den folgenden einleitenden Verben und Ausdrücken vor:

> *believe, expect, forecast, hope, imagine, suppose, think*
> *It's clear/obvious that ..., There's no doubt that ...*

B going to

1 Look at these clouds. It**'s going to rain** soon.
2 This time I**'m going to get** good marks in the class test.
3 Tom **isn't going to work** at the club any more.
4 When **are** you **going to take** your driving test?

> Das **going to future** benutzt man für Ereignisse und Situationen, die nach Meinung des Sprechers bald eintreten werden (weil es bereits Anzeichen dafür gibt) (1).
> Es wird auch für Pläne und Absichten gebraucht (2).
> Das **going to future** wird mit *am/is/are* + *going to* + Infinitiv gebildet (1, 2).
> Die **Verneinung** bildet man durch das Einfügen von *not/n't* unmittelbar nach *am/is/are* (3).
> **Fragen** werden durch Umstellung gebildet (4).

⚠ Der **Gebrauch des Futurs** hängt in gewissem Maße von der Absicht oder Sichtweise des Sprechers ab. Dies gilt insbesondere für das **going to future** und für zukünftige Ereignisse. Daher ist es im Zweifelsfall ratsam, das neutralere **will future** zu benutzen.

C The present progressive / The simple present

1 We'**re leaving** the house at 10.30.
2 The bus **goes** at 11 o'clock.

> Man kann das **present progressive** auch **mit einer Zeitbestimmung der Zukunft** (*at 10.30, this afternoon, on Sunday*) für bereits feststehende Pläne und Verabredungen verwenden (1).
> Genau wie im Deutschen wird auch im Englischen das **simple present mit einer Zeitangabe** benutzt, um fest terminierte Vorgänge (Fahrpläne, Stundenpläne, Programme usw.) anzugeben (2).

MODAL AUXILIARY VERBS

1 He **can speak** several languages.
2 You **must accept** your new situation.
3 We **needn't go** to work today.
4 **May** I **interrupt** you?

> Um zu sagen, was geschehen kann, muss, darf, soll usw., benutzt man ein modales Hilfsverb in Verbindung mit einem Vollverb (1-4).

⚠ Im Englischen steht ein Hilfsverb - anders als im Deutschen - nie ohne Vollverb:
- Lena kann Spanisch. ⟶ *Lena can speak Spanish.* NICHT: ~~Lena can Spanish.~~

> Modale Hilfsverben - nicht jedoch die Ersatzverben (siehe unten) - haben bei allen Personen immer die gleiche Form, einschließlich der 3. Person Singular (keine *-s*-Endung) (1, 2).
> Die **Verneinung** wird durch das Einfügen von *not/n't* unmittelbar nach dem Hilfsverb gebildet (3).
> **Fragen** bildet man durch Umstellung (4).
> Abgesehen von *could* (wenn damit eine Fähigkeit ausgedrückt werden soll) kann man modale Hilfsverben nur im Präsens und - mit einer geeigneten Zeitangabe - mit zukünftiger Bedeutung benutzen, zum Beispiel:
- *You **can go** home now.* (Präsens)
  *You **can go** home an hour early tomorrow.* (Futur)
- *I **must write** these letters now.* (Präsens)
  *I **must write** a long report next week.* (Futur)

⚠ Um andere Zeitformen bei modalen Hilfsverben zu bilden, z. B. die Vergangenheit, muss ein geeignetes Ersatzverb gebraucht werden:

must *The provider **had to block** access to the internet last December.*
can *I **couldn't start** the car yesterday.* (Fähigkeit)
*We **weren't allowed to go** home early last Friday.* (Erlaubnis)

Übersicht der modalen Hilfsverben nach Funktion

Funktion	Modale(s) Hilfsverb(en)	
Fähigkeit	*He **can** speak several languages.* *The first satellites **could** only transmit sound.*	
Möglichkeit	*With your qualifications you **could** work abroad.* *The boss **may** come in at any moment.* *He **might** ask you what you are doing.*	
Bitte	***Can** I have a word with Ms Sims, please?* ***Could** I speak to Ms Sims, please?* ***May** I interrupt you?* ***Might** I ask you a personal question?*	(neutral) (höflich) (betont höflich) (äußerst höflich)
Erlaubnis	*You **can** go in now.* *The boss is free. You **may** go in now.*	(neutral) (gefällig)
Verbot	*We **mustn't** be late for work tomorrow.*	
Pflicht	*You **must** wear a hard hat in the factory.*	
Wahl	*Most shop workers **needn't** work on Sundays.*	
Empfehlung	*You **should** get better qualifications.* *You **ought to** get better qualifications.* *You **must** get better qualifications.*	(neutral) (betont) (streng)

REPORTED SPEECH

A Aussagesätze

1 Some people **claim** that 'servant' robots **are putting** people out of work.
2 The speaker **reminded** his audience that there **were** some jobs robots **couldn't do**.

> Wenn man einem Dritten berichten möchte, was während eines Gespräches gesagt wurde, benutzt man die **indirekte Rede**.

> Bei Verwendung der indirekten Rede benutzt man ein einleitendes Verb wie *claim, say, remind, answer, think, mention* usw., um zu verdeutlichen, dass eine Äußerung wiedergegeben wird.
Steht das einleitende Verb in der Vergangenheit – also *said, answered, mentioned* usw. –, dann verschieben sich die Zeiten wie folgt:

direkte Rede		indirekte Rede
simple present *she works hard*	→	**simple past** *she worked hard*
present progressive *she is working hard*	→	**past progressive** *she was working hard*
simple past *she worked hard*	→	**past perfect** *she had worked hard*
past progressive *she was working hard*	→	**past perfect progressive** *she had been working hard*
present perfect *she has worked hard*	→	**past perfect** *she had worked hard*

present perfect progressive *she has been working hard*	→	**past perfect progressive** *she had been working hard*
past perfect *she had worked hard*		(keine Verschiebung) –
past perfect progressive *she had been working hard*		(keine Verschiebung) –
will *she will work hard*	→	**would** *she would work hard*
am/is/are going to *she is going to work hard*	→	**was/were going to** *she was going to work hard*
would/might etc. *she would work hard*		(keine Verschiebung) –
would have/might have etc. *she had been working hard*		(keine Verschiebung) –

⚠ Die modalen Hilfsverben werden folgendermaßen verschoben:

Modalverb	Bedeutung	indirekte Rede
can	Fähigkeit	*could, was/were able to*
can	Erlaubnis	*was/were allowed to*
may	Möglichkeit	*might*
may	Erlaubnis	*was/were allowed to*
must	Pflicht	*had to*
mustn't	Verbot	*was/were not allowed to*
needn't	freie Wahl	*did not/didn't have to*

> Außer wenn man über ein Gespräch berichtet, das am selben Tag stattgefunden hat, müssen fast alle **Zeit**- und einige **Ortsangaben** entsprechend der folgenden Tabelle geändert werden. (Angaben, die nicht aufgeführt sind, bleiben unverändert.)

direkte Rede		indirekte Rede
today	→	*on that day*
tomorrow	→	*the next day*
yesterday	→	*the day before*
the day after tomorrow	→	*two days later*
the day before yesterday	→	*two days before*
next day/Friday/week/Christmas/...	→	*the following day/Friday/week/Christmas/...*
last Friday/week/summer/...	→	*the Friday/week/summer/... before*
two years/months/weeks/... ago	→	*two years/months/weeks/... before*
now, at present	→	*then*
at the moment	→	*at that moment*
at this time	→	*at that time*
here	→	*there*
in this place	→	*at that place*
this	→	*that*
these	→	*those*

B Fragesätze

1 A member of the audience **asked what had led** to the widespread use of robots in factories.
2 She **wanted to know if/whether** her job **was endangered**.

> Bei indirekten **Fragen** unterscheidet man zwischen Fragen mit Fragewort (1) und Fragen ohne Fragewort (2).
> Bei Fragen **mit Fragewort** wird das Fragewort übernommen (1).
> Bei Fragen **ohne Fragewort** benutzt man *if* bzw. *whether* (= ob), um zu verdeutlichen, dass es sich um eine Frage handelt (2).
> Alle anderen Änderungen erfolgen wie bei den Aussagesätzen (siehe **Aussagesätze** S. 242).

C Bitten, Aufforderungen und Befehle

1 Lucy **asked the engineer to show her** the robot.
2 He **told her not to go** too close to it.

> **Bitten** werden meist durch *asked* (= bitten) (1), **Aufforderungen** und **Befehle** durch *told* (= sagen) (2) eingeleitet.
> Bei **positiven Sätzen** erscheint das Verb als *to* + Infinitiv (1).
> Bei **negativen Sätzen** wird *not* unmittelbar vor *to* gesetzt (2).

⚠ Die beiden Verben *to tell* und *to ask* stehen immer mit einem Objekt, das die angesprochene Person erwähnt (1, 2). Ist dies vom Kontext her nicht erkennbar, wird einfach ein passender Begriff eingesetzt:

> *Ben said, 'Don't enter the studio when the red light is on.'*
> *Ben **told everybody** not to enter the studio when the red light was on.*

THE PASSIVE

1 Measures **are being introduced** to reduce traffic pollution.
2 Pollution **is caused by** some thoughtless people.

> Ist der Verursacher einer Handlung unbekannt oder zweitrangig, benutzt man das Passiv. Im Vordergrund steht also das Ergebnis des Vorgangs (1).
> Möchte man den Verursacher doch angeben, benutzt man einen *by agent* (2).
⚠ Der Verursacher wird mit *by* – auf keinen Fall mit *from* – eingeleitet.
> Das Passiv wird mit einer Zeitform von *to be* und der 3. Form des Vollverbs gebildet:

Zeit	Zeitform von *to be*	3. Form
simple present	*am/is/are*	*caused*
present progressive	*am/is/are being*	*introduced*
simple past	*was/were*	*buried*
past progressive	*was/were being*	*built*
present perfect	*has/have been*	*installed*
will-Futur	*will be*	*blocked*
going to-Futur	*am/is/are going to be*	*sacked*

> Beim Gebrauch von modalen Hilfsverben wird nach folgendem Muster verfahren:

bei Aussagen	Hilfsverb + *to be* + 3. Form	*must be displayed*
bei Fragen	Hilfsverb + Subjekt + *to be* + 3. Form	*Can … be persuaded?*

⚠ Das Verb *to be* bleibt im Infinitiv immer unverändert.

THE IMPERSONAL PASSIVE

1 **It is said that** petrol will soon cost more.
2 He **is thought** to have completed the training course.

> Das **impersonal passive** wird vor allem dann benutzt, wenn man sich objektiv bzw. unbeteiligt ausdrücken möchte. Daher kommt diese Struktur oft in Polizeiberichten, seriösen Zeitungsartikeln usw. vor.

> Bei Verben des Berichtens, Denkens usw. benutzt man häufig das Satzmuster:
It is/was/… + 3. Form des einleitenden Verbs + *that*-Satz (1).
Hier sind weitere Beispiele dieses Musters:

Aktiv	*Some **say** that companies which cause pollution should be heavily fined.*
Passiv	***It is said that** companies which cause pollution should be heavily fined.*
Aktiv	*Experts **recommended** that more be spent on public transport.*
Passiv	***It was recommended** that more be spent on public transport.*

> Um das Subjekt des *that*-Satzes zu betonen, kann man folgendes Muster benutzen:
Subjekt + *is/was/…* + 3. Form + *to be* + andere Satzteile (2):

Aktiv	*Many **believe** that the minister is thinking of raising fuel taxes.*
Passiv	*The minister **is believed to be** thinking of raising fuel taxes.*

⚠ Der *by agent* wird in solchen Passivsätzen folgendermaßen verwendet:

Aktiv	*The speaker felt that the idea was too radical.*
Passiv	*The idea was felt to be too radical **by** the speaker.*

IF-SENTENCES

1 If we **invest** in new technology, a lot of people **will lose** their jobs.
2 A lot of people **will lose** their jobs if we **invest** in new technology.
3 If more people **took part** in re-training schemes, they **wouldn't have to worry** about finding new employment.
4 We **won't have** political censorship if we **don't start** to censor the internet.
5 **Will** we soon **have** political censorship if we **start** to censor the internet?

> Ein **Konditionalsatz** besteht aus zwei Teilen: dem ***if*-Teil** und dem **Hauptteil**.
Der ***if*-Teil** drückt eine **Bedingung** aus, der Hauptteil eine **Folge**.

> Bei **Konditionalsätzen** kommen folgende **Zeitmuster** am häufigsten vor:

Typ I	*If + simple present*	+	*will*-Futur
Typ II	*If + simple past*	+	*would* + Infinitiv
Typ III	*If + past perfect*	+	*would have* + 3. Form des Verbs

> Der *if*-Teil kann hinter dem Hauptteil stehen. In diesem Fall steht kein Komma dazwischen (2, 4, 5).

> Je nach Sinn kann der *if*-Teil, der Hauptteil oder beide Teile des Satzes **verneint** werden (3, 4).

> Bei **Fragen** kann nur der **Hauptteil** zu einer Frage geformt werden. Dann steht dieser Teil **an erster Stelle** (5).

> *if*-Sätze werden gemäß der **Wahrscheinlichkeit** der zu erwartenden Folge eingesetzt:
Typ I: Folge (fast) sicher.
*If we **invest in** new technology, a lot of people **will lose** their jobs.*
D.h. viele Leute werden (vermutlich) ihre Stellen verlieren, da wir (sehr wahrscheinlich) in die neue Technologie investieren werden.
Typ II: Folge theoretisch möglich, aber kaum wahrscheinlich.
*If we **invested in** new technology, a lot of people **would lose** their jobs.*
D.h. es ist kaum zu erwarten, dass viele Leute ihre Stellen verlieren werden, da wir (wahrscheinlich) nicht in die neue Technologie investieren werden.
Typ III: Folge unmöglich, da die Bedingung nicht erfüllt wurde und bereits in der Vergangenheit liegt.
*If we **had invested in** new technology, a lot of people **would have lost** their jobs.*
D.h. der Sprecher weiß schon, dass keiner den Job verloren hat, da wir in die neue Technologie nicht investiert haben.

GERUND/INFINITIVE

1 Max **enjoys visiting** his customers.
2 Can you **afford to buy** that new computer software?
3 Cem and Julie **continued to meet** even though they were no longer business partners.
4 Cem and Julie **continued meeting** even though they were no longer business partners.
5 Alison **normally likes meeting** clients, but **today** she would **prefer to stay** in the office.

> Nach einigen Verben folgt immer die *-ing*-Form **(gerund)** (1).
Am wichtigsten sind:

admit, avoid, consider, deny, enjoy, finish, give up, imagine, mention, (not) mind (etwas/nichts dagegen haben), *miss, practise, recommend, risk, stop, suggest*

> **Nach einigen Verben** folgt immer der Infinitiv **(infinitive)** (2).
Die **wichtigsten** Verben dieser Gruppe sind:

afford, choose, decide, expect, hope, manage, mean, plan, promise, refuse, want

⚠ Nach den Verben *begin, continue, intend* und *start* kann der **Infinitiv** oder die ***-ing*-Form beliebig benutzt werden** (3, 4).

> Einige Verben werden **je nach Bedeutung** entweder mit dem **Infinitiv** oder mit der ***-ing*-Form** benutzt. Die **wichtigsten** Verben dieser Gruppe sind:

like, dislike, love, hate, prefer

> Wenn von einer **allgemeingültigen Situation** die Rede ist, folgt auf diese Verben die ***-ing*-Form**. Handelt es sich aber um eine **Ausnahmesituation**, dann verwendet man den **Infinitiv** (5).

advise, allow, encourage, forbid, permit, recommend

Handelt es sich um einen **konkreten Einzelfall**, wird mit diesen Verben ein **Objekt + Infinitiv** verwendet.
*I strongly **advise you to** be more polite to people.*
Wenn es sich aber um eine **allgemeine Situation** handelt, dann steht das nachfolgende Verb in der ***-ing*-Form**.
*Most firms don't **allow smoking** in their offices.*

forget/remember

Die Struktur ***forget/remember*** **+ *-ing*-Form** bezieht sich auf die Vergangenheit. Sie drückt etwa die Idee „Ich werde nie vergessen ..." aus.

⚠ „Vergangenheit" bezieht sich hier nicht auf *forget/remember*, sondern auf das nachfolgende Verb.

I still ***remember getting*** *my first job.*
I'll never ***forget going*** *to the Japanese headquarters last year.*

Die Struktur ***forget/remember*** **+ Infinitiv** dagegen bezieht sich auf die Zukunft. Sie drückt etwa die Idee aus „Ich darf nicht vergessen, etwas zu tun" bzw. „Ich habe noch etwas zu tun, weil ich es bis jetzt vergessen habe".

Dad, please ***remember / don't forget to pick me up*** *from the station.*
Oh dear. I ***forgot / didn't remember to pick Sally up*** *from the station.*

regret

Die Struktur ***regret*** **+ *-ing*-Form** drückt Bedauern über eine vergangene Situation bzw. einen vergangenen Vorfall aus. Häufig geht es dabei um verpasste Chancen.

I really ***regret leaving*** *school without any qualifications.*
I know they will ***regret buying*** *such a big, expensive car.*

Die Struktur ***regret*** **+ Infinitiv** – fast immer mit einem Verb des Mitteilens wie *inform, say, tell* kombiniert – drückt eine schlechte Nachricht aus.

I ***regret to say*** *that I can't attend the meeting tomorrow.*
We ***regret to inform*** *you that the vacancy has now been filled.*

stop

Bedeutet ***stop*** „aufhören, etwas zu tun", steht das nachfolgende Verb in der ***-ing*-Form**.
Bedeutet ***stop*** aber „kurz anhalten, um etwas anderes zu tun", folgt ein Verb im **Infinitiv**.

For heaven's sake ***stop shouting*** *at me.*
I'm a little late because I ***stopped to give*** *somebody a lift.*

try

Bedeutet ***try*** „etwas ausprobieren", steht das nachfolgende Verb in der ***-ing*-Form**.
Bedeutet ***try*** aber „sich anstrengen, etwas zu tun", folgt ein Verb im **Infinitiv**.

I ***tried phoning*** *Ellie, but she wasn't at home.*
We'll ***try to repair*** *your computer by the weekend.*

ADJECTIVES AND ADVERBS

1 John has a **new** printer.
2 He always buys **expensive** equipment.
3 My computer has become **very slow**.
4 That CD sounds **terrible**.
5 We can make printouts **quickly** and **cheaply**.

> Um **Personen** oder **Sachen** näher zu beschreiben, benutzt man **Adjektive** (1–4).
> Adjektive stehen **unmittelbar** vor Substantiven oder **unmittelbar nach** einer Form von *be* (bzw. *become* oder *seem*, die *be* ersetzen können) (3).
> **Adjektive** können mit Verben wie *feel, look* (aussehen), *sound, smell* und *taste* eine **sinnliche Wahrnehmung** ausdrücken (4).
> Um einen **Tätigkeitsverb** näher zu beschreiben, setzt man ein Adverb **unmittelbar hinter das Verb** bzw. Verb + Objekt (5).

⚠ Im Englischen können ein Verb und sein Objekt – anders als im Deutschen – nicht durch ein Adverb getrennt werden. Also NICHT: ~~We can make quickly printouts~~. (siehe **Word order** unten)

> Adverbien werden auch benutzt, um **Adjektive, andere Adverbien** und **ganze Sätze** näher zu bestimmen:
MP3 players have become ***surprisingly cheap****.* (Adverb + Adjektiv)
My fax machine prints out ***terribly slowly****.* (Adverb + Adverb)
Luckily *Gerd left a message on my mailbox.* (Satzadverb)

> Die meisten Adverbien werden durch Anhängen von *-ly* an das Adjektiv gebildet (5). Eine kleine Anzahl von Adverbien hat dieselbe Form wie Adjektive; die häufigsten sind *fast, hard, early late, long, daily*.

COMPARISON OF ADJECTIVES AND ADVERBS

1 A hundred years ago life was **slower** and people may have been **happier**.
2 Which technological innovation is the **most/least important**?
3 Today you can copy data **more easily than** ever before.

> **Einsilbige** und **zweisilbige Adjektive**, die auf *-y* enden – zum Beispiel *easy, happy* und *lucky* –, werden mit *-(i)er*/*-(i)est* gesteigert (1).

> **Mehrsilbige Adjektive** und **Adverbien**, die auf *-ly* enden, werden mit *more/most* gesteigert (2, 3).
⚠ Die Adverbien, die dieselbe Form wie das entsprechende Adjektiv haben (*fast, hard, early* usw.), werden mit *-er*/*-est* gesteigert.

> Um Personen oder Sachen im Satz miteinander zu vergleichen, gibt es folgende Möglichkeiten:

Kein Unterschied	*as good as*	genau so gut wie
Unterschied	*not as good as*	nicht so gut wie
Unterschied	*better than*	besser als

WORD ORDER

positions of adverbs of time, place and frequency

1 She stays in hotels **every week**.
2 The company is based in a small town **outside of Frankfurt**.
3 **Last year** we went to an Italian restaurant for our department Christmas party.
4 Paul and Emily went to **the USA last year**.
5 She **always finishes** work early on Fridays.
6 He **is never** in the office when I call.
7 I like to work at home **now and then**.
8 Gina acted **strangely at the trade show last week**.

> Zeitangaben (Wann?) und Ortsangaben (Wo?, Wohin?) stehen in der Regel am Satzende (1, 2).

> Um die Zeit eines bestimmten Ereignisses hervorzuheben, kann man die Zeitangabe an die erste Stelle setzen (3).

> Stehen eine Zeitangabe und eine Ortsangabe zusammen am Satzende, dann gilt die Reihenfolge Ort vor Zeit (alphabetisch merken: O vor Z!) (4).

> Besteht eine Häufigkeitsangabe aus einem Wort, z.B. *always, often, sometimes*, steht sie unmittelbar vor dem Vollverb (5).

> Lautet das Vollverb *to be*, steht das Adverb direkt dahinter (6).

- Besteht die Häufigkeitsangabe aus mehreren Wörtern, z.B. *every day, now and then*, steht sie wie eine Zeitangabe am Satzende (7).
- Adverbien der Art und Weise stehen in der Regel am Satzende. Kommen noch Zeit- oder Ortsadverbien hinzu, lautet die Reihenfolge: Art und Weise - Ort - Zeit (AOZ) (8).

RELATIVE CLAUSES AND CONTACT CLAUSES

1 Car manufacturers are designing cars **which/that** can use hydrogen fuel cells.
2 Wildernesses are being spoiled by tourists **who/that** want to go to 'unspoiled' places.
3 Tony filled in a job satisfaction questionnaire **(which/that)** he found on the internet.
4 Fred Foley is a business tycoon **whose** fortune amounts to over €400 million.
5 Call centre employees, most **of whom** come from India, work long hours.
6 Some non-GM crops are attacked by pests **against which** they have no resistance.

- Relativsätze werden benutzt, um den Hauptsatz durch zusätzliche Informationen genauer zu bestimmen.
- Für **Sachen** benutzt man das Relativpronomen *which* bzw. *that* (1) und für Personen *who* bzw. *that* (2).
- Steht das Relativpronomen für das **Objekt des Hauptsatzes**, dann kann man es weglassen (3). Solche Relativsätze heißen **contact clauses**.
- Um **Besitz** bzw. **Zugehörigkeit** anzuzeigen, gebraucht man *whose* unmittelbar vor dem **Substantiv** bei Personen und Sachen (4).
- Steht eine **Präposition** vor dem **Relativpronomen**, wird *whom* für Personen und *which* für Sachen benutzt (5, 6). In solchen Fällen ist der Gebrauch von *that* nicht möglich.

DEFINING AND NON-DEFINING RELATIVE CLAUSES

1 The first Europeans **who** settled in Australia came from Britain.
2 Sydney, **which** is famous for its unusually designed opera house, is situated on the south-eastern coast of Australia.

- Im **ersten Beispielsatz** ist der Sinn des Hauptsatzes *The first Europeans came from Britain* ohne den Relativsatz *who settled in Australia* offensichtlich falsch bzw. unvollständig. Relativsätze dieser Art - die wesentlich für das Verständnis des gesamten Satzes sind - nennt man **defining relative clauses** (notwendige oder bestimmende Relativsätze).
- Im **zweiten Beispielsatz** ist die Aussage des Hauptsatzes *Sydney is situated on the south-eastern coast of Australia* ohne den Relativsatz völlig verständlich, weil der Relativsatz *which is famous for its unusually designed opera house* eine zusätzliche, also nebensächliche, Information enthält. Daher werden solche Relativsätze ***non-defining relative clauses*** (nicht notwendige oder nicht bestimmende Relativsätze) genannt.
  ⚠ Notwendige Relativsätze werden immer **ohne** trennende **Kommas** benutzt. Dies signalisiert, dass sie fester Bestandteil der Hauptaussage sind.

PARTICIPLE CONSTRUCTIONS

1 Malaria, preventable with a treated bed net **costing** less than one pound, is endemic.
2 Many men believe that any work **involved** with cooking is a woman's chore.
3 **Losing** more and more people to AIDS, Africa now needs effective help more urgently than ever before.

4 **Burdened** with declining life expectancy, large parts of Africa are caught in a poverty trap.
5 **Having fetched** water from a river for many years, some women in developing countries are now happy to be able to use the Hippo Roller.
6 **Despite facing** extreme destitution, many rural residents haven't given up hope.
7 Donors should invest in projects that help local inhabitants become self-supporting, **thereby making** sure that the money isn't wasted.
8 Poor infrastructure is a key barrier to economic growth in Nepal, **thus causing** huge additional costs to the transport of commercial goods.
9 Life is becoming hard in the developing countries, **with** many small farmers **going** out of business.
10 AIDS represents a major challenge to sub-Saharan Africa, currently **killing** more than two million people every year.

Die englische Sprache ist geprägt durch die häufige Verwendung von Partizipialkonstruktionen. Diese ermöglichen einen eleganteren Sprachfluss.

> Partizipialkonstruktionen verkürzen Relativsätze; dabei kann entweder das **present participle** (1) oder das **past participle** (2) verwendet werden.
> Sie werden auch verwendet, um adverbiale Nebensätze zu vekürzen. In diesen Fällen unterscheidet man zwischen Partizipialkonstruktionen ohne Konjunktion (3-5) und solchen mit Konjunktion (6-9). In Sätzen ohne Konjunktion ist der Inhalt des Satzes auch ohne eine solche klar. Dagegen sind Konjunktionen nötig, um zu verhindern, dass der logische Zusammenhang des Satzes verloren geht. Zum Beispiel wird der Inhalt von Satz 6 unklar, wenn die Konjunktion *despite* ausgelassen wird.
> Wie bei der Verkürzung von Relativsätzen kommen auch bei der Verkürzung von adverbialen Nebensätzen das **present participle** (3, 6-9) und das **past participle** (4) zur Anwendung. Darüber hinaus wird hier auch noch das **perfect participle** verwendet (5), und zwar um die Vorzeitigkeit der Handlung im Nebensatz auszudrücken. *(Nachdem sie jahrelang Wasser aus dem Fluss geholt hatten, ...)*
> Schließlich verknüpft man mit einer Partizipialkonstruktion zwei Hauptsätze zu einem einzigen Satz, und zwar ausnahmslos mittels **present participle** (10).

COUNTABLE AND UNCOUNTABLE NOUNS

1	Visit our website for more **information** on our firm.	NICHT ~~informations~~
2	Have you read the paper today? The political **news** is interesting.	NICHT ~~news are~~
3	Where can I get some **advice**?	NICHT ~~an advice~~

> Einige wichtige **Substantive** sind **zählbar im Deutschen, nicht jedoch im Englischen**. Diese Substantive können also nicht ohne weiteres mit dem unbestimmten Artikel *a/an* oder mit einem Zahlwort benutzt werden.
Hier ist eine Liste solcher Wörter, die Sie auswendig lernen sollten:

advice, baggage, damage, data, equipment, evidence, furniture, information, knowledge, luck, luggage, machinery, news, progress, research, rubbish, work (housework, homework)

> Um diese Substantive im Plural zu verwenden, muss *some, a bit of* bzw. *a piece of* hinzugefügt werden (3).

SOME AND *ANY*

1 **Some** departments prefer to hold regular weekly meetings.
2 They haven't got **any** women working in their company.
3 Have you got **any** information about arrival times?
4 Can I have **some** more coffee, please?
5 Would you like **some** mineral water?
6 There's **something** I need to do but I can't remember what it is.
7 He can't find that letter **anywhere**. Maybe **somebody** took it.

> Wir verwenden *some* in **bejahten Aussagen** (1) und *any* in **verneinten Aussagen** (2) und **„echten" Fragen** (3).
> Drückt die Frage eine höfliche **Bitte** (4) bzw. ein **Angebot** (5) aus, worauf eine positive Antwort erwartet wird, verwenden wir ebenfalls *some*.
> Wir verwenden die Zusammensetzungen von *some* and *any* - also *somebody/someone, something, somewhere, anybody/anyone, anything* und *anywhere* - in genau derselben Art und Weise (6-7).

THE DEFINITE ARTICLE

1 **Sociologists** say that **violence** is increasing among young people.
2 Is **the current trend** partly caused by **the violent films** they watch?
3 **Most sentences** are not tough enough.
4 Nearly **half the prisoners** in **British prisons** are under 25.
5 **Spring** is my favourite season but **the spring** we're having this year is more like **winter**.
6 We had **breakfast** late this morning so we came to work **by car** instead of **by bus**.
7 They are thinking of legalizing soft drugs in **the Netherlands**.

> Hat ein Substantiv eine allgemeine, uneingeschränkte Bedeutung - also „alle ohne Ausnahme" - dann steht es ohne Artikel (1, 5).
> Ist die Bedeutung eines Substantives auf bestimmte Fälle eingeschränkt, benutzt man den Artikel (2, 5).
> Ferner wird der Artikel in den folgenden Fällen und Wendungen im Englischen - z. T. anders als im Deutschen - nicht gebraucht:
- bei *most* in der Bedeutung „die meisten" (3),
- bei öffentlichen Gebäuden im allgemeinen Sinn (4),
- bei Mahlzeiten (6),
- bei Verkehrsmitteln (6),
- bei Straßennamen,
- bei Tageszeiten, Wochentagen, Monaten und Jahreszeiten im allgemeinen Sinn (5).

> Der Artikel wird verwendet nach *all* und *half* (4) und mit den Pluralnamen von Staaten (7).
⚠ Der bestimmte Artikel steht im Englischen (viel) seltener als im Deutschen. Daher: *When in doubt, leave it out!*

THE INDEFINITE ARTICLE

1 Yesterday I met **a woman** who works for **a friend** of my father's.
2 We'll have to buy **a** new **computer**.
3 That's **an** interesting **idea**.
4 Jane's **an accountant**? I thought she was **a sales rep**.
5 My father has been **a non-smoker** all his life.
6 How much does petrol cost **a liter**?
7 We have planning meetings four times **a month**.

> Der unbestimmten Artikel a/an steht bei einer einzelnen, nicht näher bestimmten Person (1), einer Sache (2), oder einem Begriff (3).

> Anders als im Deutschen verwenden wir im Englischen den unbestimmten Artikel in folgenden Fällen:
- bei Berufsangaben (4),
- bei Angaben über Nationalität, Religion, Politik oder Gruppenzugehörigkeit (5)
- bei Maß- (6), Verpackungs-, und Zeitangaben (7)
- bei den folgenden Wendungen:

to be in a hurry	in Eile sein, es eilig haben
to come to an end	enden
to have a bath/shower/...	sich baden/duschen/...
to have a go	es ausprobieren
to have a turn at (+ -ing-Form)	an der Reihe sein, etwas zu tun
to make a noise	Lärm machen
to take a seat	Platz nehmen
for a change	zur Abwechslung
for a long/short time	lange/kurze Zeit
in a loud/quiet voice	mit lauter/ruhiger Stimme
What a pity!	Wie schade!
without a break	ohne Pause

⚠ Bei *half, quite, rather* und *such* wird der unbestimmte Artikel nachgestellt:

> The meeting starts in half **an** hour.

> We had quite **a** successful year in 2005.

> Jack can be rather **an** idiot sometimes.

> We've never had such **a** big order.

Basic word list

Diese Liste enthält ca. 900 Grundwörter, die in **Focus on Business 4th Edition** als bekannt vorausgesetzt werden. Nicht aufgeführt, jedoch vorausgesetzt sind einige sehr elementare Wörter wie einfache Präpositionen, Pronomen, Farben, Zahlen, Tage, Jahreszeiten, Staaten usw. sowie internationale Wörter wie z. B. *hotel*, *restaurant*, *e-mail*.

able: to **be ~ to** können
about um, über, ungefähr
above über, oben, oberhalb
abroad im/ins Ausland
absolute(ly) absolut, völlig
to **accept** akzeptieren, annehmen
accident Unfall
across (hin)über; quer durch
active aktiv
activity Tätigkeit, Beschäftigung
actual(ly) eigentlich, tatsächlich
to **add** hinzufügen
to **address** adressieren, anreden; Adresse, Anrede
advice Rat(schlag)
afraid: I'm ~ leider
after nach
afternoon Nachmittag
afterwards nachher, danach
again wieder
against gegen
age Alter, Zeitalter
ago vor
to **agree** zustimmen, sich einigen, vereinbaren
ahead voraus, vorn
air Luft
airline Fluggesellschaft
airport Flughafen
all alle
to **allow** erlauben, gestatten
to **allow:** to **be ~ed to** etw dürfen
almost fast, beinah
alone allein(e)
along entlang, weiter, vorwärts
already schon, bereits
also auch, außerdem
although obwohl
always immer
amazing erstaunlich, fantastisch
ambulance Krankenwagen
among unter, zwischen
amusing lustig
angry böse, zornig, ärgerlich
animal Tier
another noch eine/r/s, ein/e andere/r/s
to **answer; answer** (be)antworten; Antwort, Lösung
any irgendetwas, irgendwelche
anybody (irgend)jemand, jeder
anymore: not ~ nicht mehr
anyone jede/r
anything (irgend)etwas
anyway trotzdem, sowieso
anywhere irgendwo
apartment Wohnung
apple Apfel
to **argue** sich streiten; argumentieren
around ungefähr, zirka; um (... herum)
to **arrive** ankommen, eintreffen
as well (as) ebenso (wie)
to **ask** fragen, bitten
at least zumindest, wenigstens
to **attack; attack** angreifen; Angriff
to **attend** teilnehmen, besuchen, absolvieren
aunt Tante
away weg, entfernt
back Rücken; zurück
bad(ly) schlecht
bag Tasche, Tüte
to **bake** backen
basic Grund-, Haupt-, grundsätzlich
basically im Prinzip, im Grunde
bathroom Badezimmer
beach Strand
beautiful(ly) schön, herrlich
because weil, da
to **become** werden
bed Bett
beer Bier
before vor, vorher, zuvor, bevor
to **begin** anfangen, beginnen
behind hinter, hinten
to **believe** glauben, meinen
below unter(halb), unten
between zwischen
beyond darüber hinaus
bicycle Fahrrad
big groß
bike (Fahr-, Motor-)Rad
birthday Geburtstag
bit: a ~ ein wenig, etwas
body Körper
to **book; book** buchen; Buch
bored: to **be/get ~** sich langweilen
boring langweilig
born geboren
boss Chef/in
both beide
bottle Flasche
box Kiste, Kasten, Karton
boy Junge
boyfriend Freund
bread Brot
breakfast Frühstück
bright hell, strahlend, glänzend
brilliant glänzend, genial, super
to **bring** bringen, mitbringen
brother Bruder
to **build** (auf)bauen
building Gebäude
to **burn** (ver)brennen
business Geschäft(e), Unternehmen, Wirtschafts-
busy beschäftigt, verkehrsreich, besetzt
but aber, sondern
to **buy** kaufen
calendar Kalender
to **call; call** (an)rufen; Anruf
to **call:** to **be ~ed** heißen
caller Anrufer/in
can können; Dose
car Auto
card Karte
careful(ly) vorsichtig, sorgfältig
to **carry** tragen, befördern
to **catch** fangen; packen; erreichen
to **cause; cause** hervorrufen, verursachen; Ursache, Grund
central zentral
centre Mitte, Mittelpunkt, Zentrum
certain(ly) sicher(lich), gewiss, bestimmt
chance Gelegenheit, Chance
to **change; change** wechseln, (sich ver)ändern, umsteigen; Veränderung
to **chat; chat** (mit jdm) plaudern, sich unterhalten; Schwätzchen
cheap billig, preiswert
cheese Käse
to **check** (über)prüfen, kontrollieren
child, children Kind, Kinder
choice Wahl, Auswahl
to **choose** wählen, aussuchen
Christmas Weihnachten
city Stadt
class Klasse, Kurs, Unterricht
to **clean; clean** putzen, säubern; sauber
clear(ly) klar, deutlich

clever(ly) klug, gescheit, raffiniert
to **climb** klettern, steigen
to **close** schließen, zumachen
clothes Kleidung, Kleider
coast Küste
cold Kälte; kalt
to **collect** (ein)sammeln; abholen
college Hochschule, Berufsschule, Universität
colour Farbe
colourful bunt, farbenfroh
to **come** kommen, geliefert werden
comfortable bequem, angenehm, komfortabel
common üblich, verbreitet, gemeinsam
to **communicate** sich verständigen, kommunizieren
communication Kommunikation, Verständigung
to **complete; complete(ly)** abschließen, ausfüllen, vervollständigen; völlig, vollständig, komplett
conference Tagung, Konferenz
context Zusammenhang, Kontext
to **continue** weitergehen, fortsetzen, weitermachen
contract Vertrag
conversation Gespräch, Unterhaltung
to **cook** kochen, braten
cool kühl, cool
to **copy; copy** kopieren, abschreiben; Kopie, Exemplar
to **correct; correct(ly)** berichtigen; richtig, genau
corridor Gang, Flur
to **cost; cost** kosten; Kosten
to **count** zählen
country Land, Staat
countryside Land(schaft), Natur
couple (Ehe-)Paar
couple: a ~ ein paar, einige
course Kurs, Studiengang
course: of ~ natürlich, selbstverständlich
crazy verrückt
creative kreativ, schöpferisch
crowd Menge, Menschenmasse
customer Kunde/Kundin
to **cut** schneiden
to **cycle** radeln
daily täglich
to **dance; dance** tanzen; Tanz
danger Gefahr
dangerous gefährlich
date Datum, Verabredung
daughter Tochter
day Tag
dear liebe/r
to **decide** (sich) entscheiden, beschließen, sich entschließen
decision Entscheidung, Beschluss
deep tief
to **describe** beschreiben
desert Wüste
detail Einzelheit, Detail, Angabe(n)
to **develop** (sich) entwickeln
development Entwicklung
dialogue Dialog
diary Tagebuch, Terminkalender
dictionary Wörterbuch
to **die** sterben
difference Unterschied
different(ly) verschieden, unterschiedlich
difficult schwierig, schwer
difficulty Schwierigkeit
dinner Abendessen
direct(ly) direkt
direction Richtung
direction: to **give ~s** den Weg beschreiben
to **discuss** diskutieren, besprechen, erörtern
to **do** tun, machen
doctor Arzt/Ärztin
dog Hund
door Tür
double doppelt, Doppel-
down her-/hinunter
to **dress** sich kleiden, sich anziehen
to **drink; drink** trinken; Getränk
to **drive** fahren
driver Fahrer/in
during während
each jede/r/s, jeweils
each: ~ other einander
early früh
to **earn** verdienen
Easter Ostern
eas(il)y einfach, leicht
to **eat** essen
edition Ausgabe
effect Auswirkung, Effekt
egg Ei
either: ~ ... or entweder ... oder
either: not ... ~ auch nicht, auch kein/e
else sonst (noch), andere/r/s
empty leer
to **end; end** (be)enden; Ende, Schluss
engine Motor
to **enjoy** genießen, gefallen
to **enjoy doing sth** etw gern tun
enough genug
even sogar, noch
event Ereignis, Veranstaltung
ever je(mals)
every jede/r/s
everybody jede/r
everyone jede/r
everything alles
everywhere überall(hin)
exact(ly) genau, exakt
exam Prüfung
example Beispiel
example: for ~ zum Beispiel
excellent ausgezeichnet, hervorragend
except außer
excited (freudig) aufgeregt
exciting aufregend, spannend
to **excuse; excuse** entschuldigen; Ausrede
to **exercise; exercise** üben, trainieren; Übung, Training
exercise book (Schul-)Heft
to **expect** erwarten
expensive teuer
to **explain** erklären, erläutern
expression Ausdruck
extreme(ly) äußerst, extrem
eye Auge
fact Tatsache
factory Fabrik
fair Messe; fair, gerecht
fairly ziemlich
to **fall; fall** sinken, fallen; Rückgang
false falsch
family Familie
famous berühmt
fantastic fantastisch, großartig
far weit
farm Bauernhof
farmer Bauer/Bäuerin
fascinating faszinierend
fast schnell
fat dick
father Vater
favourite Lieblings-
to **feel** (sich) fühlen, glauben
feeling Gefühl, Ansicht
few wenige
few: a ~ einige, ein paar
field Feld
to **fight; fight** (be)kämpfen; Kampf
to **file; file** ablegen; Ordner, Akte
to **fill** (aus-, be-)füllen; übernehmen; erledigen
to **fill: ~ in** ausfüllen
final letzte/r/s, End-
finally endlich, schließlich, zuletzt
financial(ly) finanziell
to **find (out)** (heraus)finden, feststellen
fine gut, schön, in Ordnung
finger Finger
to **finish; finish** zu Ende bringen, (be-, ab)schließen; Schluss
fire Feuer, Brand
first name Vorname
fish Fisch
flat Wohnung; flach
floor Etage
flower Blume, Blüte
to **fly** fliegen
following folgende/r/s

food Essen, Lebensmittel
foot, feet Fuß, Füße
to **forget** vergessen
forward vorwärts, nach vorn
free frei, umsonst
freedom Freiheit
fresh frisch
friend Freund/in
friendly freundlich
front: in ~ vorne, davor
front: in ~ of vor
fruit Obst, Frucht
full(y) voll, völlig
fun Spaß
funny lustig, seltsam
furniture Möbel
further weiter/e/s
future Zukunft, zukünftige/r/s
game Spiel
garden Garten
gate Tor; Flugsteig
general(ly) allgemein, generell
to **get** bekommen, werden, gelangen
to **get on** vorankommen
to **get up** aufstehen
giant Riese; riesig
girl Mädchen
girlfriend Freundin
to **give** geben, schenken
to **give up** aufgeben, aufhören mit
glad froh
glass Glas
to **go** gehen, fahren
to **go on** weitermachen, fortfahren
good gut
goodbye auf Wiedersehen
grammar Grammatik
grandchildren Enkelkinder
great groß, großartig, toll
group Gruppe
to **grow** (an)wachsen
to **grow up** aufwachsen
guest Gast
hair Haar, Haare
half Hälfte, halb
ham Schinken
hand Hand
hand: on the one ~, on the other ~ einerseits, andererseits
to **happen** passieren, geschehen
happy glücklich, zufrieden
hard hart, schwer, schwierig
harmless harmlos
to **have to** müssen
head Kopf
health Gesundheit(szustand)
healthy gesund
to **hear** hören
heart Herz, Zentrum
heavy schwer
to **help; help** helfen; Hilfe
helpful hilfreich, hilfsbereit
here hier
high hoch
to **hold** halten
holiday Ferien, Urlaub, Feiertag
home zu/nach Hause, Zuhause
homework Hausaufgaben
to **hope; hope** hoffen; Hoffnung
hour Stunde
house Haus
how wie
however doch, jedoch, aber; egal wie
hungry hungrig
ice Eis
idea Idee, Gedanke, Vorstellung
if wenn, falls
ill krank
immediate(ly) unmittelbar, umgehend, sofort
important wichtig
to **improve** (sich) verbessern
indoors drinnen
to **inform** informieren, unterrichten
inside in, innen, hinein
to **interest; interest** interessieren; Interesse
interested: to be ~ in interessiert sein an, sich interessieren für
interesting interessant
to **introduce** einführen, vorstellen, bekanntmachen
introduction(s) Einleitung, Einführung, Vorstellung, Bekanntmachen
to **invite** einladen
island Insel
jacket Jacke, Jackett
jam Marmelade, Konfitüre
job Arbeit, Stelle, Arbeitsplatz
to **join** verbinden, beitreten, sich anschließen
journey Fahrt, Reise
just einfach, gerade
to **keep** bleiben, halten, behalten, aufbewahren, etw weiter tun
kids Kinder
kind Sorte; freundlich
king König
kitchen Küche
to **know** wissen, kennen
knowledge Wissen, Kenntnis
lady Dame
lake See
to **land; land** landen; Land
language Sprache
large groß, bedeutend
last: at ~ endlich
to **last; last** dauern; letzte/r/s
late spät
to **lead** führen
to **learn** lernen
to **leave** (ver-, hinter-, da)lassen, weggehen, abfahren
to **lend** leihen
less weniger
to **let** lassen
letter Brief, Buchstabe
to **lie** liegen
life Leben
lift Aufzug
light hell, leicht; Licht
to **like; like** mögen, gern haben; (ähnlich) wie
line Linie, Zeile, Leitung
to **list; list** auflisten; Liste
to **listen (to)** (zu-, an)hören
little klein, wenig
little: a ~ ein bisschen
to **live** leben
lonely einsam
long lang
to **look; look** ansehen, aussehen; Blick
to **look after** sich kümmern um
lorry Lastwagen
to **lose** verlieren
lot: a ~ (of) viel, viele
lots of viel, viele
to **love; love** lieben, sehr gern mögen; Liebe
lovely hübsch, nett
low niedrig
luck Glück
luckily glücklicherweise
lucky glücklich
lucky: to **be ~** Glück haben
lunch Mittagessen
lunch break Mittagspause
madam gnädige Frau
magazine Zeitschrift
main Haupt-, hauptsächliche/r/s
to **make** machen
man, men Mann, Männer
many viele
map Stadtplan, Landkarte
to **market; market** vermarkten; Markt
married verheiratet
may dürfen, können
maybe vielleicht
to **mean** bedeuten, heißen, meinen
meaning Bedeutung, Sinn
meat Fleisch
to **meet** treffen, kennen lernen
meeting Sitzung, Besprechung, Konferenz
member Mitglied
message Nachricht, Botschaft
midday Mittag
middle mittlere/r/s
midnight Mitternacht
might könnte
mile Meile
milk Milch
minute Minute
mirror Spiegel
to **miss** vermissen, verpassen

missing fehlend
mistake Fehler
to **mix; mix** mischen; Mischung
model Modell, Beispiel
moment Moment, Augenblick
moment: at the ~ im Augenblick
money Geld
month Monat
more mehr
morning Morgen
most der/die/das meiste, die meisten
mostly größtenteils
mother Mutter
motorbike Motorrad
mountain Berg
to **move** (sich) bewegen, umziehen, verlegen, versetzen
much viel
must müssen
must not nicht dürfen
to **name; name** (be)nennen; Name
nature Nature
near nahe, in der Nähe von
nearly beinahe, fast
necessary notwendig, nötig
to **need; need** brauchen, benötigen; Bedarf, Bedürfnis
neighbour Nachbar/in
neither keines (von beiden), auch nicht
never nie(mals)
new neu
news Neuigkeit(en), Nachricht(en)
newspaper Zeitung
next nächste/r/s, danach
nice schön, nett
night Nacht
nobody niemand
none keine/r/s
normal(ly) normal(erweise)
north (nach) Norden, Nord
to **note; note** notieren, zur Kenntnis nehmen; Notiz
nothing nichts
to **notice** beachten, bemerken
now nun, jetzt
nowhere nirgends
number Zahl, (Telefon-)Nummer
obvious(ly) offensichtlich, klar, deutlich, natürlich
occasional(ly) gelegentlich
to **offer; offer** (an)bieten; Angebot
office Büro, Amt
often oft, häufig
oil Öl
old alt
once einmal; sobald
only nur
to **open; open** (sich) öffnen, eröffnen; offen
opinion Meinung
opportunity Gelegenheit
opposite Gegenteil; gegenüber(liegend)
or oder
order: in ~ to um ... zu
to **order; order** bestellen; Bestellung, Auftrag, Reihenfolge
ordinary gewöhnlich, normal
other andere/r/s, weitere/r/s
otherwise sonst, ansonsten
ought to sollte
outside Außenseite; außerhalb von, draußen
over über, vorüber
to **own; own** besitzen; eigene/r/s
page Seite
paint Farbe
pair Paar
paragraph Absatz, Abschnitt
parents Eltern
part Teil
particular bestimmt, besondere/r/s, speziell
particularly besonders, vor allem, insbesondere
partner Partner, Gesellschafter/in
past Vergangenheit; vorbei (an), hinter
path Weg, Pfad
to **pay; pay** (be)zahlen; Bezahlung, Gehalt
people Leute, Menschen
per cent Prozent
perfect vollkommen, perfekt
perhaps vielleicht
period Zeit(raum), Frist
permanent(ly) dauerhaft, bleibend
person Person
to **phone; phone** telefonieren, anrufen; Telefon
photo Foto
phrase Ausdruck, Redewendung
to **pick up** abholen
picture Bild
piece Stück, Teil
place Stelle, Platz, Ort
to **plan; plan** planen; Plan
plane Flugzeug
planet Planet
to **play** spielen
pleasant angenehm, freundlich, nett
please bitte
pleased froh, erfreut
pleasure Vergnügen
pocket Tasche
to **point; point** zeigen, richten; Punkt, Argumente, Seite
police Polizei
pool Schwimmbad, Pool
poor arm, schlecht
popular beliebt, populär
possible möglich, denkbar
possibly möglicherweise
post Post
pound Pfund
practice Praxis, Verfahrensweise
to **practise** üben, trainieren
to **prefer** vorziehen, lieber mögen
to **prepare** (sich) vorbereiten
present Gegenwart, Geschenk
pretty hübsch; ziemlich
price Preis
private privat, persönlich
probably wahrscheinlich
programme (TV-, Radio-)Sendung, Programm, Plan
to **promise; promise** versprechen; Versprechen
proper(ly) richtig, ordnungsgemäß
to **protect** schützen, beschützen
pub Kneipe
to **pull** ziehen
pupil Schüler/in
to **put** setzen, stellen, legen
to **put on** anziehen
quality Qualität, Eigenschaft
queen Königin
question Frage
quick(ly) schnell
quiet(ly) still, ruhig, leise
quite ziemlich, ganz
to **race; race** rennen; Rennen
to **rain; rain** regnen; Regen
rather ziemlich
to **reach; reach** erreichen; Reichweite
to **read** lesen, vorlesen
ready bereit
real(ly) echt, wirklich, sehr
to **receive** erhalten, empfangen
recent jüngst, aktuell
recently neulich, kürzlich, in letzter Zeit
regular(ly) regelmäßig
to **relax** sich entspannen
to **remember** sich an etw erinnern, daran denken
to **rent; rent** mieten; Miete
to **reply; reply** antworten; Antwort
to **report; report** berichten; Bericht
to **reserve** reservieren, buchen
rest Rest
result Folge, Ergebnis
to **return** zurückkehren, zurückgeben, -senden
rich reich, wohlhabend
right richtig; rechts; Recht
to **risk; risk** riskieren; Risiko
river Fluss
road Straße
role Rolle
room Zimmer, Raum
round rund; (um/in ...) herum
rule Regel, Vorschrift
to **run** laufen, rennen
sad traurig

safe sicher
safety Sicherheit
to **sail; sail** segeln, zur See fahren; Segel
salad Salat
salt Salz
same gleiche/r/s, der-, die-, dasselbe
to **say** sagen
school Schule
sea Meer, See
season Saison
seat Sitz, Platz
second-hand gebraucht, aus zweiter Hand
secretary Sekretär/in
to **see** sehen
to **seem** scheinen
to **sell** verkaufen
to **send** senden, schicken
sentence Satz
serious(ly) ernst(haft)
several etliche, einige, mehrere
shelf Regal
ship Schiff
shirt Hemd
shoe Schuh
to **shop; shop** einkaufen; Laden, Geschäft
short kurz
should sollte
shoulder Schulter
to **show** zeigen
sightseeing Besichtigungen
to **sign; sign** unterschreiben, unterzeichnen; Zeichen, Schild
silly albern, doof
simple (simply) einfach, schlicht
since seit, seitdem, da, weil
to **sing** singen
sir mein Herr
to **sit** sitzen
to **sit down** sich setzen
size Größe
slow(ly) langsam
small klein
to **smell; smell** riechen; Duft, Geruch
to **smile; smile** lächeln; Lächeln
to **smoke; smoke** rauchen; Rauch
snow Schnee
so so, also
soap Seife
some etwas, einige, irgendein
somebody jemand
something etwas
sometimes manchmal
somewhere irgendwo(hin)
son Sohn
song Lied
soon bald
(I'm) sorry (es) tut mir leid
sort Art, Sorte
to **sound; sound** klingen; Klang
soup Suppe
to **speak** sprechen
special besondere/r/s, Sonder-
spend *(Zeit)* verbringen, *(Geld)* ausgeben
sport Sport(art)
stairs Treppe
to **stand** stehen
star Stern, Star
to **start; start** beginnen, eröffnen; Anfang
station Bahnhof
to **stay** bleiben, wohnen
still noch immer
to **stop** aufhören, anhalten
storm Sturm, Unwetter
story Geschichte
straight direkt, gerade
strange seltsam
stranger Fremde/r
street Straße
strong stark
to **study** lernen, studieren, sich etw genau ansehen, durchlesen
subject Thema; (Schul-)Fach; Betreff
success Erfolg
successful(ly) erfolgreich
such solche/r/s
sudden(ly) plötzlich
sugar Zucker
summer Sommer
sun Sonne
to **suppose** glauben, annehmen, vermuten
sure sicher, freilich
to **surprise; surprise** überraschen; Überraschung
sweet süß
sweets Süßigkeiten
to **swim** schwimmen
table Tisch; Tabelle
to **take** (an-, ein-, mit)nehmen, dauern
to **talk** reden, sprechen
tall groß, hoch
task Aufgabe
tea Tee
to **tell** sagen
tent Zelt
terrible furchtbar, schrecklich
than als
to **thank** danken
thanks danke
that dies; der, die, das; dass; jene/r/s
then dann
there da, dort, dorthin
therefore deshalb
these diese
thief Dieb
thing Sache, Ding
to **think (of)** denken (an), halten von
this dies, diese/r/s
those jene
though obwohl, doch
through durch, hindurch
time Zeit, Mal
title Titel, Anrede, Bezeichnung
today heute
together zusammen
tomorrow morgen
tonight heute Abend
too zu, auch
toothpaste Zahncreme
top Spitze, Anfang; Spitzen-, oberste/r/s
total(ly) völlig, total, Gesamt
towards gegen, auf ... zu, (in) Richtung
town Stadt
toy Spielzeug
traffic Verkehr
train Zug
trainee Auszubildende/r
to **translate** übersetzen
to **travel; travel** reisen, fahren; Reisen
tree Baum
trip Reise, Ausflug
trouble Problem(e), Schwierigkeiten, Mühe(n)
truck Lastwagen
true wahr
to **try** versuchen, probieren
twice zweimal
twin Zwilling, Zwillings-
to **type; type** tippen; Art, Sorte, Typ
ugly hässlich
under unter
to **understand** verstehen, begreifen
unfortunately leider, unglücklicherweise
unfriendly unfreundlich
unhappy unzufrieden, unglücklich
unhealthy ungesund
unit Einheit, Lektion, Stück
university Universität
unless wenn nicht; es sei denn, dass
unnecessary unnötig
until bis
unusual ungewöhnlich, unüblich
to **use; use** gebrauchen, benutzen; Verwendung, Gebrauch
useful nützlich
usual(ly) normal(erweise), gewöhnlich
vegetable Gemüse
very sehr
via über, per
village Dorf
to **visit; visit** besuchen, besichtigen; Besuch, Besichtigung
visitor Besucher/in

to **wait** warten
waiter, waitress Kellner/in
to **wake up** aufwachen
to **walk; walk** (zu Fuß) gehen; Spaziergang, Fußweg
wall Wand
to **want** wollen, mögen
warm warm
to **warn** warnen
to **watch** zusehen, beobachten, anschauen
way Weg, Methode
way: this ~ hier entlang
weak schwach
to **wear** tragen
week Woche
weekday Wochentag
weekend Wochenende
weight Gewicht
to **welcome; welcome** willkommen heißen; willkommen
well also; gut
what was, welche/r/s
whatever was auch immer
wheel Rad
when wenn, als, wann
where wo, wohin
whether ob
which welche/r/s
while während, solange; Weile
who wer, die, der
whoever wer auch immer
whole ganze/r/s
why warum, weshalb
why: that's ~ deshalb, darum
will will, wollen, werden; Wille
to **win** gewinnen, siegen
to **wish; wish** wünschen; Wunsch
with mit, bei
within innerhalb, binnen, in
without ohne
woman, women Frau
to **wonder (about); wonder** sich (etw) fragen; Wunder
wonderful wunderbar
word Wort
to **work; work** arbeiten, funktionieren; Arbeit
world Welt
to **worry; worry** sich Sorgen machen; Sorge
to **write (down)** (auf-, ab)schreiben
wrong falsch
year Jahr
yesterday gestern
yet schon, bereits
young jung

Unit word list

Dieses Wörterverzeichnis enthält alle Wörter in **Focus on Business 4th Edition** in der Reihenfolge ihres Auftretens. Nicht aufgeführt sind die Wörter aus der *Basic word list* sowie internationale Wörter wie *hotel*, *e-mail* usw. Wörter, die in den Hörverständnisübungen vorkommen, sind mit einem orangefarbenen Balken, und Wörter, die in den *Partner files* vorkommen, mit einem blauen Balken gekennzeichnet.

TOPIC 1

page 6

position [pə'zɪʃn]	Position, Stellung, (Arbeits-)Stelle
automobile sales management assistant [ɔ:təməbi:l 'seɪlz mænɪdʒmənt əˌsɪstənt]	Automobilkaufmann/-frau
bank business management assistant [bæŋk 'bɪznəs mænɪdʒmənt əˌsɪstənt]	Bankkaufmann/-frau
hotel management assistant [həʊ'tel mænɪdʒmənt əˌsɪstənt]	Hotelkaufmann/-frau
information technology officer [ɪnfəˌmeɪʃn tek'nɒlədʒi ɒfɪsə]	Informatikkaufmann/-frau
management assistant for retail services [ˌmænɪdʒmənt əsɪstənt fə 'ri:teɪl sɜ:vɪsəz]	Kaufmann/-frau im Einzelhandel
management assistant in freight forwarding [ˌmænɪdʒmənt əsɪstənt ɪn 'freɪt fɔ:wədɪŋ]	Speditionskaufmann/-frau
to **deal with sb/sth** ['di:l wɪð]	es mit jdm/etw zu tun haben
paperwork ['peɪpəwɜ:k]	Formalitäten, Büroarbeit
form [fɔ:m]	Formular
to **make sure** [ˌmeɪk 'ʃʊə]	sicherstellen, sich vergewissern
goods [gʊdz]	Güter, Ware(n)
up to date [ˌʌp tə 'deɪt]	aktuell; auf dem neuesten Stand
current ['kʌrənt]	aktuell
to **advise** [əd'vaɪz]	(be)raten
proper(ly) ['prɒpə]	richtig
to **prepare sth** [prɪ'peə]	etw erstellen
credit ['kredɪt]	Kredit
contract ['kɒntrækt]	Vertrag; Auftrag
to **run tests** [ˌrʌn 'tests]	Tests/Untersuchungen durchführen

page 7

experience [ɪk'spɪəriəns]	Erfahrung
work experience ['wɜ:k ɪkspɪəriəns]	Praktikum
post [pəʊst]	Eintrag, Post (in einem Blog)
weekly ['wi:kli]	wöchentlich
archive ['ɑ:kaɪv]	Archiv
comment ['kɒment]	Kommentar
to **contact sb** ['kɒntækt]	sich mit jdn in Verbindung setzen
tired ['taɪəd]	müde
to **be in a hurry** [bi ɪn ə 'hʌri]	es eilig haben
Wait a minute. ['weɪt ə mɪnɪt]	Moment mal!
student ['stju:dnt]	Schüler/in, Berufsschüler/in
college ['kɒlɪdʒ]	Berufsschule, Berufsfachschule
employer [ɪm'plɔɪə]	Arbeitgeber/in
interview ['ɪntəvju:]	Vorstellungsgespräch
work placement ['wɜ:k pleɪsmənt]	Praktikum
store [stɔ:]	Geschäft, Laden
retail ['ri:teɪl]	Einzelhandel
purchasing ['pɜ:tʃəsɪŋ]	Einkauf, Beschaffung
department [dɪ'pɑ:tmənt]	Abteilung
purchasing department ['pɜ:tʃəsɪŋ dɪpɑ:tmənt]	Einkaufsabteilung, Beschaffungsabteilung
stock [stɒk]	Ware(n), Bestand
customer service [ˌkʌstəmə 'sɜ:vɪs]	Kundendienst, Kundenbetreuung
to **handle sth** ['hændl]	etw bearbeiten
query ['kwɪəri]	Anfrage, Frage
accounts [ə'kaʊnts]	Buchführung, Buchhaltung
financial [faɪ'nænʃl]	Finanz-, finanziell
surprising [sə'praɪzɪŋ]	erstaunlich
behind the scenes [bɪˌhaɪnd ðə 'si:nz]	hinter den Kulissen
rare(ly) ['reə]	selten
personnel [ˌpɜ:sə'nel]	Personal
employee [ɪm'plɔɪi:]	Angestellte/r, Beschäftigte/r
job advertisement ['dʒɒb ədvɜ:tɪsmənt]	Stellenanzeige
to **update** [ˌʌp'deɪt]	auf den neusten Stand bringen, aktualisieren
records ['rekɔ:dz]	Daten, Akten, Unterlagen
form letter ['fɔ:m letə]	Formbrief, Serienbrief
to **photocopy** ['fəʊtəʊkɒpi]	fotokopieren
paperwork ['peɪpəwɜ:k]	Unterlagen
to **answer the phone** [ˌɑ:nsə ðə 'fəʊn]	ans Telefon gehen
not yet [nɒt 'jet]	noch nicht
honest ['ɒnɪst]	ehrlich
folks [fəʊks]	Leute
I'm off to bed. [aɪm ˌɒf tə 'bed]	Ich gehe dann mal ins Bett.

page 8

staff [stɑ:f]	Personal, Belegschaft
to **treat** [tri:t]	behandeln
administrative [əd'mɪnɪstrətɪv]	Verwaltungs-

to **organize** ['ɔ:gənaɪz]	organisieren
advantage [əd'vɑ:ntɪdʒ]	Vorteil
disadvantage [,dɪsəd'vɑ:ntɪdʒ]	Nachteil
in my opinion [ɪn ,maɪ ə'pɪniən]	meiner Meinung nach
view [vju:]	Ansicht
to **replace** [rɪ'pleɪs]	ersetzen, austauschen
in italics [ɪn ɪ'tælɪks]	kursiv
similar ['sɪmələ]	ähnlich
company ['kʌmpəni]	Unternehmen, Gesellschaft, Firma
to **deal with sth** ['di:l wɪð]	etw erledigen, etw bearbeiten
complaint [kəm'pleɪnt]	Reklamation; Beschwerde, Klage
purchase ['pɜ:tʃəs]	Kauf
to **involve** [ɪn'vɒlv]	mit sich bringen, einbeziehen, beinhalten
the public [ðə 'pʌblɪk]	die Öffentlichkeit
concerning [kən'sɜ:nɪŋ]	betreffend
notice ['nəʊtɪs]	Hinweis, Bekanntmachung
to **contain** [kən'teɪn]	enthalten
latest ['leɪtɪst]	neueste/r/s
gap [gæp]	Lücke, Zwischenraum
to **fill in** [,fɪl 'ɪn]	ausfüllen
printed ['prɪntɪd]	gedruckt

page 9

accounts manager [ə'kaʊnts mænɪdʒə]	Leiter/in der Buchhaltung
purchasing manager ['pɜ:tʃəsɪŋ mænɪdʒə]	Einkaufsleiter/in
personnel assistant [,pɜ:sə'nel əsɪstənt]	Personalassistent/in
employee records [ɪm'plɔɪi: rekɔ:dz]	Personalakte
sales [seɪlz]	Verkauf, Vertrieb
sales assistant ['seɪlz əsɪstənt]	Verkäufer/in
to **serve sb** [sɜ:v]	jdn bedienen
accounts assistant [ə'kaʊnts əsɪstənt]	Buchhaltungsassistent/in
representative [,reprɪ'zentətɪv]	Vertreter/in
personnel manager [,pɜ:sə'nel mænɪdʒə]	Personalchef/in
purchasing assistant ['pɜ:tʃəsɪŋ əsɪstənt]	Einkaufsassistent/in
present ['preznt]	Gegenwart
coffee break ['kɒfi breɪk]	Kaffeepause
keyboard ['ki:bɔ:d]	Tastatur
cash register ['kæʃ redʒɪstə]	Registrierkasse
training course ['treɪnɪŋ kɔ:s]	Lehrgang
to **make friends** [meɪk 'frendz]	Freunde finden, Freundschaft(en) schließen
boss [bɒs]	Chef/in

page 10

currently ['kʌrəntli]	derzeit, zurzeit
enjoyable [ɪn'dʒɔɪəbl]	angenehm, schön
law firm ['lɔ: fɜ:m]	Anwaltskanzlei
high street ['haɪ stri:t]	Hauptgeschäftsstraße
translation [træns'leɪʃn]	Übersetzung
appropriate [ə'prəʊpriət]	passend, angemessen
duty ['dju:ti]	Pflicht
career [kə'rɪə]	Karriere, Laufbahn, Beruf
freight forwarding company ['freɪt fɔ:wədɪŋ kʌmpəni]	Speditionsunternehmen
importer [ɪm'pɔ:tə]	Importeur
exporter [ɪk'spɔ:tə]	Exporteur
shipment ['ʃɪpmənt]	Versand
customs (authority) ['kʌstəmz ɔ:θɒrəti]	Zoll(behörde)
insurance [ɪn'ʃʊərəns]	Versicherung
suitable ['su:təbl]	geeignet, passend
packing ['pækɪŋ]	Verpackung, Versandverpackung
to **keep track of sth** [,ki:p 'træk əv]	den Überblick behalten bei etw, etw im Auge behalten
to **summarize** ['sʌməraɪz]	zusammenfassen
ability [ə'bɪləti]	Fähigkeit, Können, Talent
to **switch between (languages)** [swɪtʃ]	wechseln, umschalten zwischen (Sprachen)
Turkish ['tɜ:kɪʃ]	Türkisch; türkisch
efficient [ɪ'fɪʃnt]	effizient, rationell
available [ə'veɪləbl]	verfügbar, erhältlich
close(ly) [kləʊs]	eng
smooth(ly) [smu:ð]	glatt, reibungslos, problemlos
(job) satisfaction [,sætɪs'fækʃn]	Zufriedenheit (am/mit dem Arbeitsplatz)
to **research sth** [rɪ'sɜ:tʃ]	Nachforschungen über etw anstellen, etw recherchieren

page 11

to **share** [ʃeə]	teilen
pay [peɪ]	Bezahlung, Lohn
qualification [,kwɒlɪfɪ'keɪʃn]	Qualifikation, Zeugnis
various ['veəriəs]	unterschiedlich
to **go places** [,gəʊ 'pleɪsɪz]	herumkommen
office management assistant ['ɒfɪs mænɪdʒmənt ə,sɪstənt]	Bürokaufmann/-frau
careers officer [kə'rɪəz ɒfɪsə]	Berufsberater/in
enquiry [ɪn'kwaɪəri]	Anfrage
employment [ɪm'plɔɪmənt]	Anstellung, Beschäftigung, Arbeit
employment agency [ɪm'plɔɪmənt eɪdʒənsi]	Arbeitsvermittlung, Arbeitsamt
to **take sb on** [,teɪk 'ɒn]	jdn annehmen, übernehmen
to **offer sb sth** ['ɒfə]	jdm etw anbieten
to **be keen on sth / to do sth** [bi 'ki:n ɒn]	auf etw wild sein, etw unbedingt wollen
well paid (a well-paid job) [,wel 'peɪd]	gut bezahlt
Dream on. ['dri:m ,ɒn]	Träum weiter!
low-paying sector [ləʊ ,peɪɪŋ 'sektə]	Niedriglohnsektor
wage [weɪdʒ]	Lohn, Gehalt
minimum wage [,mɪnɪməm 'weɪdʒ]	Mindestlohn
though [ðəʊ]	allerdings, aber, jedoch
negative ['negətɪv]	verneinend
to **check sb/sth out** [,tʃek 'aʊt]	sich jdn/etw ansehen
employment record [ɪm'plɔɪmənt rekɔ:d]	berufliche Laufbahn, Erwerbstätigkeit
professional [prə'feʃənl]	beruflich, Berufs-; professionell
official(ly) [ə'fɪʃl]	offiziell

to **recognize** ['rekəgnaɪz]	anerkennen; (wieder) erkennen
to **complete** [kəm'pli:t]	abschließen, beenden
apprenticeship [ə'prentɪʃɪp]	Lehre, Ausbildung
training course ['treɪnɪŋ kɔ:s]	Ausbildung
TOEFL (Test of English as a Foreign Language) ['təʊfl,,test əv ,ɪŋglɪʃ əz ə fɒrən 'læŋgwɪdʒ]	TOEFL (standardisierter Test der engl. Sprache)
certificate [sə'tɪfɪkət]	Zeugnis, Bescheinigung
to **prove** [pru:v]	nachweisen, beweisen
to **apply for sth** [ə'plaɪ fə]	sich für/auf etw bewerben
skill [skɪl]	Fähigkeit, Fertigkeit
a must [mʌst]	ein Muss, eine Notwendigkeit
voluntary ['vɒləntri]	freiwillig; ehrenamtlich
gap year ['gæp jɪə]	das Jahr zwischen Schulabgang und Studienbeginn
refugee [,refju'dʒi:]	Flüchtling
to **volunteer** [,vɒlən'tɪə]	sich freiwillig melden; ehrenamtlich arbeiten
positive [,pɒzətɪv]	positiv

page 12

response [rɪ'spɒns]	Antwort
so far [səʊ 'fɑ:]	bis jetzt, bis hierher
business administration ['bɪznəs ədmɪnɪstreɪʃn]	Betriebswirtschaft
vocational (training) college (BE) [vəʊ,keɪʃənl 'treɪnɪŋ kɒlɪdʒ]	Berufsschule, Berufskolleg, Gewerbliche Schule
to **attend** [ə'tend]	(hin)gehen zu, besuchen
firm [fɜ:m]	Firma
to **train as** [treɪn]	eine Ausbildung machen als/zu
part-time job [,pɑ:t 'taɪm dʒɒb]	Teilzeitjob, -stelle
final exam [,faɪnl ɪg'zæm]	Abschlussprüfung
to **include** [ɪn'klu:d]	aufnehmen; einbeziehen, einschließen
typing course ['taɪpɪŋ kɔ:s]	Computerschreibkurs
bracket ['brækɪt]	Klammer
foreign ['fɒrən]	Auslands-, ausländisch, fremd
reply [rɪ'plaɪ]	Antwort
to **sit an exam** [,sɪt ən ɪg'zæm]	eine Prüfung machen
to **pass an exam** [,pɑ:s ən ɪg'zæm]	eine Prüfung bestehen
figure ['fɪgə]	Zahl
grade [greɪd]	Note, Zensur

page 13

to **supply** [sə'plaɪ]	zur Verfügung stellen; liefern, anbieten
proof *(no pl)* [pru:f]	Nachweis(e), Beweis(e)
complicated ['kɒmplɪkeɪtɪd]	kompliziert
trainee [treɪ'ni:]	Auszubildende/r
extract ['ekstrækt]	Auszug
(bank) account [ə'kaʊnt]	(Bank-)Konto, (Giro-)Konto
teller ['telə]	Kassierer/in
anything [eniθɪŋ]	alles; egal, was
bookkeeping ['bʊkki:pɪŋ]	(die) Buchhaltung, (Abteilung für) Rechnungswesen
internal [ɪn'tɜ:nl]	intern
training ['treɪnɪŋ]	Ausbildung

page 14

permanent ['pɜ:mənənt]	(Stelle:) unbefristet
advertisement, advert, ad [əd'vɜ:tɪsmənt, 'ædvɜ:t, æd]	Anzeige, Annonce
to **view sth** [vju:]	sich etw anschauen, etw betrachten
freight forwarding ['freɪt fɔ:wədɪŋ]	Spedition, Gütertransport
information technology, IT [ɪnfə,meɪʃn tek'nɒlədʒi, ,aɪ 'ti:]	IT, Informationstechnologie
office management ['ɒfɪs mænɪdʒmənt]	Büroorganisation
retail business ['ri:teɪl bɪznəs]	Einzelhandel(sgeschäft)
receptionist [rɪ'sepʃənɪst]	Empfangsmitarbeiter/in
entertainment [,entə'teɪnmənt]	Unterhaltung(selektronik)
20K [keɪ]	20,000
depending on [dɪ'pendɪŋ ɒn]	abhängig von
PA (= personal assistant) [,pi: 'eɪ, ,pɜ:sənl ə'sɪstənt]	persönliche/r Assistent/in
consultancy [kən'sʌltənsi]	Beratungsbüro, -firma
salary ['sæləri]	Gehalt, Lohn
to **be negotiable** [nɪ'gəʊʃiəbl]	Verhandlungssache sein
secretary ['sekrətri]	Sekretär/in
per annum [pər 'ænəm]	pro Jahr
to **relate to** [rɪ'leɪt tə]	sich beziehen auf, im Zusammenhang stehen mit
product marketing [,prɒdʌkt 'mɑ:kɪtɪŋ]	Produktvermarktung
well-established [,wel ɪ'stæblɪʃt]	gut eingeführt, etabliert
to **be based in** ['beɪst ɪn]	seinen Sitz haben in
benefits ['benɪfɪts]	Zusatzleistungen, Vergünstigungen
co-ordinator [kəʊ'ɔ:dɪneɪtə]	Koordinator/in
commission [kə'mɪʃn]	Provision
telesales ['teliseɪlz]	Tele(fon)verkauf
on-the-job training [ɒn ðə ,dʒɒb 'treɪnɪŋ]	Ausbildung während der Arbeit
hint [hɪnt]	Hinweis
to **earn** [ɜ:n]	verdienen
health insurance ['helθ ɪnʃʊərəns]	Krankenversicherung
payment ['peɪmənt]	(Be-)Zahlung
pension fund ['penʃn fʌnd]	Rentenversicherung, Pensionskasse
amount [ə'maʊnt]	Menge, Betrag
to **receive** [rɪ'si:v]	erhalten, empfangen
to **contrast** [kən'trɑ:st]	einander gegenüberstellen
working hours [,wɜ:kɪŋ 'aʊəz]	Arbeitszeiten
responsibility [rɪ,spɒnsə'bɪləti]	Aufgabenbereich, Zuständigkeit
reference ['refərəns]	Erwähnung, Verweis; Bezug
personal(ly) ['pɜ:sənl]	persönlich
quality ['kwɒləti]	Qualität; Eigenschaft
manner ['mænə]	Art (und Weise)
professional manner [prə,feʃənl 'mænə]	Professionalität
to **brainstorm** ['breɪnstɔ:m]	Ideen sammeln

characteristic [ˌkærəktəˈrɪstɪk]	Eigenschaft, (charakteristisches) Merkmal

page 15

manufacturer [ˌmænjuˈfæktʃərə]	Hersteller
to **focus on sth** [ˈfəʊkəs ɒn]	sich auf etw konzentrieren
results oriented [rɪˌzʌlts ˈɔːriəntɪd]	ergebnisorientiert
to **demonstrate** [ˈdemənstreɪt]	vorführen, zeigen
automotive [ˌɔːtəˈməʊtɪv]	Automobil-
follow-up [ˈfɒləʊ ʌp]	Anschluss-
enthusiastic [ɪnˌθjuːziˈæstɪk]	begeistert
commercial [kəˈmɜːʃl]	kaufmännisch, Geschäfts-; kommerziell
effective [ɪˈfektɪv]	wirkungsvoll, effektiv
negotiation [nɪˌgəʊʃiˈeɪʃn]	Verhandlung
persuasion [pəˈsweɪʒn]	Überzeugung, Überredung
to **influence** [ˈɪnfluəns]	beeinflussen
opportunity [ˌɒpəˈtjuːnəti]	Gelegenheit, Chance; freie Stelle
within [wɪˈðɪn]	innerhalb von, in
fringe benefits [ˈfrɪndʒ benɪfɪts]	Zusatzleistungen, freiwillige Sozialleistungen
property [ˈprɒpəti]	Immobilie, Haus
property management [ˌprɒpəti ˈmænɪdʒmənt]	Immobilienverwaltung
temporary [ˈtemprəri]	vorübergehend, befristet
polite [pəˈlaɪt]	höflich
adaptable [əˈdæptəbl]	anpassungsfähig, flexibel
to **cope with** [ˈkəʊp wɪð]	zurechtkommen, fertig werden mit
environment [ɪnˈvaɪrənmənt]	Umfeld, Umgebung
to **provide** [prəˈvaɪd]	zur Verfügung stellen, anbieten
refreshment [rɪˈfreʃmənt]	Erfrischung
incoming [ˈɪnkʌmɪŋ]	eingehend, ankommend
to **transfer** [ˈtrænsfɜː]	weiterleiten, weiterverbinden (Telefonanruf)
to **require** [rɪˈkwaɪə]	erfordern, verlangen, benötigen
to **assist (with)** [əˈsɪst]	assistieren, helfen (bei)
outgoing [ˈaʊtgəʊɪŋ]	abgehend, Ausgangs-
knowledge [ˈnɒlɪdʒ]	Wissen, Kenntnis(se)
working knowledge [ˌwɜːkɪŋ ˈnɒlɪdʒ]	praktische/grundlegende Kenntnisse
previous [ˈpriːviəs]	vorige/r/s, vorherige/r/s, früherer/r/s

page 16

mediation [miːdiˈeɪʃn]	Sprachmittlung, Vermittlung
preference [ˈprefrəns]	Vorliebe
introduction [ˌɪntrəˈdʌkʃn]	Einleitung
shift [ʃɪft]	Schicht, Schicht-
factory [ˈfæktəri]	Fabrik

page 17

perks [pɜːks]	Zusatzvergünstigungen, freiwillige Sonder-/Sozialleistungen
to **keep doing sth** [kiːp]	etw dauernd/immer wieder tun
to **come across sth** [ˈkʌm əkrɒs]	auf etw stoßen, etw (zufällig) finden
term [tɜːm]	Begriff
colleague [ˈkɒliːg]	Kollege/-in
to **lay sth down** [ˌleɪ ˈdaʊn]	etw festlegen, vorschreiben
law [lɔː]	Gesetz
unemployment [ˌʌnɪmˈplɔɪmənt]	Arbeitslosigkeit
benefit [ˈbenɪfɪt]	Unterstützung, Beihilfe
medical leave [ˌmedɪkl ˈliːv]	krankheitsbedingte Beurlaubung
to **supplement** [ˈsʌplɪment]	ergänzen
childcare [ˈtʃaɪld keə]	Kinderbetreuung
discount [ˈdɪskaʊnt]	Rabatt, Nachlass
common(ly) [ˈkɒmən]	häufig, verbreitet
fee [fiː]	Gebühr
paid leave of absence [ˌpeɪd liːv əv ˈæbsəns]	bezahlter Urlaub
health club [ˈhelθ klʌb]	Fitnessstudio
membership [ˈmembəʃɪp]	Mitgliedschaft
to **subsidize** [ˈsʌbsɪdaɪz]	subventionieren, finanziell unterstützen
luncheon [ˈlʌntʃən]	Mittagessen
voucher [ˈvaʊtʃə]	Gutschein
luncheon voucher [ˈlʌntʃən vaʊtʃə]	Essensmarke
to **exchange** [ɪksˈtʃeɪndʒ]	austauschen, eintauschen
to **aim at** [ˈeɪm ət]	zielen auf, sich richten an
specific, specifically [spəˈsɪfɪk, spəˈsɪfɪkli]	speziell, spezifisch
to **care for** [ˈkeə fə]	sich kümmern um, aufpassen auf
altogether [ˌɔːltəˈgeðə]	insgesamt

page 18

to **make sth up** [ˌmeɪk ˈʌp]	etw ausmachen, bilden
workforce [ˈwɜːkfɔːs]	Beschäftigte, Erwerbstätige; Belegschaft
to **rely on** [rɪˈlaɪ ɒn]	sich verlassen auf
to **grant** [grɑːnt]	gewähren, einräumen
to **guarantee** [ˌgærənˈtiː]	garantieren
as far as ... is/are concerned [kənˈsɜːnd]	was ... betrifft/angeht
to **provide** [prəˈvaɪd]	bieten
on-site [ɒn ˈsaɪt]	vor Ort; im Betrieb
to **breastfeed** [ˈbrestfiːd]	stillen
workplace [ˈwɜːkpleɪs]	Arbeitsplatz
working conditions [ˌwɜːkɪŋ kənˈdɪʃnz]	Arbeitsbedingungen
to **improve** [ɪmˈpruːv]	(sich) verbessern
expression [ɪkˈspreʃn]	Ausdruck
nowadays [ˈnaʊədeɪz]	heutzutage

page 19

to **register with sth** [ˈredʒɪstə wɪð]	sich bei etw anmelden
recruitment [rɪˈkruːtmənt]	Personalbeschaffung
agency [ˈeɪdʒənsi]	Agentur
hospitality [ˌhɒspɪˈtæləti]	Hotel- und Gaststättengewerbe
entry level [ˈentri levl]	Einstiegsniveau
full-time [ˌfʊl ˈtaɪm]	Vollzeit-
venue [ˈvenjuː]	Veranstaltungsort, -stätte
major [ˈmeɪdʒə]	groß, bedeutend
desirable [dɪˈzaɪərəbl]	wünschenswert
promotion [prəˈməʊʃn]	Beförderung, Aufstieg
promotion prospects [prəˈməʊʃn prɒspekts]	Beförderungsaussichten, Aufstiegschancen
to **review** [rɪˈvjuː]	bewerten, prüfen
rise [raɪz]	Erhöhung, Anstieg; Aufstieg

pay rise ['peɪ raɪz]	Gehaltserhöhung
uniform ['ju:nɪfɔ:m]	Uniform
command [kə'mɑ:nd]	Beherrschung
appearance [ə'pɪərəns]	Erscheinung(sbild), Auftreten, Aussehen
passion ['pæʃn]	Leidenschaft
customer care ['kʌstəmə keə]	Kundendienst
(job) application [,æplɪ'keɪʃn]	Bewerbung
to **quote sth** [kwəʊt]	nennen, angeben
human resources (HR) [,hju:mən rɪ'sɔ:sɪz]	Personalabteilung
human resources manager [,hju:mən rɪ'sɔ:sɪz mænɪdʒə]	Personalleiter/in

page 20

location [ləʊ'keɪʃn]	Ort, Platz; Lage
increase ['ɪŋkri:s]	Zunahme, Steigerung
enthusiasm [ɪn'θju:ziæzəm]	Begeisterung, Enthusiasmus
CV (= curriculum vitae) (BE) [,si: 'vi, kə,rɪkjələm 'vi:taɪ]	Lebenslauf
résumé (AE) ['rezjumeɪ]	Lebenslauf
font [fɒnt]	Schrift, Zeichensatz
to **tailor** ['teɪlə]	individuell anpassen
cover letter ['kʌvə letə]	Anschreiben, Begleitschreiben
statement ['steɪtmənt]	Aussage
heading ['hedɪŋ]	Überschrift
to **advertise a job** [,ædvətaɪz ə 'dʒɒb]	eine Stelle ausschreiben
chronological [,krɒnə'lɒdʒɪkl]	chronologisch
reverse [rɪ'vɜ:s]	umgekehrt, entgegengesetzt
attention [ə'tenʃn]	Aufmerksamkeit
profile ['prəʊfaɪl]	Porträt, Profil
to **catch sb's attention** [kætʃ ə'tenʃn]	jds Aufmerksamkeit erregen
fluent(ly) ['flu:ənt]	(Sprache:) fließend
basic ['beɪsɪk]	Grund-, grundlegend; wesentlich
primary school ['praɪməri sku:l]	Grundschule
referee [,refə'ri:]	Referenzgeber/in

page 21

ambition [æm'bɪʃn]	Ehrgeiz, Bestreben
to motivate ['məʊtɪveɪt]	motivieren
hard-working [,hɑ:d 'wɜ:kɪŋ]	fleißig
responsible [rɪ'spɒnsəbl]	verantwortungsbewusst, zuverlässig
reliable [rɪ'laɪəbl]	zuverlässig
native speaker [,neɪtɪv 'spi:kə]	Muttersprachler/in
to **obtain sth** [əb'teɪn]	etw erhalten, etw beziehen
higher education entrance qualifications [,haɪə edʒu,keɪʃn 'entrəns kwɒlɪfɪkeɪʃnz]	Fachhochschulreife
selective secondary school [sɪ,lektɪv'sekəndri sku:l]	Realschule
housekeeping ['haʊski:pɪŋ]	Hauswirtschaft
back office [,bæk 'ɒfɪs]	Abwicklungsabteilung (ohne Kundenkontakt)
extra-curricular [,ekstrə kə'rɪkjulə]	außerschulisch

ballroom dancing ['bɔ:lru:m dɑ:nsɪŋ]	Gesellschaftstanz
date of birth [,deɪt əv'bɜ:θ]	Geburtsdatum
marital status [,mærɪtl 'steɪtəs]	Familienstand
nationality [,næʃə'næləti]	Staatsangehörigkeit
request [rɪ'kwest]	Anfrage, Wunsch, Bitte

page 22

driving licence ['draɪvɪŋ laɪsns]	Führerschein
school leaving certificate [,sku:l li:vɪŋ sə'tɪfɪkət]	Schulabgangszeugnis
Red Cross [,red 'krɒs]	Rotes Kreuz
secondary school ['sekəndri sku:l]	weiterführende Schule
goal [gəʊl]	Ziel
to **gain** [geɪn]	erwerben, gewinnen, sammeln
to **invent** [ɪn'vent]	erfinden
to **refer to sth** [rɪ'fɜ: tə]	auf etw verweisen, sich auf etw beziehen
equivalent [ɪ'kwɪvələnt]	Entsprechung, Übersetzung
grammar school ['græmə sku:l]	Gymnasium
university entrance qualifications [ju:nɪ,vɜ:səti 'entrəns kwɒlɪfɪkeɪʃnz]	Abitur, Hochschulreife
conflict mediator [,kɒnflɪkt 'mi:dieɪtə]	Streitschlichter/in
vocational school (AE) [vəʊ,keɪʃənl 'sku:l]	Berufsschule, Berufskolleg, Gewerbliche Schule

page 23

vacancy ['veɪkənsi]	freie/offene Stelle
post [pəʊst]	Stelle
by [baɪ]	bis
commerce ['kɒmɜ:s]	Handel
to **entitle sb to sth** [ɪn'taɪtl]	jdn zu etw berechtigen
to **enclose** [ɪn'kləʊz]	beifügen, beilegen
at short notice [ət ,ʃɔ:t 'nəʊtɪs]	kurzfristig
to **be delighted** [bi dɪ'laɪtɪd]	sich freuen
to **consider** [kən'sɪdə]	in Betracht ziehen

page 24

summary ['sʌməri]	Zusammenfassung
animator ['ænɪmeɪtə]	Animateur/in
requirements [rɪ'kwaɪəmənts]	Anforderungen
attitude ['ætɪtju:d]	Einstellung, Haltung
board and lodging [,bɔ:d ənd 'lɒdʒɪŋ]	Kost und Logis
applicant ['æplɪkənt]	Bewerber/in
face-to-face [,feɪs tə 'feɪs]	persönlich
to **accompany** [ə'kʌmpəni]	begleiten
destination [,destɪ'neɪʃn]	Reiseziel
accommodation [ə,kɒmə'deɪʃn]	Unterkunft
to **ensure** [ɪn'ʃʊə]	sicherstellen, gewährleisten, dafür sorgen
well-being ['wel bi:ɪŋ]	Wohlbefinden
participant [pɑ:'tɪsɪpənt]	Teilnehmer/in
specification [,spesɪfɪ'keɪʃn]	(detaillierte) Beschreibung
charming ['tʃɑ:mɪŋ]	charmant
well-groomed [,wel 'gru:md]	gepflegt

(for the) attention (of) (Attn.) [ə'tenʃn]	zu Händen
to re-write [ˌriː'raɪt]	neu schreiben, umformulieren

page 25

to enable sb to do sth [ɪ'neɪbl tə duː]	jdm etw ermöglichen
immediately [ɪ'miːdiətli]	sofort, umgehend, unmittelbar
as from ... / as of ... ['æz frəm, 'æz əv]	ab ..., von ... an
to attach [ə'tætʃ]	(E-Mail:) anhängen
to be pleased to do sth [bi 'pliːzd tə]	etw gern tun
to look forward to sth [ˌlʊk 'fɔːwəd tə]	sich auf etw freuen
convenience [kən'viːniəns]	Bequemlichkeit, Annehmlichkeit
at your earliest convenience [ət jər ˌɜːliəst kən'viːniəns]	zeitnah, so bald wie möglich

page 26

to come up with sth [ˌkʌm 'ʌp wɪð]	sich etw einfallen lassen, sich etw ausdenken
desire (for sb/sth) [dɪ'zaɪə]	Verlangen, Wunsch (nach jdm/etw)
connection [kə'nekʃn]	Verbindung, Anschluss
written correspondence [ˌrɪtn kɒrɪ'spɒndəns]	Schriftverkehr
dress [dres]	Kleiderordnung, Kleidung
casual ['kæʒuəl]	leger
to dress up [ˌdres 'ʌp]	sich schick anziehen, sich professionell kleiden
suit [suːt]	Anzug, Hosenanzug, Kostüm
to appreciate [ə'priːʃieɪt]	schätzen, zu schätzen wissen
effort ['efət]	Bemühen, Bemühungen
to take place [ˌteɪk 'pleɪs]	stattfinden
tidy ['taɪdi]	aufgeräumt, ordentlich
at sb's end [ət sʌmbədiz 'end]	bei jdm
lighting ['laɪtɪŋ]	Beleuchtung, Licht
attractive [ə'træktɪv]	attraktiv
to pass sth out [ˌpɑːs 'aʊt]	etw verteilen
corner ['kɔːnə]	Ecke
to distribute [dɪ'strɪbjuːt]	verteilen
nevertheless [ˌnevəðə'les]	nichtsdestotrotz, dennoch
to approach sb [ə'prəʊtʃ]	auf jdn zugehen, jdn ansprechen
to give the impression that ... [ˌgɪv ði ɪm'preʃn ðət]	den Eindruck erwecken, dass ...
to quit [kwɪt]	kündigen

page 27

strength [streŋθ]	Stärke
weakness ['wiːknəs]	Schwäche
to recharge [ˌriː'tʃɑːdʒ]	aufladen
battery ['bætəri]	Akku
to role-play ['rəʊl pleɪ]	mit verteilten Rollen spielen
to perform sth [pə'fɔːm]	etw aufführen
to judge [dʒʌdʒ]	beurteilen
to swap [swɒp]	tauschen

page 28

instead of [ɪn'sted əv]	statt, an Stelle von
headquarters [ˌhed'kwɔːtəz]	Zentrale
to put sth to good use [ˌpʊt tə gʊd 'juːs]	etw gut nutzen
to be pleased (with sth) [pliːzd]	sich freuen, froh sein (über etw)
independent [ˌɪndɪ'pendənt]	unabhängig
stables (pl) ['steɪbzl]	(Reit-)Stall
at the bottom [ət ðə 'bɒtəm]	(ganz) unten
to work your way up [ˌwɜːk jə weɪ 'ʌp]	sich hocharbeiten
course [kɔːs]	Studium, Studiengang
to arrange [ə'reɪndʒ]	vereinbaren, planen, abmachen, arrangieren
chain [tʃeɪn]	Kette
pleasure ['pleʒə]	Vergnügen
My pleasure. [maɪ 'pleʒə]	Es war mir ein Vergnügen. (höfliche Antwort, wenn sich jemand bedankt hat)

page 29

leisure ['leʒə]	Freizeit
cycle ['saɪkl]	Fahrrad(-)
wear [weə]	Bekleidung
accessory [ək'sesəri]	Accessoire, Zubehör(teil)
to expand [ɪk'spænd]	ausweiten
order ['ɔːdə]	Auftrag, Bestellung
preferably ['prefrəbli]	vorzugsweise, am liebsten

TOPIC 2

page 31

chart [tʃɑːt]	Tabelle; Schaubild, Diagramm
total ['təʊtl]	Gesamt-
to divide sth up (into) [dɪˌvaɪd 'ʌp]	etw (auf)teilen (in)
quantity ['kwɒntəti]	Menge
performance [pə'fɔːməns]	Leistung
line chart ['laɪn tʃɑːt]	Liniendiagramm
crude oil [ˌkruːd 'ɔɪl]	Rohöl
barrel ['bærəl]	Fass; Barrel (Maß für Erdöl)
gross [grəʊs]	brutto, Brutto-
monthly ['mʌnθli]	monatlich
horizontal [ˌhɒrɪ'zɒntl]	waagerecht, horizontal
bar chart ['bɑː tʃɑːt]	Balkendiagramm, Säulendiagramm
vertical ['vɜːtɪkl]	senkrecht, vertikal
growth [grəʊθ]	Wachstum
to announce [ə'naʊns]	ankündigen, bekanntgeben
to launch sth [lɔːntʃ]	etw auf den Markt bringen
pie chart ['paɪ tʃɑːt]	Tortendiagramm
federal ['fedərəl]	Bundes-
budget ['bʌdʒɪt]	Budget, Haushalt, Etat
labour ['leɪbə]	Arbeit, Arbeitskraft
social affairs *(pl)* [ˌsəʊʃl ə'feəz]	Soziales
billion, bn ['bɪliən]	Milliarde
contribution [ˌkɒntrɪ'bjuːʃn]	Beteiligung
interest ['ɪntrəst]	Zins(en)
research [rɪ'sɜːtʃ]	Forschung
defence [dɪ'fens]	Verteidigung

relative ['relətɪv]	relativ
to present ['preznt]	vorstellen, präsentieren

page 32

on the move [ɒn ðə 'mu:v]	unterwegs
the pros and cons [ˌprəʊz ənd 'kɒnz]	das Für und Wider, das Pro und Kontra
in order to [ɪn 'ɔ:də tə]	um ... zu
search [sɜ:tʃ]	Suche
in search of [ɪn 'sɜ:tʃ əv]	auf der Suche nach
to face sth [feɪs]	vor etw stehen
to migrate [maɪ'greɪt]	(aus-/ein-)wandern
immigrant ['ɪmɪgrənt]	Einwanderer/-in
to cause sth [kɔ:z]	etw verursachen
debt [det]	Schuld(en)
crisis, *pl* **crises** ['kraɪsɪs, 'kraɪsi:z]	Krise
migration [maɪ'greɪʃn]	Migration
citizen ['sɪtɪzn]	Bürger/in
member state ['membə steɪt]	Mitgliedsstaat
decade ['dekeɪd]	Jahrzehnt
century ['sentʃəri]	Jahrhundert
mainly ['meɪnli]	hauptsächlich
dependent on [dɪ'pendənt ɒn]	abhängig von
agriculture ['ægrɪkʌltʃə]	Landwirtschaft
building trade ['bɪldɪŋ treɪd]	Baugewerbe, Bausektor
trade [treɪd]	Handel, Handelsverkehr
diagram ['daɪəgræm]	Grafik, Diagramm
taste [teɪst]	Geschmack; Kostprobe

page 33

economy [ɪ'kɒnəmi]	Wirtschaft
government ['gʌvənmənt]	Regierung, öffentliche Verwaltung
insolvent [ɪn'sɒlvənt]	zahlungsunfähig, insolvent
bubble ['bʌbl]	Blase
to burst [bɜ:st]	platzen
homeless ['həʊmləs]	obdachlos
austerity [ɒ'sterəti]	wirtschaftliche Einschränkung, Entbehrung
to cut [kʌt]	senken
spending ['spendɪŋ]	Ausgaben, Etat
consequence ['kɒnsɪkwəns]	Folge, Konsequenz
wherever [weər'evə]	überall, wo
immigration [ˌɪmɪ'greɪʃn]	Einwanderung
emigration [ˌemɪ'greɪʃn]	Auswanderung
inhabitant [ɪn'hæbɪtənt]	Einwohner/in
to emigrate ['emɪgreɪt]	auswandern
as regards [əz rɪ'gɑ:dz]	hinsichtlich, bezüglich

page 34

qualified ['kwɒlɪfaɪd]	ausgebildet, mit Abschluss
to struggle ['strʌgl]	kämpfen, sich abmühen
rate [reɪt]	Rate, Quote
avalanche ['ævəlɑ:nʃ]	Lawine
to take up (a story) [ˌteɪk 'ʌp]	(eine Geschichte) aufgreifen, weitererzählen
to flood [flʌd]	überschwemmen, überfluten
to sort out [ˌsɔ:t 'aʊt]	sortieren; klären, lösen
unemployed [ˌʌnɪm'plɔɪd]	arbeitslos
to turn up [ˌtɜ:n 'ʌp]	erscheinen, auftauchen
a planeload of ... ['pleɪnləʊd]	ein Flugzeug voller ..., eine Flugzeugladung ...
engineer [ˌendʒɪ'nɪə]	Ingenieur/in; Techniker/in
to hire sb ['haɪə]	jdn engagieren, beauftragen, einstellen
to make money [meɪk 'mʌni]	Geld verdienen
laboratory, lab [lə'bɒrətri, læb]	Labor
technician [tek'nɪʃn]	Techniker/in
whoever [hu:'evə]	wer/wen/wem auch immer
Take ... [teɪk]	Zum Beispiel ...
opening ['əʊpnɪŋ]	freie Stelle; Chance
specialist ['speʃəlɪst]	Spezialist/in, Fachmann/-frau
expert ['ekspɜ:t]	Fachmann, Experte/-in
to complain [kəm'pleɪn]	sich beschweren
lecturer ['lektʃərə]	Dozent/in, Hochschullehrer/in
brain drain ['breɪn dreɪn]	Abwanderung von hochqualifizierten Arbeitskräften ins Ausland
graduate ['grædʒuət]	Hochschulabsolvent/in, Akademiker/in
expertise [ˌekspɜ:'ti:z]	Fachkenntnisse, Sachverstand
to train sb [treɪn]	jdn schulen, jdn ausbilden
return [rɪ'tɜ:n]	Ertrag
investment [ɪn'vestmənt]	Geldanlage; Investition(en)
to reap [ri:p]	ernten, einstreichen
benefit ['benɪfɪt]	Nutzen, Vorteil
to reap the benefit [ˌri:p ðə 'benɪfɪt]	profitieren
spokesperson ['spəʊkspɜ:sn]	Sprecher/in
resentment [rɪ'zentmənt]	Unmut, Groll, Ressentiment
to point out [ˌpɔɪnt 'aʊt]	darauf hinweisen
to benefit from ['benɪfɪt frəm]	profitieren von
to headhunt ['hedhʌnt]	abwerben
to relieve [rɪ'li:v]	erleichtern; (Druck) verringern, lindern
pressure ['preʃə]	Druck
welfare state [ˌwelfeə 'steɪt]	Sozialstaat, Wohlfahrtsstaat
conflict ['kɒnflɪkt]	Streit(igkeiten), Konflikt
conflict of interest [kɒnflɪkt əv 'ɪntrəst]	Interessenkonflikt

page 35

to recover [rɪ'kʌvə]	sich erholen
new arrival [nju: ə'raɪvl]	Neuankömmling
turnaround ['tɜ:nəraʊnd]	Aufschwung; Kehrtwendung
economist [ɪ'kɒnəmɪst]	Wirtschaftswissenschaftler/in
professional [prə'feʃənl]	Fachmann/-frau, in einem gehobenen Beruf Tätige/r
recession [rɪ'seʃn]	Rezession
to hold on [ˌhəʊld 'ɒn]	durchhalten; erhalten bleiben
to settle (down) [ˌsetl 'daʊn]	sich niederlassen
to rebuild [ˌri'bɪld]	wieder aufbauen
to envision [ɪn'vɪʒn]	sich vorstellen; vorhaben
to retain [rɪ'teɪn]	behalten

industry ['ɪndəstri]	Industrie
party ['pɑ:ti]	Partei; Beteiligte/r
equal ['i:kwəl]	gleich
condition(s) [kən'dɪʃn]	Bedingung(en)
presentation [prezn'teɪʃn]	Referat; Präsentation
to **give a presentation** [ˌgɪv ə prezn'teɪʃn]	ein Referat halten
to **draw sth up** [ˌdrɔ: 'ʌp]	etw erstellen
gender ['dʒendə]	Geschlecht
level ['levl]	Niveau

page 36

host [həʊst]	Gastgeber/in; (Talkshow-) Moderator/in
to **slide** [slaɪd]	rutschen, gleiten
market research [ˌmɑ:kɪt rɪ'sɜ:tʃ]	Marktforschung
analyst ['ænəlɪst]	Experte/Expertin
finance ['faɪnæns]	Finanzen, Finanzwirtschaft
banking ['bæŋkɪŋ]	Bankwesen
interviewee [ˌɪntəvju:'i:]	Befragte/r (im Interview)
challenge ['tʃælɪndʒ]	Herausforderung, (schwierige) Aufgabe
to **be stuck** [stʌk]	stecken bleiben, festsitzen, nicht weiterkommen
to **start off (as)** [ˌstɒ:t 'ɒf]	anfangen (als)
to **get in touch with sb** [ˌget ɪn 'tʌtʃ wɪð]	sich mit jdm in Verbindung setzen
notice ['nəʊtɪs]	Kündigung
to **hand in one's notice** [hænd ˌɪn wʌnz 'nəʊtɪs]	die Kündigung einreichen, kündigen
building site ['bɪldɪŋ saɪt]	Baustelle
engineering [endʒɪ'nɪərɪŋ]	Ingenieurwesen; Maschinenbau
to **comment on sth** ['kɒment ɒn]	etw kommentieren
to **blame sb** [bleɪm]	jdm die Schuld geben, es jdm übelnehmen
to **stick it out** [ˌstɪk ɪt 'aʊt]	durchhalten
last but not least [ˌlɑ:st bʌt nɒt 'li:st]	nicht zuletzt
whichever [wɪtʃ'evə]	wer/was (auch immer), egal welche/r/s

page 37

outsourcing ['aʊtsɔ:sɪŋ]	Auslagern, Outsourcen
globalization [ˌgləʊbəlaɪ'zeɪʃn]	Globalisierung
to **outsource** ['aʊtsɔ:s]	(Arbeit) auslagern, outsourcen
hourly wage [ˌaʊəli 'weɪdʒ]	Stundenlohn
external [ɪk'stɜ:nl]	extern
provider [prə'vaɪdə]	Anbieter
to **lay sb off** [ˌleɪ 'ɒf]	jdn entlassen, jdm betriebsbedingt kündigen
to **meet (sth)** [mi:t]	(Bedarf, Norm etc.) erfüllen, befriedigen, entsprechen
need [ni:d]	Bedarf, Bedürfnis, Notwendigkeit
value ['vælju:]	Wert
to **estimate** ['estɪmeɪt]	schätzen
popularity [ˌpɒpju'lærəti]	Beliebtheit
to **adapt (to sth)** [ə'dæpt]	sich anpassen (an etw)
competitive [kəm'petətɪv]	(Preis:) günstig
public sector [ˌpʌblɪk 'sektə]	öffentliche Hand, öffentlicher Dienst
communications (pl) [kəˌmju:nɪ'keɪʃnz]	Kommunikationsnetz, Verbindung(en)
infrastructure ['ɪnfrəstrʌktʃə]	Infrastruktur
application management [ˌæplɪ'keɪʃn mænɪdʒmənt]	Anwendungsentwicklung
geek [gi:k]	Nerd, Freak
suit [su:t]	Anzugträger/in (Geschäftsperson)
to **manage** ['mænɪdʒ]	verwalten, regeln; leiten
relationship [rɪ'leɪʃnʃɪp]	Beziehung
valuable ['væljuəbl]	wertvoll
to **go way beyond sth** [gəʊ ˌweɪ bɪ'jɒnd]	weit über etw hinausgehen
typical ['tɪpɪkl]	typisch

page 38

project ['prɒdʒekt]	Projekt
management ['mænɪdʒmənt]	Leitung, (Geschäfts-) Führung, Management, Verwaltung
supplier [sə'plaɪə]	Lieferant, Zulieferer
anxious(ly) ['æŋkʃəs]	besorgt, beunruhigt, ängstlich
to **predict** [prɪ'dɪkt]	vorhersehen, abschätzen
flexibility [ˌfleksə'bɪləti]	Flexibilität
to **pass a law** [ˌpɑ:s ə 'lɔ:]	ein Gesetz verabschieden
minor ['maɪnə]	klein, unbedeutend
to **increase** ['ɪŋkri:s]	steigern, erhöhen
data storage ['deɪtə stɔ:rɪdʒ]	Datenspeicherung, Speicherplatz
freelancer ['fri:lɑ:nsə]	Freiberufler/in
freelance ['fri:lɑ:ns]	selbstständig, freiberuflich
food chain ['fu:d tʃeɪn]	Nahrungskette
drawback (to) ['drɔ:bæk]	Schattenseite, Nachteil (von/bei)
retirement [rɪ'taɪəmənt]	Ruhestand
schedule ['ʃedju:l]	Terminplan, Zeitplan
to **fire sb** ['faɪə]	jdn (fristlos) entlassen, jdn feuern
client ['klaɪənt]	Kunde/Kundin
base of clients [ˌbeɪs əv 'klaɪənts]	Kundenstamm
overseas [ˌəʊvə'si:z]	Auslands-
to **fulfil** [fʊl'fɪl]	erfüllen
to **coordinate** [kəʊ'ɔ:dɪneɪt]	koordinieren
whenever [wen'evə]	immer, wenn; jedes Mal, wenn
to **take time off** [teɪk ˌtaɪm 'ɒf]	sich frei nehmen

page 39

to **visualize** ['vɪʒuəlaɪz]	bildlich darstellen, visualisieren
to **reduce** [rɪ'dju:s]	senken, reduzieren
cause and effect [ˌkɔ:z ənd ɪ'fekt]	Ursache und Wirkung
underlined [ˌʌndə'laɪnd]	unterstrichen
domestically [də'mestɪkli]	im Inland

page 40

to **sort sth** [sɔ:t]	etw einsortieren, einordnen
whomever [ˌhu:m'evə]	wen/wem auch immer
routine [ru:'ti:n]	Tagesablauf, Routine
to **found** [faʊnd]	gründen
decent ['di:snt]	anständig, ordentlich
to **cut costs** [ˌkʌt 'kɒsts]	Kosten senken

tempting ['temptɪŋ]	verlockend
to sack sb [sæk]	jdn entlassen, rausschmeißen
unfair [ˌʌn'feə]	unfair
unwise [ˌʌn'waɪz]	unklug
to suffer ['sʌfə]	leiden
top priority [ˌtɒp praɪ'ɒrəti]	oberste Priorität
slave [sleɪv]	Sklave
to support sb/sth [sə'pɔːt]	jdn/etw unterstützen
productivity [ˌprɒdʌk'tɪvəti]	Produktivität
perspective [pə'spektɪv]	Perspektive
to deserve sth [dɪ'zɜːv]	etw verdienen
competitor [kəm'petɪtə]	Konkurrent/in
in-house [ˌɪn 'haʊs]	betriebsintern
according to [ə'kɔːdɪŋ tə]	gemäß, nach, zufolge

page 41

demand [dɪ'mɑːnd]	Nachfrage
stage [steɪdʒ]	Abschnitt, Etappe, Stadium, Schritt
labour intensive [ˌleɪbər ɪn'tensɪv]	arbeitsintensiv
to manufacture [ˌmænju'fæktʃə]	herstellen, fertigen
material [mə'tɪəriəl]	materiell
society [sə'saɪəti]	Gesellschaft
agricultural [ˌægrɪ'kʌltʃərəl]	landwirtschaftlich, Agrar-
to industrialize [ɪn'dʌstriəlaɪz]	industrialisieren
technology [tek'nɒlədʒi]	Technik, Technologie
to disappear [ˌdɪsə'pɪə]	verschwinden
service ['sɜːvɪs]	Dienstleistung
per capita [pə 'kæpɪtə]	pro Kopf
income ['ɪnkʌm]	Einkommen
to contribute [kən'trɪbjuːt]	beitragen
medic ['medɪk]	Arzt/Ärztin
exceptional [ɪk'sepʃənl]	außergewöhnlich
to maintain [meɪn'teɪn]	behalten, beibehalten

page 42

item of clothing [ˌaɪtəm əf 'kləʊðɪŋ]	Kleidungsstück
fashionista [fæʃə'nɪstə]	Modefan, Modefreak
to linger ['lɪŋgə]	im Raum stehen
label ['leɪbl]	Etikett
cotton ['kɒtn]	Baumwolle
earnings ['ɜːnɪŋz]	Einnahmen
to be expected to do sth [ɪk'spektɪd]	etw tun sollen/müssen; es wird erwartet, dass man etw tut
to contribute [kən'trɪbjuːt]	einen/seinen/ihren Beitrag leisten
to harvest ['hɑːvɪst]	ernten
pesticide ['pestɪsaɪd]	Schädlingsbekämpfungsmittel
to spray [spreɪ]	sprühen
crop [krɒp]	Pflanzen (auf einem Feld), Ernte
fortunate ['fɔːtʃənət]	glücklich, vom Glück begünstigt
to pick [pɪk]	pflücken
to maintain [meɪn'teɪn]	(nach wie vor) behaupten
child labor (AE), labour (BE) ['tʃaɪld leɪbə]	Kinderarbeit
come September [kʌm]	wenn der September kommt, im September
to head [hed]	(in Richtung von etw) gehen, fahren
diligent(ly) ['dɪlɪdʒənt]	gewissenhaft, fleißig
to ship sth off [ˌʃɪp 'ɒf]	etw verschicken
to grow sth [grəʊ]	etw anbauen
textile ['tekstaɪl]	Textil-
raw material [ˌrɔː mə'tɪəriəl]	Rohstoff(e)
massive ['mæsɪv]	riesig
multiple ['mʌltɪpl]	vielfach
to transform [træns'fɔːm]	verwandeln
laborer (AE), labourer (BE) ['leɪbərə]	Arbeiter/in
cloth [klɒθ]	Stoff
discounted [dɪs'kaʊntɪd]	billig, Billig-
to pass sth on [ˌpɑːs 'ɒn]	etw weitergeben, -leiten
garment ['gɑːmənt]	Kleidungsstück
to employ [ɪm'plɔɪ]	beschäftigen, anstellen

page 43

sewing machine ['səʊɪŋ məʃiːn]	Nähmaschine
to surround [sə'raʊnd]	umgeben
legal age [ˌliːgl 'eɪdʒ]	gesetzliches Mindestalter
barely ['beəli]	kaum
to afford sth [ə'fɔːd]	sich etw leisten
squalid ['skwɒlɪd]	ärmlich, menschenunwürdig
hunger ['hʌŋgə]	Hunger
dockworker ['dɒkwɜːkə]	Hafenarbeiter/in
to load [ləʊd]	verladen, laden
to unload [ˌʌn'ləʊd]	entladen
rack [ræk]	Kleiderstange; Regal
to be likely to do sth ['laɪkli]	etw wahrscheinlich tun werden
annual(ly) ['ænjuəl]	jährlich
to throw [θrəʊ]	werfen
to beg the question [ˌbeg ðə 'kwestʃən]	die Frage aufwerfen
consumer [kən'sjuːmə]	Verbraucher/in
hanger ['hæŋə]	Kleiderbügel
chances are [ˌtʃɑːnsɪz 'ɑː]	sehr wahrscheinlich
to cross [krɒs]	überqueren
border ['bɔːdə]	(Landes-)Grenze
flowchart ['fləʊtʃɑːt]	Flussdiagramm
supply chain [sə'plaɪ tʃeɪn]	Lieferkette
charge [tʃɑːdʒ]	Preis, Gebühr
ingredient [ɪn'griːdiənt]	Bestandteil
circumstances ['sɜːkəmstənsɪz]	Umstände

page 44

to stuff one's pockets [stʌf]	sich die Taschen vollstopfen, sich eine goldene Nase verdienen
to protect [prə'tekt]	schützen, beschützen
to exploit [ɪk'splɔɪt]	ausbeuten
corporation [ˌkɔːpə'reɪʃn]	Konzern
to pocket ['pɒkɪt]	einstecken, einstreichen, einsacken
partly ['pɑːtli]	teilweise
lorry ['lɒri]	Lastwagen, Lkw
to record [rɪ'kɔːd]	aufnehmen
vehicle ['viːəkl]	Fahrzeug
safety ['seɪfti]	Sicherheit
precaution [prɪ'kɔːʃn]	Vorsichtsmaßnahme
security [sɪ'kjʊərəti]	Sicherheit
security guard [sɪ'kjʊərəti gɑːd]	Wachposten
exit ['eksɪt]	Ausgang
faulty ['fɔːlti]	fehlerhaft, defekt
electricity [ɪˌlek'trɪsəti]	Strom, Elektrizität

generator ['dʒenəreɪtə]	Generator (Gerät zur Stromerzeugung)
emergency [ɪ'mɜːdʒənsi]	Notfall
emergency call [ɪ'mɜːdʒənsi kɔːl]	Notruf
fire brigade ['faɪə brɪgeɪd]	Feuerwehr
to **damage** ['dæmɪdʒ]	schaden, (be)schädigen

page 45

environmental [ɪnˌvaɪrən'mentl]	Umwelt-
issue ['ɪʃuː]	Frage, Streitpunkt, Problem
to **take sth into consideration** [kənˌsɪdə'reɪʃn]	etw berücksichtigen
ethical ['eθɪkl]	ethisch, (moralisch) verantwortlich
label ['leɪbl]	Kennzeichnung; Marke
versus ['vɜːsəs]	gegen
to **reassure** [ˌriːə'ʃʊə]	beruhigen
packet ['pækɪt]	Packung
organic [ɔː'gænɪk]	Bio-
bean [biːn]	Bohne
trolley ['trɒli]	Einkaufswagen
distance ['dɪstəns]	Entfernung
to **emit** [ɪ'mɪt]	emittieren, ausstoßen
refrigerated [rɪ'frɪdʒəreɪtɪd]	gekühlt, Kühl-
to **spew** [spjuː]	spucken, speien
fumes [fjuːmz]	Abgase
apart from [ə'pɑːt frəm]	außer, abgesehen von
pollution [pə'luːʃn]	Verschmutzung
to **destroy** [dɪ'strɔɪ]	zerstören
transportation [ˌtrænspɔː'teɪʃn]	Beförderung, Transport(wesen)
packaging ['pækɪdʒɪŋ]	Verpackung
to **campaign (for/against)** [kæm'peɪn]	kämpfen, sich einsetzen (für/gegen)
regional ['riːdʒənl]	regional
concerned [kən'sɜːnd]	besorgt, beunruhigt
to **assess** [ə'ses]	einschätzen, beurteilen
classmate ['klɑːsmeɪt]	Klassenkamerad/in
consumption [kən'sʌmpʃn]	Verbrauch, Konsum
consideration [kənˌsɪdə'reɪʃn]	Erwägung, Überlegung
counter-argument [ˌkaʊtər 'ɑːgjumənt]	Gegenargument
awareness [ə'weənəs]	Bewusstsein

page 46

fearless ['fɪələs]	furchtlos
entrepreneur [ˌɒntrəprə'nɜː]	Unternehmer/in
to **take a risk** [ˌteɪk ə 'rɪsk]	ein Risiko eingehen
to **go wrong** [ˌgəʊ 'rɒŋ]	schiefgehen
to **run sth** [rʌn]	etw führen, etw betreiben
chairman ['tʃeəmən]	Vorsitzende/r
liability [ˌlaɪə'bɪləti]	Haftung
mail order [ˌmeɪl 'ɔːdə]	Versandhandel
profit ['prɒfɪt]	Gewinn
public(ly) ['pʌblɪk]	öffentlich
responsibility [rɪˌspɒnsə'bɪləti]	Verantwortung, Haftung
to **set up a business** [set ˌʌp ə 'bɪznəs]	ein Unternehmen gründen
shareholder ['ʃeəhəʊldə]	Aktionär/in; Teilhaber/in, Gesellschafter/in
to **invest** [ɪn'vest]	investieren
public limited company *(plc)* (UK) [ˌpʌblɪk ˌlɪmɪtɪd 'kʌmpəni]	Aktiengesellschaft (AG)
to **finance** ['faɪnæns]	finanzieren
head [hed]	Leiter/in, Chef/in
loss [lɒs]	Verlust

page 47

group [gruːp]	Konzern
inventor [ɪn'ventə]	Erfinder/in
brand [brænd]	Marke
empire ['empaɪə]	Reich
to **include** [ɪn'kluːd]	umfassen
approximately (approx.) [ə'prɒksɪmətli]	ungefähr, zirka
to **plant** [plɑːnt]	pflanzen, anpflanzen
technically speaking ['teknɪkli spiːkɪŋ]	genau genommen
sole trader (UK) [ˌsəʊl 'treɪdə]	Einzelunternehmer/in
to **intend** [ɪn'tend]	beabsichtigen
unlimited [ˌʌn'lɪmɪtɪd]	unbegrenzt, unbeschränkt
to **bear sth** [beə]	etw tragen
rabbit ['ræbɪt]	Kaninchen
to **fail** [feɪl]	Pleite gehen, es nicht schaffen, scheitern
record label ['rekɔːd leɪbl]	Plattenfirma
to **sign sb up** [ˌsaɪn 'ʌp]	jdn unter Vertrag nehmen
unknown [ˌʌn'nəʊn]	unbekannt
private limited company (Ltd) (UK) [ˌpraɪvət ˌlɪmɪtɪd 'kʌmpəni]	Gesellschaft mit beschränkter Haftung (GmbH)
limited ['lɪmɪtɪd]	begrenzt, beschränkt
investment [ɪn'vestmənt]	Einlage
in contrast [ɪn 'kɒntrɑːst]	im Gegensatz (dazu)
electrician [ɪˌlek'trɪʃn]	Elektriker/in
to **burn down** [ˌbɜːn 'daʊn]	abbrennen
damage ['dæmɪdʒ]	Schaden
property ['prɒpəti]	Eigentum
to **fear** [fɪə]	fürchten, befürchten
cash [kæʃ]	Geld, Bargeld, liquide Mittel
to **fund** [fʌnd]	finanzieren
to **form** [fɔːm]	bilden
share [ʃeə]	Aktie
stock exchange ['stɒk ɪkstʃeɪndʒ]	Börse
bankruptcy ['bæŋkrʌpsi]	Konkurs, Pleite
serious ['sɪəriəs]	ernst(zunehmend)

page 48

sole proprietor (AE) [ˌsəʊl prə'praɪətə]	Einzelunternehmer/in, Alleininhaber/in
to **take a decision** [ˌteɪk ə dɪ'sɪʒn]	eine Entscheidung fällen
limited liability company (LLC) (US) [ˌlɪmɪtɪd ˌlaɪə'bɪləti kʌmpəni]	Gesellschaft mit beschränkter Haftung (GmbH)
circle ['sɜːkl]	Kreis
corporation (Corp./Inc.) (US) [ˌkɔːpə'reɪʃn]	Aktiengesellschaft (AG)
director [də'rektə]	Vorstandsmitglied
proprietary limited company (Pty Ltd) (Aus, NZ) [prəˌpraɪətri ˌlɪmɪtɪd 'kʌmpəni]	Gesellschaft mit beschränkter Haftung (GmbH)
solar power [ˌsəʊlə 'paʊə]	Solarenergie, Solarstrom
trekking ['trekɪŋ]	Wandern
mountaineering [ˌmaʊntə'nɪərɪŋ]	Bergsteigen

politics ['pɒlətɪks]	Politik
to generate ['dʒenəreɪt]	erzeugen
environmentally friendly [ɪn,vaɪrən,mentəli 'frendli]	umweltfreundlich
distant ['dɪstənt]	entfernt, fern, entlegen
to import [ɪm'pɔ:t]	importieren, einführen
dress [dres]	Kleid
to cut off the phone [kʌt ˌɒf ðə 'fəʊn]	das Telefon abstellen
to go bankrupt [ˌgəʊ'bæŋkrʌpt]	Pleite gehen

page 49

minimalism ['mɪnɪməlɪzəm]	Minimalismus
passenger ['pæsɪndʒə]	Fahrgast, Passagier/in
economical [ˌi:kə'nɒmɪkl]	sparsam
fuel ['fju:əl]	Treibstoff
recyclable [ˌri:'saɪkləbl]	recycelbar
environment [ɪn'vaɪrənmənt]	Umwelt
feature ['fi:tʃə]	Merkmal, Kennzeichen
to waste [weɪst]	verschwenden, vergeuden
corporate ['kɔ:pərət]	Unternehmens-, Geschäfts-
identity [aɪ'dentəti]	Identität
concept ['kɒnsept]	Idee, Konzept
sustainability [səˌsteɪnə'bɪləti]	Nachhaltigkeit
efficiency [ɪ'fɪʃnsi]	Effizienz, Leistungsfähigkeit
commitment (to) [kə'mɪtmənt]	Engagement (für); Bekenntnis (zu)
economy [ɪ'kɒnəmi]	Sparsamkeit, Wirtschaftlichkeit

page 51

sustainable [sə'steɪnəbl]	nachhaltig
importance [ɪm'pɔ:tns]	Bedeutung, Wichtigkeit
to entitle [ɪn'taɪtl]	betiteln
mission ['mɪʃn]	Auftrag, Mission
coal [kəʊl]	Kohle
to heat [hi:t]	(be)heizen
chemicals ['kemɪklz]	Chemikalien
to pump [pʌmp]	pumpen
asbestos [æs'bestəs]	Asbest
to insulate ['ɪnsjuleɪt]	isolieren
to carry on [ˌkæri 'ɒn]	weitermachen
to realize sth ['rɪəlaɪz]	etw erkennen, wissen
to define [dɪ'faɪn]	definieren, festlegen
development [dɪ'veləpmənt]	Entwicklung
economic [ˌi:kə'nɒmɪk]	wirtschaftlich
to connect [kə'nekt]	anschließen, verbinden
In simple terms, ... [tɜ:mz]	Einfach ausgedrückt ...
backyard [ˌbæk'jɑ:d]	(Hinter-)Hof, Garten hinter dem Haus
to affect sb/sth [ə'fekt]	sich auf jdn/etw auswirken
therefore ['ðeəfɔ:]	deswegen
to balance ['bæləns]	im Gleichgewicht halten
to achieve [ə'tʃi:v]	erzielen
biofuel [ˌbaɪəʊ'fju:əl]	Biokraftstoff
biodegradable [ˌbaɪəʊdɪ'greɪdəbl]	biologisch abbaubar

page 52

building material ['bɪldɪŋ mətɪəriəl]	Baumaterial, Baustoff
cosmetics *(pl)* [kɒz'metɪks]	Kosmetikprodukte, Kosmetika
findings ['faɪndɪŋz]	Ergebnisse
beliefs (pl) [bɪ'li:fs]	Ansichten
disability [ˌdɪsə'bɪləti]	Behinderung
resource [rɪ'sɔ:s]	Ressource, Rohstoff
diversity [daɪ'vɜ:səti]	Vielfalt
to force [fɔ:s]	zwingen
forced labour [ˌfɔ:st 'leɪbə]	Zwangsarbeit

page 53

contribution [ˌkɒntrɪ'bju:ʃn]	Beitrag
on air [ˌɒn 'eə]	auf Sendung (z.B. Radio)
to follow sth up [ˌfɒləʊ 'ʌp]	etw einer Sache folgen lassen; etw weiterverfolgen

page 54

distribution [ˌdɪstrɪ'bju:ʃn]	Verteilung
to store [stɔ:]	lagern
warehouse ['weəhaʊs]	Lager
to deliver [dɪ'lɪvə]	liefern
van [væn]	Lieferwagen
network ['netwɜ:k]	Netzwerk
folder ['fəʊldə]	Mappe, Ordner
Sunday trading [ˌsʌndeɪ 'treɪdɪŋ]	verkaufsoffene Sonntage
to keep to [ˌki:p tə]	sich halten an
union ['ju:niən]	Gewerkschaft
racial ['reɪʃl]	Rassen-, rassisch
equality [i'kwɒləti]	Gleichberechtigung, Gleichheit
skin [skɪn]	Haut
first name ['fɜ:st neɪm]	Vorname
surname ['sɜ:neɪm]	Nachname
managing director [ˌmænɪdʒɪŋ də'rektə]	Geschäftsführer/in
chief executive officer (CEO) [ˌtʃi:f ɪg'zekjətɪv ɒfɪsə]	Vorstandsvorsitzende/r
president ['prezɪdənt]	Präsident/in
location [ləʊ'keɪʃn]	Standort
turnover ['tɜ:nəʊvə]	Umsatz (UK)
profit margin ['prɒfɪt mɑ:dʒɪn]	Gewinnspanne
to be located in ... [bi ləʊ'keɪtɪd ɪn]	in ... ansässig sein, seinen/ihren Sitz in ... haben
head office [ˌhed 'ɒfɪs]	Zentrale
parent company [ˌpeərənt 'kʌmpəni]	Muttergesellschaft
subsidiary [səb'sɪdiəri]	Tochtergesellschaft
agent ['eɪdʒənt]	Vertreter, Vertretung
pure [pjʊə]	rein
wool [wʊl]	Wolle
steel [sti:l]	Stahl
to export [ɪk'spɔ:t]	exportieren, ausführen

page 55

answerphone ['ɑ:nsəfəʊn]	Anrufbeantworter
video conferencing ['vɪdiəʊ kɒnfərənsɪŋ]	Videokonferenz(schaltung)
advance [əd'vɑ:ns]	Fortschritt
telework(ing) ['teliwɜ:kɪŋ]	Telearbeit
to commute [kə'mju:t]	pendeln (lange Strecke zur Arbeit fahren)
tool [tu:l]	Werkzeug
option ['ɒpʃn]	(Wahl-)Möglichkeit
suited to/for sth ['su:tɪd]	für etw geeignet
to access ['ækses]	zugreifen auf

platform ['plætfɔːm]	Plattform
distraction [dɪ'strækʃn]	Ablenkung
to concentrate ['kɒnsntreɪt]	sich konzentrieren
in charge (of) [ɪn 'tʃɑːdʒ]	verantwortlich, zuständig für
pharmaceutical [ˌfɑːmə'suːtɪkl]	Pharma-
sales representative ['seɪlz reprɪzentətɪv]	Außendienstmitarbeiter/in
out and about [ˌaʊt ənd ə'baʊt]	unterwegs
to interest ['ɪntrəst]	interessieren
appointment [ə'pɔɪntmənt]	Termin
to hand sth out [ˌhænd 'aʊt]	etw aushändigen, verteilen
sample ['sɑːmpl]	Muster, Probe
questionnaire [ˌkwestʃə'neə]	Fragebogen
feedback ['fiːdbæk]	Rückmeldung
to collate [kə'leɪt]	zusammentragen, zusammenstellen
recommendation [ˌrekɒmən'deɪʃn]	Empfehlung
to split [splɪt]	aufteilen
commute [kə'mjuːt]	Fahrt zur Arbeit
petrol ['petrəl]	Benzin
productive [prə'dʌktɪv]	produktiv

page 56

occupation [ˌɒkju'peɪʃn]	Beruf
to pamper ['pæmpə]	verwöhnen
to trust [trʌst]	vertrauen; hoffen
to resist [rɪ'zɪst]	widerstehen
to pressurize ['preʃəraɪz]	unter Druck setzen
(un)supervised ['suːpəvaɪzd, ʌn'suːpəvaɪzd]	(un)beaufsichtigt, (nicht) überwacht
temptation [temp'teɪʃn]	Versuchung
internship ['ɪntɜːnʃɪp]	Praktikum
to outline ['aʊtlaɪn]	skizzieren, beschreiben, darstellen

page 57

to conduct [kən'dʌkt]	durchführen
to throw sth up [ˌθrəʊ 'ʌp]	aufwerfen, zu Tage bringen
to discover [dɪ'skʌvə]	entdecken
percentage [pə'sentɪdʒ]	Anteil, Prozentsatz
real estate ['rɪəl əsteɪt]	Immobilien(handel)
senior ['siːniər]	leitende/r
to top a list [ˌtɒp ə 'lɪst]	eine Liste anführen, ganz oben auf einer Liste stehen
construction [kən'strʌkʃn]	Bau
wholesale ['həʊlseɪl]	Großhandel
clerical worker [ˌklerɪkl 'wɜːkə]	Büroangestellte/r, Sachbearbeiter/in
skilled [skɪld]	qualifiziert, Fach-
unskilled [ˌʌn'skɪld]	ungelernt
to mention ['menʃn]	erwähnen
facilities [fə'sɪlətiz]	Anlage(n)
to indicate ['ɪndɪkeɪt]	(an)zeigen, darauf hindeuten
to rise (by) [raɪz]	steigen, ansteigen (um)
to interrupt [ˌɪntə'rʌpt]	unterbrechen
to appear [ə'pɪə]	(er)scheinen
to call in sick [ˌkɔːl ɪn 'sɪk]	sich krankmelden
in the course of ... [kɔːs]	im (Ver-)Lauf von ...
increasingly [ɪn'kriːsɪŋli]	zunehmend
carbon (dioxide) ['kɑːbən]	Kohlenstoff, Kohlendioxid
emission [ɪ'mɪʃn]	Emission
to boast (about) [bəʊst]	prahlen, angeben (mit)
carbon footprint [ˌkɑːbən 'fʊtprɪnt]	CO_2-Fußabdruck
to delegate ['delɪgeɪt]	delegieren
to check up on [ˌtʃek 'ʌp ɒn]	kontrollieren; Nachforschungen anstellen über
policy ['pɒləsi]	Politik, Vorgehensweise, Regelung
to be committed to [kə'mɪtɪd]	sich engagieren für, engagiert sein für
supervision [ˌsuːpə'vɪʃn]	Beaufsichtigung, Aufsicht
to mind [maɪnd]	etwas dagegen haben

page 58

to cover ['kʌvə]	abdecken, (Thema) behandeln
oral(ly) ['ɔːrəl]	mündlich
to assign [ə'saɪn]	zuweisen, zuteilen
moderator ['mɒdəreɪtə]	Vermittler/in; Moderator/in

page 59

availability [əˌveɪlə'bɪləti]	Verfügbarkeit
24/7 [ˌtwenti ˌfɔː 'sevn]	rund um die Uhr
to be on call [ɒn 'kɔːl]	in Bereitschaft sein, Bereitschaftsdienst haben
stereotypical [ˌsteriə'tɪpɪkl]	stereotyp, klischeehaft
to raise (children) [reɪz]	(Kinder) erziehen, aufziehen
feminist ['femənɪst]	Feminist/in; feministisch
to be better off [ˌbetər 'ɒf]	besser dran sein, besser bedient sein
female ['fiːmeɪl]	weiblich; Frau
diploma [dɪ'pləʊmə]	Diplom, Abschlusszeugnis
competence ['kɒmpɪtəns]	Kompetenz
to disagree with sb [ˌdɪsə'griː wɪð]	anderer Meinung als jd sein, jdm nicht zustimmen
I'm afraid [aɪm ə'freɪd]	leider, ich fürchte
clarification [ˌklærɪfɪ'keɪʃn]	Erklärung, Erläuterung(en)
repetition [ˌrepə'tɪʃn]	Wiederholung
to repeat [rɪ'piːt]	wiederholen
conclusion [kən'kluːʒn]	Fazit, Schluss

TOPIC 3

page 62

good value for money [gʊd ˌvæljuː fə 'mʌni]	preiswert
influence ['ɪnfluəns]	Einfluss
advertising ['ædvətaɪzɪŋ]	Werbung
to impress [ɪm'pres]	beeindrucken
to care about sb/sth ['keər əbaʊt]	sich um jdn/etw kümmern, am Herzen liegen
to associate [ə'səʊʃiət]	verbinden, assoziieren
to brainwash sb ['breɪnwɒʃ]	jdn einer Gehirnwäsche unterziehen
athletics [æθ'letɪks]	Sport, Leichtathletik
athlete ['æθliːt]	Sportler/in
vintage ['vɪntɪdʒ]	nostalgisch, Retro-
exception [ɪk'sepʃn]	Ausnahme
toothpaste ['tuːθpeɪst]	Zahncreme
victim ['vɪktɪm]	Opfer
to admit [əd'mɪt]	zugeben
Shame on you. ['ʃeɪm ɒn juː]	Schäm dich!
glasses (pl) ['glɑːsɪz]	Brille

stereo system ['steriəʊ sɪstəm]	Stereoanlage
survey ['sɜːveɪ]	Umfrage
item ['aɪtəm]	Artikel, Gegenstand
to survey sb [sə'veɪ]	jdn befragen

page 63

dispatch [dɪ'spætʃ]	Versand
logistics (pl) [lə'dʒɪstɪks]	Logistik
quality control ['kwɒləti kəntrəʊl]	Qualitätskontrolle
research and development (R&D) [rɪˌsɜːtʃ ən dɪ'veləpmənt]	Forschung(s-) und Entwicklung(sabteilung)
instruction [ɪn'strʌkʃn]	Anweisung, Anleitung
booklet ['bʊklət]	Broschüre
transport ['trænspɔːt]	Beförderung, Transport
to design [dɪ'zaɪn]	konstruieren, entwickeln, entwerfen
to fill an order [ˌfɪl ən 'ɔːdə]	eine Bestellung erledigen
ad(vertising) agency ['ædvətaɪzɪŋ eɪdʒənsi]	Werbeagentur
to package ['pækɪdʒ]	(ver)packen
to decorate ['dekəreɪt]	einrichten, gestalten
to inspire [ɪn'spaɪə]	anregen, inspirieren
creativity [ˌkriːeɪ'tɪvəti]	Kreativität
print [prɪnt]	Druck
work of art [ˌwɜːk əv 'ɑːt]	Kunstwerk
to be on display [bi ˌɒn dɪ'spleɪ]	ausgestellt sein/werden, zu sehen sein
broad(ly) [brɔːd]	breit
department store [dɪ'pɑːtmənt stɔː]	Warenhaus
account services [ə'kaʊnt sɜːvɪsɪz]	Kundenbetreuung
ad(vertising) campaign ['ædvətaɪzɪŋ kæmpeɪn]	Werbekampagne
account executive [ə'kaʊnt ɪgzekjətɪv]	Kundenberater/in
brief [briːf]	Dossier, Anweisungen

page 64

to brew [bruː]	sich zusammenbrauen, gären
creative (department) [kri'eɪtɪv]	Kreation
to propose [prə'pəʊz]	vorschlagen
commercial [kə'mɜːʃl]	Werbespot
to feature ['fiːtʃə]	haben, aufweisen; vorkommen, eine Rolle spielen
mermaid ['mɜːmeɪd]	Meerjungfrau
longing(ly) ['lɒŋɪŋ]	sehnsüchtig
seductive(ly) [sɪ'dʌktɪv]	verführerisch
to remove [rɪ'muːv]	(Kleidung:) ausziehen
underwear ['ʌndəweə]	Unterwäsche
shot [ʃɒt]	(Film:) Einstellung, Aufnahme
myth [mɪθ]	Mythos, Märchen, Legende
unoriginal [ˌʌnə'rɪdʒənl]	herkömmlich, unoriginell
to make an impact [ˌmeɪk ən 'ɪmpækt]	einen Eindruck hinterlassen
twinkle ['twɪŋkl]	Zwinkern
to shoot [ʃuːt]	(Film:) drehen, Aufnahmen machen
dozen ['dʌzn]	Dutzend
graphic artist [ˌgræfɪk 'ɑːtɪst]	Grafiker/in
buyer ['baɪə]	Einkäufer/in
copy editor ['kɒpi edɪtə]	Redakteur/in
to exist [ɪg'zɪst]	es geben, existieren
to have sth in common [həv ˌɪn 'kɒmən]	etw gemeinsam haben
effectiveness [ɪ'fektɪvnəs]	Wirksamkeit, Effektivität
customer satisfaction [ˌkʌstəmə ˌsætɪs'fækʃn]	Kundenzufriedenheit
whirlwind ['wɜːlwɪnd]	Wirbelwind, Trubel
strategist ['strætədʒɪst]	Stratege/-in
among [ə'mʌŋ]	(mitten) in
chaos ['keɪɒs]	Chaos
to strategize ['strætədʒaɪz]	(die strategisch besten Lösungen) finden
method ['meθəd]	Methode, Art (und Weise)
health-conscious ['helθ kɒnʃəs]	gesundheitsbewusst
target audience [ˌtɑːgɪt 'ɔːdiəns]	Zielpublikum, -gruppe
along with [ə'lɒŋ wɪð]	zusammen mit
to be considered sth [bi kən'sɪdəd]	als etw gelten
pillar ['pɪlə]	Säule
to purchase ['pɜːtʃəs]	kaufen
ad(vertising) space ['ædvətaɪzɪŋ speɪs]	Werbefläche(n), Werbezeit(en)
channel ['tʃænl]	Sender
cable channel ['keɪbl tʃænl]	Kabelsender
audience ['ɔːdiəns]	Publikum
component [kəm'pəʊnənt]	Bestandteil, Komponente
application [ˌæplɪ'keɪʃn]	Anwendung
to create [kri'eɪt]	schaffen, kreieren, (Eindruck) hinterlassen
industry ['ɪndəstri]	Branche
constant ['kɒnstənt]	konstant, gleichbleibend
shopping mall ['ʃɒpɪŋ mɔːl]	Einkaufszentrum, -passage
to enquire about sth [ɪn'kwaɪər əbaʊt]	sich nach etw erkundigen
boring ['bɔːrɪŋ]	langweilig

page 65

to limit ['lɪmɪt]	beschränken
explicit(ly) [ɪk'splɪsɪt]	ausdrücklich, wörtlich
to analyse ['ænəlaɪz]	analysieren, untersuchen
billboard ['bɪlbɔːd]	Reklametafel, Plakatwand
brochure ['brəʊʃə]	Prospekt
mail shot ['meɪlʃɒt]	Mailing (Versenden von Werbematerial durch die Post)
full-page [ˌfʊl 'peɪdʒ]	ganzseitig
poster ['pəʊstə]	Plakat
leaflet ['liːflət]	Faltblatt, Informationsblatt
classified (ad) ['klæsɪfaɪd]	Kleinanzeige
clever ['klevə]	klug, geschickt
disgusting [dɪs'gʌstɪŋ]	ekelhaft
glamorous ['glæmərəs]	glanzvoll
lifestyle ['laɪfstaɪl]	Lebensweise, Lebensführung
rhetorical question [rɪˌtɒrɪkl 'kwestʃən]	rhetorische Frage
to hint [hɪnt]	andeuten, durchblicken lassen
to escape (from) [ɪ'skeɪp]	fliehen (vor/aus), entkommen (aus)
romance [rəʊ'mæns]	Romantik
adventure [əd'ventʃə]	Abenteuer
aimed at sb ['eɪmd ət]	an jdn gerichtet, für jdn
to rub off on [ˌrʌb 'ɒf ɒn]	abfärben auf
rebel ['rebəl]	Rebell/in

outsider [ˌaʊt'saɪdə]	Außenseiter/in
to convince [kən'vɪns]	überzeugen

page 66

to touch [tʌtʃ]	berühren, anfassen
screen [skriːn]	Bildschirm
headphones ['hedfəʊnz]	Kopfhörer
peace [piːs]	Frieden
sun roof ['sʌn ruːf]	Schiebedach
remote [rɪ'məʊt]	Fern-
seat heating ['siːt hiːtɪŋ]	Sitzheizung
to be sick [bi 'sɪk]	sich übergeben (müssen)

page 67

featuring ['fiːtʃərɪŋ]	(Film:) mit
to have a hard time [həv ə ˌhɑːd 'taɪm]	es schwer haben, schwerfallen
mythology [mɪ'θɒlədʒi]	Mythologie
magic ['mædʒɪk]	Zauberei, Magie
copywriter ['kɒpiraɪtə]	Werbetexter/in
to get sb's attention [ˌgett ə'tenʃn]	jds Aufmerksamkeit wecken/fesseln
comical ['kɒmɪkl]	komisch, lustig
to act [ækt]	handeln
action ['ækʃn]	Handlung, Aktion, Maßnahme(n)
model ['mɒdl]	Modell
engaging [ɪn'geɪdʒɪŋ]	fesselnd
to arouse [ə'raʊz]	wecken, erregen
to get sb involved in sth [ˌget ɪn'vɒlvd ɪn]	jdn an etw beteiligen, jdn in etw einbeziehen
to solve [sɒlv]	lösen
to approve of sth [ə'pruːv əv]	etw gut finden
to encourage [ɪn'kʌrɪdʒ]	fördern

page 68

duchess ['dʌtʃəs]	Herzogin
frozen foods [ˌfrəʊzn 'fuːdz]	Tiefkühlkost
grocery store ['grəʊsəristɔː]	Lebensmittelgeschäft
responsible [rɪ'spɒnsəbl]	verantwortlich, zuständig
investigation [ɪnˌvestɪ'geɪʃn]	Forschung, Ermittlung(en)
improvement [ɪm'pruːvmənt]	Verbesserung
process ['prəʊses]	Verfahren, Ablauf, Prozess
on time [ɒn 'taɪm]	pünktlich
strategy ['strætədʒi]	Strategie
to promote sth [prə'məʊt]	etw bewerben
to distribute [dɪ'strɪbjuːt]	vertreiben
to set a price [ˌset ə 'praɪs]	einen Preis festlegen/festsetzen
product launch ['prɒdʌkt lɔːntʃ]	Produkteinführung
product brief ['prɒdʌkt briːf]	Produktbeschreibung
question mark ['kwestʃən mɑːk]	Fragezeichen
intern ['ɪntɜːn]	Praktikant/in
to determine [dɪ'tɜːmɪn]	ermitteln, bestimmen
to figure out [ˌfɪgər 'aʊt]	herausfinden
to write sth up [ˌraɪt 'ʌp]	etw ausarbeiten, erstellen
minutes (pl) ['mɪnɪts]	Protokoll
permission [pə'mɪʃn]	Erlaubnis, Genehmigung
novelty ['nɒvlti]	Neuheit
shape [ʃeɪp]	Form
excited about sth [ɪk'saɪtɪd əbaʊt]	von etw begeistert
to schedule ['ʃedjuːl]	(Termin) ansetzen
schedule ['ʃedjuːl]	Terminkalender
excuse [ɪk'skjuːs]	Ausrede
to familiarize oneself/sb with sth [fə'mɪliəraɪz wʌnself wɪð]	sich/jdn mit etw vertraut machen

page 69

target group ['tɑːgɪt gruːp]	Zielgruppe
to carry sth out [ˌkæri 'aʊt]	etw durchführen
to market ['mɑːkɪt]	vermarkten
share [ʃeə]	Anteil
to be conceived for sb [bi kən'siːvd fə]	für jdn gedacht sein
Unique Selling Point/Proposition (USP) [juˌniːk 'selɪŋ pɔɪnt, juˌniːk 'selɪŋ prɒpəzɪʃn]	Alleinstellungsmerkmal
practical ['præktɪkl]	praktisch
aspect ['æspekt]	Aspekt, Seite
to ship [ʃɪp]	versenden
to display [dɪ'spleɪ]	ausstellen, präsentieren
preparation [ˌprepə'reɪʃn]	Zubereitung
standpoint ['stændpɔɪnt]	Standpunkt
crazy ['kreɪzi]	verrückt
heart [hɑːt]	Herz
shamrock ['ʃæmrɒk]	Kleeblatt
star [stɑː]	Stern
sex [seks]	Geschlecht
male [meɪl]	männlich; Mann
purchasing power ['pɜːtʃəsɪŋ paʊə]	Kaufkraft
education [ˌedʒu'keɪʃn]	Schulbildung
habit ['hæbɪt]	Gewohnheit
wrap [ræp]	Folie
sticker ['stɪkə]	Aufkleber

page 70

original [ə'rɪdʒənl]	originell
excerpt ['eksɜːpt]	Auszug, Ausschnitt
chairperson ['tʃeəpɜːsn]	Vorsitzende/r
attendee [ə'tendiː]	Anwesende/r
pumpkin ['pʌmpkɪn]	Kürbis
primarily [praɪ'merəli]	hauptsächlich, vorrangig
to double ['dʌbl]	sich verdoppeln
realistic [ˌriːə'lɪstɪk]	realistisch
to bake [beɪk]	backen
That's the whole point. [ˌhəʊl 'pɔɪnt]	Darum geht es gerade.
oven ['ʌvn]	Ofen, Herd
stem [stem]	Stängel, Stiel
to burn [bɜːn]	anbrennen
bear [beə]	Bär
to turn out great [ˌtɜːn aʊt 'greɪt]	sehr gut gelingen
upright ['ʌpraɪt]	aufrecht
square [skweə]	quadratisch
uniform ['juːnɪfɔːm]	einheitlich, Einheits-
brief(ly) [briːf]	kurz
to proofread ['pruːfriːd]	Korrektur lesen
punctuation [ˌpʌŋktʃu'eɪʃn]	Interpunktion
to draw sb's attention to sth [ˌdrɔː sʌmbədiz ə'tenʃn tə]	jdn auf etw aufmerksam machen
to state [steɪt]	erklären, angeben, sagen
to suggest [sə'dʒest]	vorschlagen
to recommend [ˌrekə'mend]	empfehlen
to confirm [kən'fɜːm]	bestätigen
concern [kən'sɜːn]	Befürchtung, Bedenken, Sorge

to **express** [ɪk'spres]	ausdrücken, zum Ausdruck bringen

page 71

to **congratulate sb on sth** [kən'grætʃuleɪt]	jdn für etw beglückwünschen
fish fingers [ˌfɪʃ 'fɪŋgəz]	Fischstäbchen
energy ['enədʒi]	Energie
ready meal [ˌredi 'miːl]	Fertiggericht
pricing ['praɪsɪŋ]	Preisgestaltung
to **advertise sth** ['ædvətaɪz]	für etw Werbung machen, etw anbieten
artwork ['ɑːtwɜːk]	Bildmaterial, Illustrationen
to **preheat** [ˌpriː'hiːt]	vorheizen
to **remove sth** [rɪ'muːv]	etw entfernen

page 72

edition [ɪ'dɪʃn]	Ausgabe (z. B. einer Zeitschrift)
range (of products) [reɪndʒ]	Sortiment, Angebot, Palette
throughout [θruː'aʊt]	überall, in ganz
buffet car ['bʊfeɪ kɑː]	Bordrestaurant, Büffetwagen
trial run ['traɪəl rʌn]	Probelauf
to **place an order** [ˌpleɪs ən 'ɔːdə]	einen Auftrag erteilen, eine Bestellung aufgeben
initial order [ɪˌnɪʃl 'ɔːdə]	Erstbestellung, Erstauftrag
favourable ['feɪvərəbl]	günstig
quotation [kwəʊ'teɪʃn]	Preisangebot
terms [tɜːmz]	Bedingungen, Konditionen
terms of delivery [ˌtɜːmz əv dɪ'lɪvəri]	Lieferbedingungen
terms of payment [ˌtɜːmz əf 'peɪmənt]	Zahlungsbedingungen
delivery [dɪ'lɪvəri]	Lieferung
to **be in a position to do sth** [pə'zɪʃn]	in der Lage sein, etw zu tun
Yours faithfully [ˌjɔːz 'feɪθfəli]	Mit freundlichen Grüßen (Briefschluss)
residential home [ˌrezɪ'denʃl həʊm]	Wohnheim
care home ['keə həʊm]	Pflegeheim
to **range (from ... to ...)** [reɪndʒ]	reichen (von ... bis ...)
diabetes [ˌdaɪə'biːtiːz]	Diabetes (Zuckerkrankheit)
allergy ['ælədʒi]	Allergie
it goes without saying [ɪt ˌgəʊz wɪðaʊt 'seɪɪŋ]	es ist selbstverständlich
to **serve** [sɜːv]	servieren
(easily) digestible [daɪ'dʒestəbl]	(leicht) verdaulich
to **note** [nəʊt]	feststellen
regards [rɪ'gɑːdz]	Grüße

page 73

to **be in the process of doing sth** [ɪn ðə 'prəʊses əv]	gerade dabei sein, etw zu tun
to **hand sth over** [ˌhænd 'əʊvə]	etw übergeben
conversation [ˌkɒnvə'seɪʃn]	Gespräch
musician [mju'zɪʃn]	Musiker/in
do [duː]	Veranstaltung, Fete
ground [graʊnd]	Gelände
display [dɪ'spleɪ]	Anzeige, Display; Bildschirm

page 74

labour-saving ['leɪbə seɪvɪŋ]	arbeitssparend
device [dɪ'vaɪs]	Gerät, Apparat
first-rate [ˌfɜːst 'reɪt]	erstklassig
to **minimize** ['mɪnɪmaɪz]	auf ein Minimum beschränken, minimieren
long-term [ˌlɒŋ 'tɜːm]	langfristig
cream [kriːm]	Rahm
unwittingly [ˌʌn'wɪtɪŋli]	ohne es zu ahnen
social ['səʊʃl]	gesellschaftlich
back-breaking ['bæk breɪkɪŋ]	äußerst anstrengend
time-consuming ['taɪm kənsjuːmɪŋ]	zeitraubend
to **heat** [hiːt]	erhitzen
to **liberate** ['lɪbəreɪt]	befreien
pill [pɪl]	Pille
right to work [ˌraɪt tə 'wɜːk]	Recht auf Arbeit
to **diversify** [daɪ'vɜːsɪfaɪ]	verbreitern, auffächern, diversifizieren
core business ['kɔː bɪznəs]	Kerngeschäft
medical insurance [ˌmedɪkl ɪn'ʃʊərəns]	Krankenversicherung
pension scheme ['penʃnskiːm]	betriebliche Altersversorgung, Rentenversicherung
housing ['haʊzɪŋ]	Wohnungen, Wohnraum, Unterkunft
contented [kən'tentɪd]	zufrieden
loyal ['lɔɪəl]	treu, loyal
life expectancy ['laɪf ɪkspektənsi]	Lebenserwartung
limited partnership [ˌlɪmɪtɪd 'pɑːtnəʃɪp]	Kommanditgesellschaft (KG)
founder ['faʊndə]	Gründer/in
publicly owned [ˌpʌblɪkli 'əʊnd]	börsennotiert
quarter ['kwɔːtə]	Quartal
to **buy sth up** [ˌbaɪ 'ʌp]	etw aufkaufen
production facilities [prə'dʌkʃn fəsɪlətiz]	Produktionsstätte(n), Werk(e)
unlike [ˌʌn'laɪk]	anders als, im Gegensatz zu
low-wage country [ˌləʊ weɪdʒ 'kʌntri]	Niedriglohnland
plant [plɑːnt]	Werk, Betrieb, Anlage
control [kən'trəʊl]	Steuerung
appliance [ə'plaɪəns]	Gerät, Haushaltsgerät
sales [seɪlz]	Verkaufsumsatz

page 75

to **operate** ['ɒpəreɪt]	(geschäftlich) tätig sein
short-term [ʃɔːt 'tɜːm]	kurzfristig, Kurzzeit-
after-sales service [ˌɑːftə ˌseɪlz 'sɜːvɪs]	Kundendienst
toll-free [ˌtəʊl 'friː]	gebührenfrei (z. B. Telefonanruf)
to **be prepared to do sth** [bi prɪ'peəd tə]	bereit sein, etw zu tun
dryer ['draɪə]	Trockner
celebrity [sə'lebrəti]	Prominente/r
endorsement [ɪn'dɔːsmənt]	Werbung; Unterstützung

page 76

household ['haʊshəʊld]	Haushalt, Haushalts-
to **break down** [ˌbreɪk 'daʊn]	kaputtgehen

washing machine ['wɒʃɪŋ məʃi:n]	Waschmaschine
dealer ['di:lə]	Händler
adapter [ə'dæptə]	Passstück, Adapter
Dear Sir or Madam [dɪə ˌsɜ: ɔ: 'mædəm]	Sehr geehrte Damen und Herren
supply [sə'plaɪ]	(Strom, Wasser etc.:) Anschluss, Versorgung
installation guide [ˌɪnstə'leɪʃn gaɪd]	Aufbauanleitung
hose [həʊz]	Schlauch
water intake hose ['wɔ:tərɪnteɪk həʊz]	Wasserzulaufschlauch
to attach [ə'tætʃ]	anschließen, anbringen
valve [vælv]	Ventil
hardware store ['hɑ:dweə stɔ:]	Eisenwarenhandlung, Baumarkt
source [sɔ:s]	Quelle
to function ['fʌŋkʃn]	funktionieren
out of stock [ˌaʊt əf 'stɒk]	nicht lieferbar, nicht vorrätig
design [dɪ'zaɪn]	Konstruktion
to include [ɪn'klu:d]	beifügen
Sincerely (AE) [sɪn'sɪəli]	Mit freundlichen Grüßen (Briefschluss)
proprietor [prə'praɪətə]	Inhaber/in
All rights reserved. [ɔ:l ˌraɪts rɪ'zɜ:vd]	Alle Rechte vorbehalten.

page 77

urgent(ly) ['ɜ:dʒənt]	dringend, eilig
matter ['mætə]	Angelegenheit, Sache
to structure ['strʌktʃə]	strukturieren
apology [ə'pɒlədʒi]	Entschuldigung
explanation [ˌeksplə'neɪʃn]	Erläuterung, Erklärung
ending ['endɪŋ]	Schluss, Ende
to take turns [ˌteɪk 'tɜ:nz]	sich abwechseln
anyway ['eniweɪ]	wie dem auch sei
suggestion [sə'dʒestʃən]	Vorschlag
to consider sth [kən'sɪdə]	etw berücksichtigen
to get to know sb [ˌget tə 'nəʊ]	jdn kennenlernen
to call by [ˌkɔ:l 'baɪ]	vorbeikommen
convenient [kən'vi:niənt]	passend, praktisch, angenehm
to stop by [ˌstɒp 'baɪ]	vorbeischauen

page 78

cup tray ['kʌp treɪ]	Tassenabstellfläche
container [kən'teɪnə]	Behälter; Container
fitted ['fɪtɪd]	Einbau-
countertop ['kaʊntətɒp]	Ladentisch, Theke; Arbeitsfläche
removable [rɪ'mu:vəbl]	entnehmbar
capsule chamber ['kæpsju:l tʃeɪmbə]	Kapselmagazin
ground [graʊnd]	gemahlen
flavour [flɔ:]	Geschmack(svariation)
adjustable [ə'dʒʌstəbl]	(höhen)verstellbar, einstellbar
spout [spaʊt]	(Kaffee-)Auslauf
capsule ['kæpsju:l]	Kapsel
multilingual [ˌmʌlti'lɪŋgwəl]	mehrsprachig
frothy milk [ˌfrɑθi 'mɪlk]	Milchschaum
instant coffee [ˌɪnstənt 'kɒfi]	Pulverkaffee, löslicher Kaffee
free-standing [ˌfri: 'stændɪŋ]	Stand-, frei stehend

page 80

electronics *(pl)* [ɪˌlek'trɒnɪks]	Elektronik
drive [draɪv]	Antrieb
lithium ion battery ['lɪθiəm aɪən bætəri]	Lithium-Ionen-Akku
rpm (= revolutions per minute) [ˌɑ: pi: 'əm, revəˌlu:ʃnz pə 'mɪnɪt]	Umdrehungen (pro Minute), Drehzahl
engine ['endʒɪn]	Motor, Maschine
dual ['dju:əl]	Doppel-, doppelt
clutch [klʌtʃ]	Kupplung
transmission [træns'mɪʃn]	Übertragung
race car ['reɪs kɑ:]	Rennwagen
technical ['teknɪkl]	technisch
chassis ['ʃæsi]	Fahrgestell
speed [spi:d]	Geschwindigkeit
miles per hour (mph) [ˌmaɪlz pər 'aʊə]	Meilen pro Stunde
hybrid ['haɪbrɪd]	Hybrid-
mode [məʊd]	Modus, Art
rocket ['rɒkɪt]	Rakete
to pass [pɑ:s]	vorbeifahren, überholen
to overtake [ˌəʊvə'teɪk]	überholen
mileage ['maɪlɪdʒ]	Spritverbrauch
miles per gallon (mpg) [ˌmaɪlz pɜ: 'gælən]	Meilen pro Gallone (1 gallon = 4,5 l)
win [wɪn]	Sieg
awesome ['ɔ:səm]	fantastisch
Just kidding. [ˌdʒʌst 'kɪdɪŋ]	Kleiner Scherz.
to picture sb ['pɪktʃə]	sich jdn vorstellen
to consider sth sth [kən'sɪdə]	etw für etw halten
racing ['reɪsɪŋ]	Rennen, Renn-
wheel [wi:l]	Rad
to power ['paʊə]	antreiben
to maximize ['mæksɪmaɪz]	maximieren
bloody ['blʌdi]	verdammt
button ['bʌtn]	Knopf, Taste
gorgeous ['gɔ:dʒəs]	(wunder)schön, prächtig
to sacrifice ['sækrɪfaɪs]	opfern
looks [lʊks]	(gutes) Aussehen
environmentalist [ɪnˌvaɪrən'mentəlɪst]	Umweltschützer/in
to beat [bi:t]	schlagen
area ['eəriə]	Gebiet, Bereich, Feld
medicine ['medsn]	Medizin
illustration [ˌɪlə'streɪʃn]	Abbildung, Illustration

page 81

solution [sə'lu:ʃn]	Lösung
business card ['bɪznəs kɑ:d]	Visitenkarte
to look into [ˌlʊk 'ɪntə]	prüfen, untersuchen; sich kümmern um
business plan ['bɪznəs plæn]	Geschäftsplan
branding ['brændɪŋ]	Markenaufbau, Branding
to participate in [pɑ:'tɪsɪpeɪt ɪn]	teilnehmen an
disappointed (with sb/sth) [ˌdɪsə'pɔɪntɪd]	enttäuscht (von jdm/etw)
advice [əd'vaɪs]	Rat, Ratschlag/Ratschläge
charity shop ['tʃærəti ʃɒp]	Laden einer Wohltätigkeitsorganisation
car boot sale [ˌkɑ: 'bu:t seɪl]	Trödel, Flohmarkt
fashion ['fæʃn]	Mode
to sell [sel]	sich verkaufen (lassen)

spreadsheet ['spredʃi:t]	Tabellenkalkulationsdatei
to **go wrong** [ˌgəʊ 'rɒŋ]	einen Fehler machen
Best wishes [best 'wɪʃɪz]	Mit den besten Grüßen
to **wonder** ['wʌndə]	sich fragen
to **be delighted to do sth** [bi dɪ'laɪtɪd tə du:]	etw gern tun
structure ['strʌktʃə]	Struktur
to **be worth** [wɜ:θ]	wert sein
wide [waɪd]	groß, weit; breit
marketplace ['mɑ:kɪtpleɪs]	Marktplatz
sale [seɪl]	Verkauf
antique [æn'ti:k]	antik
jewellery ['dʒu:əlri]	Schmuck

page 82

in my view [vju:]	meiner Ansicht nach
to concern sb [kən'sɜ:n]	jdm Sorgen machen
mixed [mɪkst]	gemischt
recently ['ri:sntli]	neulich, jüngst
gear [gɪə]	Ausrüstung
to **introduce sb to sth** [ˌɪntrə'dju:s]	jdm etwas näherbringen, jdn in etw einführen
suspicious [sə'spɪʃəs]	misstrauisch
buy [baɪ]	Kauf
ever since [ˌevə 'sɪns]	seitdem
experience [ɪk'spɪəriəns]	Erlebnis
helmet ['helmɪt]	Helm
seller ['selə]	Verkäufer/in
speedy [spi:di]	schnell, zügig
return label [rɪˌtɜ:n 'leɪbl]	Rücksendeaufkleber, Retourenetikett
replacement [rɪ'pleɪsmənt]	Ersatz(teil)
satisfied ['sætɪsfaɪd]	unzufrieden
occasionally [ə'keɪʒənəli]	gelegentlich
in terms of ... [ɪn 'tɜ:mz əv]	was ... angeht
competition [ˌkɒmpə'tɪʃn]	Wettbewerb

page 83

package ['pækɪdʒ]	Paket
parcel ['pɑ:sl]	Paket
despite [dɪ'spaɪt]	trotz
claim [kleɪm]	Behauptung
electrically powered [ɪˌlektrɪkli 'paʊəd]	elektrisch betrieben, elektrisch angetrieben
to **fit sb out (with)** [ˌfɪt 'aʊt]	jn ausstatten, ausrüsten (mit)
to **design** [dɪ'zaɪn]	gestalten
to **aim to do sth** [eɪm]	bestrebt sein etw zu tun, etw tun wollen
to **please sb** [pli:z]	jdn zufriedenstellen
to **notify sb (of sth)** ['nəʊtɪfaɪ]	jdn (über etw) benachrichtigen
fragile ['frædʒaɪl]	(leicht) zerbrechlich
to **ring** [rɪŋ]	klingeln, läuten (an)
rear-view mirror [ˌrɪə vju: 'mɪrə]	Rückspiegel
to **sweat** [swet]	schwitzen
to **bark** [bɑ:k]	brüllen
exhaust fumes [ɪg'zɔ:st fju:mz]	Abgase

page 84

to **text** [tekst]	SMS schicken
to **keep in touch** [ˌki:p ɪn 'tʌtʃ]	in Verbindung/Kontakt bleiben
allowance [ə'laʊəns]	erlaubte Menge
to **jumble sth up** [ˌdʒʌmbl 'ʌp]	etw (kunterbunt) durcheinanderwerfen
to **upload** [ˌʌp'ləʊd]	hochladen
to **turn on** [ˌtɜ:n 'ɒn]	einschalten
to **synchronize** ['sɪŋkrənaɪz]	synchronisieren
file [faɪl]	Datei
automatically [ˌɔ:tə'mætɪkli]	automatisch
to **select** [sɪ'lekt]	auswählen
to **press** [pres]	drücken
to **hook sth up to sth** [ˌhʊk 'ʌp]	etw an etw anschließen
forever [fər'evə]	ewig (lange)

page 85

coach [kəʊtʃ]	Bus
to **welcome** ['welkʌm]	begrüßen, willkommen heißen
(tour) guide [gaɪd]	Reiseleiter/in; Fremdenführer/in
to **board** [bɔ:d]	einsteigen (in); an Bord gehen
destination [ˌdestɪ'neɪʃn]	Bestimmungsort
via (Dover) ['vaɪə]	über (Dover)
to **set off** [ˌset 'ɒf]	aufbrechen, losfahren
experienced [ɪk'spɪəriənst]	erfahren (Adj)
to **put up (a tent)** [ˌpʊt 'ʌp]	(ein Zelt) aufbauen
to **take down (a tent)** [ˌteɪk 'daʊn]	(ein Zelt) abbauen
self-catering [ˌself 'keɪtərɪŋ]	Selbstversorgung, für Selbstversorger
luggage ['lʌgɪdʒ]	Gepäck
to **transfer (sb/sth from A to B)** ['trænsfɜ:]	(jdn/etw von A nach B) fahren, bringen
individual [ˌɪndɪ'vɪdʒuəl]	individuell
self-guided [ˌself 'gaɪdɪd]	selbst geführt
guesthouse ['gesthaʊs]	(Fremden-)Pension
transfer ['trænsfɜ:]	Transfer, Weitertransport
(fully-)guided [ˌfʊli 'gaɪdɪd]	geführt
travel ['trævl]	Reise
travel arrangements ['trævl əreɪndʒmənts]	Reisevorbereitungen
top of the range [ˌtɒp əv ðə 'reɪndʒ]	Spitzen-
region ['ri:dʒən]	Region
to **apply (to sth)** [ə'plaɪ tə]	gelten (für etw)
surcharge ['sɜ:tʃɑ:dʒ]	Aufpreis

TOPIC 4

page 87

FOB (free on board) Mumbai [ˌef əʊ 'bi:, ˌfri: ɑn 'bɔ:d]	frei an Bord in Mumbai
on board [ɒn 'bɔ:d]	an Bord
at the latest [ət ðə 'leɪtɪst]	spätestens
to **arrange for sth** [ə'reɪndʒ fə]	etw arrangieren, vereinbaren
premises ['premɪsɪz]	Geschäftsräume
to **request sth** [rɪ'kwest]	etw anfordern, erbitten
to **submit** [səb'mɪt]	(Angebot) unterbreiten
unit ['ju:nɪt]	Einheit, Stück
to **escape one's notice** [ɪˌskeɪp wʌnz 'nəʊtɪs]	entgehen, übersehen
above-mentioned [ə'bʌv 'menʃnd]	oben genannt
invoice ['ɪnvɔɪs]	Rechnung
due [dju:]	fällig
receipt of order [rɪˌsi:t əv 'ɔ:də]	Auftragseingang, Auftragserhalt
sum [sʌm]	Summe, Betrag
in question [ɪn 'kwestʃən]	betreffend, fraglich
stand [stænd]	Stand
fair [feə]	Messe

dated ['deɪtɪd] | (Datum:) vom
discrepancy [dɪs'krepənsi] | Diskrepanz
ready for dispatch [ˌredi fə dɪ'spætʃ] | versandbereit, versandfertig
to remit [rɪ'mɪt] | überweisen
description [dɪ'skrɪpʃn] | Beschreibung
unit price [ˌju:nɪt 'praɪs] | Stückpreis
to label ['leɪbl] | beschriften, etikettieren
transaction [træn'zækʃn] | Geschäft, Transaktion
acknowledgement [ək'nɒlɪdʒmənt] | Auftragsbestätigung
reminder [rɪ'maɪndə] | Mahnung

page 88

letterhead ['letəhed] | Briefkopf
reference ['refərəns] | Zeichen, Referenz
special marking [ˌspeʃl 'mɑ:kɪŋ] | Vermerk, Kennzeichnung
salutation [ˌsælju'teɪʃn] | (Brief:) Anrede
subject line ['sʌbdʒɪkt laɪn] | Betreffzeile
body ['bɒdi] | (Brief:) Haupttext
complimentary close [ˌkɒmplɪˌmentri 'kləʊz] | (Brief:) Schlussformel
signature ['sɪgnətʃə] | Unterschrift
enclosure(s) (Enc, Encs) [ɪn'kləʊʒə] | Anlage(n)
complimentary [ˌkɒmplɪ'mentri] | Frei-
Yours sincerely [jɔ:z sɪn'sɪəli] | Mit freundlichen Grüßen (Briefschluss)

page 89

left aligned ['left əlaɪnd] | linksbündig
sender ['sendə] | Absender/in
postal address [ˌpəʊstl ə'dres] | Postadresse
to misunderstand [ˌmɪsʌndə'stænd] | falsch verstehen
confidential [ˌkɒnfɪ'denʃl] | vertraulich
air mail ['eə meɪl] | Luftpost
registered (letter) ['redʒɪstəd] | Einschreiben
recorded delivery [rɪˌkɔ:dɪd dɪ'lɪvəri] | Einschreiben mit Rückschein
envelope ['envələʊp] | Briefumschlag
recipient [rɪ'sɪpiənt] | Empfänger/in
capital letter [ˌkæpɪtl 'letə] | Großbuchstabe
postcode ['pəʊstkəʊd] | Postleitzahl
separate ['seprət] | getrennt
close [kləʊs] | nahe, in der Nähe
bold [bəʊld] | fett (gedruckt)
to separate ['seprət] | trennen

page 90

signatory ['sɪgnətri] | Unterzeichner/in
to dictate [dɪk'teɪt] | diktieren
export sales director [ˌekspɔ:t 'seɪlz dərektə] | Vertriebsleiter/in Export
perfume ['pɜ:fju:m] | Parfüm
photocopy ['fəʊtəʊkɒpi] | Fotokopie
reaction [ri'ækʃn] | Reaktion

page 91

conference ['kɒnfərəns] | Konferenz
convention [kən'venʃn] | Tagung, Konferenz
passionate(ly) ['pæʃənət] | leidenschaftlich
access ['ækses] | Zugriff, Zugang
charity ['tʃærəti] | Kampagne, Aktion (für wohltätige Zwecke)
fee [fi:] | Honorar
expenses [ɪk'spensɪz] | Kosten, Auslagen
to sign off [ˌsaɪn 'ɒf] | (Brief:) beenden, unterschreiben

page 92

informal [ɪn'fɔ:ml] | informell, zwanglos, locker
formal ['fɔ:ml] | formell, förmlich
by mistake [baɪ mɪ'steɪk] | irrtümlich
initiative [ɪ'nɪʃətɪv] | Eigeninitiative, Initiative
to take the initiative [ˌteɪk ði ɪ'nɪʃətɪv] | die Initiative ergreifen
cheers [tʃɪəz] | tschüs, danke
text message ['tekst mesɪdʒ] | SMS
in capitals [ɪn 'kæpɪtls] | in Großbuchstaben
exclamation mark [eksklə'meɪʃn mɑ:k] | Ausrufezeichen

page 93

rapid(ly) ['ræpɪd] | schnell, rasch
wholesaler ['həʊlseɪlə] | Großhändler
at present [ət 'preznt] | gegenwärtig
reasonable ['ri:znəbl] | vernünftig, angemessen
delivery period [dɪ'lɪvəri pɪəriəd] | Lieferzeit

page 94

reduction [rɪ'dʌkʃn] | Nachlass, Reduzierung

page 95

long-standing [ˌlɒŋ 'stændɪŋ] | langjährig, schon lange bestehend
considerable [kən'sɪdərəbl] | erheblich, beträchtlich
DDP (delivery duty paid) [ˌdi: di: 'pi:, dɪˌlɪvəri dju:ti 'peɪd] | frei verzollt

page 96

costume jewellery ['kɒstju:m dʒu:əlri] | Modeschmuck
to extend [ɪk'stend] | erweitern, ausdehnen
comprehensive [ˌkɒmprɪ'hensɪv] | umfassend
entire [ɪn'taɪə] | gesamte/r/s

page 97

to call on sb ['kɔ:l ɒn] | jdn besuchen
substantial [səb'stænʃl] | beträchtlich, erheblich
to last [lɑ:st] | halten; (Vorrat, Warenbestand:) reichen
while stocks last [waɪl ˌstɒks 'lɑ:st] | solange der Vorrat reicht
portable ['pɔ:təbl] | tragbar
lightweight ['laɪtweɪt] | leicht
to fold [fəʊld] | falten, zusammenklappen; sich zusammenfalten/-klappen lassen
storage ['stɔ:rɪdʒ] | Aufbewahrung
trade show ['treɪd ʃəʊ] | Messe
foldable ['fəʊldəbl] | zusammenklappbar, faltbar
compact [kəm'pækt] | kompakt
robust [rəʊ'bʌst] | widerstandsfähig, robust
aluminium [ˌæljə'mɪniəm] | Aluminium
frame [freɪm] | Rahmen

page 98

fabulous ['fæbjələs] | fantastisch, sagenhaft, fabelhaft

line [laɪn] — Sortiment
to fall in love with sb/sth [ˌfɔːl ɪn 'lʌv wɪð] — sich in jdn/etw verlieben
earring ['ɪərɪŋ] — Ohrring
bracelet ['breɪslət] — Armband, Armreifen

page 99

trial order ['traɪəl ɔːdə] — Probebestellung, Probeauftrag
in stock [ɪn 'stɒk] — vorrätig, auf Lager
to pick sb/sth up [ˌpɪk 'ʌp] — jdn/etw abholen
pleasant ['pleznt] — angenehm, nett
in writing [ɪn 'raɪtɪŋ] — schriftlich, in Schriftform
distributor [dɪ'strɪbjətə] — Großhändler
reputation [ˌrepju'teɪʃn] — Ruf
CIP (carriage and insurance paid) [ˌsiː aɪ 'piː, ˌkærɪdʒ ənd ɪnˌʃʊərəns 'peɪd] — Fracht und Versicherung bezahlt bis
CWO (cash with order) [ˌsiː dʌbljuː 'əʊ, ˌkæʃ wɪð 'ɔːdə] — Vorauskasse; (Bar-)Zahlung bei Auftragserteilung
net [net] — netto
open account [ˌəʊpən ə'kaʊnt] — offenes Zahlungsziel
Incoterm ['ɪnkəʊtɜːm] — Internationale Handelsklausel

page 101

in the meantime [ɪn ðə 'miːntaɪm] — in der Zwischenzeit
letter of credit (L/C) [ˌletər əv 'kredɪt] — Akkreditiv
bank transfer ['bæŋk trænsfɜː] — Überweisung
regular customer [ˌregjələ 'kʌstəmə] — Stammkunde/-in, Bestandskunde
preferential terms [prefəˌrenʃl 'tɜːmz] — Sonderkonditionen, bevorzugte (Zahlungs-)Bedingungen

page 102

pre-carriage [ˌpriː 'kærɪdʒ] — Vorlauf
carriage ['kærɪdʒ] — Beförderung, Transport
loading ['ləʊdɪŋ] — Verladung
contract of carriage [ˌkɒntrækt əv 'kærɪdʒ] — Beförderungsvertrag
export clearance ['ekspɔːt klɪərəns] — (Erledigung der) Ausfuhrformalitäten
port [pɔːt] — Hafen
port of shipment [ˌpɔːt əf 'ʃɪpmənt] — Verladehafen
port of destination [ˌpɔːt əv destɪ'neɪʃn] — Bestimmungshafen
unloading [ˌʌn'ləʊdɪŋ] — Entladung
post-carriage [ˌpəʊst 'kærɪdʒ] — Nachlauf
customs clearance ['kʌstəmz klɪərəns] — Zollabfertigung, Verzollung
main carriage [ˌmeɪn 'kærɪdʒ] — Hauptlauf
import duty ['ɪmpɔːt djuːti] — Einfuhrzoll
mode of transport [ˌməʊd əf 'trænspɔːt] — Transportart
waterway ['wɔːtəweɪ] — Wasserstraße

page 103

to pack [pæk] — verpacken
carrier ['kæriə] — Frachtführer
documents ['dɒkjumənts] — Unterlagen, Papiere, Dokumente
to insure [ɪn'ʃʊə] — versichern
machinery [mə'ʃiːnəri] — Maschinen, Geräte: Anlagen
tractor ['træktə] — Traktor
beef [biːf] — Rindfleisch
consignment [kən'saɪnmənt] — Lieferung, Sendung
to transport [træn'spɔːt] — befördern, transportieren
bulky goods [ˌbʌlki 'gʊdz] — Sperrgüter, Massengüter
load [ləʊd] — Ladung
perishable ['perɪʃəbl] — verderblich
multi-modal transport [ˌmʌltiməʊdl 'trænspɔːt] — kombinierte Beförderung, multimodaler Transport
cargo ['kɑːgəʊ] — Fracht
wood [wʊd] — Holz
mine [maɪn] — Bergwerk, Mine
power station ['paʊə steɪʃn] — Kraftwerk

page 104

to calculate ['kælkjuleɪt] — ausrechnen, berechnen, kalkulieren
to collect [kə'lekt] — (ab)holen, (ein)sammeln
guarantee [ˌgærən'tiː] — Garantie

page 105

to sb's liking ['laɪkɪŋ] — nach jds Geschmack
trade discount ['treɪd dɪskaʊnt] — Handelsrabatt
quantity discount ['kwɒntəti dɪskaʊnt] — Mengenrabatt

page 106

average ['ævərɪdʒ] — Durchschnitt
average-priced [ˌævərɪdʒ 'praɪst] — zu durchschnittlichem Preis
high-end [ˌhaɪ 'end] — für gehobene Ansprüche, im gehobenen Marktsegment

page 107

beyond [bɪ'jɒnd] — darüber hinaus; über etw hinaus
grateful ['greɪtfl] — dankbar

page 108

material [mə'tɪəriəl] — Stoff, Material
roll [rəʊl] — Rolle
frontlit ['frʌntlɪt] — frontal beleuchtet
backlit ['bæklɪt] — hinterleuchtet
total ['təʊtl] — Gesamtbetrag, Summe
total price [ˌtəʊtl 'praɪs] — Gesamtpreis
completion [kəm'pliːʃn] — Fertigstellung
account (a/c) [ə'kaʊnt] — Konto
confirmation of order [kɒnfəˌmeɪʃn əv 'ɔːdə] — Auftragsbestätigung
advice of dispatch [ədˌvaɪs əv dɪ'spætʃ] — Versandanzeige, Versandmitteilung

page 109

subtotal ['sʌbtəʊtl] — Zwischensumme
value added tax (VAT) [ˌvæljuː 'ædɪd tæks] — Mehrwertsteuer, Umsatzsteuer
sturdy ['stɜːdi] — stabil, fest
carton ['kɑːtn] — Kiste, Karton
receipt of invoice [rɪˌsiːt əv 'ɪnvɔɪs] — Rechnungseingang, -erhalt

page 110
currency ['kʌrənsi] – Währung
currency sign ['kʌrənsi saɪn] – Währungssymbol

page 111
punctual(ly) ['pʌŋktʃuəl] – pünktlich

page 112
assessment [ə'sesmənt] – Einschätzung, Beurteilung, Bewertung
overview ['əʊvəvju:] – Überblick
capability [ˌkəɪpə'bɪləti] – Fähigkeit; Potenzial
capacity [kə'pæsəti] – Kapazität, Leistung
testimonial [ˌtestɪ'məʊniəl] – Bewertung(en); Zeugnis
to **rate** [reɪt] – bewerten, beurteilen
decoration [ˌdekə'reɪʃn] – Dekorierung, Verzierung
to **specialize (in)** [ˌspeʃəlaɪz] – sich spezialisieren (auf), sich spezialisiert haben (auf)
self-adhesive [ˌself əd'hi:sɪv] – selbstklebend
film [fɪlm] – Folie
tape [teɪp] – Band, Klebeband
to **browse sth** [braʊz] – etw durchsehen, durchstöbern, durchblättern

page 113
to **transfer** ['trænsfɜ:] – überweisen
to **complete an order** [kəmˌpli:t ən 'ɔ:də] – einen Auftrag fertigstellen, ausführen
to **remain** [rɪ'meɪn] – (ver)bleiben
high-resolution [ˌhaɪ reʒə'lu:ʃn] – hochauflösend
to **hesitate** ['hezɪteɪt] – zögern
to **be located in ...** [bi ləʊ'keɪtɪd ɪn] – in ... liegen

page 114
substitute ['sʌbstɪtju:t] – Ersatz(-)
rejection [rɪ'dʒekʃn] – Ablehnung
alternatively [ɔ:l'tɜ:nətɪvli] – alternativ, als weitere Möglichkeit
unable [ˌʌn'eɪbl] – nicht in der Lage, unfähig
to **execute** ['eksɪkju:t] – ausführen

page 116
silk [sɪlk] – Seide, Seiden-
scarf [skɑ:f] – Schal, Halstuch

page 118
commercial invoice [kəˌmɜ:ʃl 'ɪnvɔɪs] – Handelsrechnung

page 119
width [wɪdθ] – Breite
length [leŋθ] – Länge
area ['eəriə] – Fläche
matte [mæt] – matt
seaworthy ['si:wɜ:ði] – seetüchtig

page 120
unreliable [ˌʌnrɪ'laɪəbl] – unzuverlässig
trusted ['trʌstɪd] – zuverlässig
unpaid [ˌʌn'peɪd] – nicht bezahlt
forceful ['fɔ:sfl] – deutlich, eindringlich
final demand [ˌfaɪnl dɪ'mɑ:nd] – letzte Mahnung
deadline ['dedlaɪn] – Frist
non-payment [ˌnɒn 'peɪmənt] – Nichtzahlung
senior executive [ˌsi:niər ɪg'zekjətɪv] – leitende/r Angestellte/r
to **resolve** [rɪ'zɒlv] – lösen, auflösen
overdue [ˌəʊvə'dju:] – überfällig
whatever the case may be [wɒtevə ðə ˌkeɪs meɪ 'bi] – wie dem auch sei, in jedem Fall
to **disregard sth** [ˌdɪsrɪ'gɑ:d] – etw als gegenstandslos betrachten

page 121
to **provide for sth** [prə'vaɪd fə] – etw vorsehen
with regard to [wɪð rɪ'gɑ:d tə] – bezüglich
remittance [rɪ'mɪtns] – Überweisung
to **insist** [ɪn'sɪst] – darauf bestehen
without delay [wɪðaʊt dɪ'leɪ] – unverzüglich
to **take steps** [ˌteɪk 'steps] – Schritte einleiten
to **recover sth** [rɪ'kʌvə] – etw sicherstellen, beschaffen
owing ['əʊɪŋ] – fällig, ausstehend
to **fail to do sth** [ˌfeɪl tə 'du:] – versäumen, etw zu tun
to **discontinue sth** [ˌdɪskən'tɪnju:] – etw einstellen, abbrechen
prompt [prɒmpt] – umgehend
to **settle** ['setl] – regeln, erledigen

page 123
dissatisfied [dɪs'sætɪsfaɪd] – unzufrieden
delay [dɪ'leɪ] – Verspätung
in time (for) [ɪn 'taɪm] – rechtzeitig (für/zu)
freight [freɪt] – Fracht
air freight ['eə freɪt] – Luftfracht
not ... until [nɒt ən'tɪl] – erst (um/am)
to **unpack** [ˌʌn'pæk] – auspacken
a number of [ə 'nʌmbər əv] – eine Anzahl (von), mehrere
freight forwarder ['freɪt fɔ:wədə] – Spediteur
in transit [ɪn 'trænzɪt] – beim Transport
to **mix sth up** [ˌmɪks 'ʌp] – etw durcheinanderbringen, etw verwechseln
right away [ˌraɪt ə'weɪ] – sofort
to **rush sth** [rʌʃ] – etw auf dem schnellsten Weg hinbringen
gesture ['dʒestʃə] – Geste
inconvenience [ˌɪnkən'vi:niəns] – Unannehmlichkeiten
to **assure** [ə'ʃʊə] – versichern, zusichern

page 124
to **threaten** ['θretn] – drohen
to **cancel** ['kænsl] – stornieren
at sb's expense [ɪk'spens] – auf jds Kosten
to **have sth done by sb** [ˌhæv sʌmθɪŋ 'dʌn baɪ] – jdn etw tun lassen; veranlassen, dass jd etw tut

page 125
to **be obliged to do sth** [bi ə'blaɪdʒd tə] – sich genötigt sehen, etw zu tun

page 126
to **examine** [ɪg'zæmɪn] – untersuchen, prüfen
sleeve [sli:v] – Ärmel
neck [nek] – Hals, Halsausschnitt

narrow ['nærəʊ] — eng, schmal
to **appreciate sth** [ə'pri:ʃieɪt] — für etw Verständnis haben

page 127
sleeveless ['sli:vləs] — ärmellos
to **regret** [rɪ'gret] — bedauern
due to ['dju: tə] — aufgrund
rough handling [ˌrʌf'hændlɪŋ] — unsachgemäße Behandlung/Handhabung
wardrobe ['wɔ:drəʊb] — Kleiderschrank
discoloured [ˌdɪs'kʌləd] — verfärbt
to **be up to sth** [bi 'ʌp tə] — einer Sache entsprechen

page 128
by return [baɪ rɪ'tɜ:n] — postwendend
substandard [ˌsʌb'stændəd] — minderwertig
to **depend on sth** [dɪ'pend ɒn] — von etw abhängig sein

page 130
booking ['bʊkɪŋ] — Buchung, Reservierung
interest ['ɪntrəst] — Interesse

page 131
worrying ['wʌriɪŋ] — Besorgnis erregend, beunruhigend
apparent(ly) [ə'pærənt] — augenscheinlich
preferential [ˌprefə'renʃl] — Sonder-, bevorzugt
treatment ['tri:tmənt] — Behandlung
word-of-mouth (propaganda) [ˌwɜ:d əv 'maʊθ] — mündlich, Mund-(Propaganda)

TOPIC 5

page 132
teleconference ['tekikɒnfərəns] — Telekonferenz
video conference ['vɪdiəʊ kɒnfərəns] — Videokonferenz
straight away [ˌstreɪt ə'weɪ] — sofort, gleich
real-time [ˌrɪəl 'taɪm] — Echtzeit-
delayed [dɪ'leɪd] — verzögert, zeitversetzt; verspätet
to **remind sb** [rɪ'maɪnd] — jdn (an etw) erinnern

page 133
voicemail ['vɔɪsmeɪl] — Anrufbeantworter
developer [dɪ'veləpə] — Entwickler/in
to **be available** [ə'veɪləbl] — (Telefon:) zu sprechen sein; zur Verfügung stehen
to **be unavailable** [bi ˌʌnə'veɪləbl] — (Telefon:) nicht zu sprechen sein; nicht zur Verfügung stehen
to **leave a message** [ˌli:v ə 'mesɪdʒ] — (Telefon:) eine Nachricht hinterlassen
donation [dəʊ'neɪʃn] — Spende
to **hold the line** [həʊld ðə 'laɪn] — (Telefon:) am Apparat bleiben
to **take a message** [ˌteɪk ə 'mesɪdʒ] — (Telefon:) etw ausrichten
to **catch** [kætʃ] — verstehen, mitkriegen
You're breaking up. [jɔ: ˌbreɪkɪŋ 'ʌp] — (Telefon:) Das Netz geht weg.
Go ahead. [ˌgəʊ ə'hed] — Nur zu. / Dann mal los. / Mach weiter.

page 134
landline ['lændlaɪn] — Festnetztelefon
to **get sth** [get] — etw verstehen
office hours ['ɒfɪs aʊəz] — Bürozeiten, Arbeitszeit
to **get back to sb** [ˌget 'bæk tə] — sich bei jdm melden, jdn zurückrufen
speaker ['spi:kə] — Redner/in
unofficial [ˌʌnə'fɪʃl] — inoffiziell
to **make a note of sth** [ˌmeɪk ə 'nəʊt əv] — sich etw notieren

page 135
upper-case [ˌʌpə 'keɪs] — großgeschrieben
lower-case [ˌləʊə 'keɪs] — kleingeschrieben
to **react to sth** [ri'ækt tə] — auf etw reagieren
marvellous ['mɑ:vələs] — großartig
to **apologize** [ə'pɒlədʒaɪz] — sich entschuldigen

page 136
to **act sth out** [ˌækt 'aʊt] — etw (vor-, durch)spielen

page 137
to **be to do sth** ['bi tə] — etw tun sollen
to **hold** [həʊld] — (Veranstaltungen) abhalten; (Gespräche) führen
speech [spi:tʃ] — Rede, Vortrag
meeting ['mi:tɪŋ] — Besprechung, Sitzung
sunglasses *(pl)* ['sʌnglɑ:sɪz] — Sonnenbrille
flight [flaɪt] — Flug

page 139
to **rest** [rest] — sich ausruhen
out of action [!a8t 4v 1äkSn] — lahmgelegt
TV station [ˌti: 'vi: steɪʃn] — Fernsehsender
to **bring sth forward** [ˌbrɪŋ 'fɔ:wəd] — etw vorverlegen
to **be up and about** [bi 'ʌp ənd ə'baʊt] — auf den Beinen sein
to **decline** [dɪ'klaɪn] — ablehnen
to **have sth on** [ˌhæv 'ɒn] — etw vorhaben

page 140
Father ['fɑ:ðə] — Pater, Pfarrer
chat show ['tʃæt ʃəʊ] — Talkshow
to **autograph** ['ɔ:təgrɑ:f] — signieren
to **auction** ['ɔ:kʃn] — versteigern
charity ['tʃærəti] — Hilfsorganisation, guter Zweck
photo shoot ['fəʊtəʊ ʃu:t] — Fotoaufnahmen
to **arrange** [ə'reɪndʒ] — (Termin) ausmachen
boycott ['bɔɪkɒt] — Boykott
fur [fɜ:] — Pelz
vegetarian [ˌvedʒə'teəriən] — Vegetarier/in
statue ['stætʃu:] — Statue
Christ [kraɪst] — Christus
rehearsal [rɪ'hɜ:sl] — Probe (Theater, Chor, Orchester etc.)
appearance [ə'pɪərəns] — Auftritt

page 141
gatehouse ['geɪthaʊs] — Torhaus
invitation [ˌɪnvɪ'teɪʃn] — Einladung
reception [rɪ'sepʃn] — Empfang (auch beim Telefon); Rezeption
indeed [ɪn'di:d] — in der Tat
a shame [ə 'ʃeɪm] — schade
to **land** [lænd] — landen

underground ['ʌndəgraʊnd]	U-Bahn
the Tube [ðə tju:b]	die Londoner U-Bahn
minicab ['mɪnikæb]	Funktaxi
coach service ['kəʊtʃ sɜ:vɪs]	Busverbindung
train service ['treɪn sɜ:vɪs]	Zugverbindung
study ['stʌdi]	Arbeitszimmer

page 142

departure [dɪ'pɑ:tʃə]	Abfahrt, Abflug
arrival [ə'raɪvl]	Ankunft
carrier ['kæriə]	Fluggesellschaft
to depart [dɪ'pɑ:t]	abfahren, abfliegen
duration [dju'reɪʃn]	Dauer
connecting flight [kəˌnektɪŋ 'flaɪt]	Anschlussflug
shopping bag ['ʃɒpɪŋ bæg]	Einkaufstasche

page 143

interchange ['ɪntətʃeɪndʒ]	Übergang, Umsteigen

page 144

contactless ['kɒntæktləs]	kontaktlos
credit card ['kredɪt kɑ:d]	Kreditkarte
debit ['debɪt]	(Konto) Soll, Debet, Belastung
debit card ['debɪt kɑ:d]	Debitkarte, Geldkarte
charge card ['tʃɑ:dʒ kɑ:d]	Kundenkarte (mit der man auch bezahlen kann)
to issue ['ɪʃu:]	ausstellen
to display [dɪ'spleɪ]	zeigen, anzeigen
single journey [ˌsɪŋgl 'dʒɜ:ni]	einfache Fahrt
reader ['ri:də]	Lesegerät
(card) issuer ['ɪʃuə]	Kartenunternehmen, (Karten-)Aussteller
to charge [tʃɑ:dʒ]	(Preis) verlangen, berechnen, in Rechnung stellen
fare [feə]	Fahrpreis
fraudulent [frɔ:dʒələnt]	betrügerisch
retailer ['ri:teɪlə]	Einzelhändler/in
to enter sth ['entə]	etw eingeben
to give sb a ring [ˌgɪv ə 'rɪŋ]	jdn anrufen

page 145

reservation [ˌrezə'veɪʃn]	Reservierung
unplugged [ˌʌn'plʌgd]	ohne Strom, (Musik:) akustisch
to explore [ɪk'splɔ:]	erforschen, erkunden
to search [sɜ:tʃ]	durchsuchen, suchen
to set [set]	angeben, einstellen, festlegen
grading ['greɪdɪŋ]	Einstufung
board [bɔ:d]	Verpflegung
guide price ['gaɪd praɪs]	Richtpreis
campus ['kæmpəs]	Campus, Universitätsgelände
serviced apartment [ˌsɜ:vɪst ə'pɑ:tmənt]	Wohnung in einem Apartment-Hotel
half board [ˌhɑ:f 'bɔ:d]	Halbpension
full board [ˌfʊl 'bɔ:d]	Vollpension
to widen ['waɪdn]	verbreitern, erweitern

page 146

bread roll [ˌbred 'rəʊl]	Brötchen
jam [dʒæm]	Marmelade
cereal ['sɪəriəl]	Getreideflocken
porridge ['pɒrɪdʒ]	Haferbrei
bacon ['beɪkən]	Speck
single room [ˌsɪŋgl 'ru:m]	Einzelzimmer
to sleep (3 people) [sli:p]	Schlafmöglichkeit(en) bieten für (3 Personen)
en suite [ˌɒ 'swi:t]	mit eigenem Bad
shower ['ʃaʊə]	Dusche
bathtub ['bɑ:θtʌb]	Badewanne
furnished ['fɜ:nɪʃt]	möbliert, ausgestattet
cleaner ['kli:nə]	Reinigungskraft
amenities [ə'mi:nətiz]	Annehmlichkeiten
spa [spɑ:]	Wellnessbereich
rate [reɪt]	(Zimmer-)Preis
booking fee ['bʊkɪŋ fi:]	Buchungsgebühr
deposit [dɪ'pɒzɪt]	Anzahlung
to secure (sth) [sɪ'kjuə]	(sich etw) sichern

page 147

agent ['eɪdʒənt]	Mitarbeiter/in
booked up [ˌbʊkt 'ʌp]	ausgebucht
farther ['fɑ:ðə]	weiter
to hire sth ['haɪə]	etw mieten
confirmation [ˌkɒnfə'meɪʃn]	Bestätigung

page 148

alternative [ɔ:l'tɜ:nətɪv]	Alternative
to reject [rɪ'dʒekt]	ablehnen
cancellation [ˌkænsə'leɪʃn]	Stornierung, Absage
security number [sɪ'kjʊərəti nʌmbə]	Sicherheitsnummer

page 150

to put sth back [ˌpʊt 'bæk]	(Termin) verschieben, auf später verlegen
Must rush. [ˌmʌst 'rʌʃ]	Ich muss weg. (Brief:) In Eile
in case [ɪn 'keɪs]	für den Fall, dass
to spoil [spɔɪl]	verderben
agenda [ə'dʒendə]	Terminplan, -kalender

page 151

bumpy ['bʌmpi]	holprig, (Flug) unruhig
turbulence ['tɜ:bjələns]	Turbulenzen
comfortable ['kʌmftəbl]	bequem, angenehm, komfortabel

page 152

impolite [ˌɪmpə'laɪt]	unhöflich
to introduce oneself [ˌɪntrə'dju:s]	sich vorstellen

page 153

conference call ['kɒnfərəns kɔ:l]	Telefonkonferenz, Konferenzschaltung

page 154

quarterly ['kwɔ:təli]	vierteljährlich
branch [brɑ:ntʃ]	Filiale, Niederlassung
agenda [ə'dʒendə]	Tagesordnung
draft [drɑ:ft]	Entwurf
scheduled ['ʃedju:ld]	geplant
topic ['tɒpɪk]	Thema
to amend [ə'mend]	(ab)ändern
to circulate ['sɜ:kjəleɪt]	verschicken
in advance [ɪn əd'vɑ:ns]	im Voraus
version ['vɜ:ʃn]	Version
present ['preznt]	anwesend

page 155

expansion [ɪk'spænʃn]	Expansion
to recruit sb [rɪ'kru:t]	jdn anwerben, jdn neu einstellen
to expand [ɪk'spænd]	expandieren, (sich) erweitern, (sich) vergrößern
to vote sb sth [vəʊt]	jdn zu etw wählen
to shrink [ʃrɪŋk]	schrumpfen

page 157

absentee [,æbsən'ti:]	Abwesende/r, Fehlende/r
well received [,wel rɪ'si:vd]	gut aufgenommen, gut angenommen
crowd [kraʊd]	Menge, Menschenmasse
advance [əd'vɑ:ns]	Voraus-, Vorab-
to perform [pə'fɔ:m]	auftreten, eine Vorstellung geben
costume ['kɒstju:m]	Kostüm
luxury ['lʌkʃəri]	Luxus
promoter [prə'məʊtə]	Veranstalter/in, Promoter/in
thoroughly ['θʌrəli]	völlig, total

page 159

outward (flight) ['aʊtwəd]	Hin-(Flug)
return (flight) [rɪ'tɜ:n]	Rück-(Flug)
estimate ['estɪmət]	(Ab-)Schätzung; Kostenvoranschlag
any other business (AOB) [,eni ,ʌðə 'bɪznəs]	Verschiedenes

TOPIC 6

page 160

conflict resolution [,kɒnflɪkt rezə'lu:ʃn]	Konfliktbewältigung, -lösung
filing cabinet ['faɪlɪŋ kæbɪnət]	Aktenschrank
paper shredder ['peɪpə ʃredə]	Aktenvernichter
boxing glove ['bɒksɪŋ glʌv]	Boxhandschuh
effect [ɪ'fekt]	Auswirkung, Effekt
fortune ['fɔ:tʃu:n]	Vermögen
employment tribunal [ɪm,plɔɪmənt traɪ'bju:nl]	Arbeitsgericht

page 161

to bully ['bʊli]	mobben, tyrannisieren
supervisor ['su:pəvaɪzə]	Vorgesetzte/r
to report sb/sth [rɪ'pɔ:t]	jdn/etw melden
to get sb into trouble [,get ɪntə 'trʌbl]	jdn in Schwierigkeiten bringen
to get sb down [,get 'daʊn]	jdn bedrücken, jdn deprimieren
to give sb a hard time [gɪv ə ,hɑ:d 'taɪm]	jdm das Leben schwer machen
awful ['ɔ:fl]	furchtbar
to make sb's life a misery [meɪk ,laɪf ə 'mɪzəri]	jdm das Leben schwer/zur Hölle machen
incompetent [ɪn'kɒmpɪtənt]	inkompetent, unfähig
embarrassing [ɪm'bærəsɪŋ]	peinlich
shocked [ʃɒkt]	schockiert
in private [ɪn 'praɪvət]	unter vier Augen
chair [tʃeə]	Stuhl
to dispatch [dɪ'spætʃ]	versenden
furious ['fjʊəriəs]	wütend
sb's fault [fɔ:lt]	jds Schuld
to put up with sth [,pʊt 'ʌp wɪð]	sich etw gefallen lassen
to hand sth in [,hænd 'ɪn]	etw einreichen
resignation [,rezɪg'neɪʃn]	Kündigung
to defend [dɪ'fend]	verteidigen
for instance [fə'r ɪnstəns]	zum Beispiel
What's the point? [,wɒts ðə 'pɔɪnt]	Welchen Sinn soll das haben?
to take sb's side [,teɪk 'saɪd]	für jdn Partei ergreifen
to stick together [,stɪk tə'geðə]	zusammenhalten
grievance procedure ['gri:vəns prəsi:dʒə]	Beschwerdeverfahren
to deal with sth ['di:l wɪð]	mit etw umgehen
harassment ['hærəsmənt]	Schikane, Mobbing
to put [pʊt]	hier: formulieren, sagen
mark [mɑ:k]	Zeichen, Kreuz
extra training [,ekstrə 'treɪnɪŋ]	Fortbildung
in the end [ɪn ði 'end]	schließlich, letztendlich
It's up to you. [ɪts ,ʌp tə 'ju:]	Die Entscheidung liegt bei dir.
to respect [rɪ'spekt]	respektieren
authority [ɔ:'θɒrəti]	Autorität
to persuade [pə'sweɪd]	überreden, überzeugen
strict [strɪkt]	streng, strikt

page 162

to be involved [ɪn'vɒlvd]	involviert sein, beteiligt sein
to refrain from doing sth [rɪ'freɪn frəm]	etw unterlassen
to exceed [ɪk'si:d]	überschreiten, -steigen
authority [ɔ:'θɒrəti]	Befugnis; Kompetenz(en)
to provoke [prə'vəʊk]	provozieren
affected by sth [ə'fektɪd baɪ]	betroffen, beeinflusst, beeindruckt von etw
to justify ['dʒʌstɪfaɪ]	rechtfertigen
to spread [spred]	verbreiten, verteilen
rumour ['ru:mə]	Gerücht
accusation [,ækju'zeɪʃn]	Vorwurf, Anschuldigung
witness ['wɪtnəs]	Zeuge, Zeugin

page 163

helpline ['helplaɪn]	Telefonberatung, Telefonnotdienst
counsellor ['kaʊnsələ]	Berater/in
sexual ['sekʃuəl]	sexuell
physical(ly) ['fɪzɪkl]	körperlich
unwanted [,ʌn'wɒntɪd]	unerwünscht
to trouble [trʌbl]	bedrücken, beunruhigen
anonymous [ə'nɒnɪməs]	anonym
plenty (of) ['plenti]	reichlich, viel
to bother sb ['bɒðə]	jdm Sorgen machen, zu schaffen machen
nasty ['nɑ:sti]	gemein, fies, scheußlich, widerlich
to fall asleep [,fɔ:l ə'sli:p]	einschlafen
to party ['pɑ:ti]	feiern
lie [laɪ]	Lüge
jealous ['dʒeləs]	neidisch, eifersüchtig
flier ['flaɪə]	Handzettel, Flugblatt
confident ['kɒnfɪdənt]	zuversichtlich
satisfaction [,sætɪs'fækʃn]	Genugtuung
to be clear about ['klɪər əbaʊt]	sich im Klaren sein über
to keep a record of sth [,ki:p ə 'rekɔ:d]	etw dokumentieren, Buch führen über etw
evaluation [ɪ,vælju'eɪʃn]	Beurteilung, Bewertung

to calm [kɑːm]	(sich) beruhigen
to interact [ˌɪntərˈækt]	interagieren, miteinander umgehen

page 164

candlelight [ˈkændllaɪt]	(bei) Kerzenlicht
to break (a law) [breɪk]	verstoßen gegen (ein Gesetz), (ein Gesetz) brechen
shelter [ˈʃeltə]	Unterkunft, Obdach
to report (on) [rɪˈpɔːt]	berichten (über)
Is it any of your business? / It's none of your business. [ˈbɪznəs]	Geht dich das etwas an? / Das geht dich nichts an.
thief, *pl* **thieves** [θiːf, θiːvz]	Dieb
valuables [ˈvæljuəblz]	Wertsachen
locker [ˈlɒkə]	Spind, Schließfach
racist [ˈreɪsɪst]	rassistisch
remark [rɪˈmɑːk]	Bemerkung
to overhear [ˌəʊvəˈhɪə]	(zufällig) mithören, mit anhören
glass ceiling [ˌglɑːs ˈsiːlɪŋ]	gläserne Decke (unsichtbare Barriere, die Frauen am beruflichen Aufstieg hindert)
to pass sb over [ˌpɑːs ˈəʊvə]	jdn übergehen

page 165

practices [ˈpræktɪsɪz]	Praktiken, Verfahren
disapproval [ˌdɪsəˈpruːvl]	Missbilligung
playable [ˌpleɪəbl]	abspielbar
principle [ˈprɪnsəpl]	Prinzip, Grundsatz
to hold [həʊld]	gelten
As for me, … [ˌæz fə ˈmiː]	Was mich betrifft/angeht, …

page 166

misleading [ˌmɪsˈliːdɪŋ]	irreführend
to live up to sth [ˌlɪv ˈʌp tə]	einer Sache gerecht werden
to skim [skɪm]	überfliegen (schnell lesen)
target [ˈtɑːgɪt]	Ziel(scheibe)
crackdown (on) [ˈkrækdaʊn]	scharfes Vorgehen (gegen)
editor [ˈedɪtə]	Herausgeber/in, Redakteur/in
standards [ˈstændədz]	Prinzipien; Maßstäbe, Vorschriften
authority [ɔːˈθɒrəti]	Behörde
to target [ˈtɑːgɪt]	zielen auf
to exaggerate [ɪgˈzædʒəreɪt]	übertreiben
move [muːv]	Maßnahme, Schritt
unbiased [ʌnˈbaɪəst]	unvoreingenommen, objektiv
to represent [ˌreprɪˈzent]	vertreten, repräsentieren
unsuspecting [ˌʌnsəˈspektɪŋ]	ahnungslos
browser [ˈbraʊzə]	Mensch, der sich im Internet umschaut
nappy [ˈnæpi]	Windel
clampdown (on) [ˈklæmpdaʊn]	hartes Durchgreifen (gegen)
to broaden [ˈbrɔːdn]	ausweiten, erweitern
remit [ˈriːmɪt]	Aufgabenbereich, Auftrag
to regulate [ˈregjuleɪt]	regeln, regulieren
sphere [sfɪə]	Bereich, Sphäre
to put up (a website) [ˌpʊt ˈʌp]	(eine Website) einrichten
up and running [ˌʌp ənd ˈrʌnɪŋ]	in Betrieb
clue [kluː]	Hinweis, Anhaltspunkt
to not have a clue [kluː]	keine Ahnung haben
code [kəʊd]	Kodex, Regeln
to educate [ˈedʒukeɪt]	jdn unterweisen, aufklären
up to speed [ʌp tə ˈspiːd]	auf dem/den neuesten Stand
basics [ˈbeɪsɪks]	grundsätzliche Dinge
watchdog [ˈwɒtʃdɒg]	Überwachungsbeauftragte/r, Überwachungsgremium
to ban [bæn]	sperren; verbieten
search engine [ˈsɜːtʃ endʒɪn]	Suchmaschine
to stamp out [ˌstæmp ˈaʊt]	bekämpfen, beseitigen
owner [ˈəʊnə]	Besitzer/in, Inhaber/in
to get carried away [get kærid əˈweɪ]	sich vergessen, sich nicht mehr bremsen können
roughly [ˈrʌfli]	ungefähr
to absorb [əbˈsɔːb]	aufsaugen, aufnehmen, absorbieren
to close down (an advert on the internet) [ˌkləʊz ˈdaʊn]	(Internetwerbung) aus dem Netz nehmen, abschalten
to launch sth [lɔːntʃ]	etw ins Leben rufen, starten

page 167

behaviour [bɪˈheɪvjə]	Verhalten, Benehmen
to be concerned with [kənˈsɜːnd]	sich befassen mit
conscious(ly) [ˈkɒnʃəs]	bewusst
evidence [ˈevɪdəns]	Nachweis(e), Beweis(e)
affidavit [ˌæfəˈdeɪvɪt]	eidesstattliche Erklärung
violation [ˌvaɪəˈleɪʃn]	Verstoß, Verletzung (von Gesetzen, Rechten)

page 168

dispute [dɪˈspjuːt]	Streit, Disput, Kampf
strike [straɪk]	Streik
to bargain [ˈbɑːgɪn]	(ver)handeln
striker [ˈstraɪkə]	Streikende/r
to work to rule [wɜːk tə ˈruːl]	Dienst nach Vorschrift machen
sit-in [ˈsɪt ɪn]	Sit-in, Sitzstreik
attempt [əˈtempt]	Versuch
closure [ˈkləʊʒə]	Schließung, Stilllegung
go-slow [ˌgəʊ ˈsləʊ]	Bummelstreik
layoff [ˈleɪɒf]	Entlassung
miner [ˈmaɪnə]	Bergmann, Bergarbeiter/in
arbitration [ˌɒːbɪˈtreɪʃn]	Schlichtung
correspondent [ˌkɒrəˈspɒndənt]	Korrespondent/in
cabin [ˈkæbɪn]	Kabine, Passagierraum
cabin crew [ˈkæbɪn kruː]	Bordpersonal
sigh [saɪ]	Seufzer
relief [rɪˈliːf]	Erleichterung
to give a sigh of relief [ˌsaɪ əv rɪˈliːf]	(erleichtert) aufatmen
to return [rɪˈtɜːn]	zurückkehren
to ground [graʊnd]	am Boden lassen, nicht starten lassen (Flugzeug)
to settle [ˈsetl]	(Streit) beilegen
to call a strike [ˌkɔːl ə ˈstraɪk]	zu einem Streik aufrufen

to **call for** ['kɔːl fə]	fordern, verlangen
furthermore [ˌfɜːðə'mɔː]	außerdem, des weiteren
to demand [dɪ'mɑːnd]	fordern
flight attendant ['flaɪt ətendənt]	Flugbegleiter/in
irregular [ɪ'regjələ]	unregelmäßig
court [kɔːt]	Gericht(shof)
case [keɪs]	Fall; Prozess, Gerichtsverfahren

page 169

constructive [kən'strʌktɪv]	konstruktiv
concession [kən'seʃn]	Zugeständnis
unwilling to do sth [ˌʌn'wɪlɪŋ tə duː]	nicht bereit, etw zu tun
in return for [ɪn rɪ'tɜːn fə]	als Ausgleich/Gegenleistung für
to **initiate** [ɪ'nɪʃieɪt]	einleiten, initiieren
to **post** [pəʊst]	bekannt geben
drop [drɒp]	Rückgang
to **axe (jobs)** [æks]	(Stellen) streichen
aid [eɪd]	Hilfe
to **hit** [hɪt]	treffen; (auf)treffen auf
position [pə'zɪʃn]	Haltung, Standpunkt
majority [mə'dʒɒrəti]	größter Teil, Mehrheit
to **irritate** ['ɪrɪteɪt]	(ver)ärgern
disruption [dɪs'rʌpʃn]	Störung, Behinderung, Unterbrechung

page 170

panel discussion ['pænl dɪskʌʃn]	Podiumsdiskussion
to **disrupt** [dɪs'rʌpt]	stören, behindern
to **direct questions (at sb)** [də'rekt]	jdm Fragen stellen
fellow (strikers) ['feləʊ]	Mit- (Streikende)
to **survive** [sə'vaɪv]	überleben
to **be stranded** ['stændɪd]	festsitzen, gestrandet sein
review [rɪ'vjuː]	Besprechung, Rezension, Kritik
reviewer [rɪ'vjuːə]	Rezensent/in, Kritiker/in
critical (of/about) ['krɪtɪkl]	kritisch (gegenüber)

page 171

to **raise (a point)** [reɪz]	(einen Punkt) aufwerfen, zur Sprache bringen
standard ['stændəd]	Standard, Niveau
admittedly [əd'mɪtɪdli]	zugegeben(ermaßen)
to **result in** [rɪ'zʌlt ɪn]	führen zu
refund ['riːfʌnd]	(Kosten-)Erstattung

page 172

equipment [ɪ'kwɪpmənt]	Geräte, Ausrüstung
brand new [ˌbrænd 'njuː]	nagelneu
regular(ly) ['regjələ]	regelmäßig
up to standard [ˌʌp tə 'stændəd]	den Anforderungen genügend
unnecessary [ʌn'nesəsəri]	unnötig
to **monitor** ['mɒnɪtə]	überwachen, kontrollieren

A–Z word list

Dieses Wörterverzeichnis enthält alle Wörter in **Focus on Business 4th Edition** in alphabetischer Reihenfolge. Nicht aufgeführt sind die Wörter aus der *Basic word list* sowie internationale Wörter wie *hotel*, *e-mail* usw. Wörter, die in den Hörverständnisübungen vorkommen, sind mit einem *T*, und Wörter, die in den *Partner Files*, mit einem *F* hinter der Seitenzahl gekennzeichnet.

A

ability *10t* Fähigkeit, Können, Talent
about: out and ~ *55t* unterwegs
about: to be up and ~ *139t* auf den Beinen sein
above-mentioned *87* oben genannt
absence: paid leave of ~ *17* bezahlter Urlaub
absentee *157* Abwesende/r, Fehlende/r
to **absorb** *166* aufsaugen, aufnehmen, absorbieren
to **access** *55* zugreifen auf
access *91* Zugriff, Zugang
accessory *29* Accessoire, Zubehör(teil)
accommodation *24* Unterkunft
to **accompany** *24* begleiten
according to *40* gemäß, nach, zufolge
account: (bank) ~ *13* (Bank-)Konto, (Giro-)Konto
account (a/c) *108* Konto
account executive *63* Kundenberater/in
account services *63* Kundenbetreuung
accounts *7* Buchführung, Buchhaltung
accounts assistant *9* Buchhaltungsassistent/in
accounts manager *9* Leiter/in der Buchhaltung
accusation *162* Vorwurf, Anschuldigung
to **achieve** *51* erzielen
acknowledgement *87* Auftragsbestätigung
to **act** *67* handeln
to **act sth out** *136* etw (vor-, durch) spielen
action *67* Handlung, Aktion, Maßnahme(n)
action: out of ~ *139t* lahmgelegt
ad(vertising) agency *63* Werbeagentur
ad(vertising) campaign *63* Werbekampagne
ad(vertising) space *64* Werbefläche(n), Werbezeit(en)
to **adapt (to sth)** *37* sich anpassen (an etw)
adaptable *15* anpassungsfähig, flexibel
adapter *76* Passstück, Adapter
adjustable *78* (höhen)verstellbar, einstellbar
administration: business ~ *12* Betriebswirtschaft
administrative *8* Verwaltungs-
to **admit** *62t* zugeben
admittedly *171* zugegeben(ermaßen)
advance *55* Fortschritt
in advance *154* im Voraus
advance *157* Voraus-, Vorab-
advantage *8* Vorteil
adventure *65* Abenteuer
to **advertise a job** *20* eine Stelle ausschreiben
to **advertise sth** *71* für etw Werbung machen, etw anbieten
advertisement, advert, ad *14* Anzeige, Annonce
advertising *62* Werbung
advice *81* Rat, Ratschlag/Ratschläge
advice of dispatch *108* Versandanzeige, Versandmitteilung
to **advise** *6* (be)raten
to **affect sb/sth** *51* sich auf jdn/etw auswirken
affected by sth *162* betroffen, beeinflusst, beeindruckt von etw
affidavit *167* eidesstattliche Erklärung
to **afford sth** *43* sich etw leisten
I'm afraid *59* leider, ich fürchte
after-sales service *75* Kundendienst
agency *19* Agentur
agenda *150t* Terminplan, -kalender; *154* Tagesordnung
agent *54* Vertreter, Vertretung; *147t* Mitarbeiter/in
agricultural *41* landwirtschaftlich, Agrar-
agriculture *32* Landwirtschaft
Go ahead. *133* Nur zu. / Dann mal los. / Mach weiter.
aid *169* Hilfe
to **aim at** *17* zielen auf, sich richten an
to **aim to do sth** *83* bestrebt sein etw zu tun, etw tun wollen
aimed at sb *65* an jdn gerichtet, für jdn
on air *53* auf Sendung (z. B. Radio)
air freight *123t* Luftfracht
air mail *89* Luftpost
left aligned *89* linksbündig
allergy *72* Allergie
allowance *84* erlaubte Menge
along with *64* zusammen mit
alternative *148* Alternative
alternatively *114* alternativ, als weitere Möglichkeit
altogether *17* insgesamt
aluminium *97* Aluminium
ambition *21* Ehrgeiz, Bestreben
to **amend** *154* (ab)ändern
amenities *146* Annehmlichkeiten
among *64* (mitten) in
amount *14* Menge, Betrag
to **analyse** *65* analysieren, untersuchen
analyst *36t* Experte/Expertin
animator *24* Animateur/in
to **announce** *31* ankündigen, bekanntgeben
annual(ly) *43* jährlich
per annum *14* pro Jahr
anonymous *163t* anonym
to **answer the phone** *7* ans Telefon gehen
answerphone *55* Anrufbeantworter
antique *81* antik
anxious(ly) *38* besorgt, beunruhigt, ängstlich
any other business (AOB) *159* Verschiedenes
anything *13* alles; egal, was
anyway *77t* wie dem auch sei
apart from *45* außer, abgesehen von
apartment: serviced ~ *145* Wohnung in einem Apartment-Hotel
to **apologize** *135* sich entschuldigen
apology *77* Entschuldigung
apparent(ly) *131* augenscheinlich

to **appear** *57* (er)scheinen
appearance *19* Erscheinung(sbild), Auftreten, Aussehen; *140* Auftritt
appliance *74* Gerät, Haushaltsgerät
applicant *24* Bewerber/in
(job) application *19* Bewerbung
application *64* Anwendung
application management *37* Anwendungsentwicklung
to **apply (to sth)** *85* gelten (für etw)
to **apply for sth** *11* sich für/auf etw bewerben
appointment *55t* Termin
to **appreciate** *26* schätzen, zu schätzen wissen
to **appreciate sth** *126* für etw Verständnis haben
apprenticeship *11* Lehre, Ausbildung
to **approach sb** *26* auf jdn zugehen, jdn ansprechen
appropriate *10* passend, angemessen
to **approve of sth** *67* etw gut finden
approximately (approx.) *47* ungefähr, zirka
arbitration *168* Schlichtung
archive *7* Archiv
area *80* Gebiet, Bereich, Feld; *119* Fläche
to **arouse** *67* wecken, erregen
to **arrange** *28t* vereinbaren, planen, abmachen, arrangieren; *140* (Termin) ausmachen
to **arrange for sth** *87* etw arrangieren, vereinbaren
arrival *142* Ankunft
art: work of ~ *63* Kunstwerk
artwork *71* Bildmaterial, Illustrationen
as from ... / as of ... *25* ab ..., von ... an
As for me, ... *165* Was mich betrifft/angeht, ...
as regards *33* hinsichtlich, bezüglich
asbestos *51* Asbest
asleep: to fall ~ *163t* einschlafen
aspect *69* Aspekt, Seite
to **assess** *45* einschätzen, beurteilen
assessment *112* Einschätzung, Beurteilung, Bewertung
to **assign** *58* zuweisen, zuteilen
to **assist (with)** *15* assistieren, helfen (bei)
to **associate** *62t* verbinden, assoziieren
to **assure** *123t* versichern, zusichern
athlete *62t* Sportler/in
athletics *62t* Sport, Leichtathletik
to **attach** *25* (E-Mail:) anhängen; *76* anschließen, anbringen
attempt *168* Versuch
to **attend** *12* (hin)gehen zu, besuchen
attendee *70* Anwesende/r
attention *20* Aufmerksamkeit
attention: to catch sb's ~ *20* jds Aufmerksamkeit erregen
attention: (for the) ~ (of) (Attn.) *24* zu Händen
attention: to **get sb's ~** *67* jds Aufmerksamkeit wecken/fesseln
attention: to **draw sb's ~ to sth** *70* jdn auf etw aufmerksam machen
attitude *24* Einstellung, Haltung
attractive *26* attraktiv
to **auction** *140* versteigern
audience *64* Publikum
austerity *33* wirtschaftliche Einschränkung, Entbehrung
authority *161* Autorität; *162* Befugnis; Kompetenz(en); *166* Behörde
to **autograph** *140* signieren
automatically *84* automatisch
automobile sales management assistant *6* Automobilkaufmann/-frau
automotive *15* Automobil-
availability *59* Verfügbarkeit
available *10t* verfügbar, erhältlich
to **be available** *133* (Telefon:) zu sprechen sein; zur Verfügung stehen
avalanche *34* Lawine
average *106* Durchschnitt
awareness *45* Bewusstsein
awesome *80t* fantastisch
awful *161t* furchtbar
to **axe (jobs)** *169* (Stellen) streichen

B

back office *21* Abwicklungsabteilung (ohne Kundenkontakt)
back-breaking *74* äußerst anstrengend
backlit *108* hinterleuchtet
backyard *51* (Hinter-)Hof, Garten hinter dem Haus
bacon *146* Speck
to **bake** *70t* backen
to **balance** *51* im Gleichgewicht halten
ballroom dancing *21* Gesellschaftstanz
to **ban** *166* sperren; verbieten
bank business management assistant *6* Bankkaufmann/-frau
bank transfer *101* Überweisung
banking *36t* Bankwesen
to **go bankrupt** *48* Pleite gehen
bankruptcy *47* Konkurs, Pleite
bar chart *31* Balkendiagramm, Säulendiagramm
barely *43* kaum
to **bargain** *168* (ver)handeln
to **bark** *83* brüllen
barrel *31* Fass; Barrel (Maß für Erdöl)
base of clients *38* Kundenstamm
to **be based in** *14* seinen Sitz haben in
basic *20* Grund-, grundlegend; wesentlich
basics *166* grundsätzliche Dinge
bathtub *146* Badewanne
battery *27t* Akku
battery: lithium ion ~ *80* Lithium-Ionen-Akku
to **be to do sth** *137* etw tun sollen
to **be stranded** *170* festsitzen, gestrandet sein
bean *45* Bohne
bear *70t* Bär
to **bear sth** *47* etw tragen
to **beat** *80t* schlagen
bed: I'm off to ~. *7* Ich gehe dann mal ins Bett.
beef *103* Rindfleisch
to **beg the question** *43* die Frage aufwerfen
behaviour *167* Verhalten, Benehmen
behind the scenes *7* hinter den Kulissen
beliefs (pl) *52* Ansichten
benefit *17* Unterstützung, Beihilfe; *34* Nutzen, Vorteil
to **benefit from** *34* profitieren von
benefits *14* Zusatzleistungen, Vergünstigungen
benefits: fringe ~ *15* Zusatzleistungen, freiwillige Sozialleistungen
Best wishes *81* Mit den besten Grüßen
to **be better off** *59* besser dran sein, besser bedient sein
beyond: to **go way ~ sth** *37* weit über etw hinausgehen
beyond *107* darüber hinaus; über etw hinaus
billboard *65* Reklametafel, Plakatwand
billion, bn *31* Milliarde
biodegradable *51* biologisch abbaubar
biofuel *51* Biokraftstoff
birth: date of ~ *21* Geburtsdatum
to **blame sb** *36t* jdm die Schuld geben, es jdm übelnehmen
bloody *80t* verdammt
to **board** *85* einsteigen (in); an Bord gehen
on board *87* an Bord

board *145* Verpflegung
board and lodging *24* Kost und Logis
to **boast (about)** *57* prahlen, angeben (mit)
body *88* (Brief:) Haupttext
bold *89* fett (gedruckt)
booked up *147t* ausgebucht
booking *130* Buchung, Reservierung
booking fee *146* Buchungsgebühr
bookkeeping *13* (die) Buchhaltung, (Abteilung für) Rechnungswesen
booklet *63* Broschüre
border *43* (Landes-)Grenze
boring *64* langweilig
boss *9* Chef/in
to **bother sb** *163t* jdm Sorgen machen, zu schaffen machen
bottom: at the ~ *28t* (ganz) unten
boxing glove *160* Boxhandschuh
boycott *140* Boykott
bracelet *98* Armband, Armreifen
bracket *12* Klammer
brain drain *34* Abwanderung von hochqualifizierten Arbeitskräften ins Ausland
to **brainstorm** *14* Ideen sammeln
to **brainwash sb** *62t* jdn einer Gehirnwäsche unterziehen
branch *154* Filiale, Niederlassung
brand *47* Marke
brand new *172* nagelneu
branding *81* Markenaufbau, Branding
bread roll *146* Brötchen
to **break (a law)** *164* verstoßen gegen (ein Gesetz), (ein Gesetz) brechen
to **break down** *76* kaputtgehen
breaking up: You're ~. *133* (Telefon:) Das Netz geht weg.
to **breastfeed** *18* stillen
to **brew** *64* sich zusammenbrauen, gären
brief *63* Dossier, Anweisungen
brief(ly) *70* kurz
to **bring sth forward** *139t* etw vorverlegen
broad(ly) *63* breit
to **broaden** *166* ausweiten, erweitern
brochure *65* Prospekt
to **browse sth** *112* etw durchsehen, durchstöbern, durchblättern
browser *166* Mensch, der sich im Internet umschaut
bubble *33* Blase
budget *31* Budget, Haushalt, Etat
buffet car *72* Bordrestaurant, Büffetwagen
building material *52* Baumaterial, Baustoff
building site *36t* Baustelle
building trade *32* Baugewerbe, Bausektor
bulky goods *103* Sperrgüter, Massengüter
to **bully** *161* mobben, tyrannisieren
bumpy *151* holprig, (Flug) unruhig
to **burn** *70t* anbrennen
to **burn down** *47* abbrennen
to **burst** *33* platzen
bank business management assistant *6* Bankkaufmann/-frau
business: to **set up a ~** *46* ein Unternehmen gründen
business: any other ~ (AOB) *159* Verschiedenes
business: Is it any of your ~? / It's none of your ~. *164* Geht dich das etwas an? / Das geht dich nichts an.
business administration *12* Betriebswirtschaft
business card *81* Visitenkarte
business plan *81* Geschäftsplan
button *80t* Knopf, Taste
buy *82* Kauf
to **buy sth up** *74* etw aufkaufen
buyer *64* Einkäufer/in
by *23* bis

C

cabin *168* Kabine, Passagierraum
cabin crew *168* Bordpersonal
cable channel *64* Kabelsender
to **calculate** *104* ausrechnen, berechnen, kalkulieren
call: to **be on ~** *59* in Bereitschaft sein, Bereitschaftsdienst haben
to **call a strike** *168* zu einem Streik aufrufen
to **call by** *77t* vorbeikommen
to **call for** *168* fordern, verlangen
to **call in sick** *57* sich krankmelden
to **call on sb** *97* jdn besuchen
to **calm** *163* (sich) beruhigen
to **campaign (for/against)** *45* kämpfen, sich einsetzen (für/gegen)
campus *145* Campus, Universitätsgelände
to **cancel** *124* stornieren
cancellation *148* Stornierung, Absage
candlelight *164* (bei) Kerzenlicht
capability *112* Fähigkeit; Potenzial
capacity *112* Kapazität, Leistung
per capita *41* pro Kopf
capital letter *89* Großbuchstabe
in capitals *92* in Großbuchstaben
capsule *78* Kapsel
capsule chamber *78* Kapselmagazin
car boot sale *81* Trödel, Flohmarkt
carbon (dioxide) *57* Kohlenstoff, Kohlendioxid
carbon footprint *57* CO_2-Fußabdruck
to **care about sb/sth** *62* sich um jdn/etw kümmern, am Herzen liegen
to **care for** *17* sich kümmern um, aufpassen auf
care home *72* Pflegeheim
career *10* Karriere, Laufbahn, Beruf
careers officer *11* Berufsberater/in
cargo *103* Fracht
carriage *102* Beförderung, Transport
carriage: contract of ~ *102* Beförderungsvertrag
carried away: to get ~ *166* sich vergessen, sich nicht mehr bremsen können
carrier *103* Frachtführer; *142* Fluggesellschaft
to **carry on** *51* weitermachen
to **carry sth out** *69* etw durchführen
carton *109* Kiste, Karton
case: whatever the ~ may be *120* wie dem auch sei, in jedem Fall
in case *150* für den Fall, dass
case *168* Fall; Prozess, Gerichtsverfahren
cash *47* Geld, Bargeld, liquide Mittel
cash register *9* Registrierkasse
casual *26* leger
to **catch sb's attention** *20* jds Aufmerksamkeit erregen
to **catch** *133* verstehen, mitkriegen
cause and effect *39* Ursache und Wirkung
to **cause sth** *32* etw verursachen
glass ceiling *164* gläserne Decke (unsichtbare Barriere, die Frauen am beruflichen Aufstieg hindert)
celebrity *75* Prominente/r
century *32* Jahrhundert
cereal *146* Getreideflocken
certificate *11* Zeugnis, Bescheinigung
certificate: school leaving ~ *22* Schulabgangszeugnis
chain *28t* Kette
chair *161t* Stuhl
chairman *46* Vorsitzende/r
chairperson *70* Vorsitzende/r
challenge *36t* Herausforderung, (schwierige) Aufgabe
chances are *43* sehr wahrscheinlich
channel *64* Sender
chaos *64* Chaos
characteristic *14* Eigenschaft,

(charakteristisches) Merkmal
charge *43* Preis, Gebühr
in charge (of) *55* verantwortlich, zuständig für
to **charge** *144* (Preis) verlangen, berechnen, in Rechnung stellen
charge card *144* Kundenkarte (mit der man auch bezahlen kann)
charity *91* Kampagne, Aktion (für wohltätige Zwecke); *140* Hilfsorganisation, guter Zweck
charity shop *81* Laden einer Wohltätigkeitsorganisation
charming *24* charmant
chart *31* Tabelle; Schaubild, Diagramm
chassis *80* Fahrgestell
chat show *140* Talkshow
to **check sb/sth out** *11* sich jdn/etw ansehen
to **check up on** *57* kontrollieren; Nachforschungen anstellen über
cheers *92* tschüs, danke
chemicals *51* Chemikalien
chief executive officer (CEO) *54* Vorstandsvorsitzende/r
child labor (AE), labour (BE) *42* Kinderarbeit
childcare *17* Kinderbetreuung
Christ *140* Christus
chronological *20* chronologisch
CIP (carriage and insurance paid) *99* Fracht und Versicherung bezahlt bis
circle *48* Kreis
to **circulate** *154* verschicken
circumstances *43* Umstände
citizen *32* Bürger/in
claim *83* Behauptung
clampdown (on) *166* hartes Durchgreifen (gegen)
clarification *59* Erklärung, Erläuterung(en)
classified (ad) *65* Kleinanzeige
classmate *45* Klassenkamerad/in
cleaner *146* Reinigungskraft
to **be clear about** *163t* sich im Klaren sein über
clerical worker *57* Büroangestellte/r, Sachbearbeiter/in
clever *65* klug, geschickt
client *38* Kunde/Kundin
clients: base of ~ *38* Kundenstamm
close *89* nahe, in der Nähe
to **close down (an advert on the internet)** *166* (Internetwerbung) aus dem Netz nehmen, abschalten
close(ly) *10t* eng
closure *168* Schließung, Stilllegung
cloth *42* Stoff
clothing: item of ~ *42* Kleidungsstück
clue *166* Hinweis, Anhaltspunkt
clue: to not have a ~ *166* keine Ahnung haben
clutch *80* Kupplung
coach *85* Bus
coach service *141t* Busverbindung
coal *51* Kohle
code *166* Kodex, Regeln
coffee break *9* Kaffeepause
to **collate** *55t* zusammentragen, zusammenstellen
colleague *17* Kollege/-in
to **collect** *104* (ab)holen, (ein) sammeln
college *7* Berufsschule, Berufsfachschule
to **come across sth** *17* auf etw stoßen, etw (zufällig) finden
come September *42* wenn der September kommt, im September
to **come up with sth** *26* sich etw einfallen lassen, sich etw ausdenken
comfortable *151* bequem, angenehm, komfortabel
comical *67* komisch, lustig
command *19* Beherrschung
comment *7* Kommentar
to **comment on sth** *36t* etw kommentieren
commerce *23* Handel
commercial *15* kaufmännisch, Geschäfts-; kommerziell; *64* Werbespot
commercial invoice *118* Handelsrechnung
commission *14* Provision
commitment (to) *49* Engagement (für); Bekenntnis (zu)
to **be committed to** *57* sich engagieren für, engagiert sein für
common: to **have sth in ~** *64* etw gemeinsam haben
common(ly) *17* häufig, verbreitet
communications (pl) *37* Kommunikationsnetz, Verbindung(en)
commute *55t* Fahrt zur Arbeit
to **commute** *55* pendeln (lange Strecke zur Arbeit fahren)
compact *97* kompakt
company *8* Unternehmen, Gesellschaft, Firma
competence *59* Kompetenz
competition *82* Wettbewerb
competitive *37* (Preis:) günstig
competitor *40* Konkurrent/in
to complain *34* sich beschweren
complaint *8* Reklamation; Beschwerde, Klage
to **complete** *11* abschließen, beenden
to complete an order *113* einen Auftrag fertigstellen, ausführen
completion *108* Fertigstellung
complicated *13* kompliziert
complimentary *88* Frei-
complimentary close *88* (Brief:) Schlussformel
component *64* Bestandteil, Komponente
comprehensive *96* umfassend
to **be conceived for sb** *69* für jdn gedacht sein
to **concentrate** *55* sich konzentrieren
concept *49* Idee, Konzept
concern *70* Befürchtung, Bedenken, Sorge
to **concern sb** *82* jdm Sorgen machen
concerned: as far as ... is/are ~ *18* was ... betrifft/angeht
concerned *45* besorgt, beunruhigt
to **be concerned with** *167* sich befassen mit
concerning *8* betreffend
concession *169* Zugeständnis
conclusion *59* Fazit, Schluss
condition(s) *35* Bedingung(en)
to **conduct** *57* durchführen
conference *91* Konferenz
conference call *153* Telefonkonferenz, Konferenzschaltung
confident *163t* zuversichtlich
confidential *89* vertraulich
to **confirm** *70* bestätigen
confirmation *147t* Bestätigung
confirmation of order *108* Auftragsbestätigung
conflict *34* Streit(igkeiten), Konflikt
conflict of interest *34* Interessenkonflikt
conflict mediator *22* Streitschlichter/in
conflict resolution *160* Konfliktbewältigung, -lösung
to **congratulate sb on sth** *71* jdn für etw beglückwünschen
to **connect** *51* anschließen, verbinden
connecting flight *142* Anschlussflug
connection *26* Verbindung, Anschluss
cons: the pros and ~ *32* das Für und Wider, das Pro und Kontra
conscious(ly) *167* bewusst
consequence *33* Folge, Konsequenz
to consider *23* in Betracht ziehen
to **consider sth** *77t* etw berücksichtigen
to **consider sth sth** *80t* etw für etw halten
considerable *95* erheblich, beträchtlich

consideration: to take sth into ~ *45* etw berücksichtigen
consideration *45* Erwägung, Überlegung
to **be considered sth** *64* als etw gelten
consignment *103* Lieferung, Sendung
constant *64* konstant, gleichbleibend
construction *57* Bau
constructive *169* konstruktiv
consultancy *14* Beratungsbüro, -firma
consumer *43* Verbraucher/in
consumption *45* Verbrauch, Konsum
to **contact sb** *7* sich mit jdn in Verbindung setzen
contactless *144* kontaktlos
to **contain** *8* enthalten
container *78* Behälter; Container
contented *74* zufrieden
contract *6* Vertrag; Auftrag
contract of carriage *102* Beförderungsvertrag
to **contrast** *14* einander gegenüberstellen
in contrast *47* im Gegensatz (dazu)
to **contribute** *41* beitragen; *42* einen/seinen/ihren Beitrag leisten
contribution *31* Beteiligung; *53* Beitrag
control *74* Steuerung
convenience: at your earliest ~ *25* zeitnah, so bald wie möglich
convenience *25* Bequemlichkeit, Annehmlichkeit
convenient *77t* passend, praktisch, angenehm
convention *91* Tagung, Konferenz
conversation *73* Gespräch
to **convince** *65* überzeugen
to **coordinate** *38* koordinieren
co-ordinator *14* Koordinator/in
to **cope with** *15* zurechtkommen, fertig werden mit
copy editor *64* Redakteur/in
copywriter *67* Werbetexter/in
core business *74* Kerngeschäft
corner *26* Ecke
corporate *49* Unternehmens-, Geschäfts-
corporation *44* Konzern
corporation (Corp./Inc.) (US) *48* Aktiengesellschaft (AG)
correspondent *168* Korrespondent/in
cosmetics *(pl)* *52* Kosmetikprodukte, Kosmetika
costs: to cut ~ *40* Kosten senken
costume *157t* Kostüm
costume jewellery *96* Modeschmuck
cotton *42* Baumwolle
counsellor *163* Berater/in
counter-argument *45* Gegenargument
countertop *78* Ladentisch, Theke; Arbeitsfläche
course *28t* Studium, Studiengang
course: in the ~ of ... *57* im (Ver-)Lauf von ...
court *168* Gericht(shof)
to **cover** *58* abdecken, (Thema) behandeln
cover letter *20* Anschreiben, Begleitschreiben
crackdown (on) *166* scharfes Vorgehen (gegen)
crazy *69* verrückt
cream *74* Rahm
to **create** *64* schaffen, kreieren, (Eindruck) hinterlassen
creative (department) *64* Kreation
creativity *63* Kreativität
credit *6* Kredit
credit card *144* Kreditkarte
crisis, pl crises *32* Krise
critical (of/about) *170* kritisch (gegenüber)
crop *42* Pflanzen (auf einem Feld), Ernte
to **cross** *43* überqueren
crowd *157* Menge, Menschenmasse
crude oil *31* Rohöl
cup tray *78* Tassenabstellfläche
currency *110* Währung
currency sign *110* Währungssymbol
current *6* aktuell
currently *10* derzeit, zurzeit
customer care *19* Kundendienst
customer satisfaction *64* Kundenzufriedenheit
customer service *7* Kundendienst, Kundenbetreuung
customs (authority) *10* Zoll(behörde)
customs clearance *102* Zollabfertigung, Verzollung
to **cut** *33* senken
to **cut costs** *40* Kosten senken
to **cut off the phone** *48* das Telefon abstellen
CV (= curriculum vitae, BE) *20* Lebenslauf
CWO (cash with order) *99* Vorauskasse; (Bar-)Zahlung bei Auftragserteilung
cycle *29* Fahrrad(-)

D

to **damage** *44* schaden, (be)schädigen
damage *47* Schaden
data storage *38* Datenspeicherung, Speicherplatz
date of birth *21* Geburtsdatum
dated *87* (Datum:) vom
DDP (delivery duty paid) *95* frei verzollt
deadline *120* Frist
to **deal with sb/sth** *6* es mit jdm/etw zu tun haben
to **deal with sth** *8* etw erledigen, etw bearbeiten; *161t* mit etw umgehen
dealer *76* Händler
Dear Sir or Madam *76* Sehr geehrte Damen und Herren
debit *144* (Konto) Soll, Debet, Belastung
debit card *144* Debitkarte, Geldkarte
debt *32* Schuld(en)
decade *32* Jahrzehnt
decent *40* anständig, ordentlich
decision: to **take a ~** *48* eine Entscheidung fällen
to **decline** *139* ablehnen
to **decorate** *63* einrichten, gestalten
decoration *112* Dekorierung, Verzierung
defence *31* Verteidigung
to **defend** *161t* verteidigen
to **define** *51* definieren, festlegen
delay *123* Verspätung
delayed *132* verzögert, zeitversetzt; verspätet
to **delegate** *57* delegieren
to **be delighted** *23* sich freuen
to **be delighted to do sth** *81* etw gern tun
to **deliver** *54t* liefern
delivery: terms of ~ *72* Lieferbedingungen
delivery *72* Lieferung
delivery period *93* Lieferzeit
demand *41* Nachfrage
to **demand** *168* fordern
to **demonstrate** *15* vorführen, zeigen
to depart *142* abfahren, abfliegen
department *7* Abteilung
department store *63* Warenhaus
departure *142* Abfahrt, Abflug
to **depend on sth** *128* von etw abhängig sein
dependent on *32* abhängig von
depending on *14* abhängig von
deposit *146* Anzahlung
description *87* Beschreibung

to **deserve sth** *40* etw verdienen
to **design** *63* konstruieren, entwickeln, entwerfen; *83* gestalten
design *76* Konstruktion
desirable *19* wünschenswert
desire (for sb/sth) *26* Verlangen, Wunsch (nach jdm/etw)
despite *83* trotz
destination *24* Reiseziel; *85* Bestimmungsort
destination: port of ~ *102* Bestimmungshafen
to **destroy** *45* zerstören
to **determine** *68* ermitteln, bestimmen
developer *133* Entwickler/in
development *51* Entwicklung
development: research and ~ (R&D) *63* Forschung(s-) und Entwicklung(sabteilung)
device *74* Gerät, Apparat
diabetes *72* Diabetes (Zuckerkrankheit)
diagram *32* Grafik, Diagramm
to **dictate** *90* diktieren
digestible: (easily) ~ *72* (leicht) verdaulich
diligent(ly) *42* gewissenhaft, fleißig
diploma *59* Diplom, Abschlusszeugnis
to **direct questions (at sb)** *170* jdm Fragen stellen
director *48* Vorstandsmitglied
disability *52* Behinderung
disadvantage *8* Nachteil
to **disagree with sb** *59* anderer Meinung als jd sein, jdm nicht zustimmen
to **disappear** *41* verschwinden
disappointed (with sb/sth) *81* enttäuscht (von jdm/etw)
disapproval *165* Missbilligung
discoloured *127* verfärbt
to **discontinue sth** *121* etw einstellen, abbrechen
discount *17* Rabatt, Nachlass
discounted *42* billig, Billig-
to discover *57* entdecken
discrepancy *87* Diskrepanz
disgusting *65* ekelhaft
dispatch *63* Versand
dispatch: ready for ~ *87* versandbereit, versandfertig
dispatch: advice of ~ *108* Versandanzeige, Versandmitteilung
to **dispatch** *161t* versenden
to **display** *69* ausstellen, präsentieren; 144 zeigen, anzeigen
display *73t* Anzeige, Display; Bildschirm
display: to **be on ~** *63* ausgestellt sein/werden, zu sehen sein
dispute *168* Streit, Disput, Kampf
to **disregard sth** *120* etw als gegenstandslos betrachten
to **disrupt** *170* stören, behindern
disruption *169* Störung, Behinderung, Unterbrechung
dissatisfied *123* unzufrieden
distance *45* Entfernung
distant *48* entfernt, fern, entlegen
distraction *55* Ablenkung
to **distribute** *26* verteilen; *68* vertreiben
distribution *54t* Verteilung
distributor *99* Großhändler
to **diversify** *74* verbreitern, auffächern, diversifizieren
diversity *52* Vielfalt
to **divide sth up (into)** *31* etw (auf) teilen (in)
do *73t* Veranstaltung, Fete
dockworker *43* Hafenarbeiter/in
documents *103* Unterlagen, Papiere, Dokumente
domestically *39* im Inland
donation *133* Spende
done: to **have sth ~ by sb** *124* jdn etw tun lassen; veranlassen, dass jd etw tut
to **double** *70t* sich verdoppeln
dozen *64* Dutzend
draft *154* Entwurf
to **draw sb's attention to sth** *70* jdn auf etw aufmerksam machen
to **draw sth up** *35* etw erstellen
drawback (to) *38* Schattenseite, Nachteil (von/bei)
Dream on. *11* Träum weiter!
dress *26* Kleiderordnung, Kleidung; *48* Kleid
to **dress up** *26* sich schick anziehen, sich professionell kleiden
drive *80* Antrieb
driving licence *22* Führerschein
drop *169* Rückgang
dryer *75* Trockner
dual *80* Doppel-, doppelt
duchess *68* Herzogin
due *87* fällig
due to *127* aufgrund
duration *142* Dauer
duty *10* Pflicht

E

earliest: at your ~ convenience *25* zeitnah, so bald wie möglich
to **earn** *14* verdienen
earnings *42* Einnahmen
earring *98* Ohrring
economic *51* wirtschaftlich
economical *49* sparsam
economist *35* Wirtschaftswissenschaftler/in
economy *33* Wirtschaft; *49* Sparsamkeit, Wirtschaftlichkeit
edition *72* Ausgabe (z. B. einer Zeitschrift)
editor *166* Herausgeber/in, Redakteur/in
to **educate** *166* jdn unterweisen, aufklären
education *69* Schulbildung
effect: cause and ~ *39* Ursache und Wirkung
effect *160* Auswirkung, Effekt
effective *15* wirkungsvoll, effektiv
effectiveness *64* Wirksamkeit, Effektivität
efficiency *49* Effizienz, Leistungsfähigkeit
efficient *10t* effizient, rationell
effort *26* Bemühen, Bemühungen
electrically powered *83* elektrisch betrieben, elektrisch angetrieben
electrician *47* Elektriker/in
electricity *44* Strom, Elektrizität
electronics *(pl)* *80* Elektronik
embarrassing *161t* peinlich
emergency *44* Notfall
emergency call *44* Notruf
to **emigrate** *33* auswandern
emigration *33* Auswanderung
emission *57* Emission
to **emit** *45* emittieren, ausstoßen
empire *47* Reich
to **employ** *42* beschäftigen, anstellen
employee *7* Angestellte/r, Beschäftigte/r
employee records *9* Personalakte
employer *7* Arbeitgeber/in
employment *11* Anstellung, Beschäftigung, Arbeit
employment agency *11* Arbeitsvermittlung, Arbeitsamt
employment record *11* berufliche Laufbahn, Erwerbstätigkeit
employment tribunal *160* Arbeitsgericht
en suite *146* mit eigenem Bad
to **enable sb to do sth** *25* jdm etw ermöglichen
to **enclose** *23* beifügen, beilegen
enclosure(s) (Enc, Encs) *88* Anlage(n)
to **encourage** *67* fördern
end: at sb's ~ *26* bei jdm
end: in the ~ *161t* schließlich, letztendlich
ending *77* Schluss, Ende
endorsement *75* Werbung; Unterstützung
energy *71* Energie
engaging *67* fesselnd
engine *80* Motor, Maschine

engineer *34* Ingenieur/in; Techniker/in
engineering *36t* Ingenieurwesen; Maschinenbau
enjoyable *10* angenehm, schön
to **enquire about sth** *64* sich nach etw erkundigen
enquiry *11* Anfrage
to **ensure** *24* sicherstellen, gewährleisten, dafür sorgen
to **enter sth** *144* etw eingeben
entertainment *14* Unterhaltung(selektronik)
enthusiasm *20* Begeisterung, Enthusiasmus
enthusiastic *15* begeistert
entire *96* gesamte/r/s
to **entitle** *51* betiteln
to **entitle sb to sth** *23* jdn zu etw berechtigen
entrepreneur *46* Unternehmer/in
entry level *19* Einstiegsniveau
envelope *89* Briefumschlag
environment *15* Umfeld, Umgebung; *49* Umwelt
environmental *45* Umwelt-
environmentalist *80t* Umweltschützer/in
environmentally friendly *48* umweltfreundlich
to **envision** *35* sich vorstellen; vorhaben
equal *35* gleich
equality *54t* Gleichberechtigung, Gleichheit
equipment *172* Geräte, Ausrüstung
equivalent *22* Entsprechung, Übersetzung
to **escape (from)** *65* fliehen (vor/aus), entkommen (aus)
to **escape one's notice** *87* entgehen, übersehen
to **estimate** *37* schätzen
estimate *159* (Ab-)Schätzung; Kostenvoranschlag
ethical *45* ethisch, (moralisch) verantwortlich
evaluation *163t* Beurteilung, Bewertung
ever since *82* seitdem
evidence *167* Nachweis(e), Beweis(e)
to **exaggerate** *166* übertreiben
exam: to pass an ~ *12* eine Prüfung bestehen
exam: to sit an ~ *12* eine Prüfung machen
to **examine** *126* untersuchen, prüfen
to **exceed** *162* überschreiten, -steigen
exception *62t* Ausnahme
exceptional *41* außergewöhnlich
excerpt *70* Auszug, Ausschnitt
to **exchange** *17* austauschen, eintauschen
excited about sth *68* von etw begeistert
exclamation mark *92* Ausrufezeichen
excuse *68* Ausrede
to **execute** *114* ausführen
exhaust fumes *83* Abgase
to **exist** *64* es geben, existieren
exit *44* Ausgang
to **expand** *29* ausweiten; *155* expandieren, (sich) erweitern, (sich) vergrößern
expansion *155* Expansion
to **be expected to do sth** *42* etw tun sollen/müssen; es wird erwartet, dass man etw tut
expense: at sb's ~ *124* auf jds Kosten
expenses *91* Kosten, Auslagen
experience *7* Erfahrung; *82* Erlebnis
experienced *85* erfahren (Adj)
expert *34* Fachmann, Experte/-in
expertise *34* Fachkenntnisse, Sachverstand
explanation *77* Erläuterung, Erklärung
explicit(ly) *65* ausdrücklich, wörtlich
to **exploit** *44* ausbeuten
to **explore** *145* erforschen, erkunden
to **export** *54* exportieren, ausführen
export clearance *102* (Erledigung der) Ausfuhrformalitäten
export sales director *90* Vertriebsleiter/in Export
exporter *10* Exporteur
to **express** *70* ausdrücken, zum Ausdruck bringen
expression *18* Ausdruck
to **extend** *96* erweitern, ausdehnen
external *37* extern
extra training *161t* Fortbildung
extract *13* Auszug
extra-curricular *21* außerschulisch

F

fabulous *98* fantastisch, sagenhaft, fabelhaft
to **face sth** *32* vor etw stehen
face-to-face *24* persönlich
facilities *57* Anlage(n)
factory *16* Fabrik
to **fail** *47* Pleite gehen, es nicht schaffen, scheitern
to **fail to do sth** *121* versäumen, etw zu tun
fair *87* Messe
to **fall in love with sb/sth** *98* sich in jdn/etw verlieben
to **familiarize oneself/sb with sth** *68* sich/jdn mit etw vertraut machen
so far *12* bis jetzt, bis hierher
as far as ... is/are concerned *18* was ... betrifft/angeht
fare *144* Fahrpreis
farther *147t* weiter
fashion *81* Mode
fashionista *42* Modefan, Modefreak
Father *140* Pater, Pfarrer
sb's fault *161t* jds Schuld
faulty *44* fehlerhaft, defekt
favourable *72* günstig
to **fear** *47* fürchten, befürchten
fearless *46* furchtlos
feature *49* Merkmal, Kennzeichen
to **feature** *64* haben, aufweisen; vorkommen, eine Rolle spielen
featuring *67* (Film:) mit
federal *31* Bundes-
fee *17* Gebühr; *91* Honorar
feedback *55t* Rückmeldung
fellow (strikers) *170* Mit-(Streikende)
female *59* weiblich; Frau
feminist *59* Feminist/in; feministisch
figure *12* Zahl
to **figure out** *68* herausfinden
file *84* Datei
filing cabinet *160* Aktenschrank
to **fill an order** *63* eine Bestellung erledigen
to **fill in** *8* ausfüllen
film *112* Folie
final demand *120* letzte Mahnung
final exam *12* Abschlussprüfung
finance *36t* Finanzen, Finanzwirtschaft
to **finance** *46* finanzieren
financial *7* Finanz-, finanziell
findings *52* Ergebnisse
fire brigade *44* Feuerwehr
to **fire sb** *38* jdn (fristlos) entlassen, jdn feuern
firm *12* Firma
first name *54* Vorname
first-rate *74* erstklassig
fish fingers *71* Fischstäbchen
to **fit sb out (with)** *83* jn ausstatten, ausrüsten (mit)
fitted *78* Einbau-
flavour *78* Geschmack(svariation)
flexibility *38* Flexibilität
flier *163t* Handzettel, Flugblatt
flight *137* Flug
flight attendant *168* Flugbegleiter/in

to **flood** *34* überschwemmen, überfluten
flowchart *43* Flussdiagramm
fluent(ly) *20* (Sprache:) fließend
FOB (free on board) Mumbai *87* frei an Bord in Mumbai
to **focus on sth** *15* sich auf etw konzentrieren
to **fold** *97* falten, zusammenklappen; sich zusammenfalten/-klappen lassen
foldable *97* zusammenklappbar, faltbar
folder *54t* Mappe, Ordner
folks *7* Leute
to **follow sth up** *53* etw einer Sache folgen lassen; etw weiterverfolgen
follow-up *15* Anschluss-
font *20* Schrift, Zeichensatz
food chain *38* Nahrungskette
footprint: carbon ~ *57* CO_2-Fußabdruck
to **force** *52* zwingen
forced labour *52* Zwangsarbeit
forceful *120* deutlich, eindringlich
foreign *12* Auslands-, ausländisch, fremd
forever *84* ewig (lange)
form *6* Formular
to **form** *47* bilden
form letter *7* Formbrief, Serienbrief
formal *92* formell, förmlich
fortunate *42* glücklich, vom Glück begünstigt
fortune *160* Vermögen
to **found** *40* gründen
founder *74* Gründer/in
fragile *83* (leicht) zerbrechlich
frame *97* Rahmen
fraudulent *144* betrügerisch
freelance *38* selbstständig, freiberuflich
freelancer *38* Freiberufler/in
free-standing *78* Stand-, frei stehend
air freight *123t* Luftfracht
freight *123t* Fracht
freight forwarder *123t* Spediteur
freight forwarding: management assistant in ~ *6* Speditionskaufmann/-frau
freight forwarding *14* Spedition, Gütertransport
freight forwarding company *10* Speditionsunternehmen
friends: to **make ~** *9* Freunde finden, Freundschaft(en) schließen
fringe benefits *15* Zusatzleistungen, freiwillige Sozialleistungen
frontlit *108* frontal beleuchtet
frothy milk *78* Milchschaum
frozen foods *68* Tiefkühlkost
fuel *49* Treibstoff
to **fulfil** *38* erfüllen
full board *145* Vollpension
full-page *65* ganzseitig
full-time *19* Vollzeit-
(fully-)guided *85* geführt
fumes *45* Abgase
to **function** *76* funktionieren
to **fund** *47* finanzieren
fur *140* Pelz
furious *161t* wütend
furnished *146* möbliert, ausgestattet
furthermore *168* außerdem, des weiteren

G

to **gain** *22* erwerben, gewinnen, sammeln
gap *8* Lücke, Zwischenraum
gap year *11* das Jahr zwischen Schulabgang und Studienbeginn
garment *42* Kleidungsstück
gatehouse *141* Torhaus
gear *82* Ausrüstung
geek *37* Nerd, Freak
gender *35* Geschlecht
to generate *48* erzeugen
generator *44* Generator (Gerät zur Stromerzeugung)
gesture *123t* Geste
to **get back to sb** *134t* sich bei jdm melden, jdn zurückrufen
to **get carried away** *166* sich vergessen, sich nicht mehr bremsen können
to **get in touch with sb** *36t* sich mit jdm in Verbindung setzen
to **get sb down** *161t* jdn bedrücken, jdn deprimieren
to **get sb's attention** *67* jds Aufmerksamkeit wecken/fesseln
to **get sth** *134* etw verstehen
to **get to know sb** *77t* jdn kennenlernen
to **give the impression that ...** *26* den Eindruck erwecken, dass ...
glamorous *65* glanzvoll
glass ceiling *164* gläserne Decke (unsichtbare Barriere, die Frauen am beruflichen Aufstieg hindert)
glasses *(pl)* *62* Brille
globalization *37* Globalisierung
glove: boxing ~ *160* Boxhandschuh
it goes without saying *72* es ist selbstverständlich
Go ahead. *133* Nur zu. / Dann mal los. / Mach weiter.
to **go places** *11* herumkommen
goal *22* Ziel
good value for money *62* preiswert
goods *6* Güter, Ware(n)
gorgeous *80t* (wunder)schön, prächtig
go-slow *168* Bummelstreik
government *33* Regierung, öffentliche Verwaltung
grade *12* Note, Zensur
grading *145* Einstufung
graduate *34* Hochschulabsolvent/in, Akademiker/in
grammar school *22* Gymnasium
to **grant** *18* gewähren, einräumen
graphic artist *64* Grafiker/in
grateful *107* dankbar
great: to **turn out ~** *70t* sehr gut gelingen
grievance procedure *161t* Beschwerdeverfahren
grocery store *68* Lebensmittelgeschäft
gross *31* brutto, Brutto-
ground *73t* Gelände; *78* gemahlen
to **ground** *168* am Boden lassen, nicht starten lassen (Flugzeug)
group *47* Konzern
to **grow sth** *42* etw anbauen
growth *31* Wachstum
to **guarantee** *18* garantieren
guarantee *104* Garantie
guesthouse *85* (Fremden-)Pension
guide: (tour) ~ *85* Reiseleiter/in; Fremdenführer/in
guide price *145* Richtpreis
guided: (fully-)~ *85* geführt

H

habit *69* Gewohnheit
half board *145* Halbpension
to **hand in one's notice** *36t* die Kündigung einreichen, kündigen
to **hand sth in** *161t* etw einreichen
to **hand sth out** *55t* etw aushändigen, verteilen
to **hand sth over** *73* etw übergeben
to **handle sth** *7* etw bearbeiten
hanger *43* Kleiderbügel
harassment *161t* Schikane, Mobbing
hard time: to have a ~ *67* es schwer haben, schwerfallen
hard time: to **give sb a ~** *161t* jdm das Leben schwer machen
hardware store *76* Eisenwarenhandlung, Baumarkt
hard-working *21* fleißig
to **harvest** *42* ernten
to **have sth done by sb** *124* jdn etw tun lassen; veranlassen, dass jd etw tut
to **head** *42* (in Richtung von etw) gehen, fahren
head *46* Leiter/in, Chef/in

head office *54* Zentrale
to **headhunt** *34* abwerben
heading *20* Überschrift
headphones *66t* Kopfhörer
headquarters *28t* Zentrale
health club *17* Fitnessstudio
health insurance *14* Krankenversicherung
health-conscious *64* gesundheitsbewusst
heart *69* Herz
to **heat** *51* (be)heizen; *74* erhitzen
helmet *82* Helm
helpline *163* Telefonberatung, Telefonnotdienst
to **hesitate** *113* zögern
high street *10* Hauptgeschäftsstraße
high-end *106* für gehobene Ansprüche, im gehobenen Marktsegment
higher education entrance qualifications *21* Fachhochschulreife
high-resolution *113* hochauflösend
hint *14* Hinweis
to **hint** *65* andeuten, durchblicken lassen
to **hire sb** *34* jdn engagieren, beauftragen, einstellen
to **hire sth** *147t* etw mieten
to **hit** *169* treffen; (auf)treffen auf
to **hold** *137* (Veranstaltungen) abhalten; (Gespräche) führen; *165* gelten
to **hold on** *35* durchhalten; erhalten bleiben
to **hold the line** *133* (Telefon:) am Apparat bleiben
homeless *33* obdachlos
honest *7* ehrlich
to **hook sth up to sth** *84* etw an etw anschließen
horizontal *31* waagerecht, horizontal
hose *76* Schlauch
hose: water intake ~ *76* Wasserzulaufschlauch
hospitality *19* Hotel- und Gaststättengewerbe
host *36* Gastgeber/in; (Talkshow-) Moderator/in
hotel management assistant *6* Hotelkaufmann/-frau
hourly wage *37* Stundenlohn
household *76* Haushalt, Haushalts-
housekeeping *21* Hauswirtschaft
housing *74* Wohnungen, Wohnraum, Unterkunft
human resources (HR) *19* Personalabteilung
human resources manager *19* Personalleiter/in
hunger *43* Hunger
hurry: to **be in a ~** *7* es eilig haben
hybrid *80* Hybrid-

I

identity *49* Identität
illustration *80* Abbildung, Illustration
immediately *25* sofort, umgehend, unmittelbar
immigrant *32* Einwanderer/-in
immigration *33* Einwanderung
impolite *152* unhöflich
to **import** *48* importieren, einführen
import duty *102* Einfuhrzoll
importance *51* Bedeutung, Wichtigkeit
importer *10* Importeur
to **impress** *62* beeindrucken
impression: to **give the ~ that ...** *26* den Eindruck erwecken, dass ...
to **improve** *18* (sich) verbessern
improvement *68* Verbesserung
to **include** *12* aufnehmen; einbeziehen, einschließen; *47* umfassen; *76* beifügen
income *41* Einkommen
incoming *15* eingehend, ankommend
incompetent *161t* inkompetent, unfähig
inconvenience *123t* Unannehmlichkeiten
Incoterm *99* Internationale Handelsklausel
increase *20* Zunahme, Steigerung
to increase *38* steigern, erhöhen
increasingly *57* zunehmend
indeed *141t* in der Tat
independent *28t* unabhängig
to **indicate** *57* (an)zeigen, darauf hindeuten
individual *85* individuell
to **industrialize** *41* industrialisieren
industry *35* Industrie; *64* Branche
to **influence** *15* beeinflussen
influence *62* Einfluss
informal *92* informell, zwanglos, locker
information technology officer *6* Informatikkaufmann/-frau
information technology, IT *14* IT, Informationstechnologie
infrastructure *37* Infrastruktur
ingredient *43* Bestandteil
inhabitant *33* Einwohner/in
in-house *40* betriebsintern
initial order *72* Erstbestellung, Erstauftrag
to **initiate** *169* einleiten, initiieren
initiative: to **take the ~** *92* die Initiative ergreifen
initiative *92* Eigeninitiative, Initiative
to **insist** *121* darauf bestehen
insolvent *33* zahlungsunfähig, insolvent
to **inspire** *63* anregen, inspirieren
installation guide *76* Aufbauanleitung
for instance *161t* zum Beispiel
instant coffee *78* Pulverkaffee, löslicher Kaffee
instead of *28* statt, an Stelle von
instruction *63* Anweisung, Anleitung
to **insulate** *51* isolieren
insurance *10* Versicherung
to **insure** *103* versichern
to **intend** *47* beabsichtigen
to **interact** *163* interagieren, miteinander umgehen
interchange *143* Übergang, Umsteigen
to **interest** *55t* interessieren
interest *31* Zins(en); *130* Interesse
interest: conflict of ~ *34* Interessenkonflikt
intern *68* Praktikant/in
internal *13* intern
internship *56* Praktikum
to **interrupt** *57* unterbrechen
interview *7* Vorstellungsgespräch
interviewee *36t* Befragte/r (im Interview)
to **introduce oneself** *152* sich vorstellen
to **introduce sb to sth** *82* jdm etwas näherbringen, jdn in etw einführen
introduction *16* Einleitung
to **invent** *22* erfinden
inventor *47* Erfinder/in
to **invest** *46* investieren
investigation *68* Forschung, Ermittlung(en)
investment *34* Geldanlage; Investition(en); *47* Einlage
invitation *141t* Einladung
invoice *87* Rechnung
invoice: receipt of ~ *109* Rechnungseingang, -erhalt
to **involve** *8* mit sich bringen, einbeziehen, beinhalten
involved: to **get sb ~ in sth** *67* jdn an etw beteiligen, jdn in etw einbeziehen
to **be involved** *162* involviert sein, beteiligt sein
irregular *168* unregelmäßig
to **irritate** *169* (ver)ärgern
issue *45* Frage, Streitpunkt, Problem

to **issue** *144* ausstellen
issuer: (card) ~ *144* Kartenunternehmen, (Karten-)Aussteller
IT: information technology, ~ *14* IT, Informationstechnologie
in italics *8* kursiv
item *62* Artikel, Gegenstand
item of clothing *42* Kleidungsstück

J

jam *146* Marmelade
jealous *163t* neidisch, eifersüchtig
jewellery *81* Schmuck
job advertisement *7* Stellenanzeige
to **judge** *27* beurteilen
to **jumble sth up** *84* etw (kunterbunt) durcheinanderwerfen
Just kidding. *80t* Kleiner Scherz.
to **justify** *162* rechtfertigen

K

20K *14* 20,000
to **be keen on sth / to do sth** *11* auf etw wild sein, etw unbedingt wollen
to **keep in touch** *84* in Verbindung/Kontakt bleiben
to **keep doing sth** *17* etw dauernd/immer wieder tun
to **keep to** *54t* sich halten an
to **keep track of sth** *10* den Überblick behalten bei etw, etw im Auge behalten
keyboard *9* Tastatur
know: to **get to ~ sb** *77t* jdn kennenlernen
knowledge: working ~ *15* praktische/grundlegende Kenntnisse
knowledge *15* Wissen, Kenntnis(se)

L

label *42* Etikett; *45* Kennzeichnung; Marke
to **label** *87* beschriften, etikettieren
laboratory, lab *34* Labor
laborer (AE), labourer (BE) *42* Arbeiter/in
labour *31* Arbeit, Arbeitskraft
labour intensive *41* arbeitsintensiv
labour-saving *74* arbeitssparend
to **land** *141t* landen
landline *134* Festnetztelefon
last: while stocks ~ *97* solange der Vorrat reicht
to **last** *97* halten; (Vorrat, Warenbestand:) reichen
last but not least *36t* nicht zuletzt
latest *8* neueste/r/s
latest: at the ~ *87* spätestens
to **launch sth** *31* etw auf den Markt bringen; *166* etw ins Leben rufen, starten
law *17* Gesetz
law: to pass a ~ *38* ein Gesetz verabschieden
law firm *10* Anwaltskanzlei
to **lay sb off** *37* jdn entlassen, jdm betriebsbedingt kündigen
to **lay sth down** *17* etw festlegen, vorschreiben
layoff *168* Entlassung
leaflet *65* Faltblatt, Informationsblatt
least: last but not ~ *36t* nicht zuletzt
to **leave a message** *133* (Telefon:) eine Nachricht hinterlassen
paid leave of absence *17* bezahlter Urlaub
lecturer *34* Dozent/in, Hochschullehrer/in
left aligned *89* linksbündig
legal age *43* gesetzliches Mindestalter
leisure *29* Freizeit
length *119* Länge
letter of credit (L/C) *101* Akkreditiv
letterhead *88* Briefkopf
level *35* Niveau
liability *46* Haftung
to **liberate** *74* befreien
lie *163t* Lüge
life: to **make sb's ~ a misery** *161t* jdm das Leben schwer/zur Hölle machen
life expectancy *74* Lebenserwartung
lifestyle *65* Lebensweise, Lebensführung
lighting *26* Beleuchtung, Licht
lightweight *97* leicht
to **be likely to do sth** *43* etw wahrscheinlich tun werden
liking: to **sb's ~** *105* nach jds Geschmack
to **limit** *65* beschränken
limited *47* begrenzt, beschränkt
limited liability company (LLC) (US) *48* Gesellschaft mit beschränkter Haftung (GmbH)
limited partnership *74* Kommanditgesellschaft (KG)
line *98* Sortiment
line: to **hold the ~** *133* (Telefon:) am Apparat bleiben
line chart *31* Liniendiagramm
to **linger** *42* im Raum stehen
list: to **top a ~** *57* eine Liste anführen, ganz oben auf einer Liste stehen
lithium ion battery *80* Lithium-Ionen-Akku
to **live up to sth** *166* einer Sache gerecht werden
to **load** *43* verladen, laden
load *103* Ladung
loading *102* Verladung
to **be located in ...** *54* in ... ansässig sein, seinen/ihren Sitz in ... haben; *113* in ... liegen
location *20* Ort, Platz; Lage; *54* Standort
locker *164* Spind, Schließfach
lodging: board and ~ *24* Kost und Logis
logistics *(pl)* *63* Logistik
longing(ly) *64* sehnsüchtig
long-standing *95* langjährig, schon lange bestehend
long-term *74* langfristig
to **look forward to sth** *25* sich auf etw freuen
to **look into** *81* prüfen, untersuchen; sich kümmern um
looks *80t* (gutes) Aussehen
lorry *44* Lastwagen, Lkw
loss *46* Verlust
love: to fall in ~ with sb/sth *98* sich in jdn/etw verlieben
lower-case *135* kleingeschrieben
low-paying sector *11* Niedriglohnsektor
low-wage country *74* Niedriglohnland
loyal *74* treu, loyal
luggage *85* Gepäck
luncheon *17* Mittagessen
luncheon voucher *17* Essensmarke
luxury *157t* Luxus

M

machinery *103* Maschinen, Geräte: Anlagen
Madam: Dear Sir or ~ *76* Sehr geehrte Damen und Herren
magic *67* Zauberei, Magie
mail order *46* Versandhandel
mail shot *65* Mailing (Versenden von Werbematerial durch die Post)
main carriage *102* Hauptlauf
mainly *32* hauptsächlich
to **maintain** *41* behalten, beibehalten; *42* (nach wie vor) behaupten
major *19* groß, bedeutend
majority *169* größter Teil, Mehrheit
to **make an impact** *64* einen Eindruck hinterlassen
to **make friends** *9* Freunde finden, Freundschaft(en) schließen
to **make money** *34* Geld verdienen

to **make sb's life a misery** *161t* jdm das Leben schwer/zur Hölle machen
to **make sth up** *18* etw ausmachen, bilden
to **make sure** *6* sicherstellen, sich vergewissern
male *69* männlich; Mann
to **manage** *37* verwalten, regeln; leiten
management *38* Leitung, (Geschäfts-)Führung, Management, Verwaltung
management assistant for retail services *6* Kaufmann/-frau im Einzelhandel
management assistant in freight forwarding *6* Speditionskaufmann/-frau
management assistant: bank business ~ *6* Bankkaufmann/-frau
management assistant: automobile sales ~ *6* Automobilkaufmann/-frau
management assistant: office ~ *11* Bürokaufmann/-frau
managing director *54* Geschäftsführer/in
manner *14* Art (und Weise)
manner: professional ~ *14* Professionalität
to **manufacture** *41* herstellen, fertigen
manufacturer *15* Hersteller
marital status *21* Familienstand
mark *161t* Zeichen, Kreuz
to **market** *69* vermarkten
market research *36t* Marktforschung
marketplace *81* Marktplatz
marvellous *135* großartig
massive *42* riesig
material *41* materiell; *108* Stoff, Material
matte *119* matt
matter *77* Angelegenheit, Sache
to **maximize** *80t* maximieren
meantime: in the ~ *101* in der Zwischenzeit
mediation *16* Sprachmittlung, Vermittlung
medic *41* Arzt/Ärztin
medical insurance *74* Krankenversicherung
medical leave *17* krankheitsbedingte Beurlaubung
medicine *80* Medizin
to **meet (sth)** *37* (Bedarf, Norm etc.) erfüllen, befriedigen, entsprechen
meeting *137* Besprechung, Sitzung
member state *32* Mitgliedsstaat
membership *17* Mitgliedschaft
to **mention** *57* erwähnen
mermaid *64* Meerjungfrau
message: to **leave a ~** *133* (Telefon:) eine Nachricht hinterlassen
message: to **take a ~** *133* (Telefon:) etw ausrichten
method *64* Methode, Art (und Weise)
to **migrate** *32* (aus-/ein-)wandern
migration *32* Migration
mileage *80* Spritverbrauch
miles per gallon (mpg) *80* Meilen pro Gallone (1 gallon = 4,5 l)
miles per hour (mph) *80* Meilen pro Stunde
to **mind** *57* etwas dagegen haben
mine *103* Bergwerk, Mine
miner *168* Bergmann, Bergarbeiter/in
minicab *141t* Funktaxi
minimalism *49* Minimalismus
to **minimize** *74* auf ein Minimum beschränken, minimieren
minimum wage *11* Mindestlohn
minor *38* klein, unbedeutend
minute: Wait a ~. *7* Moment mal!
minutes *(pl)* *68* Protokoll
misery: to **make sb's life a ~** *161t* jdm das Leben schwer/zur Hölle machen
misleading *166* irreführend
mission *51* Auftrag, Mission
by mistake *92* irrtümlich
to **misunderstand** *89* falsch verstehen
to **mix sth up** *123t* etw durcheinanderbringen, etw verwechseln
mixed *82* gemischt
mode *80* Modus, Art
mode of transport *102* Transportart
model *67* Modell
moderator *58* Vermittler/in; Moderator/in
money: to **make ~** *34* Geld verdienen
money: good value for ~ *62* preiswert
to **monitor** *172* überwachen, kontrollieren
monthly *31* monatlich
to **motivate** *21* motivieren
mountaineering *48* Bergsteigen
mouth: word-of-~ (propaganda) *131* mündlich, Mund-(Propaganda)
move: on the ~ *32* unterwegs
move *166* Maßnahme, Schritt
multilingual *78* mehrsprachig
multi-modal transport *103* kombinierte Beförderung, multimodaler Transport
multiple *42* vielfach
musician *73t* Musiker/in
a must *11* ein Muss, eine Notwendigkeit
Must rush. *150* Ich muss weg. (Brief:) In Eile
My pleasure. *28t* Es war mir ein Vergnügen. (höfliche Antwort, wenn sich jemand bedankt hat)
myth *64* Mythos, Märchen, Legende
mythology *67* Mythologie

N

nappy *166* Windel
narrow *126* eng, schmal
nasty *163t* gemein, fies, scheußlich, widerlich
nationality *21* Staatsangehörigkeit
native speaker *21* Muttersprachler/in
neck *126* Hals, Halsausschnitt
need *37* Bedarf, Bedürfnis, Notwendigkeit
negative *11* verneinend
to **be negotiable** *14* Verhandlungssache sein
negotiation *15* Verhandlung
net *99* netto
network *54t* Netzwerk
nevertheless *26* nichtsdestotrotz, dennoch
new arrival *35* Neuankömmling
non-payment *120* Nichtzahlung
to **note** *72* feststellen
note: to **make a ~ of sth** *134t* sich etw notieren
notice *8* Hinweis, Bekanntmachung
notice: at short ~ *23* kurzfristig
notice *36t* Kündigung
notice: to **hand in one's ~** *36t* die Kündigung einreichen, kündigen
notice: to **escape one's ~** *87* entgehen, übersehen
to **notify sb (of sth)** *83* jdn (über etw) benachrichtigen
novelty *68* Neuheit
nowadays *18* heutzutage
a number of *123t* eine Anzahl (von), mehrere

O

to **be obliged to do sth** *125* sich genötigt sehen, etw zu tun
to **obtain sth** *21* etw erhalten, etw beziehen
occasionally *82* gelegentlich
occupation *56* Beruf
I'm off to bed. *7* Ich gehe dann mal ins Bett.
off: to **take time ~** *38* sich frei nehmen

to **offer sb sth** *11* jdm etw anbieten
office management assistant *11* Bürokaufmann/-frau
office hours *134t* Bürozeiten, Arbeitszeit
office management *14* Büroorganisation
officer: information technology ~ *6* Informatikkaufmann/-frau
official(ly) *11* offiziell
on: to **have sth ~** *139* etw vorhaben
on-site *18* vor Ort; im Betrieb
on-the-job training *14* Ausbildung während der Arbeit
open account *99* offenes Zahlungsziel
opening *34* freie Stelle; Chance
to **operate** *75* (geschäftlich) tätig sein
in my opinion *8* meiner Meinung nach
opportunity *15* Gelegenheit, Chance; freie Stelle
option *55* (Wahl-)Möglichkeit
oral(ly) *58* mündlich
order *29* Auftrag, Bestellung
in order to *32* um ... zu
order: to **fill an ~** *63* eine Bestellung erledigen
order: to **place an ~** *72* einen Auftrag erteilen, eine Bestellung aufgeben
order: receipt of ~ *87* Auftragseingang, Auftragserhalt
order: confirmation of ~ *108* Auftragsbestätigung
order: to **complete an ~** *113* einen Auftrag fertigstellen, ausführen
organic *45* Bio-
to **organize** *8* organisieren
original *70* originell
out and about *55t* unterwegs
out of action *139t* lahmgelegt
outgoing *15* abgehend, Ausgangs-
to **outline** *56* skizzieren, beschreiben, darstellen
outsider *65* Außenseiter/in
to **outsource** *37* (Arbeit) auslagern, outsourcen
outsourcing *37* Auslagern, Outsourcen
outward (flight) *159* Hin-(Flug)
oven *70t* Ofen, Herd
overdue *120* überfällig
to **overhear** *164* (zufällig) mithören, mit anhören
overseas *38* Auslands-
to **overtake** *80* überholen
overview *112* Überblick
owing *121* fällig, ausstehend
owner *166* Besitzer/in, Inhaber/in

P

PA (= personal assistant) *14* persönliche/r Assistent/in
to **pack** *103* verpacken
to **package** *63* (ver)packen
package *83* Paket
packaging *45* Verpackung
packet *45* Packung
packing *10* Verpackung, Versandverpackung
paid leave of absence *17* bezahlter Urlaub
to **pamper** *56* verwöhnen
panel discussion *170* Podiumsdiskussion
paper shredder *160* Aktenvernichter
paperwork *6* Formalitäten, Büroarbeit; *7* Unterlagen
parcel *83* Paket
parent company *54* Muttergesellschaft
participant *24* Teilnehmer/in
to **participate in** *81* teilnehmen an
partly *44* teilweise
part-time job *12* Teilzeitjob, -stelle
party *35* Partei; Beteiligte/r
to **party** *163t* feiern
to **pass** *80* vorbeifahren, überholen
to **pass a law** *38* ein Gesetz verabschieden
to **pass an exam** *12* eine Prüfung bestehen
to **pass sb over** *164* jdn übergehen
to **pass sth on** *42* etw weitergeben, -leiten
to **pass sth out** *26* etw verteilen
passenger *49* Fahrgast, Passagier/in
passion *19* Leidenschaft
passionate(ly) *91* leidenschaftlich
pay *11* Bezahlung, Lohn
pay rise *19* Gehaltserhöhung
payment *14* (Be-)Zahlung
payment: terms of ~ *72* Zahlungsbedingungen
peace *66t* Frieden
pension fund *14* Rentenversicherung, Pensionskasse
pension scheme *74* betriebliche Altersversorgung, Rentenversicherung
per annum *14* pro Jahr
per capita *41* pro Kopf
percentage *57* Anteil, Prozentsatz
to **perform** *157* auftreten, eine Vorstellung geben
to **perform sth** *27* etw aufführen
performance *31* Leistung
perfume *90* Parfüm
perishable *103* verderblich
perks *17* Zusatzvergünstigungen, freiwillige Sonder-/Sozialleistungen
permanent *14* (Stelle:) unbefristet
permission *68* Erlaubnis, Genehmigung
personal(ly) *14* persönlich
personnel *7* Personal
personnel assistant *9* Personalassistent/in
personnel manager *9* Personalchef/in
perspective *40* Perspektive
to **persuade** *161* überreden, überzeugen
persuasion *15* Überzeugung, Überredung
pesticide *42* Schädlingsbekämpfungsmittel
petrol *55t* Benzin
pharmaceutical *55* Pharma-
phone: to **answer the ~** *7* ans Telefon gehen
phone: to **cut off the ~** *48* das Telefon abstellen
photo shoot *140* Fotoaufnahmen
to **photocopy** *7* fotokopieren
photocopy *90* Fotokopie
physical(ly) *163* körperlich
to **pick** *42* pflücken
to **pick sb/sth up** *99t* jdn/etw abholen
to **picture sb** *80t* sich jdn vorstellen
pie chart *31* Tortendiagramm
pill *74* Pille
pillar *64* Säule
place: to take ~ *26* stattfinden
to **place an order** *72* einen Auftrag erteilen, eine Bestellung aufgeben
a planeload of ... *34* ein Flugzeug voller ..., eine Flugzeugladung ...
to **plant** *47* pflanzen, anpflanzen
plant *74* Werk, Betrieb, Anlage
platform *55* Plattform
playable *165* abspielbar
pleasant *99* angenehm, nett
to **please sb** *83* jdn zufriedenstellen
to **be pleased to do sth** *25* etw gern tun
to **be pleased (with sth)** *28t* sich freuen, froh sein (über etw)
pleasure *28t* Vergnügen
My pleasure. *28t* Es war mir ein Vergnügen. (höfliche Antwort, wenn sich jemand bedankt hat)
plenty (of) *163t* reichlich, viel
to **pocket** *44* einstecken, einstreichen, einsacken
pockets: to **stuff one's ~** *44* sich die Taschen vollstopfen, sich eine goldene Nase verdienen

point: That's the whole ~. *70t* Darum geht es gerade.
point: What's the ~? *161t* Welchen Sinn soll das haben?
to **point out** *34* darauf hinweisen
policy *57* Politik, Vorgehensweise, Regelung
polite *15* höflich
politics *48* Politik
pollution *45* Verschmutzung
popularity *37* Beliebtheit
porridge *146* Haferbrei
port *102* Hafen
port of destination *102* Bestimmungshafen
port of shipment *102* Verladehafen
portable *97* tragbar
position *6* Position, Stellung, (Arbeits-)Stelle
position: to **be in a ~ to do sth** *72* in der Lage sein, etw zu tun
position *169* Haltung, Standpunkt
positive *11* positiv
post *7* Eintrag, Post (in einem Blog); *23* Stelle
to **post** *169* bekannt geben
postal address *89* Postadresse
post-carriage *102* Nachlauf
postcode *89* Postleitzahl
poster *65* Plakat
to **power** *80t* antreiben
power station *103* Kraftwerk
powered: electrically ~ *83* elektrisch betrieben, elektrisch angetrieben
practical *69* praktisch
practices *165* Praktiken, Verfahren
pre-carriage *102* Vorlauf
precaution *44* Vorsichtsmaßnahme
to **predict** *38* vorhersehen, abschätzen
preferably *29* vorzugsweise, am liebsten
preference *16* Vorliebe
preferential *131* Sonder-, bevorzugt
preferential terms *101* Sonderkonditionen, bevorzugte (Zahlungs-)Bedingungen
to **preheat** *71* vorheizen
premises *87* Geschäftsräume
preparation *69* Zubereitung
to **prepare sth** *6* etw erstellen
to **be prepared to do sth** *75* bereit sein, etw zu tun
present *9* Gegenwart
to **present** *31* vorstellen, präsentieren
at present *93* gegenwärtig
present *154* anwesend
presentation: to **give a ~** *35* ein Referat halten
presentation *35* Referat; Präsentation
president *54* Präsident/in
to **press** *84* drücken
pressure *34* Druck
to **pressurize** *56* unter Druck setzen
previous *15* vorige/r/s, vorherige/r/s, früher/r/s
price: to **set a ~** *68* einen Preis festlegen/festsetzen
priced: average-~ *106* zu durchschnittlichem Preis
pricing *71* Preisgestaltung
primarily *70t* hauptsächlich, vorrangig
primary school *20* Grundschule
principle *165* Prinzip, Grundsatz
print *63* Druck
printed *8* gedruckt
top priority *40* oberste Priorität
in private *161t* unter vier Augen
private limited company (Ltd) (UK) *47* Gesellschaft mit beschränkter Haftung (GmbH)
process *68* Verfahren, Ablauf, Prozess
process: to be in the ~ of doing sth *73* gerade dabei sein, etw zu tun
product brief *68* Produktbeschreibung
product launch *68* Produkteinführung
product marketing *14* Produktvermarktung
production facilities *74* Produktionsstätte(n), Werk(e)
productive *55t* produktiv
productivity *40* Produktivität
professional *11* beruflich, Berufs-; professionell; *35* Fachmann/-frau, in einem gehobenen Beruf Tätige/r
professional manner *14* Professionalität
profile *20* Porträt, Profil
profit *46* Gewinn
profit margin *54* Gewinnspanne
project *38* Projekt
to **promote sth** *68* etw bewerben
promoter *157t* Veranstalter/in, Promoter/in
promotion *19* Beförderung, Aufstieg
promotion prospects *19* Beförderungsaussichten, Aufstiegschancen
prompt *121* umgehend
proof (no pl) *13* Nachweis(e), Beweis(e)
to **proofread** *70* Korrektur lesen
proper(ly) *6* richtig
property *15* Immobilie, Haus; *47* Eigentum
property management *15* Immobilienverwaltung
to **propose** *64* vorschlagen
proprietary limited company (Pty Ltd) (Aus, NZ) *48* Gesellschaft mit beschränkter Haftung (GmbH)
proprietor *76* Inhaber/in
the pros and cons *32* das Für und Wider, das Pro und Kontra
to **protect** *44* schützen, beschützen
to **prove** *11* nachweisen, beweisen
to **provide** *15* zur Verfügung stellen, anbieten; *18* bieten
to **provide for sth** *121* etw vorsehen
provider *37* Anbieter
to **provoke** *162* provozieren
the public *8* die Öffentlichkeit
public limited company (*plc*) (UK) *46* Aktiengesellschaft (AG)
public sector *37* öffentliche Hand, öffentlicher Dienst
public(ly) *46* öffentlich
publicly owned *74* börsennotiert
to **pump** *51* pumpen
pumpkin *70t* Kürbis
punctual(ly) *111* pünktlich
punctuation *70* Interpunktion
purchase *8* Kauf
to **purchase** *64* kaufen
purchasing *7* Einkauf, Beschaffung
purchasing assistant *9* Einkaufsassistent/in
purchasing department *7* Einkaufsabteilung, Beschaffungsabteilung
purchasing manager *9* Einkaufsleiter/in
purchasing power *69* Kaufkraft
pure *54* rein
to **put** *161t* hier: formulieren, sagen
to **put sth back** *150* (Termin) verschieben, auf später verlegen
to **put up (a tent)** *85* (ein Zelt) aufbauen
to **put up (a website)** *166* (eine Website) einrichten
to **put up with sth** *161t* sich etw gefallen lassen

Q

qualification *11* Qualifikation, Zeugnis
qualifications: higher education entrance ~ *21* Fachhochschulreife
qualifications: university entrance ~ *22* Abitur, Hochschulreife
qualified *34* ausgebildet, mit Abschluss
quality *14* Qualität; Eigenschaft
quality control *63* Qualitätskontrolle

quantity *31* Menge
quantity discount *105* Mengenrabatt
quarter *74* Quartal
quarterly *154* vierteljährlich
query *7* Anfrage, Frage
question: to **beg the ~** *43* die Frage aufwerfen
in question *87* betreffend, fraglich
question mark *68* Fragezeichen
questionnaire *55t* Fragebogen
to **quit** *26* kündigen
quotation *72* Preisangebot
to quote sth *19* nennen, angeben

R

rabbit *47* Kaninchen
race car *80* Rennwagen
racial *54t* Rassen-, rassisch
racing *80t* Rennen, Renn-
racist *164* rassistisch
rack *43* Kleiderstange; Regal
to **raise (a point)** *171* (einen Punkt) aufwerfen, zur Sprache bringen
to **raise (children)** *59* (Kinder) erziehen, aufziehen
range: top of the ~ *85* Spitzen-
to **range (from ... to ...)** *72* reichen (von ... bis ...)
range (of products) *72* Sortiment, Angebot, Palette
rapid(ly) *93* schnell, rasch
rare(ly) *7* selten
rate *34* Rate, Quote
to **rate** *112* bewerten, beurteilen
rate *146* (Zimmer-)Preis
raw material *42* Rohstoff(e)
to **react to sth** *135* auf etw reagieren
reaction *90* Reaktion
reader *144* Lesegerät
ready for dispatch *87* versandbereit, versandfertig
ready meal *71* Fertiggericht
real estate *57* Immobilien(handel)
realistic *70t* realistisch
to **realize sth** *51* etw erkennen, wissen
real-time *132* Echtzeit-
to **reap** *34* ernten, einstreichen
to reap the benefit *34* profitieren
rear-view mirror *83* Rückspiegel
reasonable *93* vernünftig, angemessen
to **reassure** *45* beruhigen
rebel *65* Rebell/in
to **rebuild** *35* wieder aufbauen
receipt of invoice *109* Rechnungseingang, -erhalt
receipt of order *87* Auftragseingang, Auftragserhalt
to **receive** *14* erhalten, empfangen
recently *82* neulich, jüngst
reception *141t* Empfang (auch beim Telefon); Rezeption
receptionist *14* Empfangsmitarbeiter/in
recession *35* Rezession
to **recharge** *27t* aufladen
recipient *89* Empfänger/in
to **recognize** *11* anerkennen; (wieder)erkennen
to **recommend** *70* empfehlen
recommendation *55t* Empfehlung
to **record** *44* aufnehmen
record: to **keep a ~ of sth** *163t* etw dokumentieren, Buch führen über etw
record label *47* Plattenfirma
recorded delivery *89* Einschreiben mit Rückschein
records *7* Daten, Akten, Unterlagen
to **recover** *35* sich erholen
to **recover sth** *121* etw sicherstellen, beschaffen
to **recruit sb** *155* jdn anwerben, jdn neu einstellen
recruitment *19* Personalbeschaffung
recyclable *49* recycelbar
Red Cross *22* Rotes Kreuz
to **reduce** *39* senken, reduzieren
reduction *94* Nachlass, Reduzierung
to **refer to sth** *22* auf etw verweisen, sich auf etw beziehen
referee *20* Referenzgeber/in
reference *14* Erwähnung, Verweis; Bezug; *88* Zeichen, Referenz
to **refrain from doing sth** *162* etw unterlassen
refreshment *15* Erfrischung
refrigerated *45* gekühlt, Kühl-
refugee *11* Flüchtling
refund *171* (Kosten-)Erstattung
with regard to *121* bezüglich
as regards *33* hinsichtlich, bezüglich
regards *72* Grüße
region *85* Region
regional *45* regional
to **register with sth** *19* sich bei etw anmelden
registered (letter) *89* Einschreiben
to **regret** *127* bedauern
regular customer *101* Stammkunde/-in, Bestandskunde
regular(ly) *172* regelmäßig
to **regulate** *166* regeln, regulieren
rehearsal *140* Probe (Theater, Chor, Orchester etc.)
to **reject** *148* ablehnen
rejection *114* Ablehnung
to **relate to** *14* sich beziehen auf, im Zusammenhang stehen mit
relationship *37* Beziehung
relative *31* relativ
reliable *21* zuverlässig
relief *168* Erleichterung
to **relieve** *34* erleichtern; (Druck) verringern, lindern
to **rely on** *18* sich verlassen auf
to **remain** *113* (ver)bleiben
remark *164* Bemerkung
to **remind sb** *132* jdn (an etw) erinnern
reminder *87* Mahnung
to **remit** *87* überweisen
remit *166* Aufgabenbereich, Auftrag
remittance *121* Überweisung
remote *66t* Fern-
removable *78* entnehmbar
to **remove** *64* (Kleidung:) ausziehen
to **remove sth** *71* etw entfernen
to **repeat** *59* wiederholen
repetition *59* Wiederholung
to **replace** *8* ersetzen, austauschen
replacement *82* Ersatz(teil)
reply *12* Antwort
to **report (on)** *164* berichten (über)
to **report sb/sth** *161* jdn/etw melden
to **represent** *166* vertreten, repräsentieren
representative *9* Vertreter/in
reputation *99* Ruf
request *21* Anfrage, Wunsch, Bitte
to **request sth** *87* etw anfordern, erbitten
to **require** *15* erfordern, verlangen, benötigen
requirements *24* Anforderungen
research *31* Forschung
research and development (R&D) *63* Forschung(s-) und Entwicklung(sabteilung)
to **research sth** *10* Nachforschungen über etw anstellen, etw recherchieren
resentment *34* Unmut, Groll, Ressentiment
reservation *145* Reservierung
reserved: All rights ~. *76* Alle Rechte vorbehalten.
residential home *72* Wohnheim
resignation *161t* Kündigung
to **resist** *56* widerstehen
resolution: conflict ~ *160* Konfliktbewältigung, -lösung
to **resolve** *120* lösen, auflösen
resource *52* Ressource, Rohstoff
to **respect** *161* respektieren
response *12* Antwort
responsibility *14* Aufgabenbereich, Zuständigkeit; *46* Verantwortung, Haftung

responsible *21* verantwortungsbewusst, zuverlässig; *68* verantwortlich, zuständig
to **rest** *139t* sich ausruhen
to **result in** *171* führen zu
results oriented *15* ergebnisorientiert
résumé (AE) *20* Lebenslauf
retail: management assistant for ~ services *6* Kaufmann/-frau im Einzelhandel
retail *7* Einzelhandel
retail business *14* Einzelhandel(sgeschäft)
retailer *144* Einzelhändler/in
to **retain** *35* behalten
retirement *38* Ruhestand
return *34* Ertrag
by return *128* postwendend
to **return** *168* zurückkehren
in return for *169* als Ausgleich/Gegenleistung für
return (flight) *159* Rück-(Flug)
return label *82* Rücksendeaufkleber, Retourenetikett
reverse *20* umgekehrt, entgegengesetzt
to **review** *19* bewerten, prüfen
review *170* Besprechung, Rezension, Kritik
reviewer *170* Rezensent/in, Kritiker/in
to **re-write** *24* neu schreiben, umformulieren
rhetorical question *65* rhetorische Frage
right away *123t* sofort
right to work *74* Recht auf Arbeit
All rights reserved. *76* Alle Rechte vorbehalten.
to **ring** *83* klingeln, läuten (an)
ring: to give sb a ~ *144* jdn anrufen
rise *19* Erhöhung, Anstieg; Aufstieg
to **rise (by)** *57* steigen, ansteigen (um)
risk: to **take a ~** *46* ein Risiko eingehen
robust *97* widerstandsfähig, robust
rocket *80* Rakete
to **role-play** *27* mit verteilten Rollen spielen
roll *108* Rolle
romance *65* Romantik
rough handling *127* unsachgemäße Behandlung/Handhabung
roughly *166* ungefähr
routine *40* Tagesablauf, Routine
rpm (= revolutions per minute) *80* Umdrehungen (pro Minute), Drehzahl
to **rub off on** *65* abfärben auf
rule: to **work to ~** *168* Dienst nach Vorschrift machen
rumour *162* Gerücht
to **run sth** *46* etw führen, etw betreiben
to **run tests** *6* Tests/Untersuchungen durchführen
running: up and ~ *166* in Betrieb
to **rush sth** *123t* etw auf dem schnellsten Weg hinbringen

S

to **sack sb** *40* jdn entlassen, rausschmeißen
to **sacrifice** *80t* opfern
safety *44* Sicherheit
salary *14* Gehalt, Lohn
sale *81* Verkauf
sales: automobile ~ management assistant *6* Automobilkaufmann/-frau
sales *9* Verkauf, Vertrieb; *74* Verkaufsumsatz
sales assistant *9* Verkäufer/in
sales representative *55* Außendienstmitarbeiter/in
salutation *88* (Brief:) Anrede
sample *55t* Muster, Probe
(job) satisfaction *10t* Zufriedenheit (am/mit dem Arbeitsplatz)
satisfaction *163t* Genugtuung
satisfied *82* unzufrieden
saying: it goes without ~ *72* es ist selbstverständlich
scarf *116* Schal, Halstuch
scenes: behind the ~ *7* hinter den Kulissen
schedule *38* Terminplan, Zeitplan; *68* Terminkalender
to **schedule** *68* (Termin) ansetzen
scheduled *154* geplant
school leaving certificate *22* Schulabgangszeugnis
screen *66t* Bildschirm
in search of *32* auf der Suche nach
search *32* Suche
to **search** *145* durchsuchen, suchen
search engine *166* Suchmaschine
seat heating *66t* Sitzheizung
seaworthy *119* seetüchtig
secondary school *22* weiterführende Schule
secretary *14* Sekretär/in
sector: low-paying ~ *11* Niedriglohnsektor
to **secure (sth)** *146* (sich etw) sichern
security *44* Sicherheit
security guard *44* Wachposten
security number *148* Sicherheitsnummer
seductive(ly) *64* verführerisch
to **select** *84* auswählen
selective secondary school *21* Realschule
self-adhesive *112* selbstklebend
self-catering *85* Selbstversorgung, für Selbstversorger
self-guided *85* selbst geführt
to **sell** *81* sich verkaufen (lassen)
seller *82* Verkäufer/in
sender *89* Absender/in
senior *57* leitende/r
senior executive *120* leitende/r Angestellte/r
to **separate** *89* trennen
separate *89* getrennt
serious *47* ernst(zunehmend)
to **serve** *72* servieren
to **serve sb** *9* jdn bedienen
service *41* Dienstleistung
serviced apartment *145* Wohnung in einem Apartment-Hotel
to **set** *145* angeben, einstellen, festlegen
to **set a price** *68* einen Preis festlegen/festsetzen
to **set off** *85* aufbrechen, losfahren
to **set up a business** *46* ein Unternehmen gründen
to **settle** *121* regeln, erledigen; *168* (Streit) beilegen
to **settle (down)** *35* sich niederlassen
sewing machine *43* Nähmaschine
sex *69* Geschlecht
sexual *163* sexuell
a shame *141t* schade
Shame on you. *62t* Schäm dich!
shamrock *69* Kleeblatt
shape *68* Form
to **share** *11* teilen
share *47* Aktie; *69* Anteil
shareholder *46* Aktionär/in; Teilhaber/in, Gesellschafter/in
shelter *164* Unterkunft, Obdach
shift *16* Schicht, Schicht-
to **ship** *69* versenden
to **ship sth off** *42* etw verschicken
shipment *10* Versand
shipment: port of ~ *102* Verladehafen
shocked *161t* schockiert
to **shoot** *64* (Film:) drehen, Aufnahmen machen
shopping bag *142* Einkaufstasche
shopping mall *64* Einkaufszentrum, -passage
at short notice *23* kurzfristig
short-term *75* kurzfristig, Kurzzeit-
shot *64* (Film:) Einstellung, Aufnahme
shower *146* Dusche
to **shrink** *155* schrumpfen

sick: to call in ~ *57* sich krankmelden
to **be sick** *66t* sich übergeben (müssen)
side: to take sb's ~ *161t* für jdn Partei ergreifen
sigh *168* Seufzer
sigh of relief: to **give a ~** *168* (erleichtert) aufatmen
to **sign off** *91* (Brief:) beenden, unterschreiben
to **sign sb up** *47* jdn unter Vertrag nehmen
signatory *90* Unterzeichner/in
signature *88* Unterschrift
silk *116* Seide, Seiden-
similar *8* ähnlich
In simple terms, ... *51* Einfach ausgedrückt ...
Sincerely (AE) *76* Mit freundlichen Grüßen (Briefschluss)
single journey *144* einfache Fahrt
single room *146* Einzelzimmer
Dear Sir or Madam *76* Sehr geehrte Damen und Herren
to **sit an exam** *12* eine Prüfung machen
sit-in *168* Sit-in, Sitzstreik
skill *11* Fähigkeit, Fertigkeit
skilled *57* qualifiziert, Fach-
to **skim** *166* überfliegen (schnell lesen)
skin *54t* Haut
slave *40* Sklave
to **sleep (3 people)** *146* Schlafmöglichkeit(en) bieten für (3 Personen)
sleeve *126* Ärmel
sleeveless *127* ärmellos
to **slide** *36t* rutschen, gleiten
smooth(ly) *10t* glatt, reibungslos, problemlos
so far *12* bis jetzt, bis hierher
social *74* gesellschaftlich
social affairs *(pl)* *31* Soziales
society *41* Gesellschaft
solar power *48* Solarenergie, Solarstrom
sole proprietor (AE) *48* Einzelunternehmer/in, Alleininhaber/in
sole trader (UK) *47* Einzelunternehmer/in
solution *81* Lösung
to **solve** *67* lösen
to **sort out** *34* sortieren; klären, lösen
to **sort sth** *40* etw einsortieren, einordnen
source *76* Quelle
spa *146* Wellnessbereich
speaker *134t* Redner/in
special marking *88* Vermerk, Kennzeichnung
specialist *34* Spezialist/in, Fachmann/-frau
to **specialize (in)** *112* sich spezialisieren (auf), sich spezialisiert haben (auf)
specific, specifically *17* speziell, spezifisch
specification *24* (detaillierte) Beschreibung
speech *137* Rede, Vortrag
speed *80* Geschwindigkeit
up to speed *166* auf dem/den neuesten Stand
speedy *82* schnell, zügig
spending *33* Ausgaben, Etat
to **spew** *45* spucken, speien
sphere *166* Bereich, Sphäre
to **split** *55t* aufteilen
to **spoil** *150t* verderben
spokesperson *34* Sprecher/in
spout *78* (Kaffee-)Auslauf
to **spray** *42* sprühen
to **spread** *162* verbreiten, verteilen
spreadsheet *81* Tabellenkalkulationsdatei
squalid *43* ärmlich, menschenunwürdig
square *70t* quadratisch
stables *(pl)* *28t* (Reit-)Stall
staff *8* Personal, Belegschaft
stage *41* Abschnitt, Etappe, Stadium, Schritt
to **stamp out** *166* bekämpfen, beseitigen
stand *87* Stand
standard *171* Standard, Niveau
up to standard *172* den Anforderungen genügend
standards *166* Prinzipien; Maßstäbe, Vorschriften
standpoint *69* Standpunkt
star *69* Stern
to **start off (as)** *36t* anfangen (als)
to **state** *70* erklären, angeben, sagen
statement *20* Aussage
statue *140* Statue
steel *54* Stahl
stem *70t* Stängel, Stiel
steps: to take ~ *121* Schritte einleiten
stereo system *62* Stereoanlage
stereotypical *59* stereotyp, klischeehaft
to **stick it out** *36t* durchhalten
to **stick together** *161t* zusammenhalten
sticker *69* Aufkleber
stock *7* Ware(n), Bestand
stock: out of ~ *76* nicht lieferbar, nicht vorrätig
in stock *99t* vorrätig, auf Lager
stock exchange *47* Börse
to **stop by** *77t* vorbeischauen
storage *97* Aufbewahrung
store *7* Geschäft, Laden
to **store** *54t* lagern
straight away *132* sofort, gleich
strategist *64* Stratege/-in
to **strategize** *64* (die strategisch besten Lösungen) finden
strategy *68* Strategie
strength *27* Stärke
strict *161* streng, strikt
strike *168* Streik
strike: to call a ~ *168* zu einem Streik aufrufen
striker *168* Streikende/r
to **structure** *77* strukturieren
structure *81* Struktur
to **struggle** *34* kämpfen, sich abmühen
to **be stuck** *36t* stecken bleiben, festsitzen, nicht weiterkommen
student *7* Schüler/in, Berufsschüler/in
study *141t* Arbeitszimmer
to **stuff one's pockets** *44* sich die Taschen vollstopfen, sich eine goldene Nase verdienen
sturdy *109* stabil, fest
subject line *88* Betreffzeile
to **submit** *87* (Angebot) unterbreiten
subsidiary *54* Tochtergesellschaft
to **subsidize** *17* subventionieren, finanziell unterstützen
substandard *128* minderwertig
substantial *97* beträchtlich, erheblich
substitute *114* Ersatz(-)
subtotal *109* Zwischensumme
to **suffer** *40* leiden
to **suggest** *70* vorschlagen
suggestion *77t* Vorschlag
suit *26* Anzug, Hosenanzug, Kostüm; *37* Anzugträger/in (Geschäftsperson)
suitable *10* geeignet, passend
suited to/for sth *55* für etw geeignet
sum *87* Summe, Betrag
to **summarize** *10* zusammenfassen
summary *24* Zusammenfassung
sun roof *66t* Schiebedach
Sunday trading *54t* verkaufsoffene Sonntage
sunglasses *(pl)* *137* Sonnenbrille
(un)supervised *56* (un)beaufsichtigt, (nicht) überwacht
supervision *57* Beaufsichtigung, Aufsicht
supervisor *161* Vorgesetzte/r
to **supplement** *17* ergänzen
supplier *38* Lieferant, Zulieferer

to **supply** *13* zur Verfügung stellen; liefern, anbieten
supply *76* (Strom, Wasser etc.:) Anschluss, Versorgung
supply chain *43* Lieferkette
to **support sb/sth** *40* jdn/etw unterstützen
surcharge *85* Aufpreis
sure: to **make ~** *6* sicherstellen, sich vergewissern
surname *54* Nachname
surprising *7* erstaunlich
to **surround** *43* umgeben
survey *62* Umfrage
to **survey sb** *62* jdn befragen
to **survive** *170* überleben
suspicious *82* misstrauisch
sustainability *49* Nachhaltigkeit
sustainable *51* nachhaltig
to **swap** *27* tauschen
to **sweat** *83* schwitzen
to **switch between (languages)** *10t* wechseln, umschalten zwischen (Sprachen)
to **synchronize** *84* synchronisieren

T

to **tailor** *20* individuell anpassen
Take ... *34* Zum Beispiel ...
to **take sb's side** *161t* für jdn Partei ergreifen
to **take a message** *133* (Telefon:) etw ausrichten
to **take down (a tent)** *85* (ein Zelt) abbauen
to **take place** *26* stattfinden
to **take sb on** *11* jdn annehmen, übernehmen
to **take steps** *121* Schritte einleiten
to **take the initiative** *92* die Initiative ergreifen
to **take time off** *38* sich frei nehmen
to **take turns** *77* sich abwechseln
to **take up (a story)** *34* (eine Geschichte) aufgreifen, weitererzählen
tape *112* Band, Klebeband
to **target** *166* zielen auf
target *166* Ziel(scheibe)
target audience *64* Zielpublikum, -gruppe
target group *69* Zielgruppe
taste *32* Geschmack; Kostprobe
technical *80* technisch
technically speaking *47* genau genommen
technician *34* Techniker/in
technology *41* Technik, Technologie
teleconference *132* Telekonferenz
telesales *14* Tele(fon)verkauf
telework(ing) *55* Telearbeit
teller *13* Kassierer/in
temporary *15* vorübergehend, befristet
temptation *56* Versuchung
tempting *40* verlockend
term *17* Begriff
terms: In simple ~, ... *51* Einfach ausgedrückt ...
terms *72* Bedingungen, Konditionen
in terms of ... *82* was ... angeht
terms of delivery *72* Lieferbedingungen
terms of payment *72* Zahlungsbedingungen
testimonial *112* Bewertung(en); Zeugnis
tests: to **run ~** *6* Tests/Untersuchungen durchführen
to **text** *84* SMS schicken
text message *92* SMS
textile *42* Textil-
therefore *51* deswegen
thief, pl thieves *164* Dieb
thoroughly *157t* völlig, total
though *11* allerdings, aber, jedoch
to **threaten** *124* drohen
throughout *72* überall, in ganz
to **throw** *43* werfen
to **throw sth up** *57* aufwerfen, zu Tage bringen
tidy *26* aufgeräumt, ordentlich
on time *68* pünktlich
in time (for) *123* rechtzeitig (für/zu)
time-consuming *74* zeitraubend
tired *7* müde
to **be to do sth** *137* etw tun sollen
TOEFL (Test of English as a Foreign Language) *11* TOEFL (standardisierter Test der engl. Sprache)
toll-free *75* gebührenfrei (z. B. Telefonanruf)
tool *55* Werkzeug
toothpaste *62t* Zahncreme
top of the range *85* Spitzen-
to **top a list** *57* eine Liste anführen, ganz oben auf einer Liste stehen
top priority *40* oberste Priorität
topic *154* Thema
total *31* Gesamt-; *108* Gesamtbetrag, Summe
total price *108* Gesamtpreis
touch: to **get in ~ with sb** *36t* sich mit jdm in Verbindung setzen
to **touch** *66t* berühren, anfassen
touch: to **keep in ~** *84* in Verbindung/Kontakt bleiben
track: to **keep ~ of sth** *10* den Überblick behalten bei etw, etw im Auge behalten
tractor *103* Traktor
trade *32* Handel, Handelsverkehr
trade discount *105* Handelsrabatt
trade show *97* Messe
trading: Sunday ~ *54t* verkaufsoffene Sonntage
to **train as** *12* eine Ausbildung machen als/zu
to **train sb** *34* jdn schulen, jdn ausbilden
train service *141t* Zugverbindung
trainee *13* Auszubildende/r
training *13* Ausbildung
training: on-the-job ~ *14* Ausbildung während der Arbeit
training course *9* Lehrgang; *11* Ausbildung
transaction *87* Geschäft, Transaktion
to **transfer** *15* weiterleiten, weiterverbinden (Telefonanruf)
transfer *85* Transfer, Weitertransport
to **transfer** *113* überweisen
to **transfer (sb/sth from A to B)** *85* (jdn/etw von A nach B) fahren, bringen
to **transform** *42* verwandeln
in transit *123t* beim Transport
translation *10* Übersetzung
transmission *80* Übertragung
transport *63* Beförderung, Transport
transport: mode of ~ *102* Transportart
to **transport** *103* befördern, transportieren
transportation *45* Beförderung, Transport(wesen)
travel *85* Reise
travel arrangements *85* Reisevorbereitungen
to **treat** *8* behandeln
treatment *131* Behandlung
trekking *48* Wandern
trial order *99t* Probebestellung, Probeauftrag
trial run *72* Probelauf
tribunal: employment ~ *160* Arbeitsgericht
trolley *45* Einkaufswagen
trouble: to **get sb into ~** *161* jdn in Schwierigkeiten bringen
to **trouble** *163t* bedrücken, beunruhigen
to **trust** *56* vertrauen; hoffen
trusted *120* zuverlässig
the Tube *141t* die Londoner U-Bahn
turbulence *151* Turbulenzen
Turkish *10t* Türkisch; türkisch
to **turn on** *84* einschalten
to **turn out great** *70t* sehr gut gelingen
to **turn up** *34* erscheinen, auftauchen

turnaround *35* Aufschwung; Kehrtwendung
turnover *54* Umsatz (UK)
turns: to **take ~** *77* sich abwechseln
TV station *139t* Fernsehsender
24/7 *59* rund um die Uhr
twinkle *64* Zwinkern
typical *37* typisch
typing course *12* Computerschreibkurs

U

unable *114* nicht in der Lage, unfähig
to **be unavailable** *133* (Telefon:) nicht zu sprechen sein; nicht zur Verfügung stehen
unbiased *166* unvoreingenommen, objektiv
underground *141t* U-Bahn
underlined *39* unterstrichen
underwear *64* Unterwäsche
unemployed *34* arbeitslos
unemployment *17* Arbeitslosigkeit
unfair *40* unfair
uniform *19* Uniform; *70t* einheitlich, Einheits-
union *54t* Gewerkschaft
Unique Selling Point/Proposition (USP) *69* Alleinstellungsmerkmal
unit *87* Einheit, Stück
unit price *87* Stückpreis
university entrance qualifications *22* Abitur, Hochschulreife
unknown *47* unbekannt
unlike *74* anders als, im Gegensatz zu
unlimited *47* unbegrenzt, unbeschränkt
to **unload** *43* entladen
unloading *102* Entladung
unnecessary *172* unnötig
unofficial *134t* inoffiziell
unoriginal *64* herkömmlich, unoriginell
to **unpack** *123t* auspacken
unpaid *120* nicht bezahlt
unplugged *145* ohne Strom, (Musik:) akustisch
unreliable *120* unzuverlässig
unskilled *57* ungelernt
(un)supervised *56* (un)beaufsichtigt, (nicht) überwacht
unsuspecting *166* ahnungslos
not ... until *123t* erst (um/am)
unwanted *163* unerwünscht
unwilling to do sth *169* nicht bereit, etw zu tun
unwise *40* unklug
unwittingly *74* ohne es zu ahnen
up: to **work your way ~** *28t* sich hocharbeiten
to **be up and about** *139t* auf den Beinen sein
up and running *166* in Betrieb
to **be up to sth** *127* einer Sache entsprechen
It's up to you. *161t* Die Entscheidung liegt bei dir.
up to date *6* aktuell; auf dem neuesten Stand
up to speed *166* auf dem/den neuesten Stand
up to standard *172* den Anforderungen genügend
to **update** *7* auf den neusten Stand bringen, aktualisieren
to **upload** *84* hochladen
upper-case *135* großgeschrieben
upright *70t* aufrecht
urgent(ly) *77* dringend, eilig
use: to **put sth to good ~** *28t* etw gut nutzen

V

vacancy *23* freie/offene Stelle
valuable *37* wertvoll
valuables *164* Wertsachen
value *37* Wert
good value for money *62* preiswert
value added tax (VAT) *109* Mehrwertsteuer, Umsatzsteuer
valve *76* Ventil
van *54t* Lieferwagen
various *11* unterschiedlich
vegetarian *140* Vegetarier/in
vehicle *44* Fahrzeug
venue *19* Veranstaltungsort, -stätte
version *154* Version
versus *45* gegen
vertical *31* senkrecht, vertikal
via (Dover) *85* über (Dover)
victim *62t* Opfer
video conference *132* Videokonferenz
video conferencing *55* Videokonferenz(schaltung)
view *8* Ansicht
in my view *82* meiner Ansicht nach
to **view sth** *14* sich etw anschauen, etw betrachten
vintage *62t* nostalgisch, Retro-
violation *167* Verstoß, Verletzung (von Gesetzen, Rechten)
to **visualize** *39* bildlich darstellen, visualisieren
vocational (training) college (BE) *12* Berufsschule, Berufskolleg, Gewerbliche Schule
vocational school (AE) *22* Berufsschule, Berufskolleg, Gewerbliche Schule
voicemail *133* Anrufbeantworter
voluntary *11* freiwillig; ehrenamtlich
to **volunteer** *11* sich freiwillig melden; ehrenamtlich arbeiten
to **vote sb sth** *155t* jdn zu etw wählen
voucher *17* Gutschein

W

wage *11* Lohn, Gehalt
Wait a minute. *7* Moment mal!
wardrobe *127* Kleiderschrank
warehouse *54t* Lager
washing machine *76* Waschmaschine
to **waste** *49* verschwenden, vergeuden
watchdog *166* Überwachungsbeauftragte/r, Überwachungsgremium
water intake hose *76* Wasserzulaufschlauch
waterway *102* Wasserstraße
way: to **work your ~ up** *28t* sich hocharbeiten
to **go way beyond sth** *37* weit über etw hinausgehen
weakness *27* Schwäche
wear *29* Bekleidung
weekly *7* wöchentlich
to **welcome** *85* begrüßen, willkommen heißen
welfare state *34* Sozialstaat, Wohlfahrtsstaat
well paid (a well-paid job) *11* gut bezahlt
well received *157* gut aufgenommen, gut angenommen
well-being *24* Wohlbefinden
well-established *14* gut eingeführt, etabliert
well-groomed *24* gepflegt
whatever the case may be *120* wie dem auch sei, in jedem Fall
wheel *80t* Rad
whenever *38* immer, wenn; jedes Mal, wenn
wherever *33* überall, wo
whichever *36* wer/was (auch immer), egal welche/r/s
while stocks last *97* solange der Vorrat reicht
whirlwind *64* Wirbelwind, Trubel
whoever *34* wer/wen/wem auch immer
whole: That's the ~ point. *70t* Darum geht es gerade.
wholesale *57* Großhandel
wholesaler *93* Großhändler
whomever *40* wen/wem auch immer

wide *81* groß, weit; breit
to **widen** *145* verbreitern, erweitern
width *119* Breite
win *80t* Sieg
within *15* innerhalb von, in
without: it goes ~ saying *72* es ist selbstverständlich
without delay *121* unverzüglich
witness *162* Zeuge, Zeugin
to **wonder** *81* sich fragen
wood *103* Holz
wool *54* Wolle
word-of-mouth (propaganda) *131* mündlich, Mund-(Propaganda)
to **work your way up** *28t* sich hocharbeiten
to **work to rule** *168* Dienst nach Vorschrift machen
work experience *7* Praktikum
work of art *63* Kunstwerk
work placement *7* Praktikum
workforce *18* Beschäftigte, Erwerbstätige; Belegschaft
working conditions *18* Arbeitsbedingungen
working hours *14* Arbeitszeiten
working knowledge *15* praktische/grundlegende Kenntnisse
workplace *18* Arbeitsplatz
worrying *131* Besorgnis erregend, beunruhigend
to **be worth** *81* wert sein
wrap *69* Folie
to **write sth up** *68* etw ausarbeiten, erstellen
in writing *99* schriftlich, in Schriftform
written correspondence *26* Schriftverkehr
to **go wrong** *46* schiefgehen; *81* einen Fehler machen

Y

not yet *7* noch nicht
Yours faithfully *72* Mit freundlichen Grüßen (Briefschluss)
Yours sincerely *88* Mit freundlichen Grüßen (Briefschluss)

Irregular verbs

be	was/were	been	*sein*
beat	beat	beaten	*schlagen, besiegen*
become	became	become	*werden*
begin	began	begun	*anfangen, beginnen*
bend	bent	bent	*(sich) beugen*
blow	blew	blown	*wehen, blasen, ziehen*
break	broke	broken	*brechen*
breed	bred	bred	*sich vermehren, sich ausbreiten*
bring	brought	brought	*(mit)bringen*
build	built	built	*bauen*
burn	burnt/ burned	burnt/ burned	*(ver)brennen*
buy	bought	bought	*kaufen*
catch	caught	caught	*fangen, fassen, erreichen*
choose	chose	chosen	*(aus)wählen*
come	came	come	*kommen*
cost	cost	cost	*kosten*
cross-breed	cross-bred	cross-bred	*kreuzen*
cut	cut	cut	*schneiden*
deal	dealt	dealt	*versetzen, verteilen*
dig	dug	dug	*graben*
do	did	done	*tun, machen*
draw	drew	drawn	*zeichnen*
dream	dreamt/ dreamed	dreamt/ dreamed	*träumen*
drink	drank	drunk	*trinken*
drive	drove	driven	*fahren*
eat	ate	eaten	*essen*
fall	fell	fallen	*fallen*
feed	fed	fed	*füttern, ernähren*
feel	felt	felt	*(sich) fühlen, empfinden*
fight	fought	fought	*kämpfen*
find	found	found	*finden*
fit	fit/fitted	fit/fitted	*passen, entsprechen, anbringen*
fly	flew	flown	*fliegen*
forbid	forbade	forbidden	*verbieten*
forget	forgot	forgotten	*vergessen*
get	got	got (*AE* gotten)	*bekommen*
give	gave	given	*geben*
go	went	gone	*gehen, fahren*
grow	grew	grown	*wachsen*
hang	hung	hung	*hängen*
have	had	had	*haben*
hear	heard	heard	*hören*
hide	hid	hidden	*(sich) verstecken*
hit	hit	hit	*schlagen*
hold	held	held	*halten, festhalten*
hurt	hurt	hurt	*verletzen*
keep	kept	kept	*behalten*
know	knew	known	*kennen, wissen*
lay	laid	laid	*legen*
lead	led	led	*führen*
lean	leant/ leaned	leant/ leaned	*sich lehnen, sich beugen*
learn	learnt/ learned	learnt/ learned	*lernen*
leave	left	left	*abfahren, verlassen, weggehen*
let	let	let	*lassen*
lie	lay	lain	*liegen*
light	lit	lit	*anzünden, beleuchten*
lose	lost	lost	*verlieren*
make	made	made	*machen*
mean	meant	meant	*meinen, bedeuten*
meet	met	met	*treffen*
overcome	overcame	overcome	*überwinden, überwältigen*
override	overrode	overridden	*sich hinwegsetzen über*
panic	panicked	panicked	*in Panik geraten*
pay	paid	paid	*bezahlen*
put	put	put	*setzen, stellen, legen*
quit	quit/ quitted	quit/ quitted	*verlassen, aufhören*
read	read	read	*lesen*
repay	repaid	repaid	*zurückzahlen*
rewrite	rewrote	rewritten	*umschreiben*
ride	rode	ridden	*reiten, fahren*
ring	rang	rung	*anrufen, läuten*
rise	rose	risen	*(an)steigen*
run	ran	run	*laufen, rennen*
say	said	said	*sagen*
see	saw	seen	*sehen*
seek	sought	sought	*suchen*
sell	sold	sold	*verkaufen*
send	sent	sent	*senden, schicken*
set	set	set	*setzen, stellen*
shake	shook	shaken	*schütteln*
shine	shone	shone	*scheinen, glänzen*
show	showed	shown	*zeigen*
shrink	shrank	shrunk	*schrumpfen, zurückgehen*
shut	shut	shut	*schließen*
sing	sang	sung	*singen*
sink	sank	sunk	*sinken*
sit	sat	sat	*sitzen*
sleep	slept	slept	*schlafen*
slide	slid	slid	*(ab)rutschen, (ab)sacken*
smell	smelt/ smelled	smelt/ smelled	*riechen*
speak	spoke	spoken	*sprechen*

spell	spelt/ spelled	spelt/ spelled	*buchstabieren*
spend	spent	spent	*ausgeben, verbringen*
spread	spread	spread	*(sich) verbreiten*
stand	stood	stood	*stehen*
steal	stole	stolen	*stehlen*
swim	swam	swum	*schwimmen*
take	took	taken	*nehmen*
teach	taught	taught	*unterrichten, beibringen*
tell	told	told	*sagen, erzählen*
think	thought	thought	*denken*
throw	threw	thrown	*werfen*
under-stand	under-stood	under-stood	*verstehen*
wake	woke	woken	*aufwachen, aufwecken*
wear	wore	worn	*tragen*
win	won	won	*gewinnen*
write	wrote	written	*schreiben*

Quellenverzeichnis

Cover: 1/shutterstock/Brian A Jackson,2/shutterstock/hxdbzxy,3/shutterstock/ wavebreakmedia,4/ Fotosearch

S.6/1/Fotofinder/ Visum/Thomas Langreder, S.6/2/Fotofinder/ Varioimages, S.6/3/Alamy/Ken Seet, S.6/4/ shutterstock/goodluz, S.6/5/ shutterstock/wavebrakmedia, S.6/6/ shutterstock/Tyler Olson, S.7/1/ Alamy/ Geoffrey Robinson, S.10/1/Alamy/Helene Rogers, S.11/Oxana Rödel, S.13/Alamy/Catchlight Visual Services, S.14/Alamy/beyond/Lava, S.17/Akg/algoba systems, S.18/Alamy/I love images, S.19/shutterstock/EDHAR, S.26/PictureAlliance/Monique Wuestenhagen, S.27/1/Corbis/S.Ocean, 27/2/Alamy/Kathy deWitt, S.28/1-2/Best Western Monbar Hotel,York, S.31/rechts unten/www.zeitbombestaatsverschuldung.de/ Siegfried Hildebrandt, Düsseldorf, Marco Schinkel, Mainhausen, S.32/Alamy/DWD-photo, S.33/ODI, S.34/1/ Fotofinder/Vario, S.34/2/Fotofinder/Visum/xinhua, S.36/Alamy/Jim Newberry, S.37/1/shutterstock/Angela Waye, S.37/2/shutterstock/Sergej Butorin, S.38/shutterstock/Monkey Business Images, S.40/Alamy/Lutz Pape, S.41/1/Akg, S.41/2/shutterstock/Worldpics, S.41/3/shutterstock/M.Jung, S.41/4/shutterstock/Amy Dunn, S.44/Fotofinder/Visum/Panos Pictures, S.45oben/Organic Soil Association, TransFair e.V., rainforest-alliance, Bundesanstalt für Landwirtschaft und Ernährung, S.45unten/ODI, S.46/1/shutterstock/Rita Manoj Jetha, S.46/2/shutterstock/ValeStock, S.46/3/shutterstock/Kipling Brock, S.46/4/shutterstock/Brian Jackson, S.47/1/Picture Alliance/Justin Lane, S.47/2/Alamy/Carlo Bolls, S.48/1/shutterstock/auremar, S.48/2/shutterstock/wavebreakmedia, S.48/3/CorbisRF/moodboard, S.48/4/shutterstock/Istvan Csak, S.48/5/shutterstock/iofoto, S.48/6/Istockphoto/Juanmonino, S.49/50 /BMW AG München, S.51/ODI, S.54/ PictureAlliance/Uwe Zucchi, S.55/1 shutterstock/RogerBrowning, S.55/2/shutterstock/Kimages, S.55/3/ shutterstock/bloomua, S.55/4/shutterstock/Yuri Arcurs, S.62oben/www.nike.com.de, Frankfurt, adidas AG, www.adidas-group.com, Herzogenaurach, Diesel Deutschland GmbH, Düsseldorf, www.diesel.com, Fossil GmbH, Grabenstätt, GABA GmbH, Lörrach, www.gaba-dent.de, Beiersdorf AG, Hamburg, S.62 unten/1/Alamy/Yuri Arcurs, S.62/2/Alamy/Form Advertising/Shoosh, S.62/3/Alamy/Montgomery Martin, S.63/1/Alamy/ Wavebreak Media ltd, S.65/1/Alamy/Chris Batson, S.66/1/Fotofinder/Joker, S.66/2/shutterstock, S.66/3/ Fotofinder/Caro/Westermann, S.67/1/ Alamy/Wavebreak Media ltd, S.67/2/ODI, S.68/1/Alamy/Huntstock, S.68/2/Alamy/image 100 Business, S.68/3/shutterstock/paulaphoto, S.68/4/shutterstock/Kary1974, S.69/1/ODI, S.71/1/shutterstock/wrangler, S.73/shutterstock/Alexander Manykin , S.74/1/Fotofinder/ TV-yesterday, S.74/2/Fotofinder/transit/Thomas Haertrich, S.76/shutterstock/Kurhan, S.79/Miele, S.80/ Porsche, S.83/1/shutterstock/trifonenko ivan ,S.83/2/Istockphoto/mattjeacock, S.94/1/shutterstock/Sam Dcruz, S.94/2/PictureAlliance/Achim Scheidemann, S.97/1/shutterstock/photo25th, S.102/1/ODI, S.103/1/ shutterstock, S.103/2/shutterstock, S.103/3/ shutterstock, S.103/4/ shutterstock, S.109/ shutterstock/ claudio zaccherini, S.113/istockphoto/gerenme, S.123/1-7/ODI, S.128/shutterstock/trekandshoot, S.129/ shutterstock/Anna Lurye, S.132/1/shutterstock/tanatat, S.132/2/ shutterstock/Adam Gregor, S.132/3/ shutterstock/Songquan Deng, S.132/4/shutterstock/S.Beagle, S.134/shutterstock, S.139/PictureAlliance/ Martin Gerten, S.142/Fotofinder/Weisflog , S.144/shutterstock, S.145/shutterstock, S.149/1/shutterstock/ Paul Prescott, S.149/2/shutterstock/Nick Hawkes, S.152/ shutterstock, S.153/1/shutterstock/AndreyPopov, S.153/2/shutterstock/ Monkey Business Images, S.153/3/shutterstock/Norman Pogson, S.153/4/ shutterstock/carlosseller, S.160/1/Randy Glasbergen, S.160/2/ cartoonstock, S.160/3/ cartoonstock, S.161/ Fotofinder/Varioimages, S.163/1/,Istockphoto/Robert Churchill, S.163/2/Istockphoto/thoughtful, S.165/ Alamy/SuperStock/Purestock, S.168/Picture Alliance, S.169/Getty images/Tim Boyle, S.176/shutterstock/ Edyta Pawlowska, S.184/1-4/Derby Cycle Werke GmbH, Cloppenburg

Texte: S.42/The Huffington Post, S.53/Adidas AG, S.57/www.eurofound.europa.eu/eiro/studies/tn0910050s/ tn0910050s_3.htm, S.58/Stiftung Jugend und Bildung in Zusammenarbeit mit dem BMAS; www.jugend-und-bildung.de, S.79/Miele, S.162/Michael Odenkirchen, Köln, S.166/Telegraph Media Group, London, S.167/ www.wettbewerbszentrale.de, S.176/Handelsblatt-Grafik